THE LEG

~ OR ~

The Remarkable Reappearance
of Santa Anna's Disembodied Limb

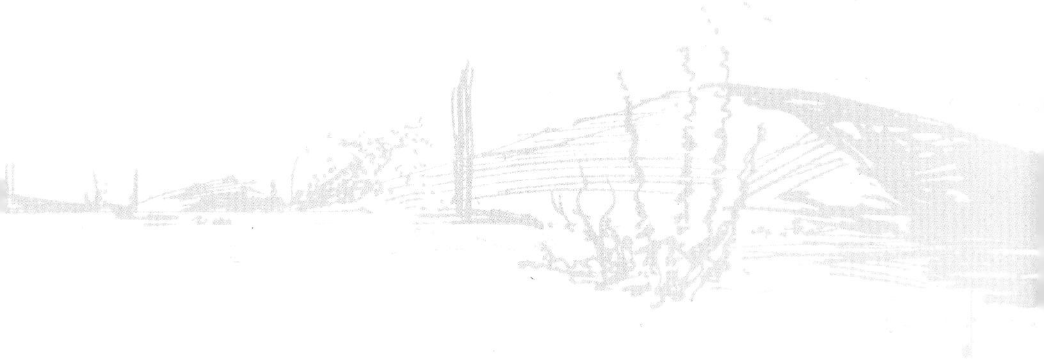

THE LEG

Written by Van Jensen
Illustrated by Jose Pimienta
Colored and Lettered by Matthew Petz
Book design by J Chris Campbell

Published by Blue Creek Creative LLC,
P.O. Box 5560, Atlanta, GA, 31107 USA.

First Printing, August 2014.
Printed in China.

ISBN 978-1-60309-354-5

1. Graphic Novels
2. Historical Fiction
3. Mexico

THE LEG

~ OR ~

**The Remarkable Reappearance of
Santa Anna's Disembodied Limb**

VAN JENSEN   **JOSE PIMIENTA**

To everyone who listened to me talk
about this story for the past decade
and didn't think I was crazy.
Also, for those of you who did.
~ Van

To my mother,
who introduced me to magic,
and to my father,
who reminds me to keep observing.
~ Jose

Chapter One

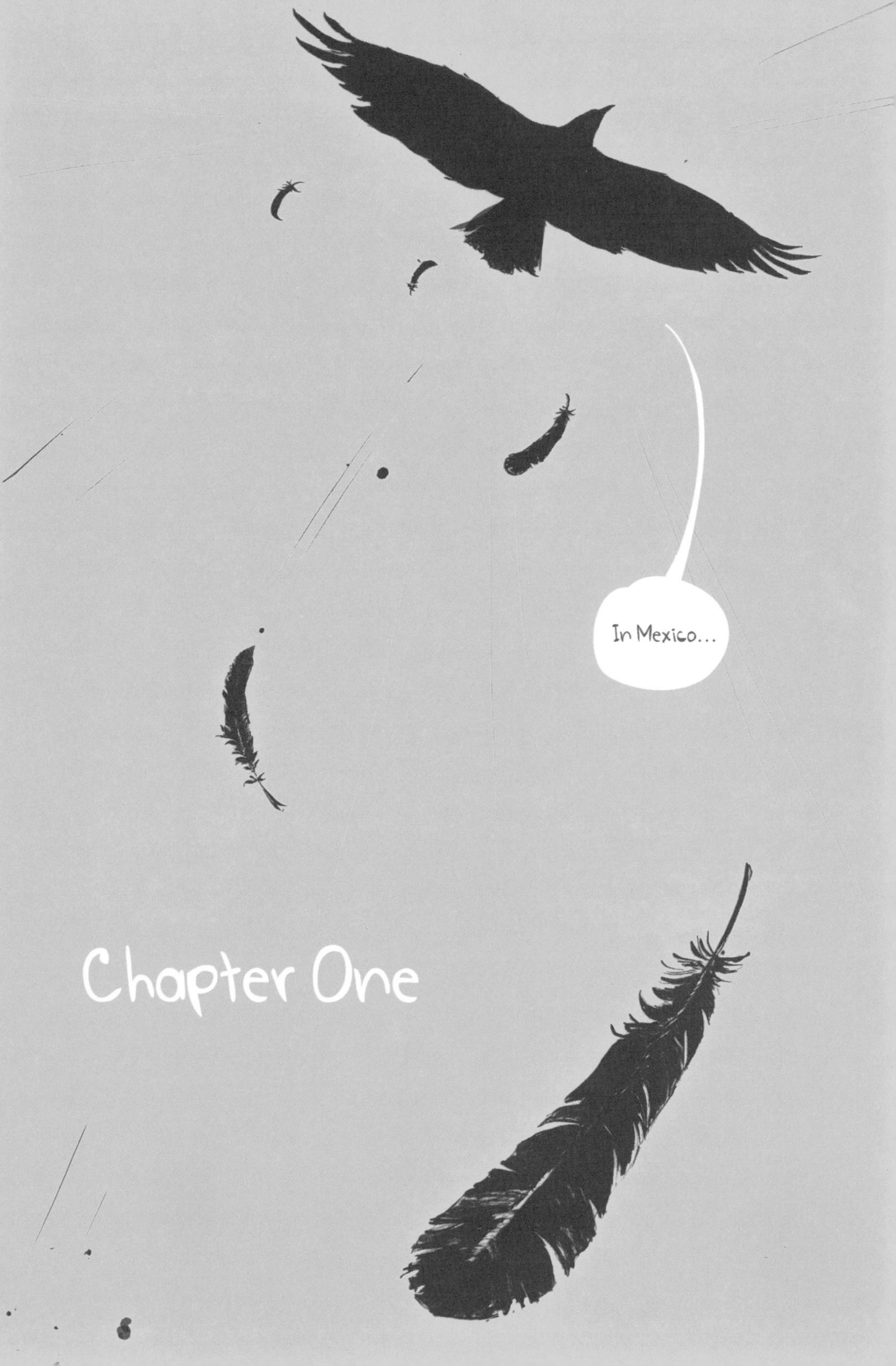
In Mexico...

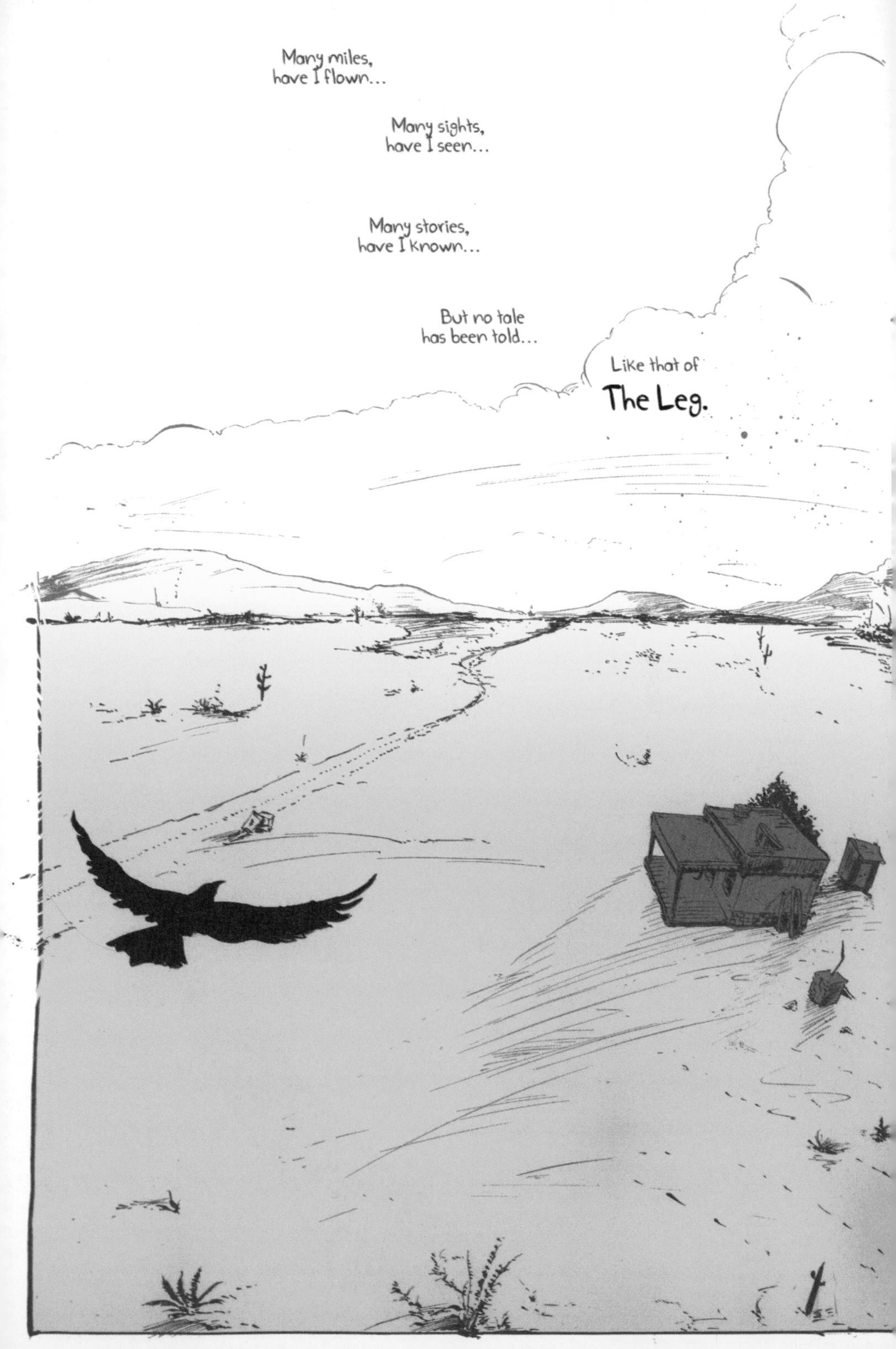
Many miles,
have I flown...
Many sights,
have I seen...
Many stories,
have I known...
But no tale
has been told...
Like that of
The Leg.

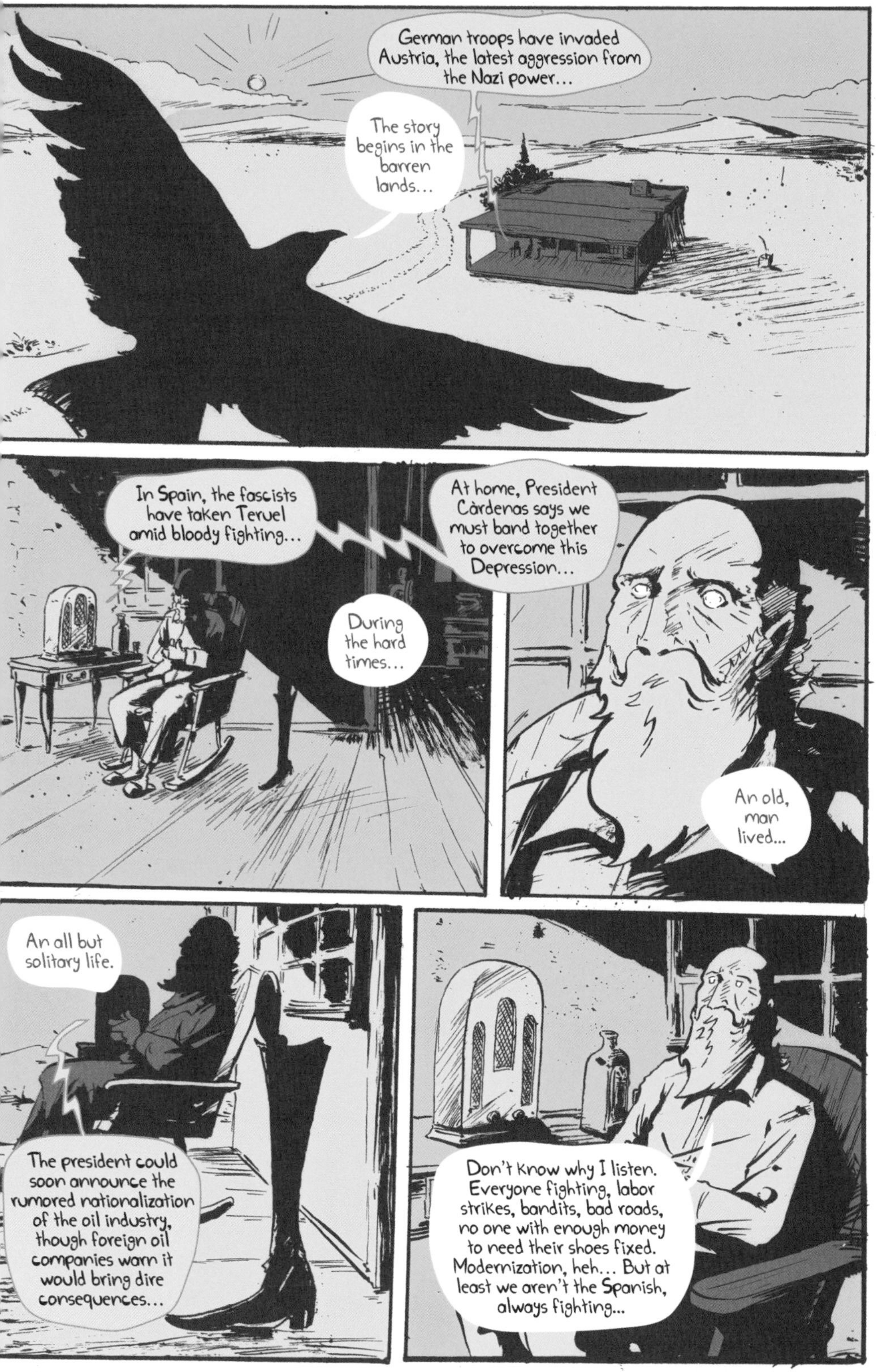

German troops have invaded Austria, the latest aggression from the Nazi power...
The story begins in the barren lands...
In Spain, the fascists have taken Teruel amid bloody fighting...
At home, President Càrdenas says we must band together to overcome this Depression...
During the hard times...
An old, man lived...
An all but solitary life.
The president could soon announce the rumored nationalization of the oil industry, though foreign oil companies warn it would bring dire consequences...
Don't know why I listen. Everyone fighting, labor strikes, bandits, bad roads, no one with enough money to need their shoes fixed. Modernization, heh... But at least we aren't the Spanish, always fighting...

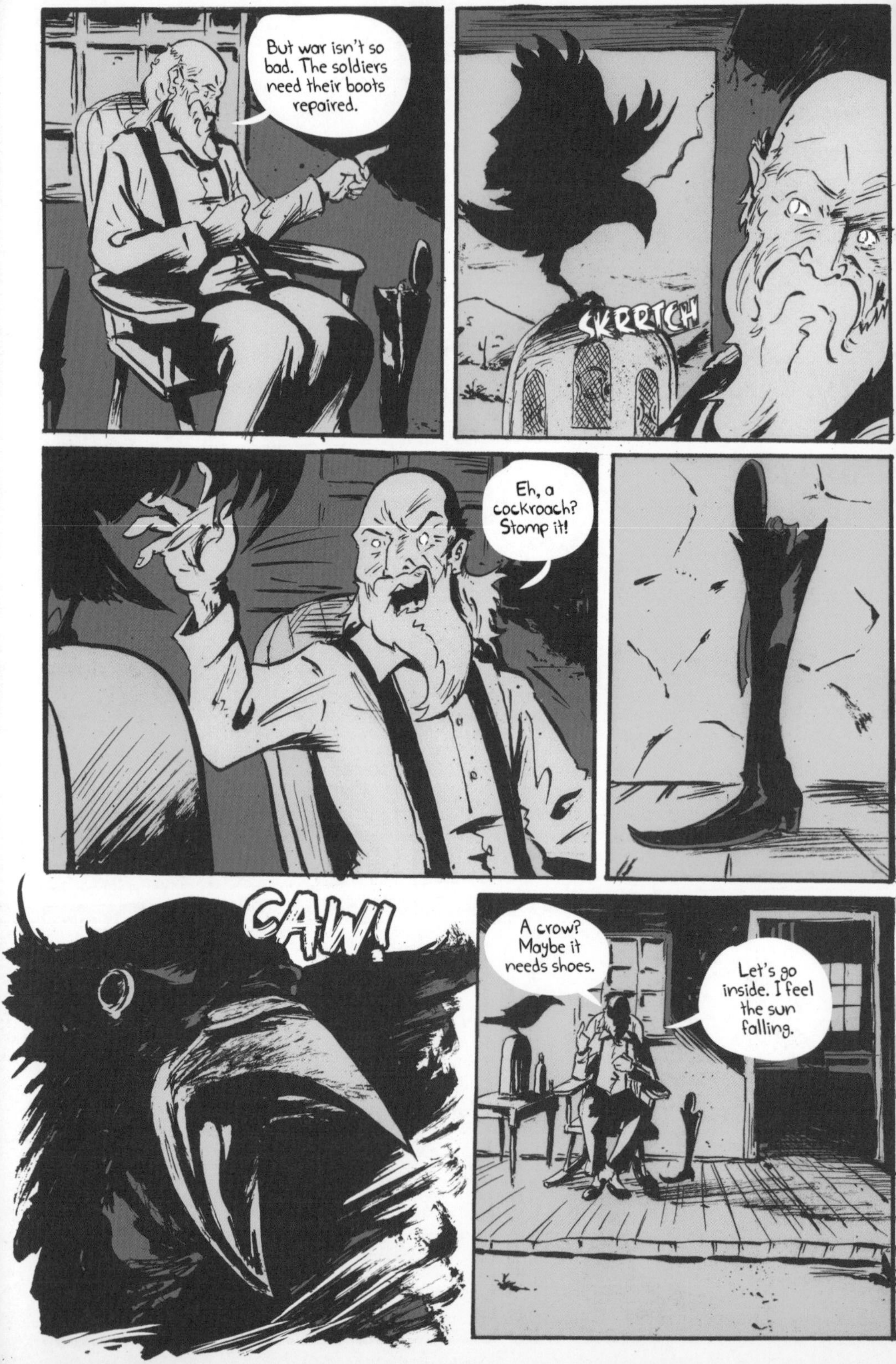
But war isn't so bad. The soldiers need their boots repaired.
SKRRTCH
Eh, a cockroach? Stomp it!
CAW!
A crow? Maybe it needs shoes.
Let's go inside. I feel the sun falling.

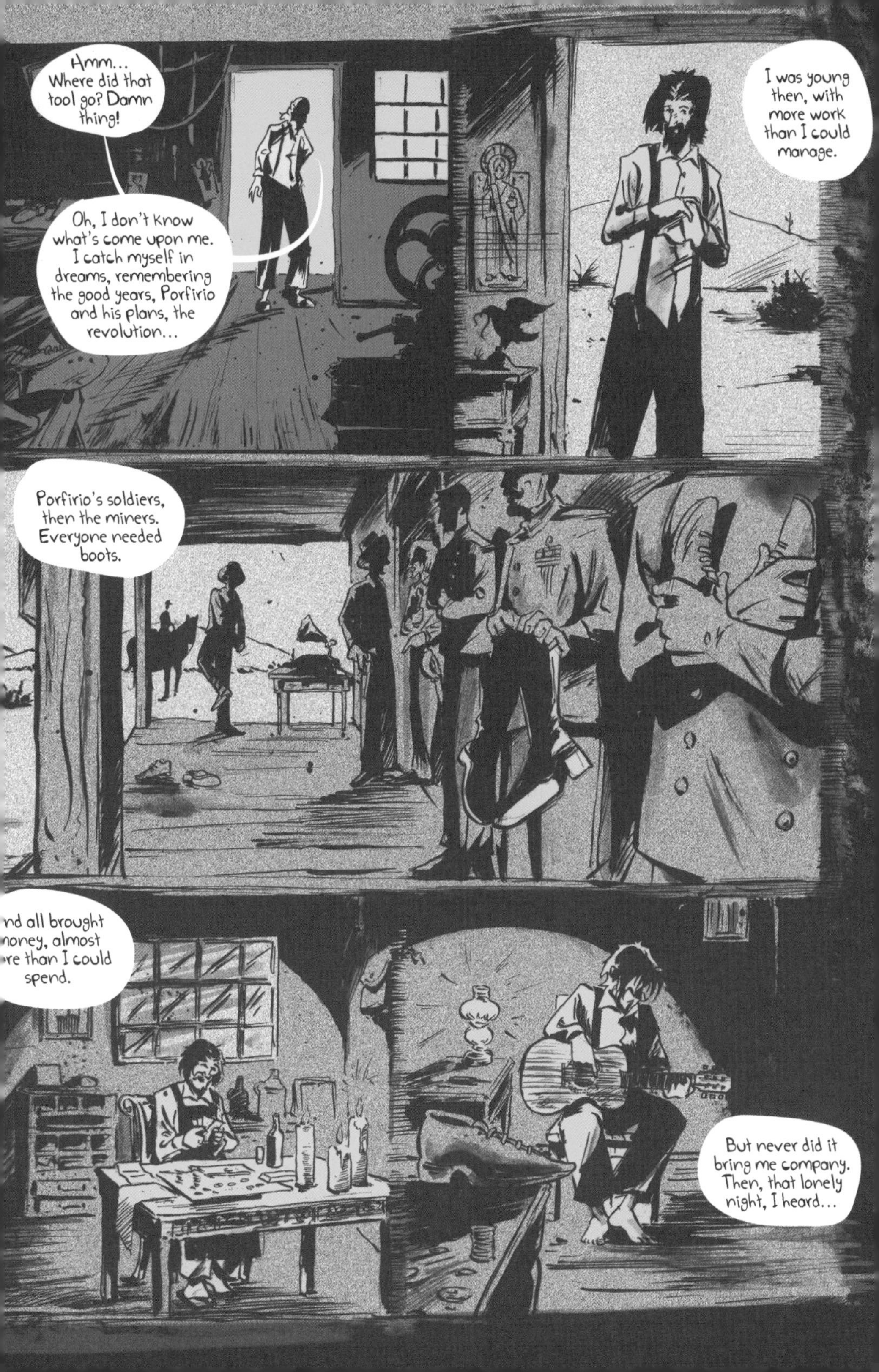
Hmm... Where did that tool go? Damn thing!
Oh, I don't know what's come upon me. I catch myself in dreams, remembering the good years, Porfirio and his plans, the revolution...
I was young then, with more work than I could manage.
Porfirio's soldiers, then the miners. Everyone needed boots.
nd all brought noney, almost re than I could spend.
But never did it bring me company. Then, that lonely night, I heard...

I brought you in, cared for you.

I couldn't have made it without you, my friend. That boot, the only perfect thing I've created.

Ah, but you know the story...

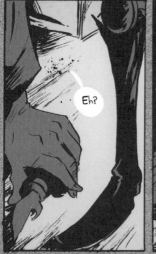

Eh?

Ah, gracias.

A story?

No, not "La Llorona" again.

I know the story for you, one you've never heard, that of "The Eagle."

Far before our time, dark years consumed Mexico. Her people lived ever afraid. Then, from the heavens, a great eagle came. Its talons and beak tore through our enemies till none stood. In thanks, the people worshiped their savior.

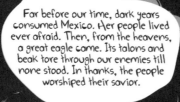

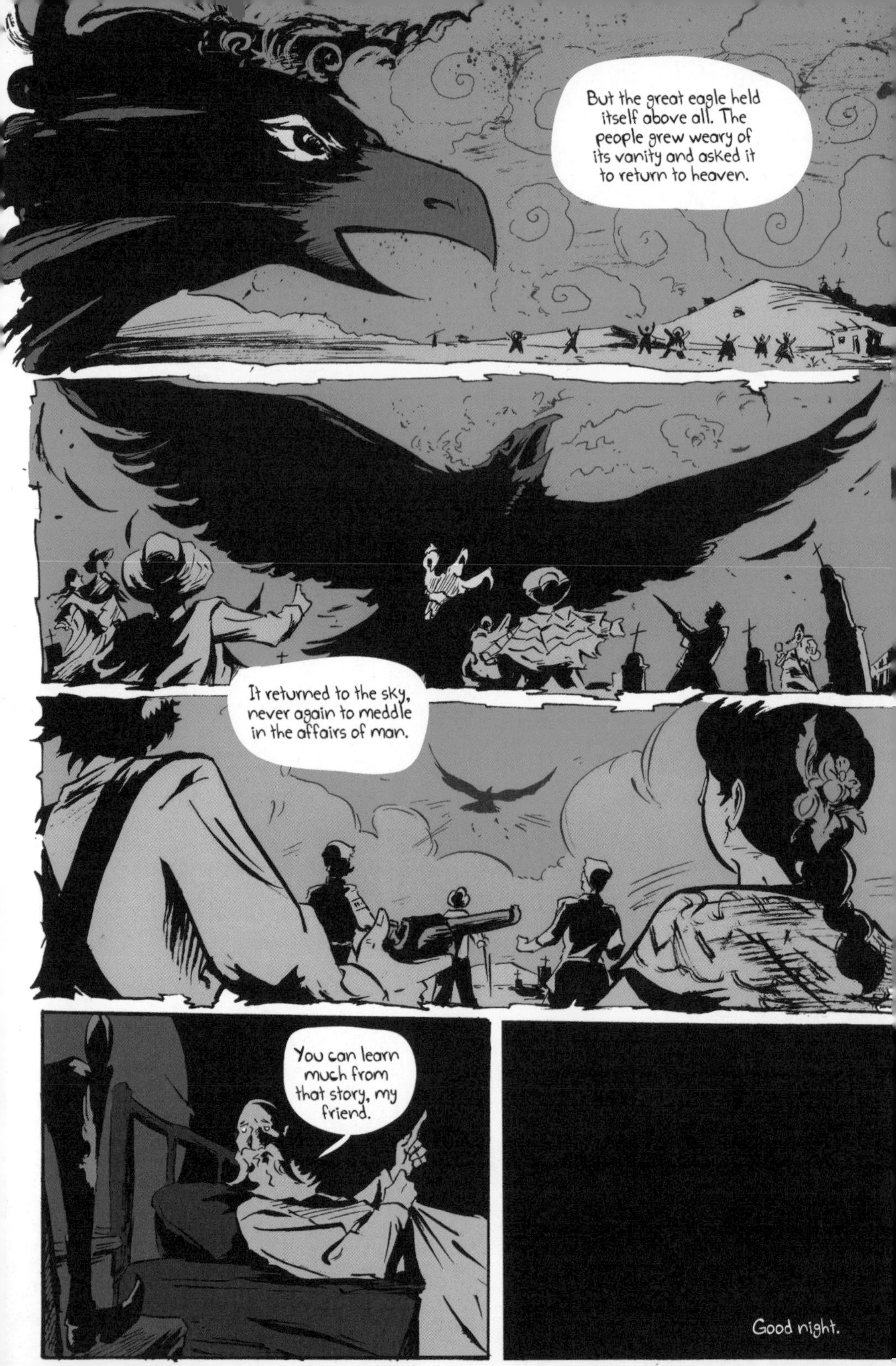
But the great eagle held itself above all. The people grew weary of its vanity and asked it to return to heaven.
It returned to the sky, never again to meddle in the affairs of man.
You can learn much from that story, my friend.
Good night.

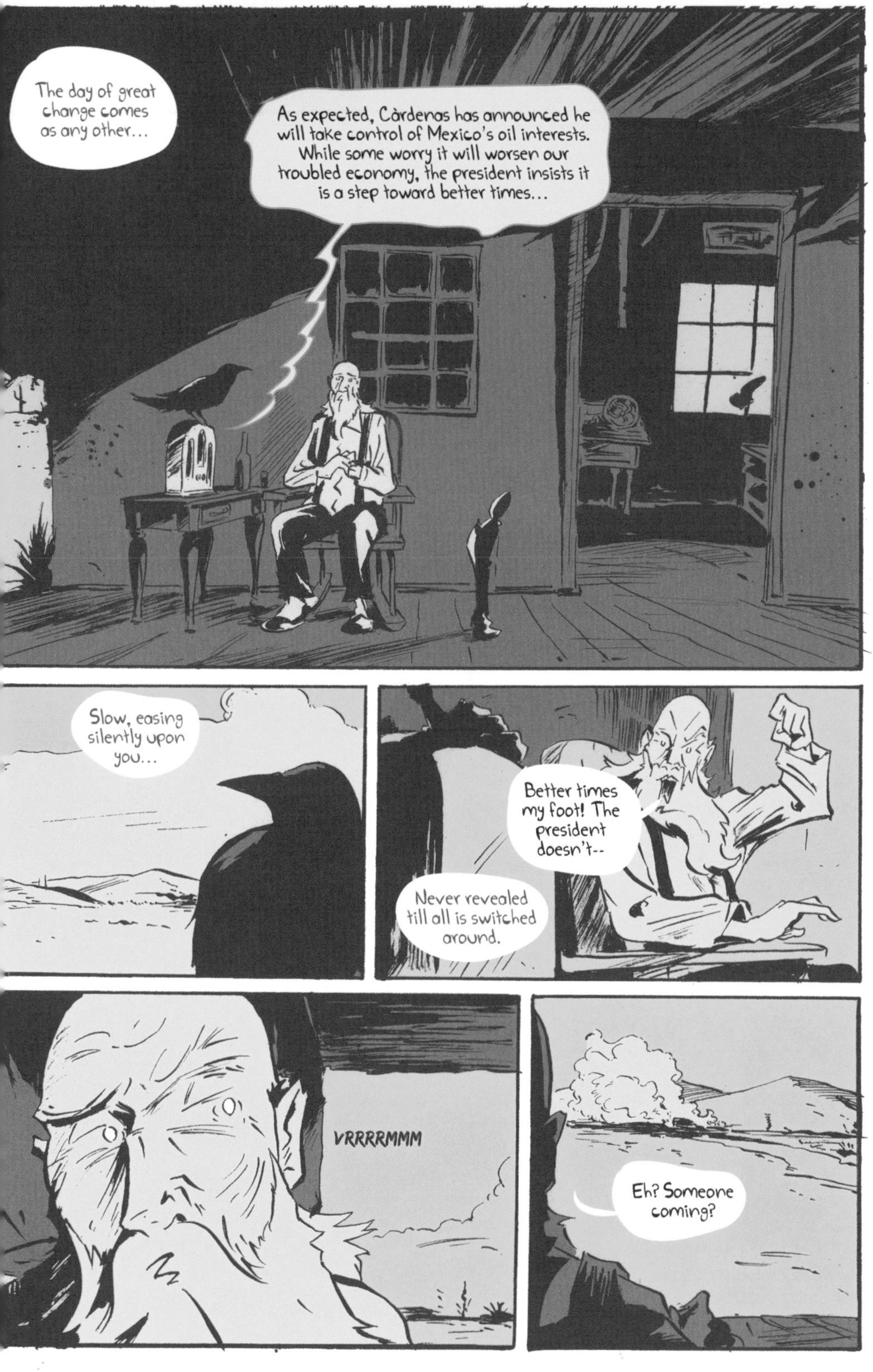
The day of great change comes as any other...
As expected, Càrdenas has announced he will take control of Mexico's oil interests. While some worry it will worsen our troubled economy, the president insists it is a step toward better times...
Slow, easing silently upon you...
Better times my foot! The president doesn't--
Never revealed till all is switched around.
VRRRRMMM
Eh? Someone coming?

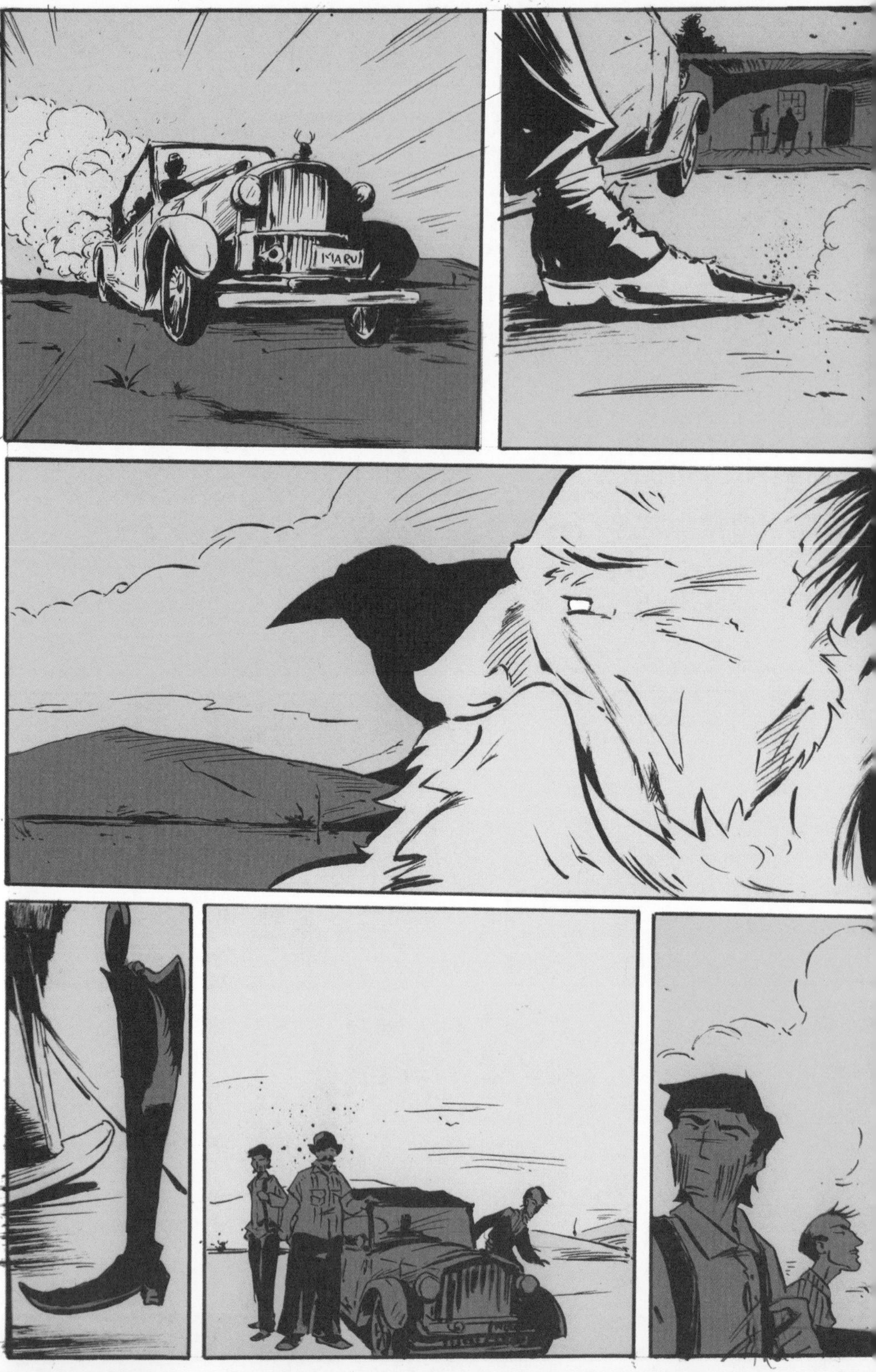
MARU

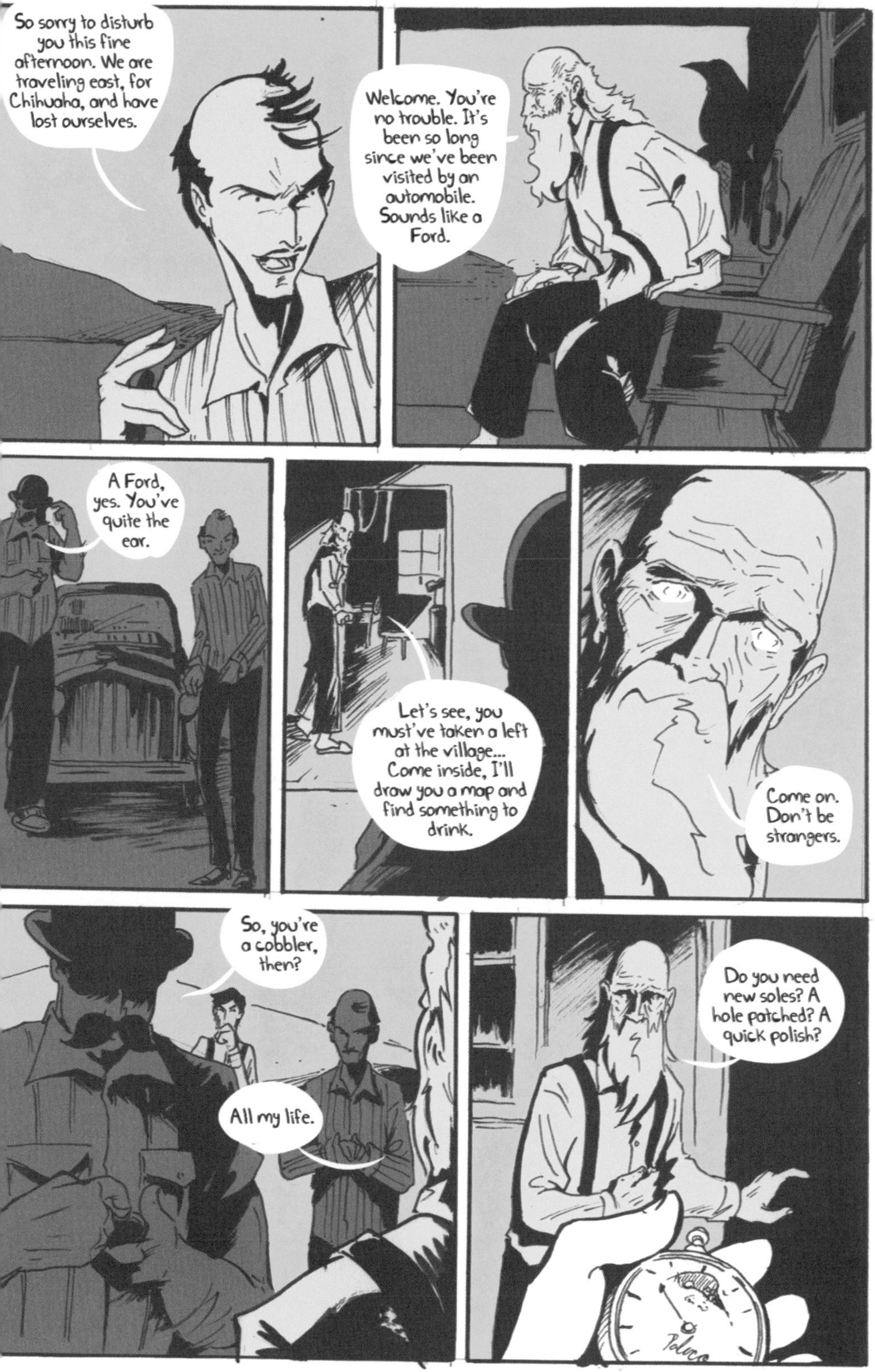
So sorry to disturb you this fine afternoon. We are traveling east, for Chihuaha, and have lost ourselves.
Welcome. You're no trouble. It's been so long since we've been visited by an automobile. Sounds like a Ford.
A Ford, yes. You've quite the ear.
Let's see, you must've taken a left at the village... Come inside, I'll draw you a map and find something to drink.
Come on. Don't be strangers.
So, you're a cobbler, then?
All my life.
Do you need new soles? A hole patched? A quick polish?
Poloco

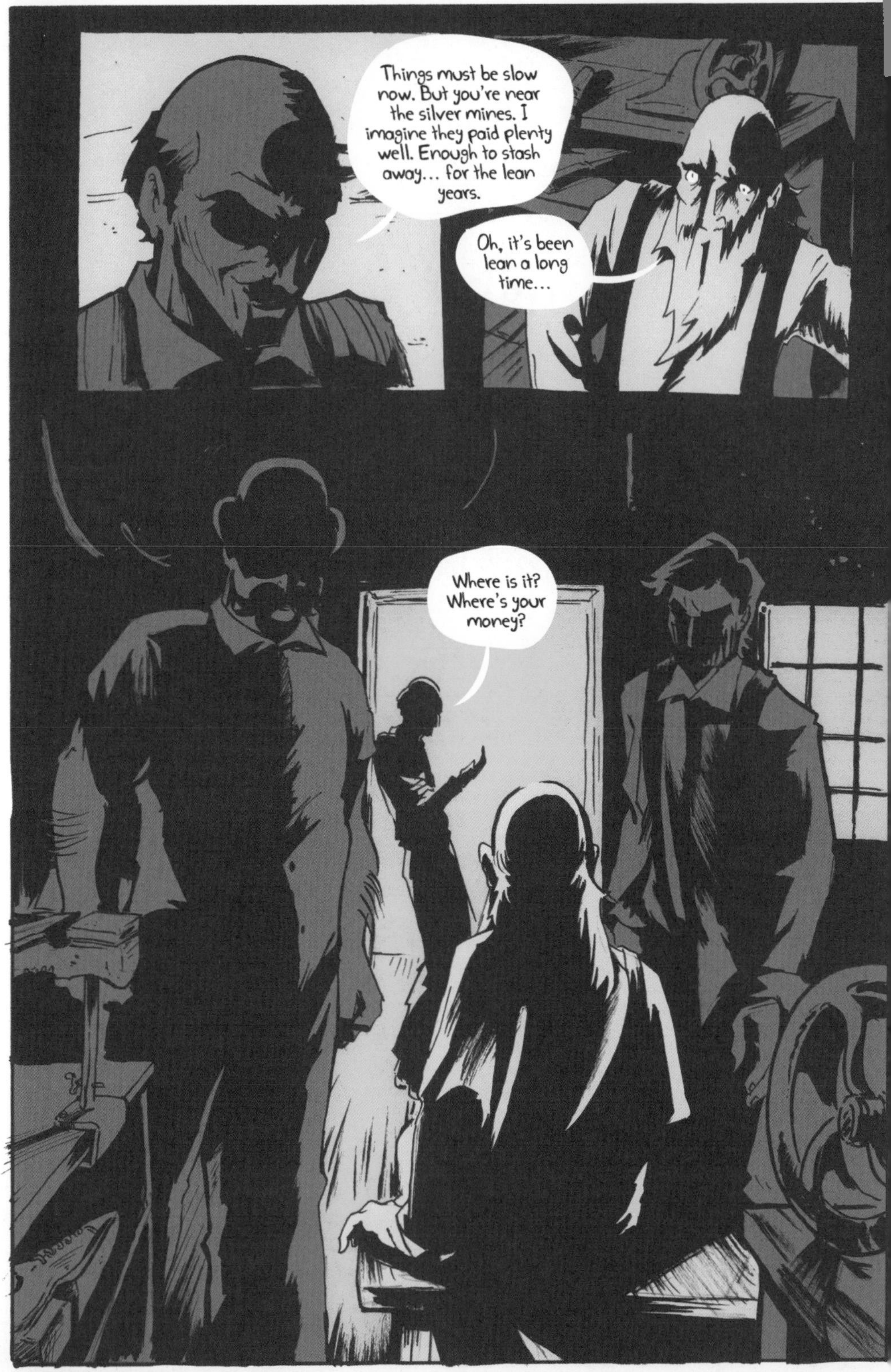
Things must be slow now. But you're near the silver mines. I imagine they paid plenty well. Enough to stash away... for the lean years.
Oh, it's been lean a long time...
Where is it? Where's your money?

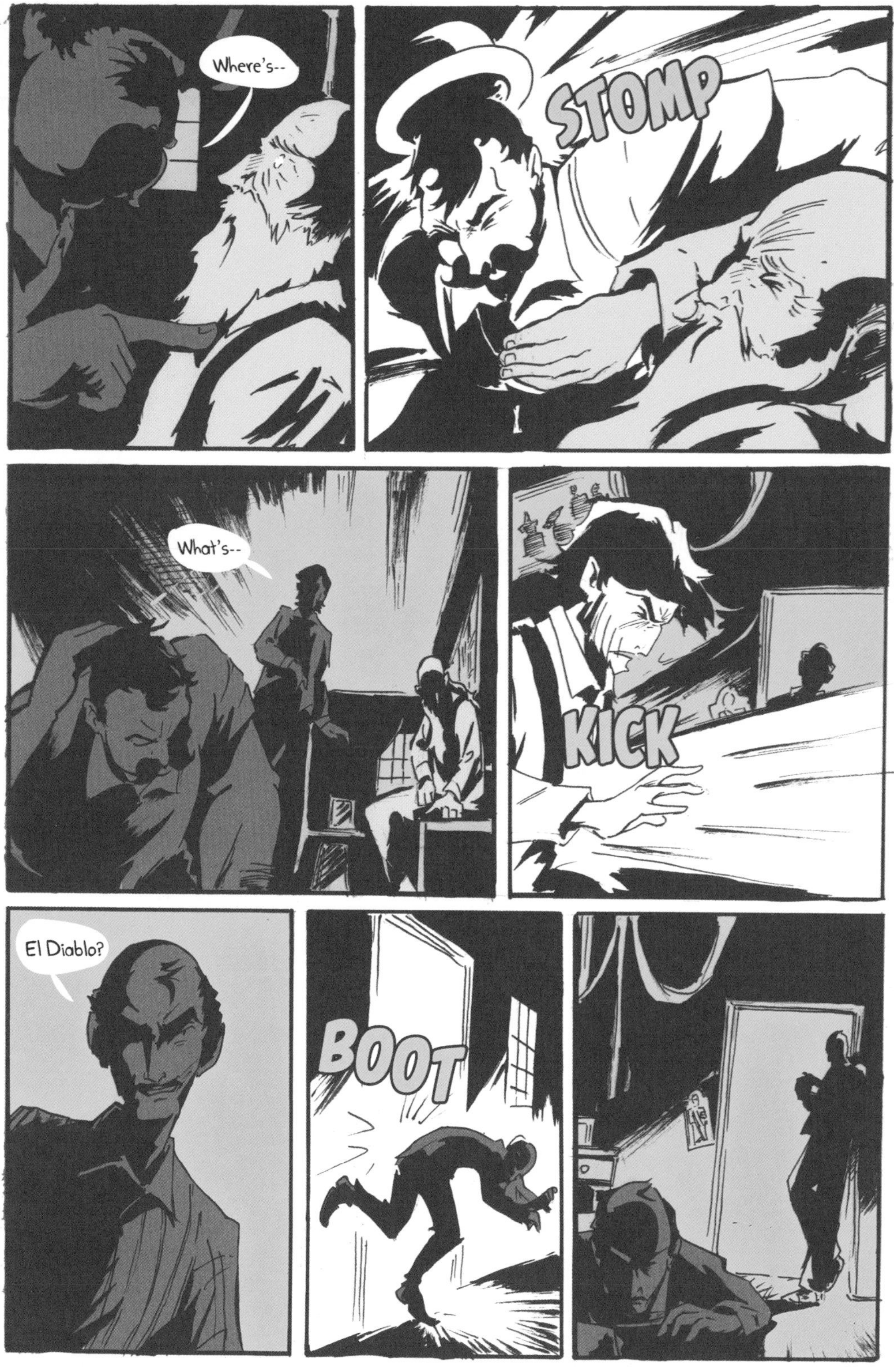
Where's--
STOMP
What's--
KICK
El Diablo?
BOOT

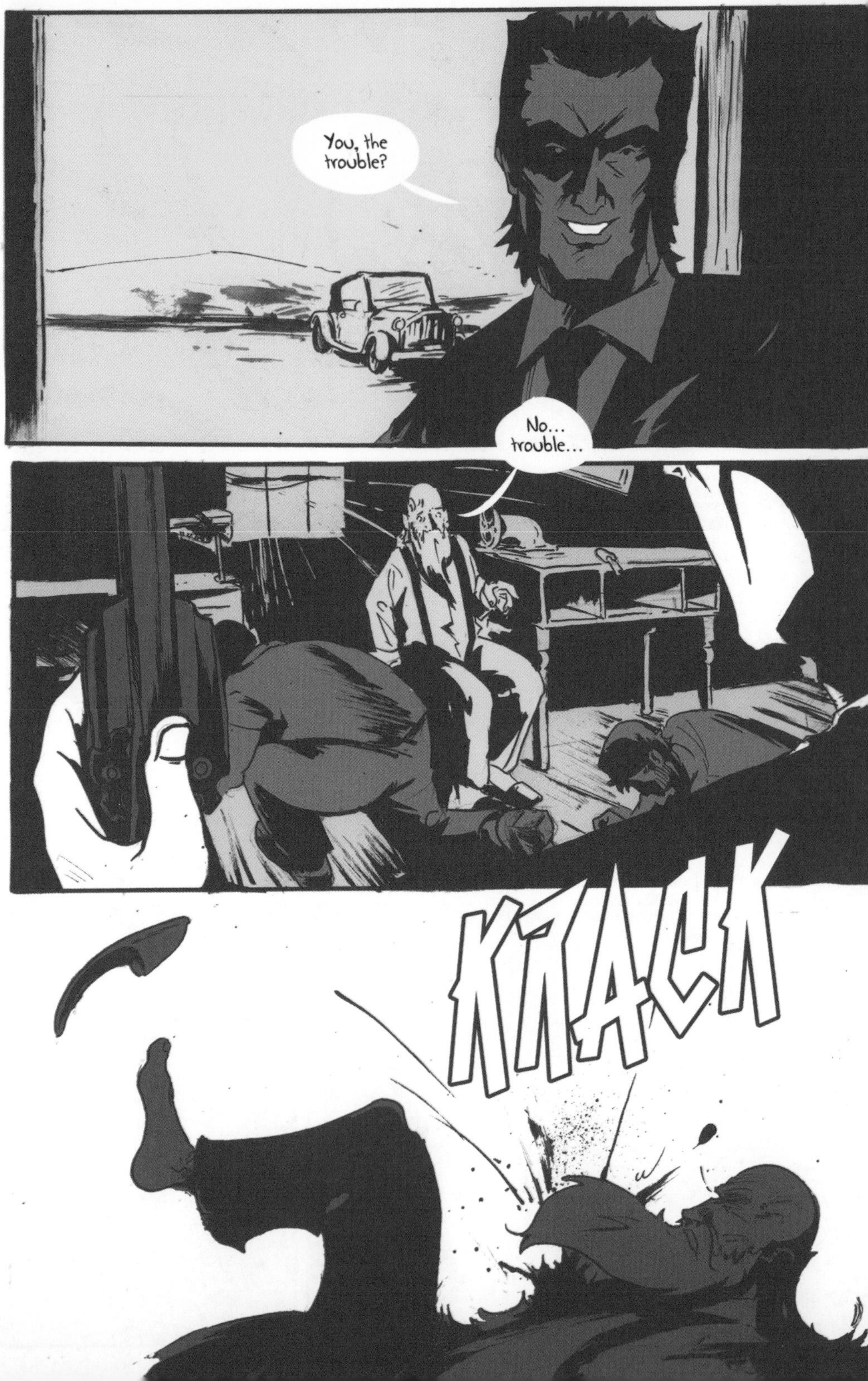
You, the trouble?
No... trouble...
KRACK

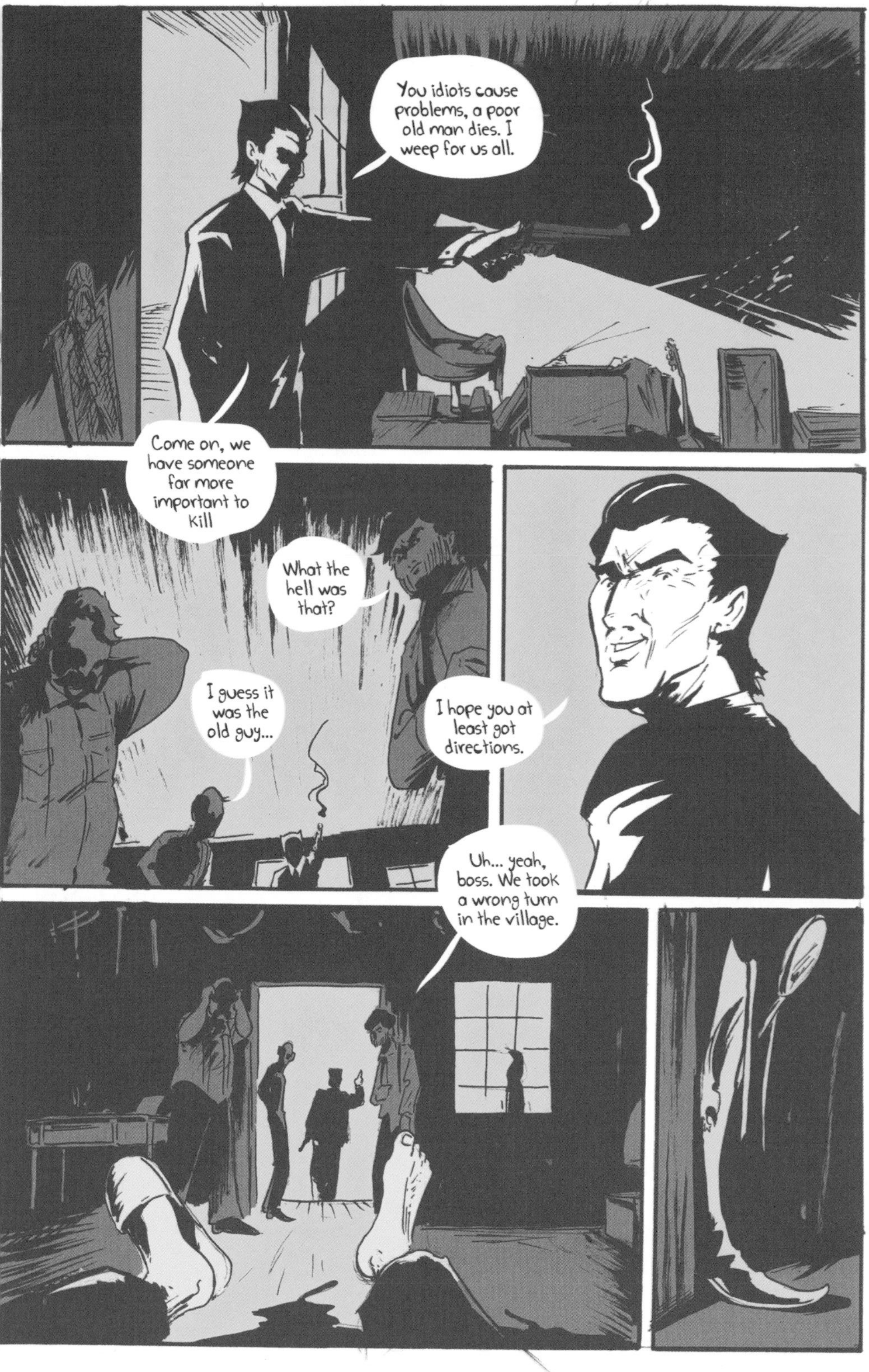
You idiots cause problems, a poor old man dies. I weep for us all.
Come on, we have someone far more important to kill
What the hell was that?
I guess it was the old guy...
I hope you at least got directions.
Uh... yeah, boss. We took a wrong turn in the village.

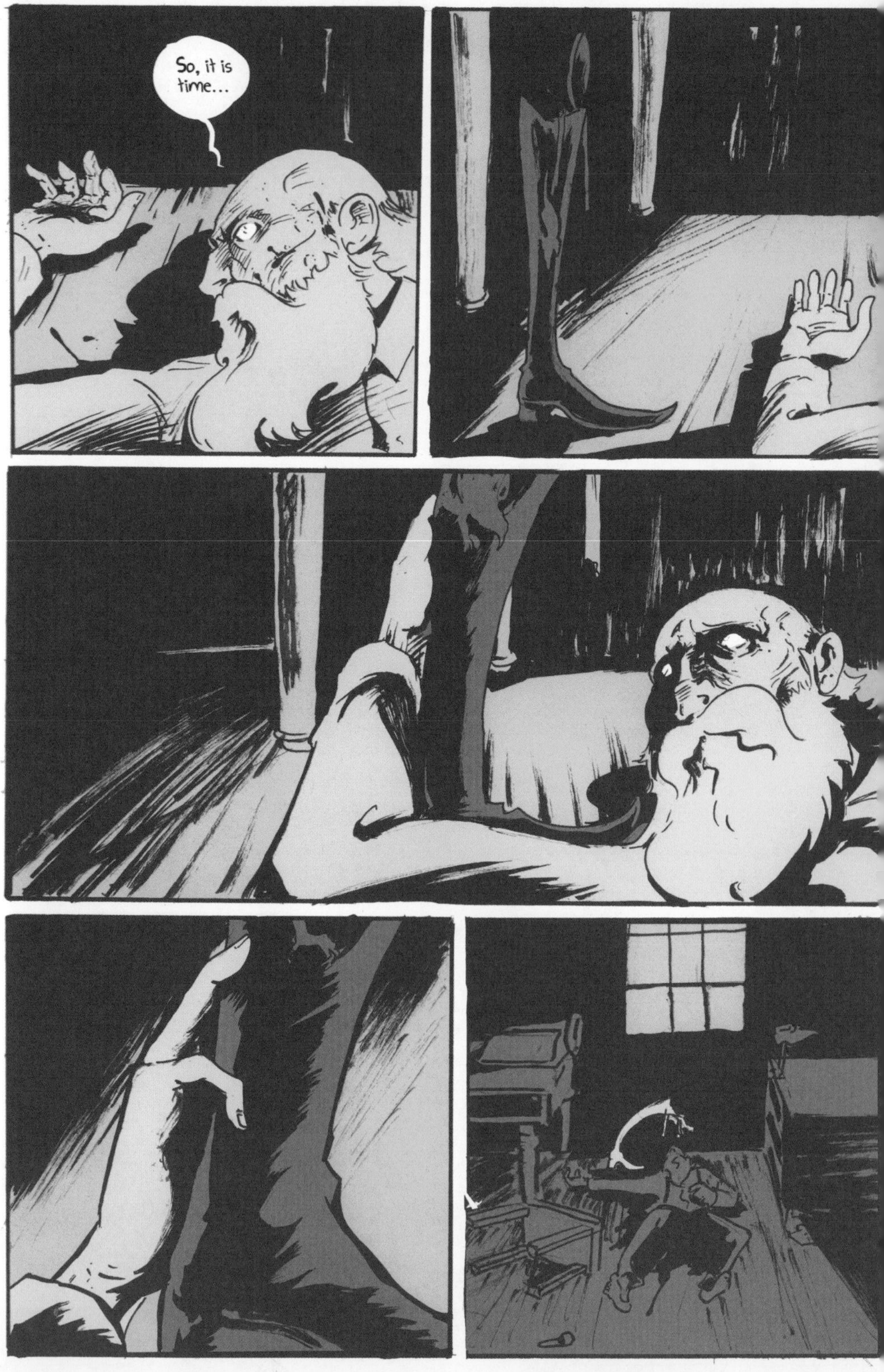
So, it is time...

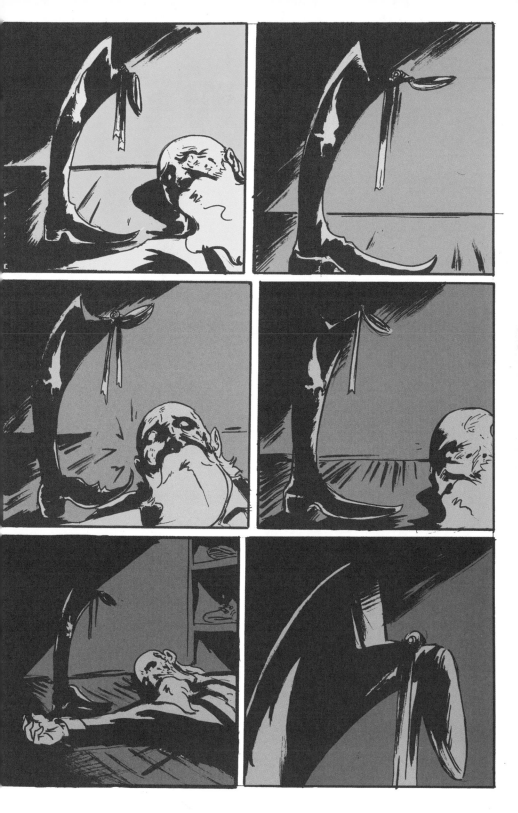

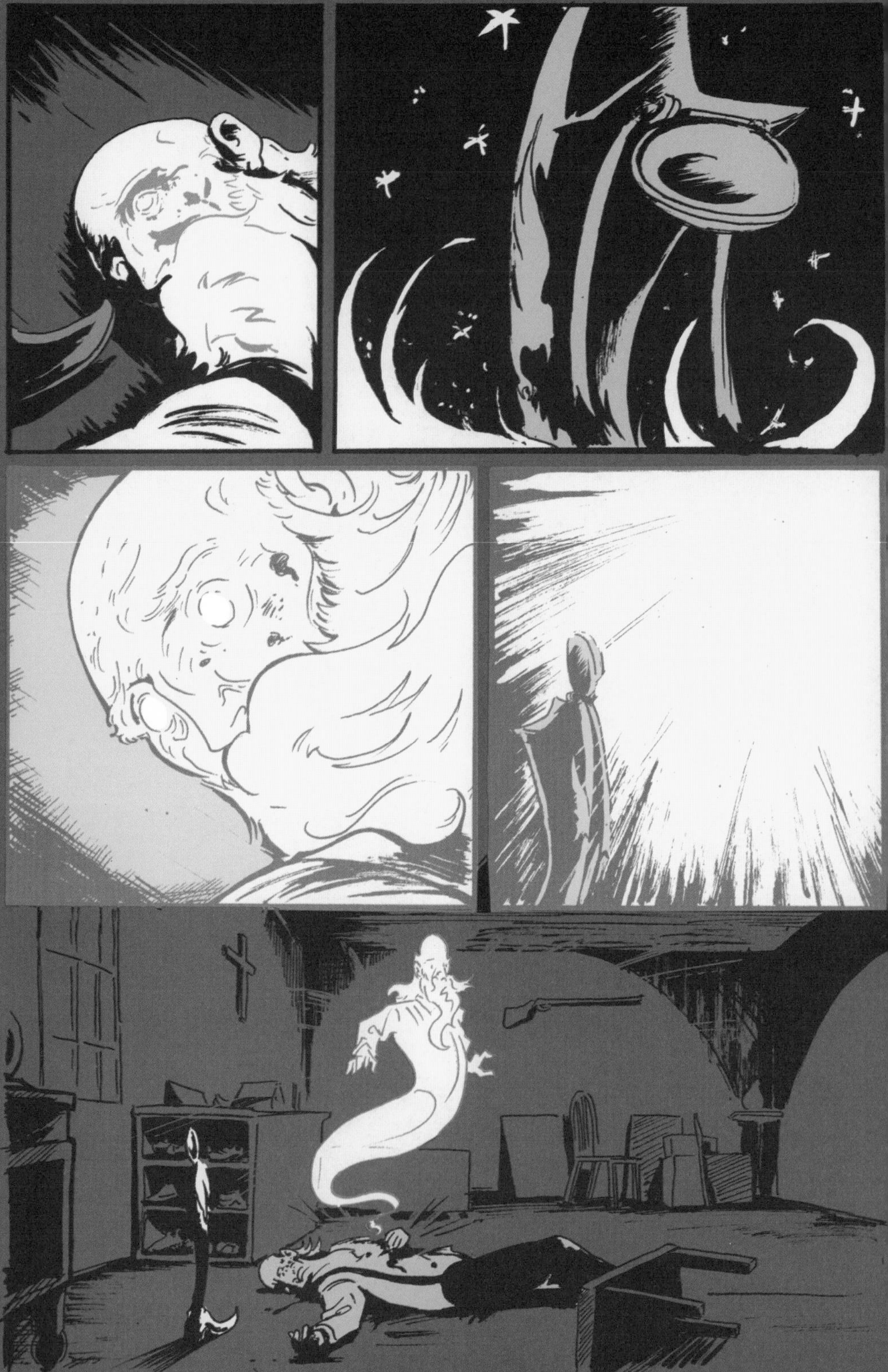

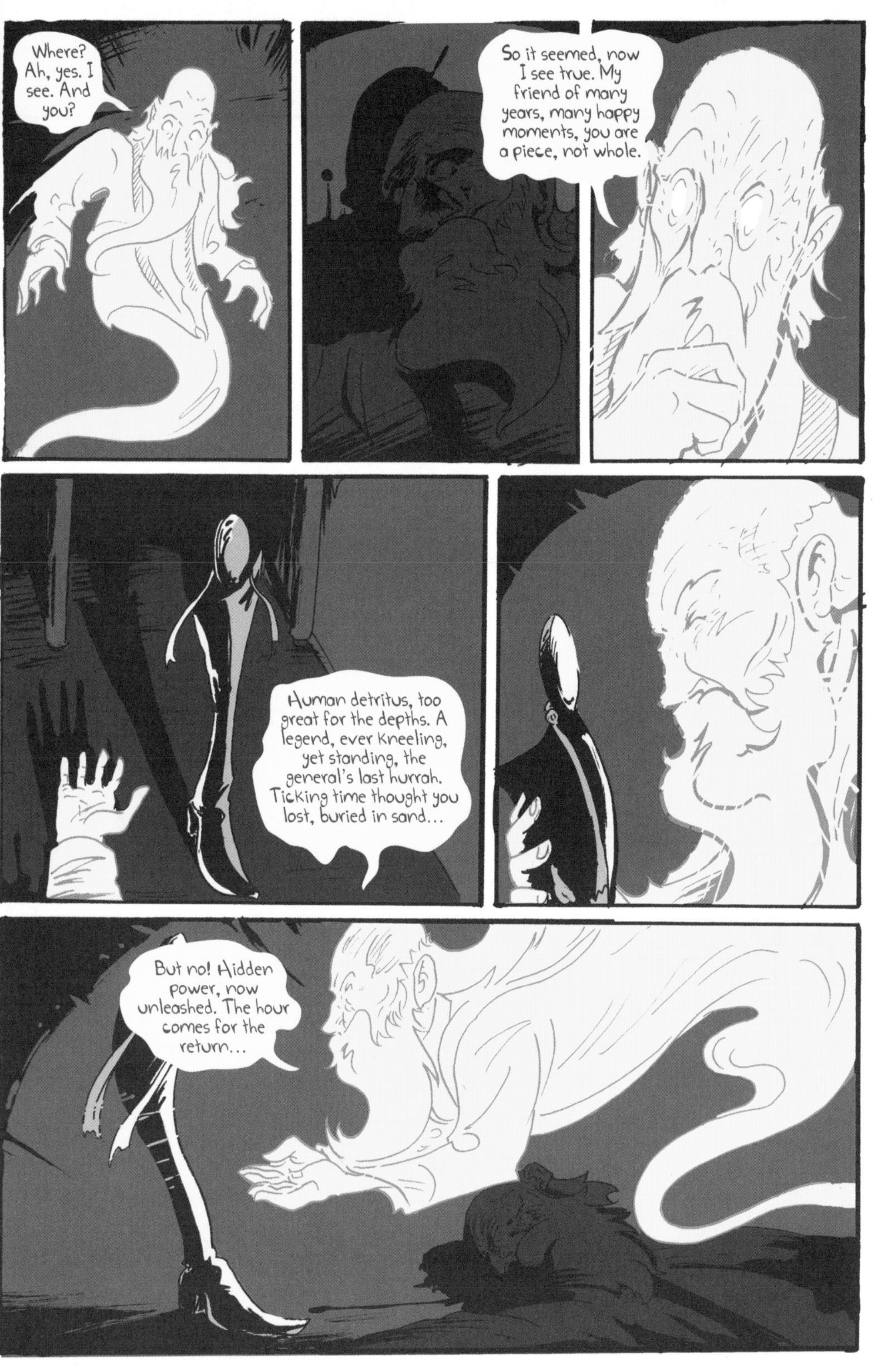
Where? Ah, yes. I see. And you?
So it seemed, now I see true. My friend of many years, many happy moments, you are a piece, not whole.
Human detritus, too great for the depths. A legend, ever kneeling, yet standing, the general's last hurrah. Ticking time thought you lost, buried in sand...
But no! Hidden power, now unleashed. The hour comes for the return...

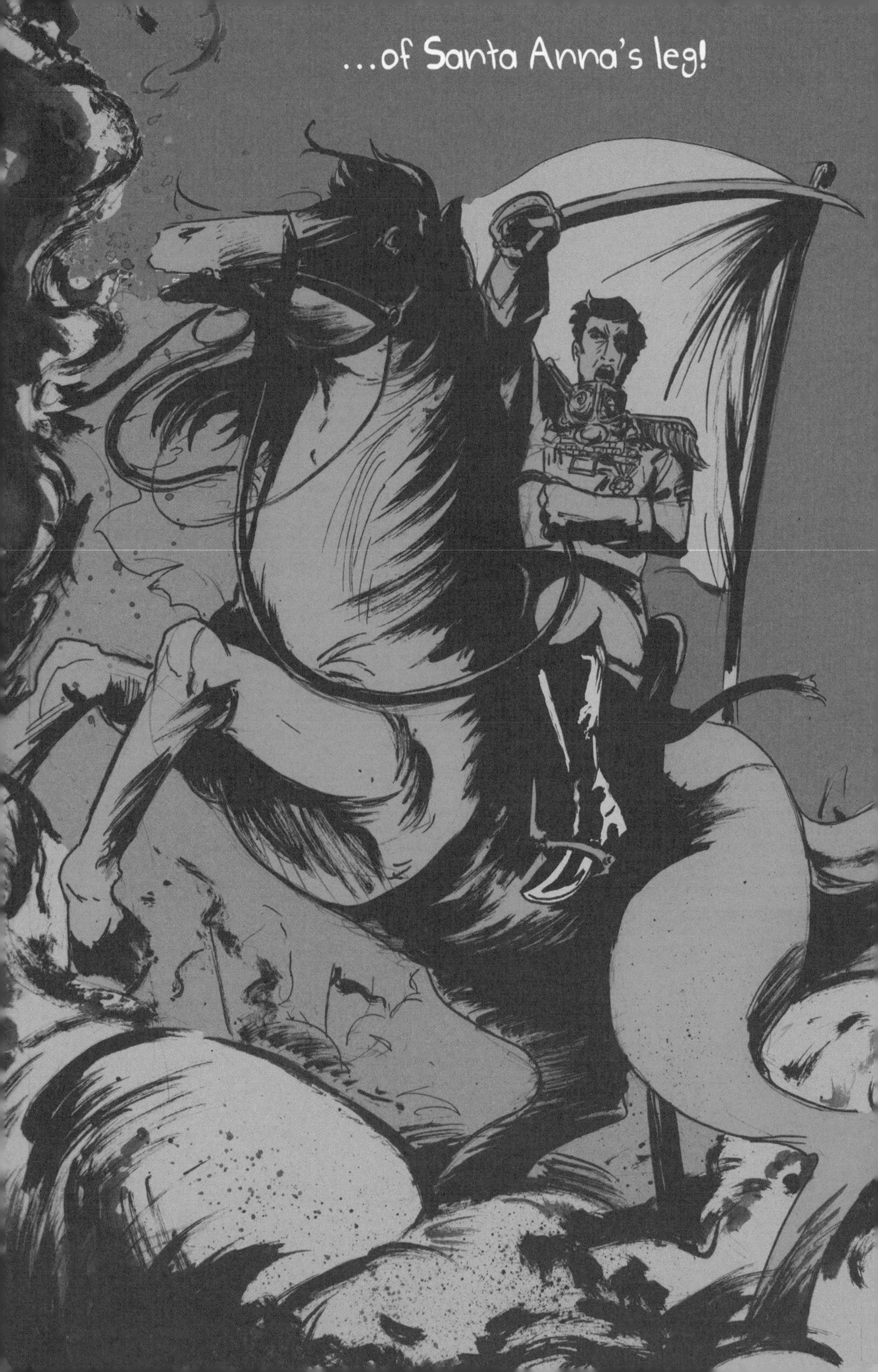
...of Santa Anna's leg!

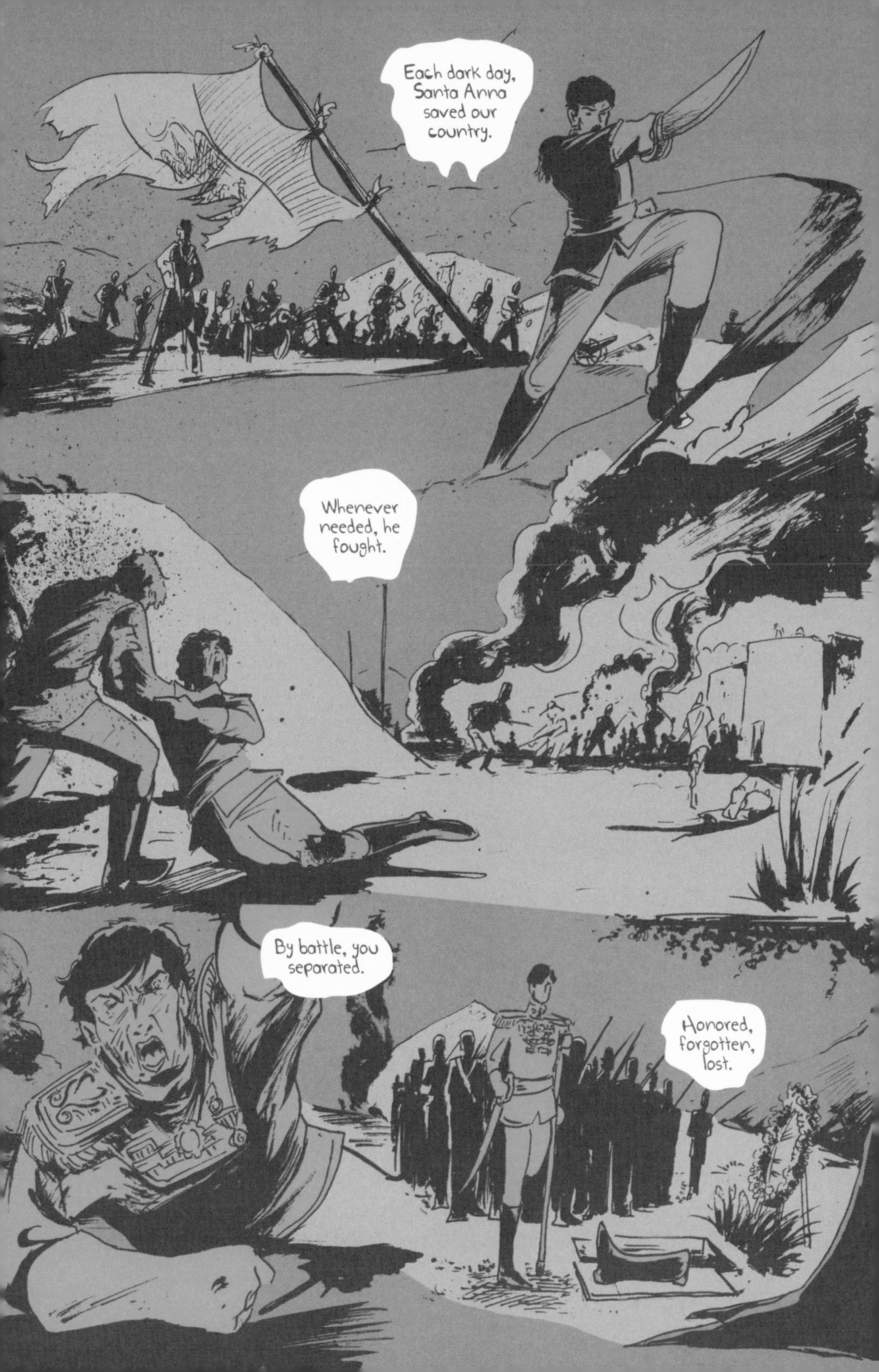
Each dark day, Santa Anna saved our country.
Whenever needed, he fought.
By battle, you separated.
Honored, forgotten, lost.

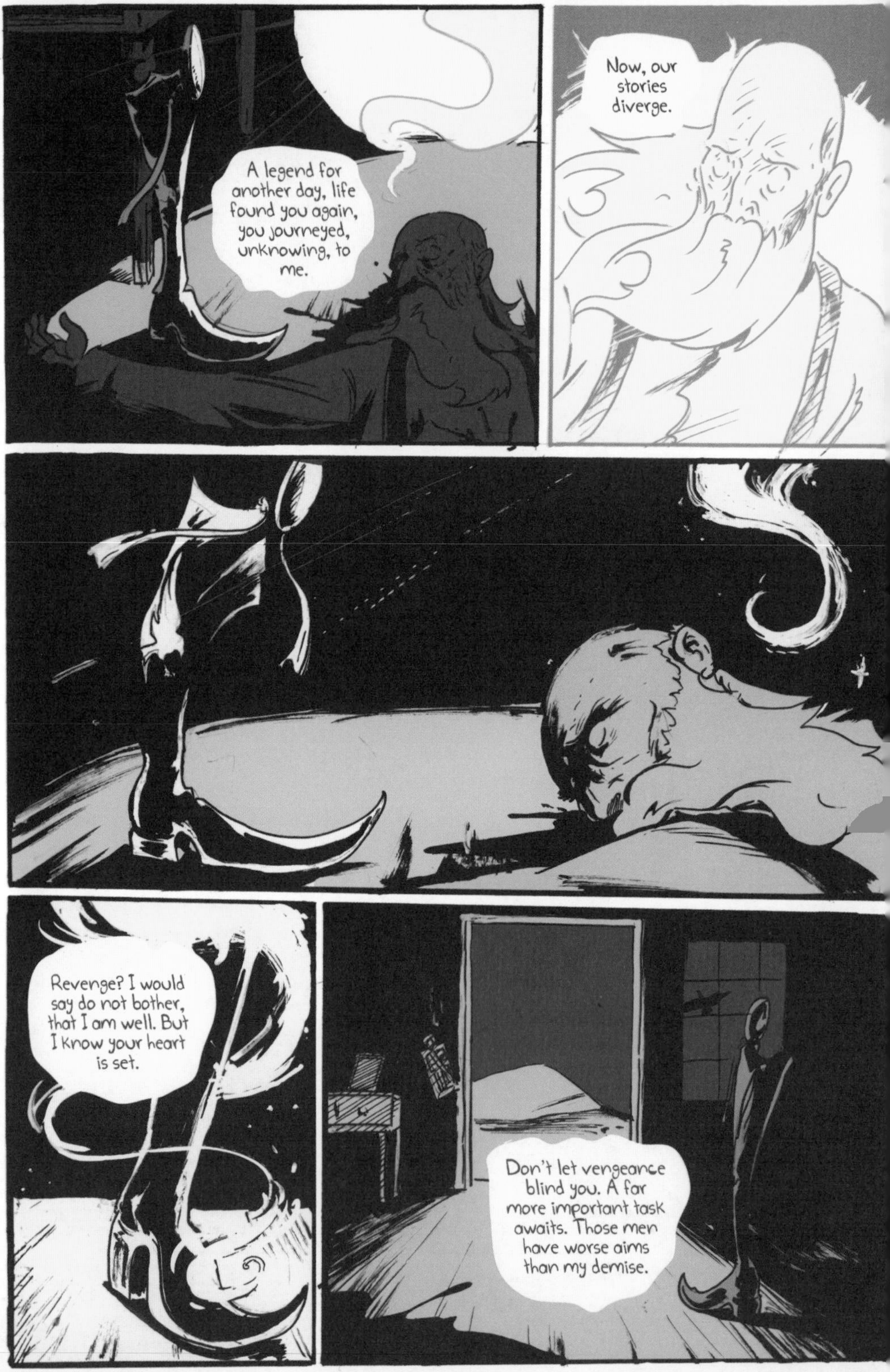
A legend for another day, life found you again, you journeyed, unknowing, to me.
Now, our stories diverge.
Revenge? I would say do not bother, that I am well. But I know your heart is set.
Don't let vengeance blind you. A far more important task awaits. Those men have worse aims than my demise.

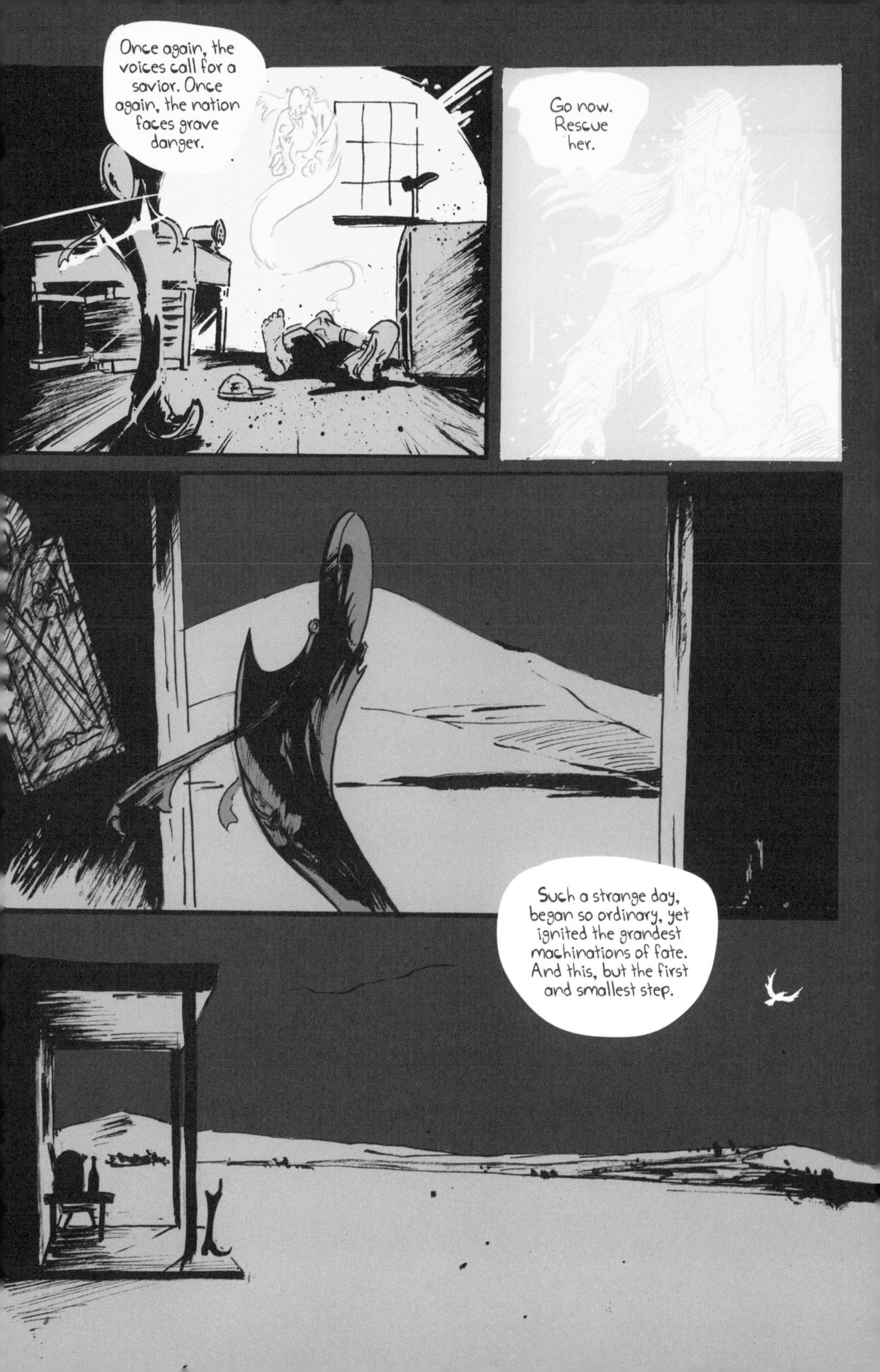
Once again, the voices call for a savior. Once again, the nation faces grave danger.
Go now. Rescue her.
Such a strange day, began so ordinary, yet ignited the grandest machinations of fate. And this, but the first and smallest step.

CHAPTER TWO

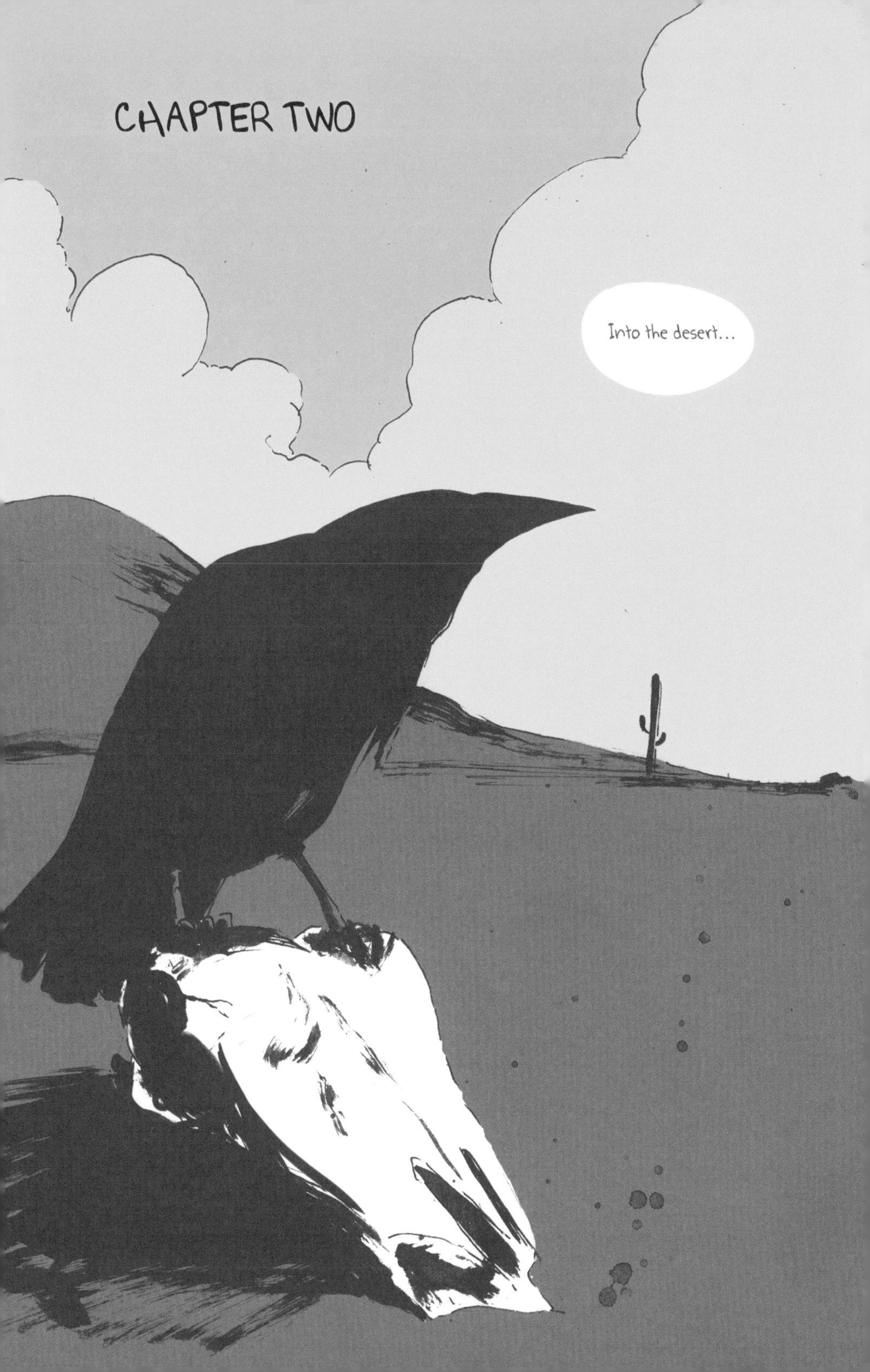
Into the desert...

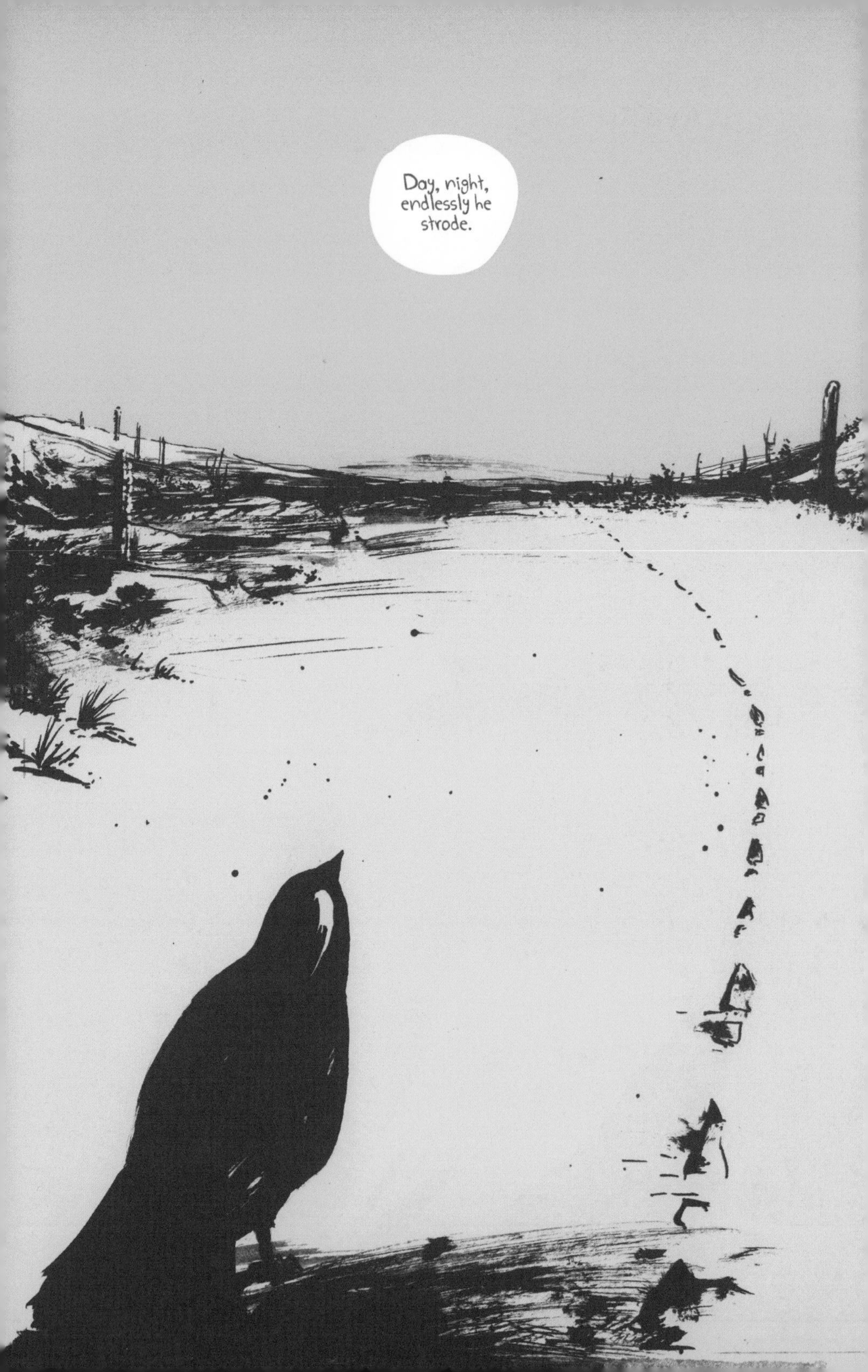
Day, night, endlessly he strode.

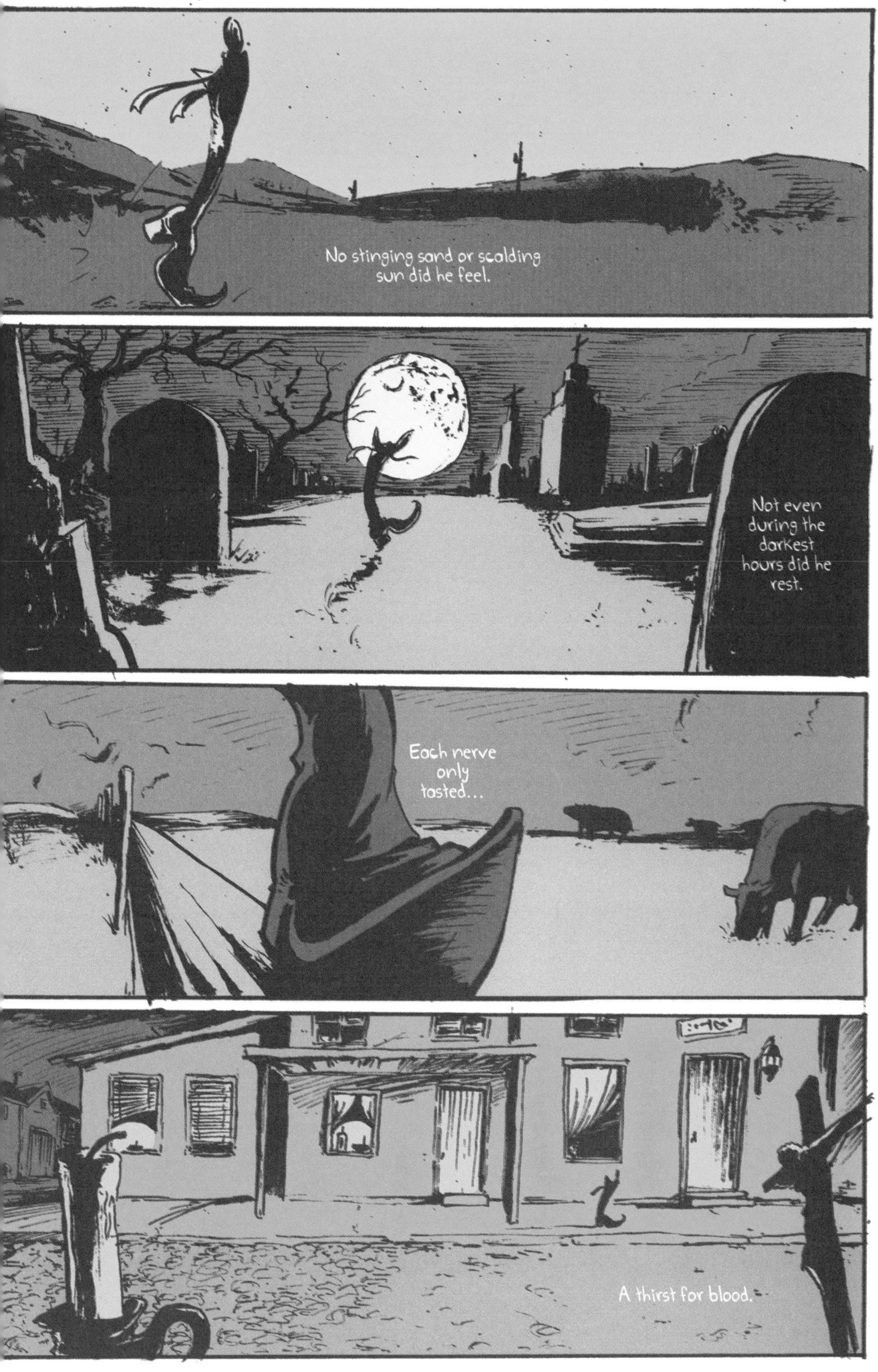
No stinging sand or scalding sun did he feel.
Not even during the darkest hours did he rest.
Each nerve only tasted...
A thirst for blood.

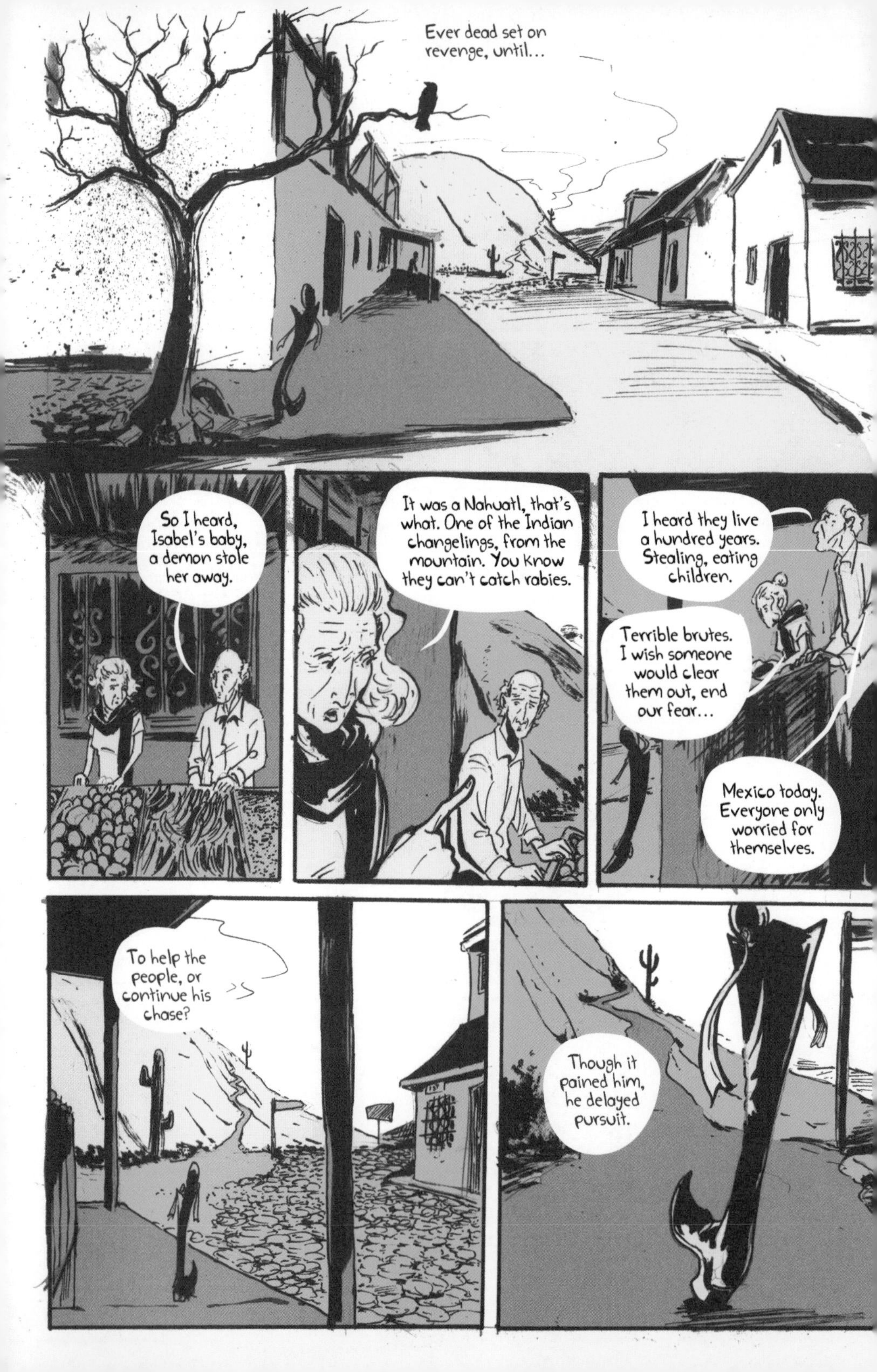
Ever dead set on revenge, until...
So I heard, Isabel's baby, a demon stole her away.
It was a Nahuatl, that's what. One of the Indian changelings, from the mountain. You know they can't catch rabies.
I heard they live a hundred years. Stealing, eating children.
Terrible brutes. I wish someone would clear them out, end our fear...
Mexico today. Everyone only worried for themselves.
To help the people, or continue his chase?
Though it pained him, he delayed pursuit.

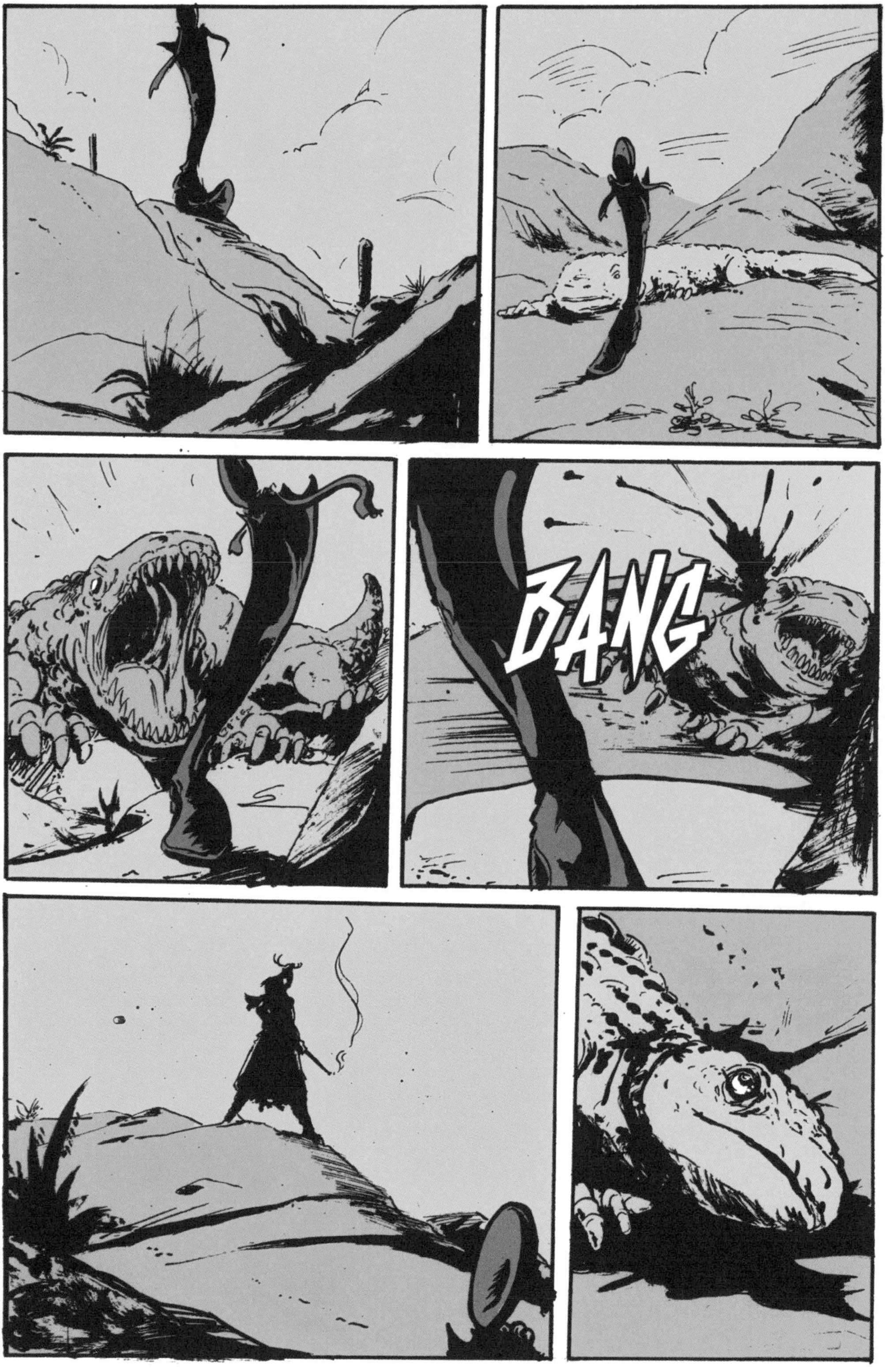
BANG

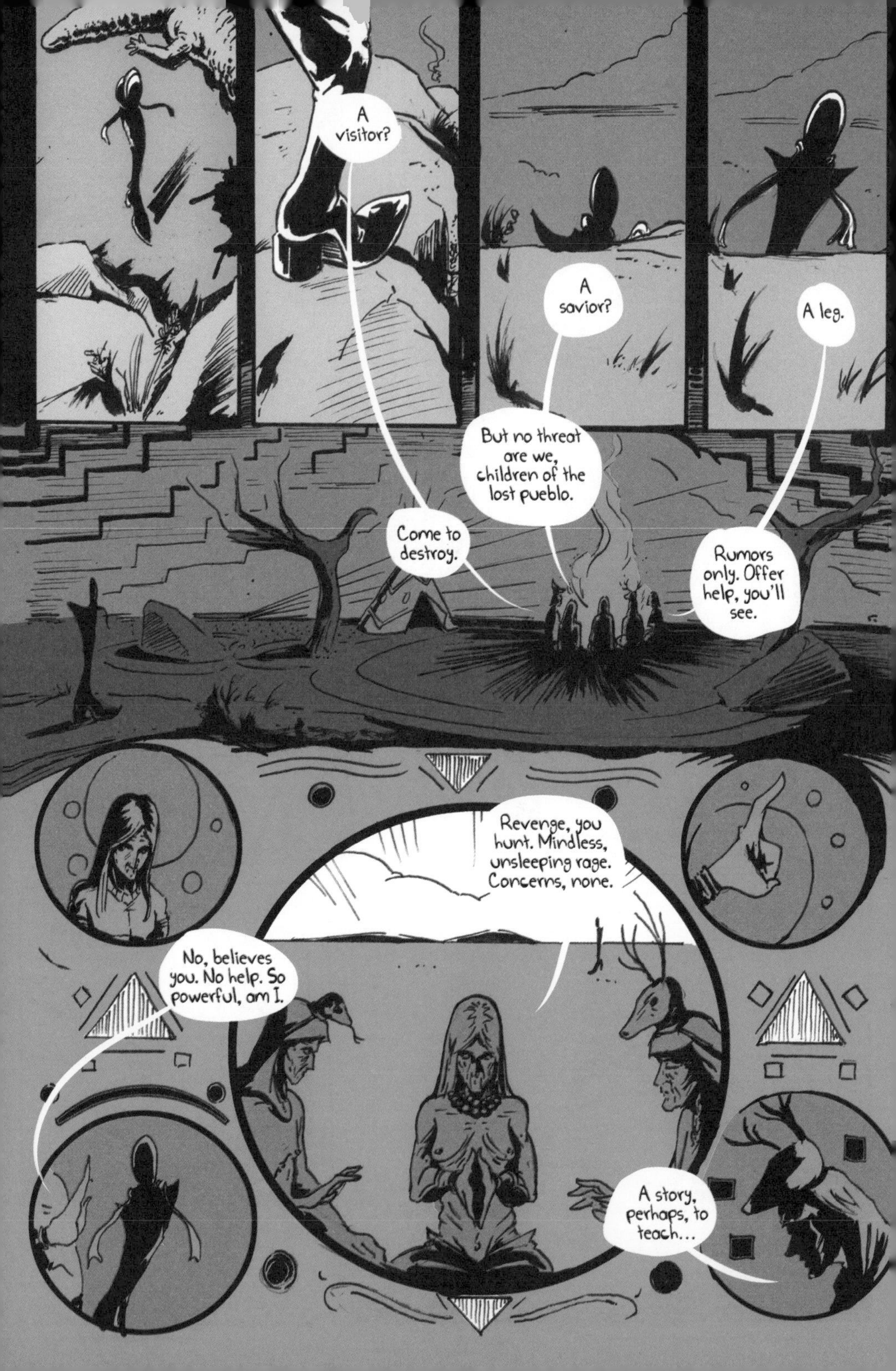
A visitor?
A savior?
A leg.
But no threat are we, children of the lost pueblo.
Come to destroy.
Rumors only. Offer help, you'll see.
Revenge, you hunt. Mindless, unsleeping rage. Concerns, none.
No, believes you. No help. So powerful, am I.
A story, perhaps, to teach…

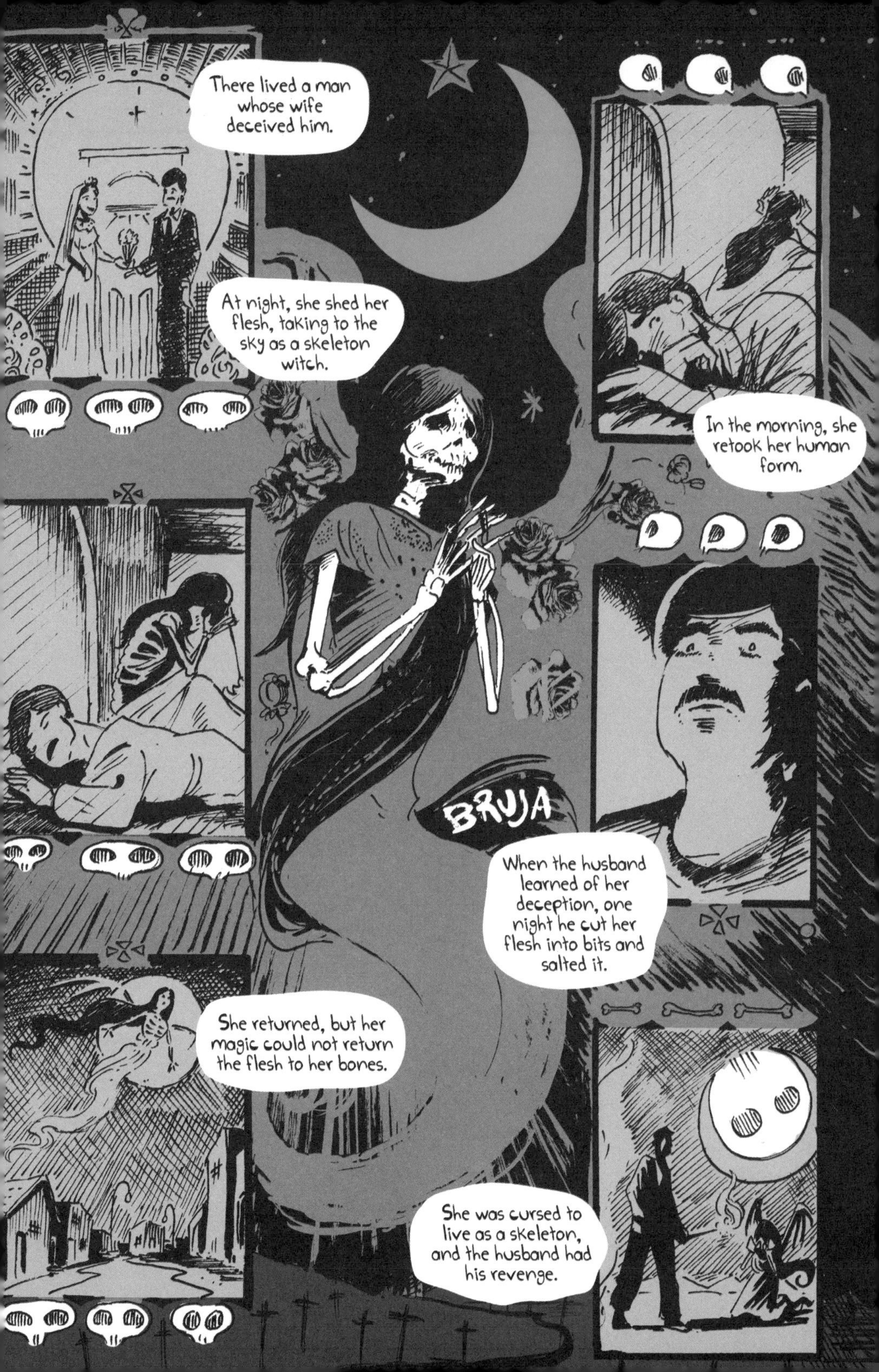

There lived a man whose wife deceived him.
At night, she shed her flesh, taking to the sky as a skeleton witch.
In the morning, she retook her human form.
BRUJA
When the husband learned of her deception, one night he cut her flesh into bits and salted it.
She returned, but her magic could not return the flesh to her bones.
She was cursed to live as a skeleton, and the husband had his revenge.

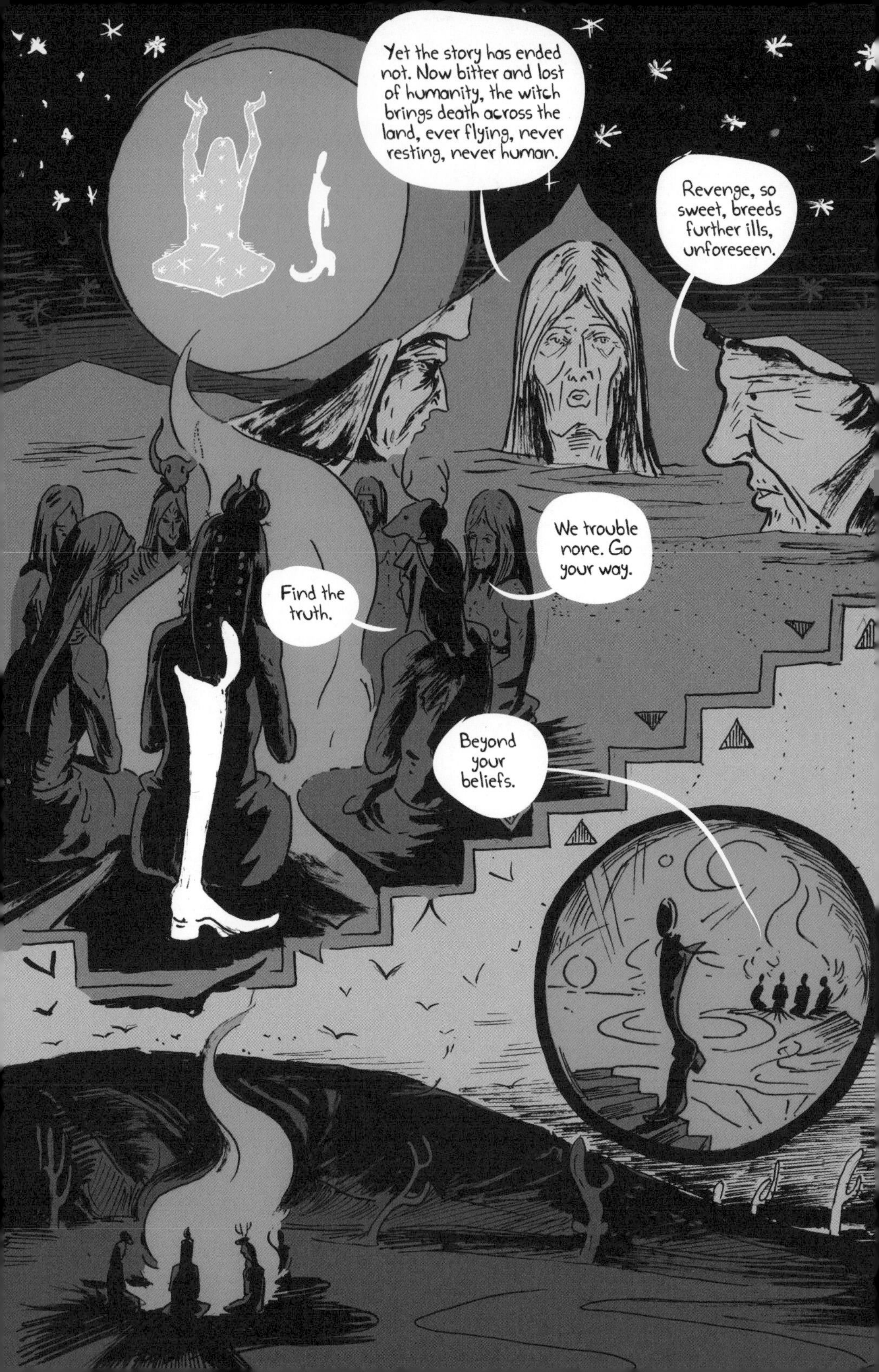
Yet the story has ended not. Now bitter and lost of humanity, the witch brings death across the land, ever flying, never resting, never human.
Revenge, so sweet, breeds further ills, unforeseen.
We trouble none. Go your way.
Find the truth.
Beyond your beliefs.

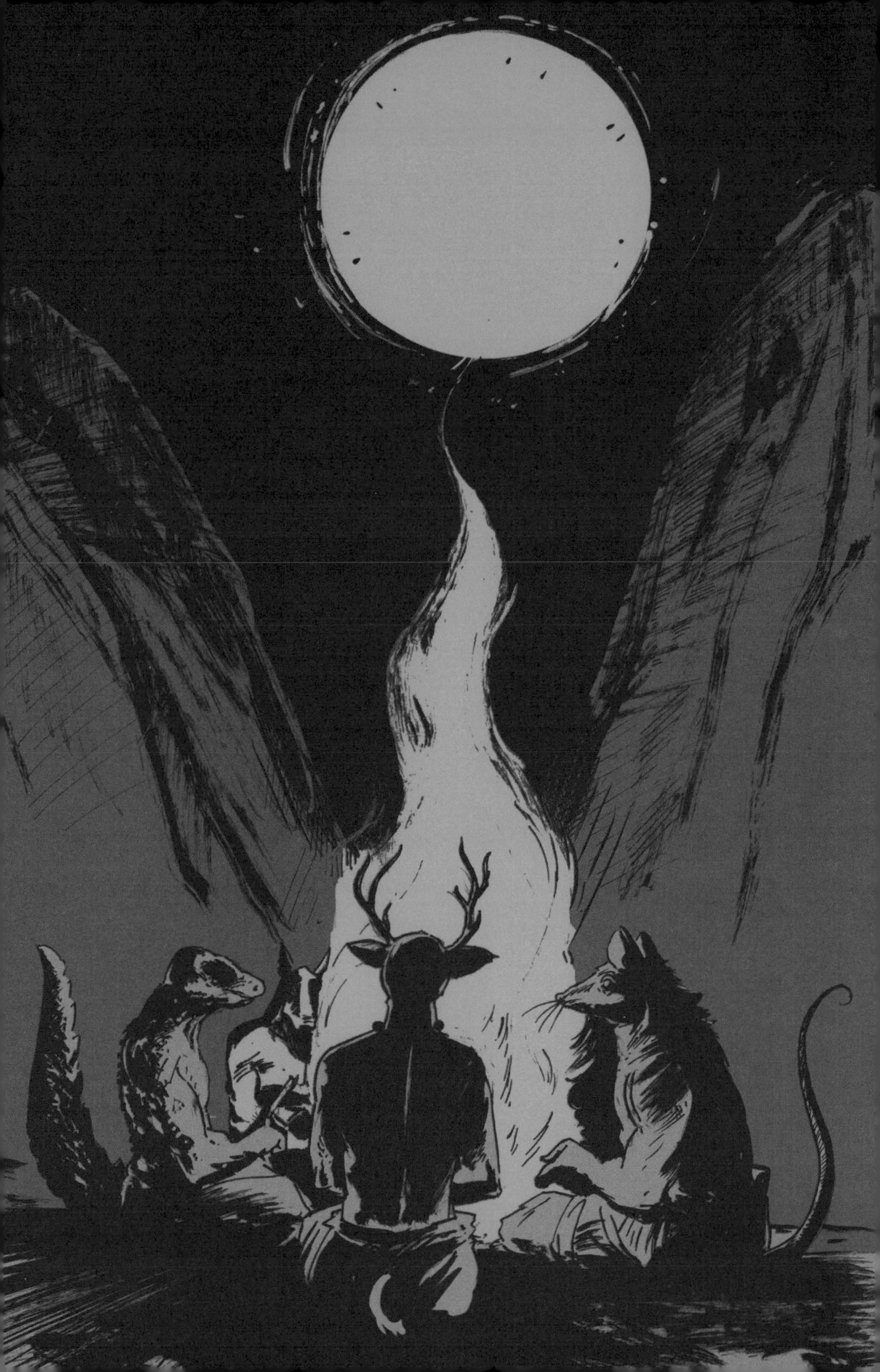

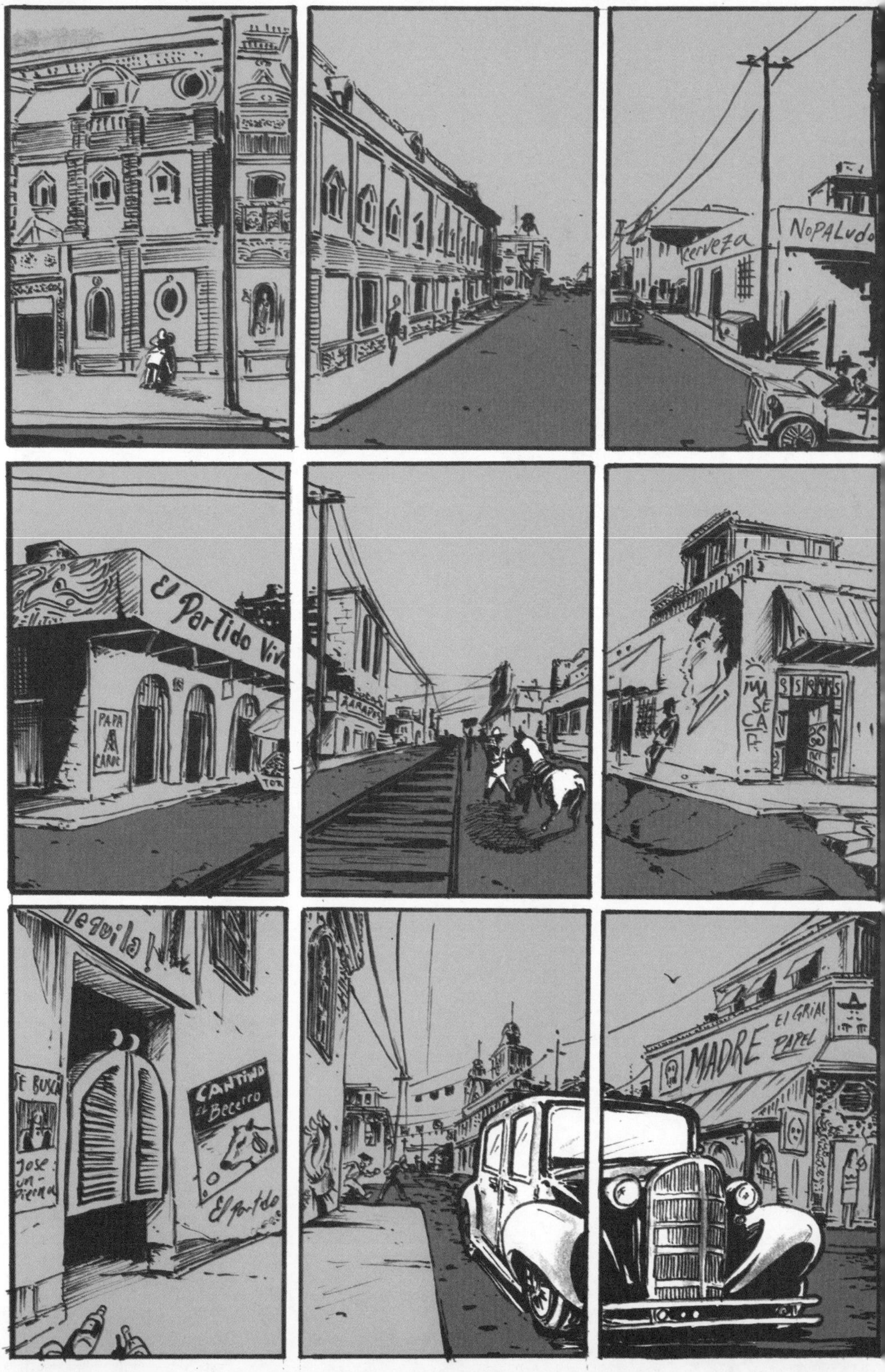
NoPALudo
Cerveza
El Partido Viv
PAPA
Tequila!
SE BUSCA
Jose
CANTINA El Becerro
El Partido
MADRE
El GRIAL
PAPEL

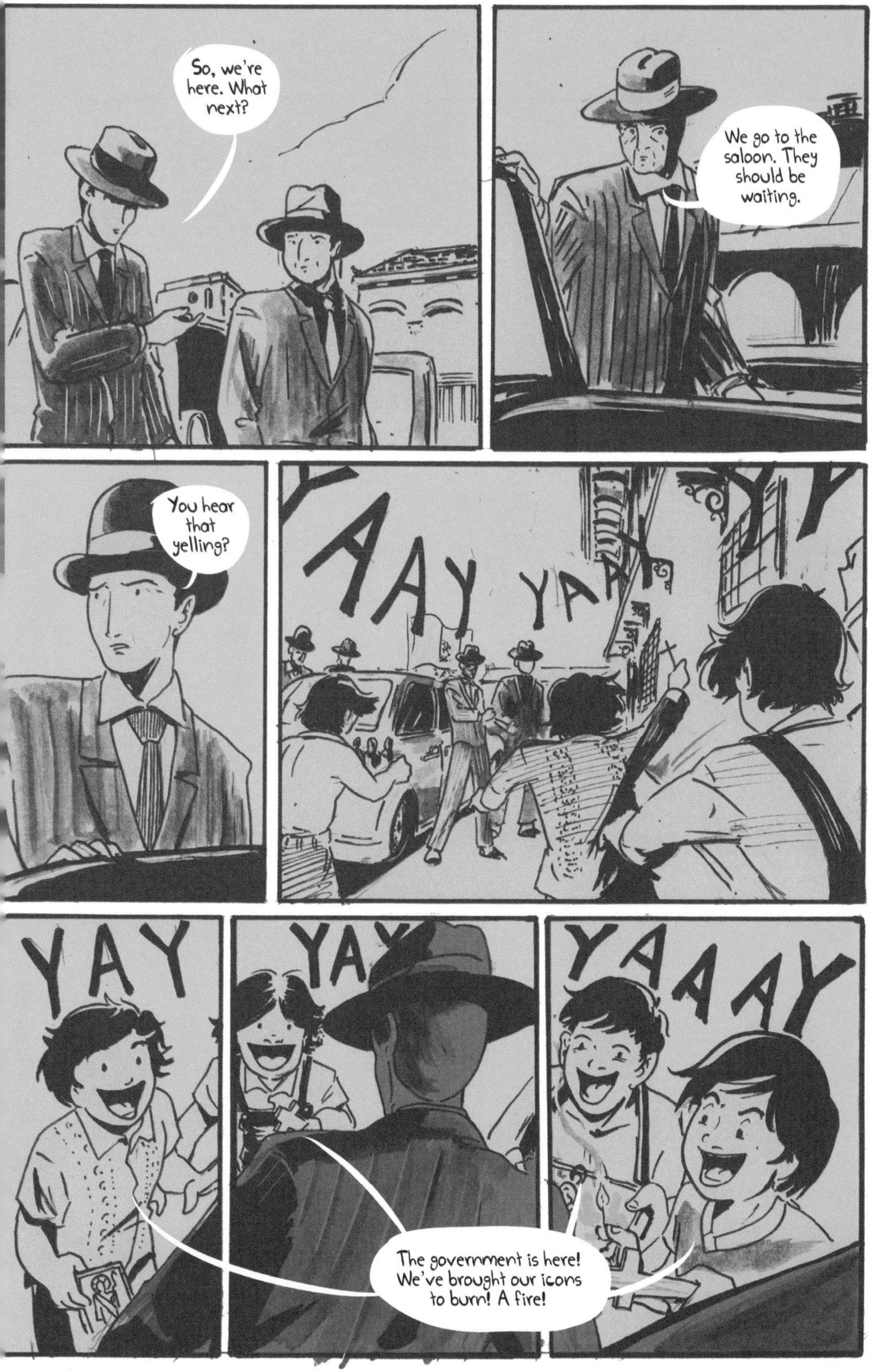
So, we're here. What next?
We go to the saloon. They should be waiting.
You hear that yelling?
YAAY YAAY
YAY
YAY
YAAAY
The government is here! We've brought our icons to burn! A fire!

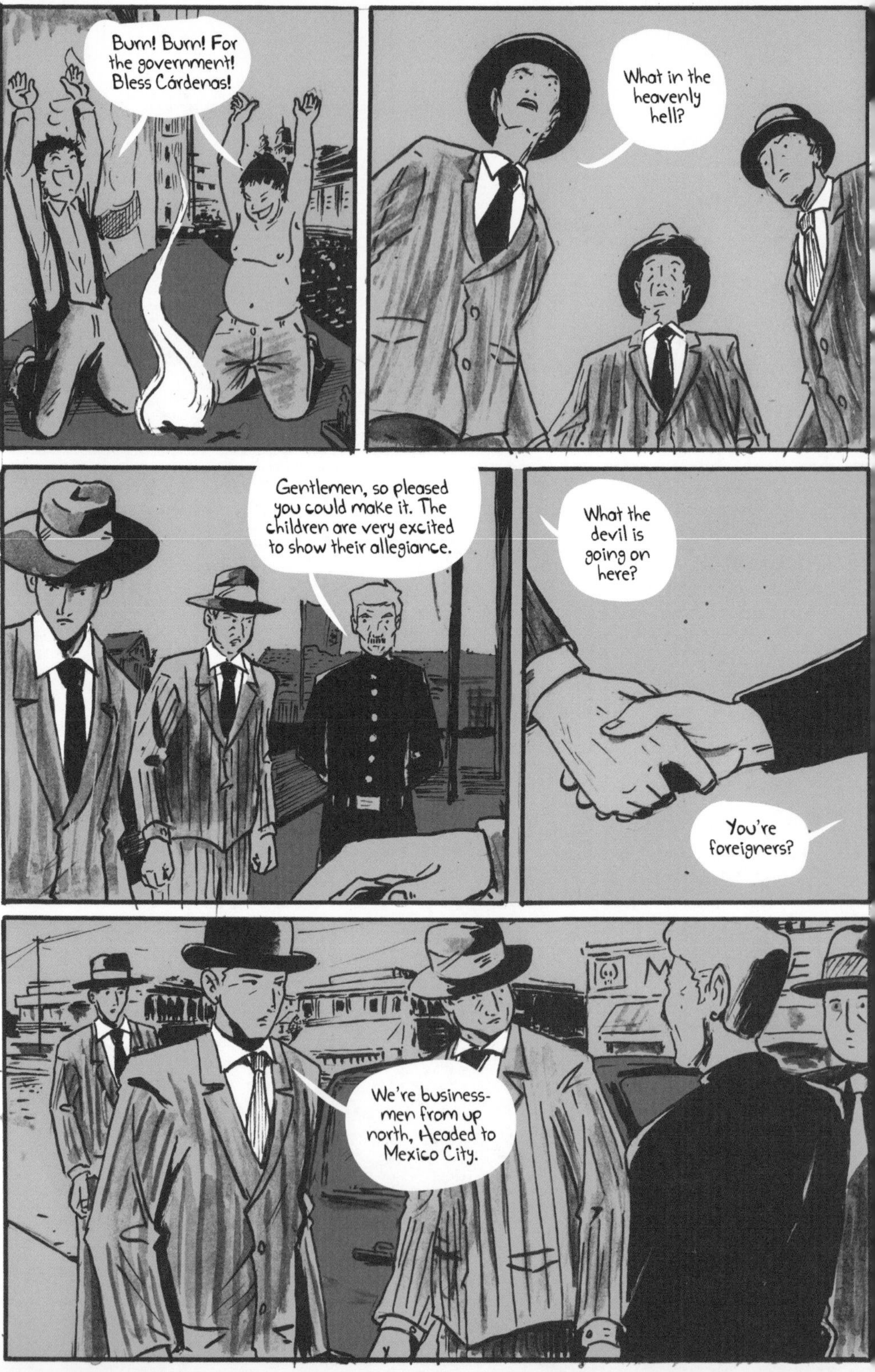
Burn! Burn! For the government! Bless Cárdenas!
What in the heavenly hell?
Gentlemen, so pleased you could make it. The children are very excited to show their allegiance.
What the devil is going on here?
You're foreigners?
We're business-men from up north, Headed to Mexico City.

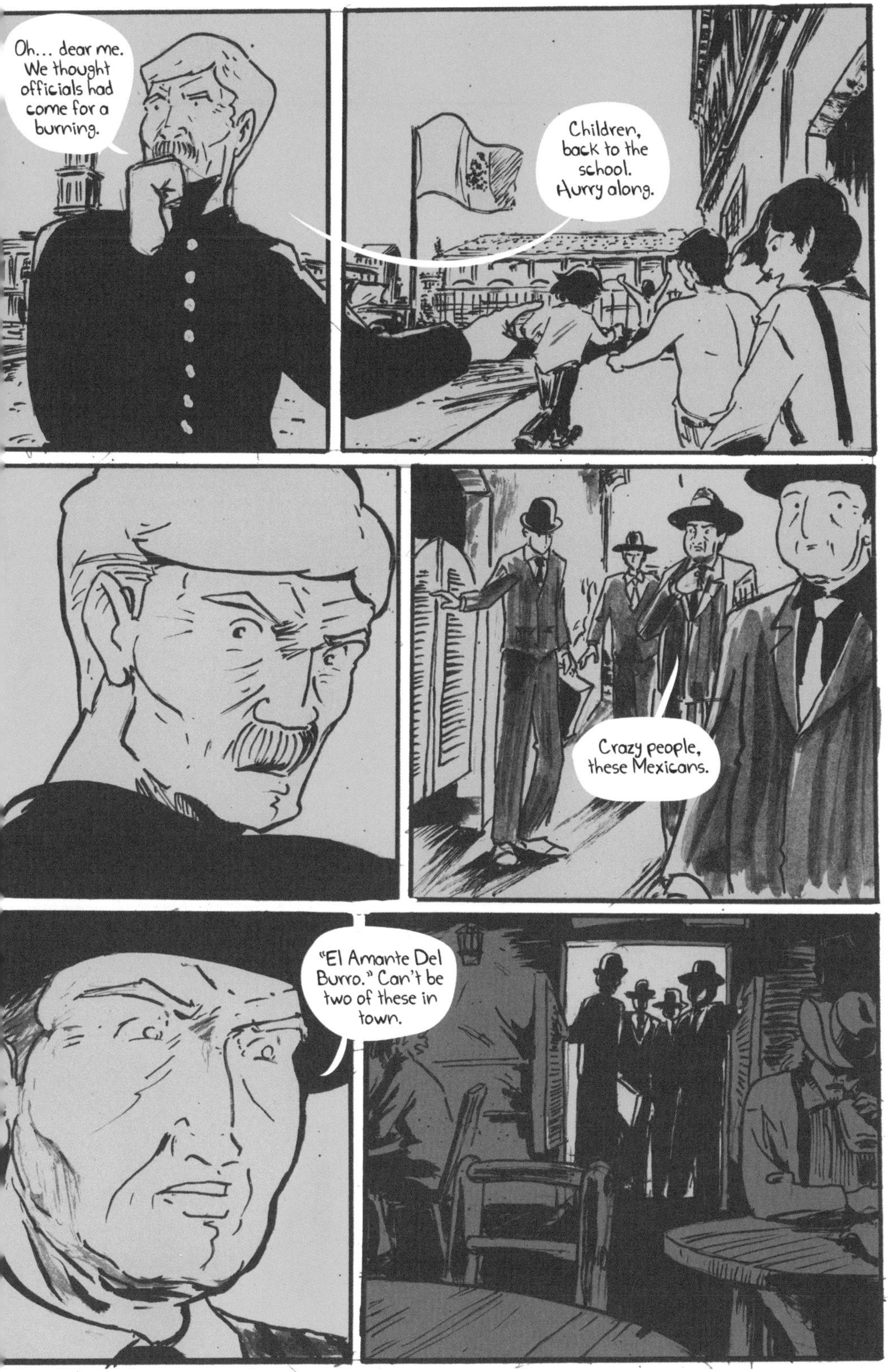
Oh... dear me. We thought officials had come for a burning.
Children, back to the school. Hurry along.
Crazy people, these Mexicans.
"El Amante Del Burro." Can't be two of these in town.

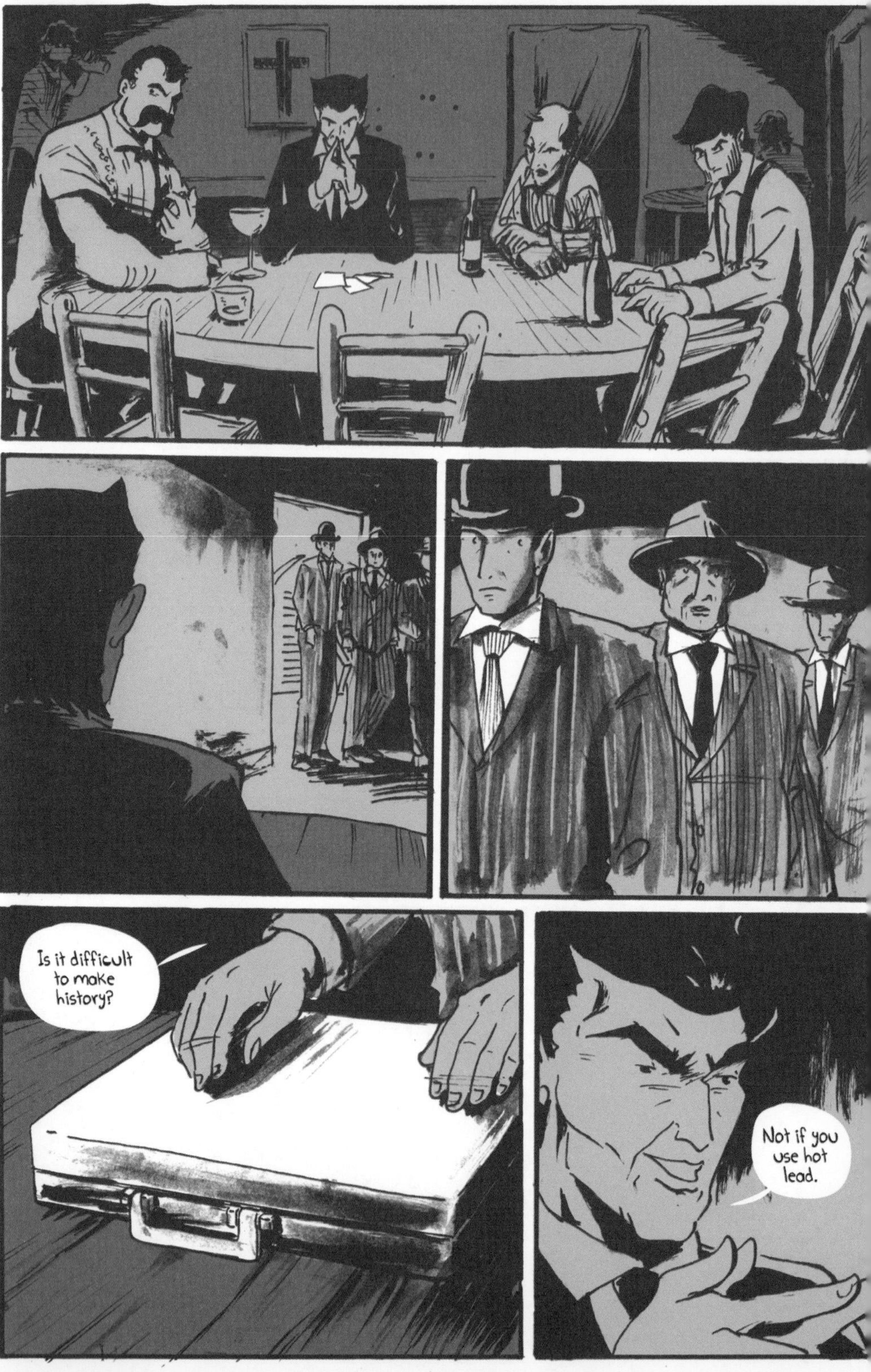
Is it difficult to make history?
Not if you use hot lead.

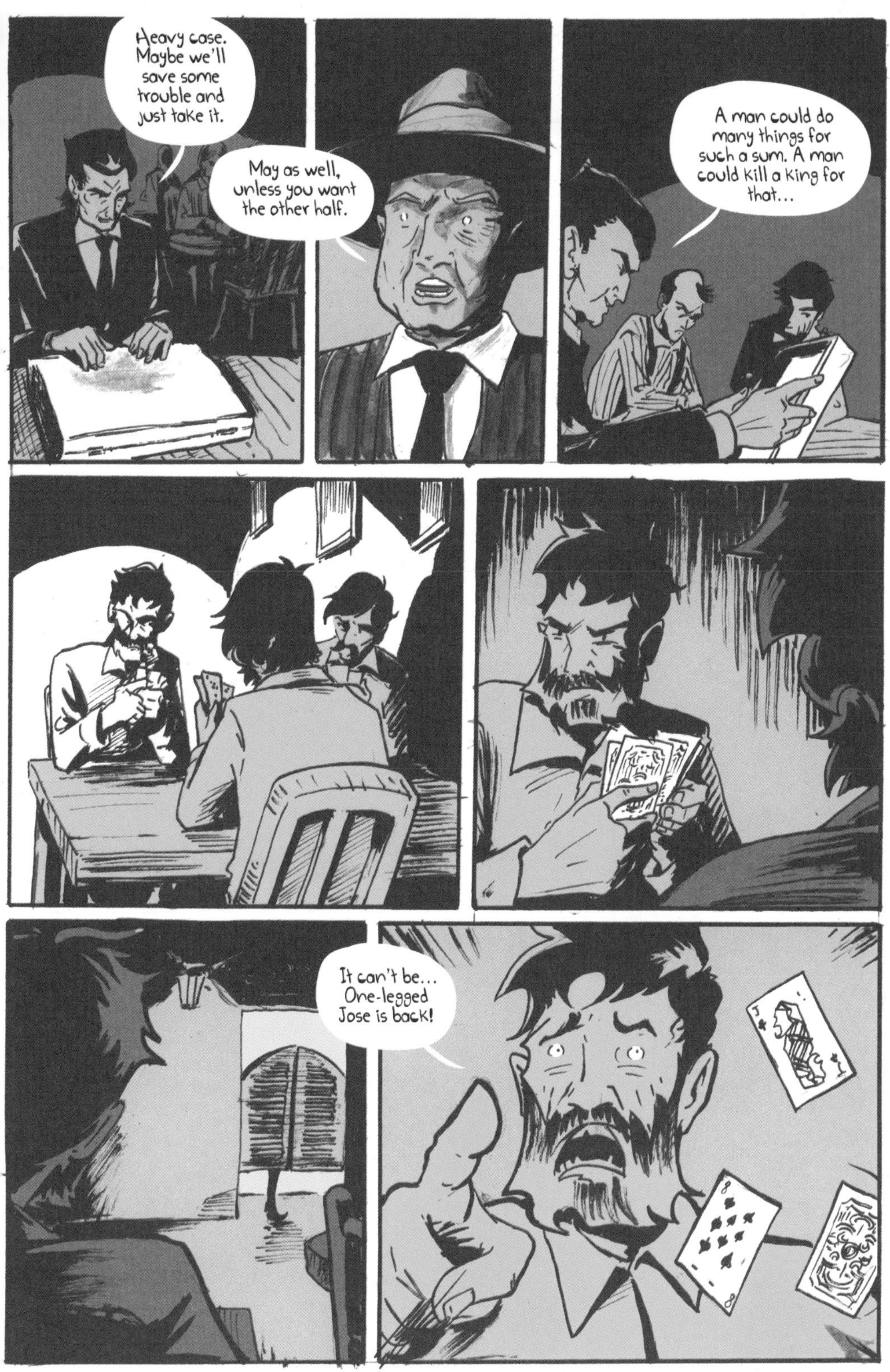
Heavy case. Maybe we'll save some trouble and just take it.
May as well, unless you want the other half.
A man could do many things for such a sum. A man could kill a king for that...
It can't be... One-legged Jose is back!

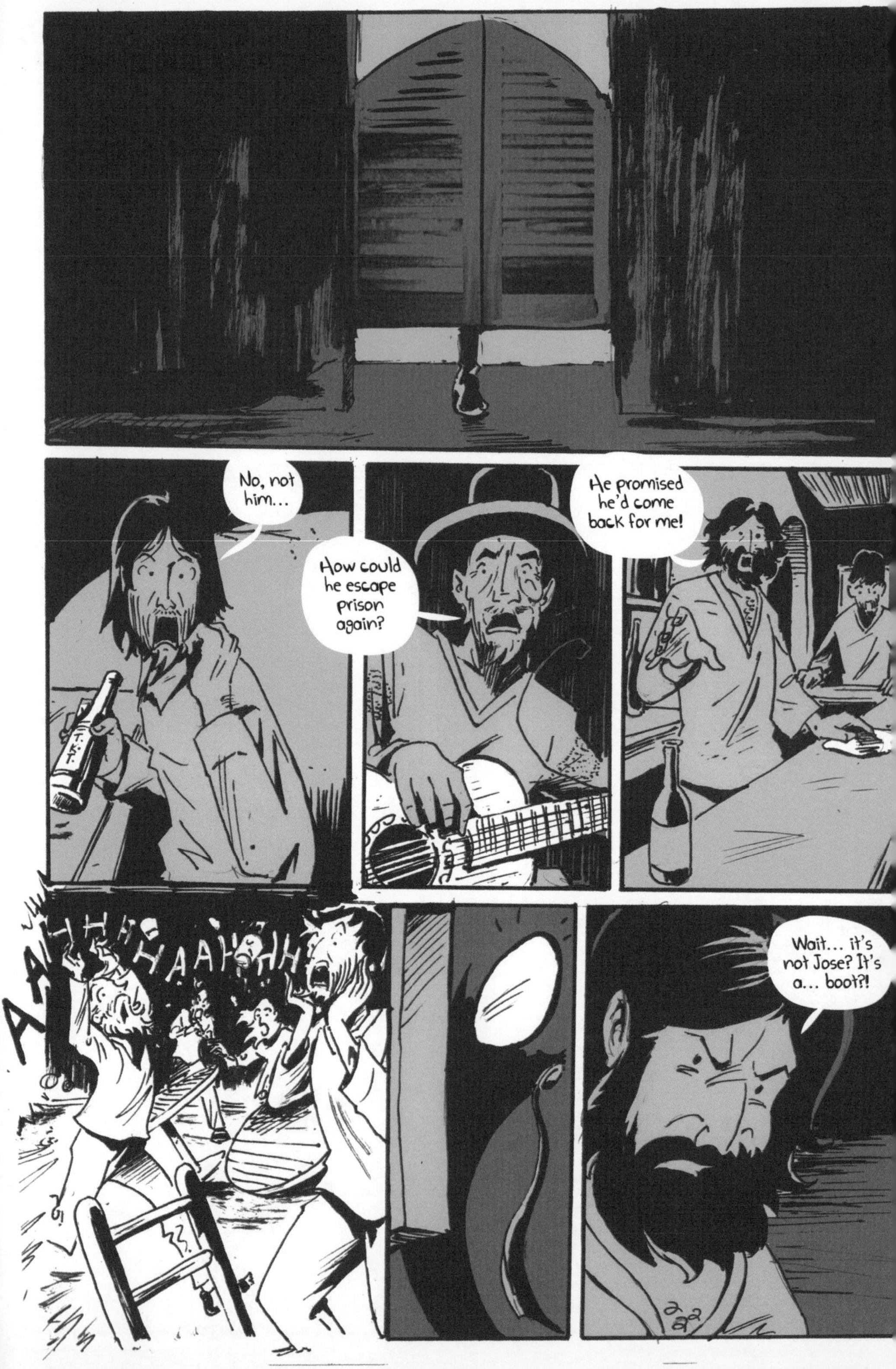
No, not him...
How could he escape prison again?
He promised he'd come back for me!
AAHHHAAAHHHH
Wait... it's not Jose? It's a... boot?!

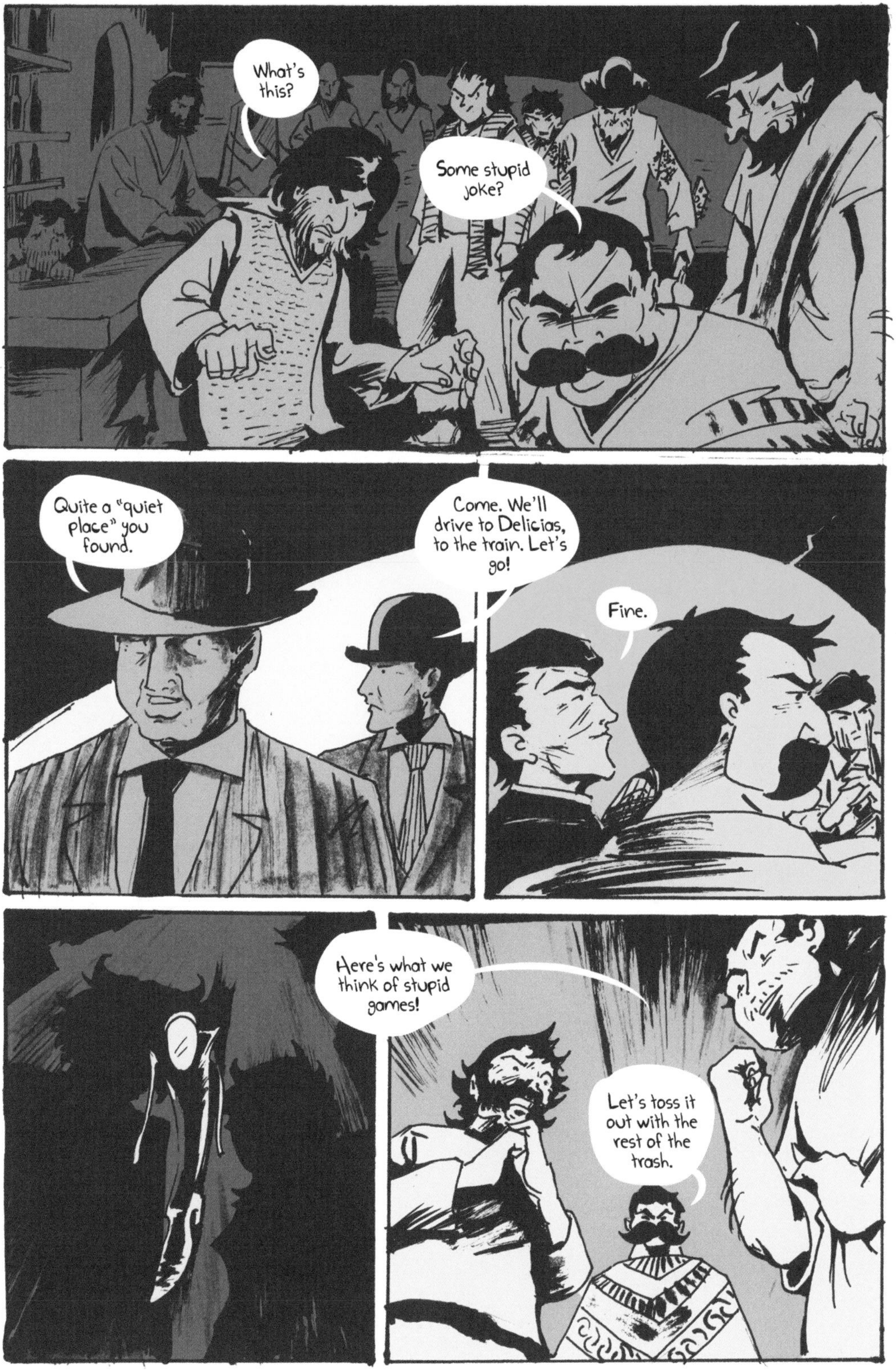
What's this?
Some stupid joke?
Quite a "quiet place" you found.
Come. We'll drive to Delicias, to the train. Let's go!
Fine.
Here's what we think of stupid games!
Let's toss it out with the rest of the trash.

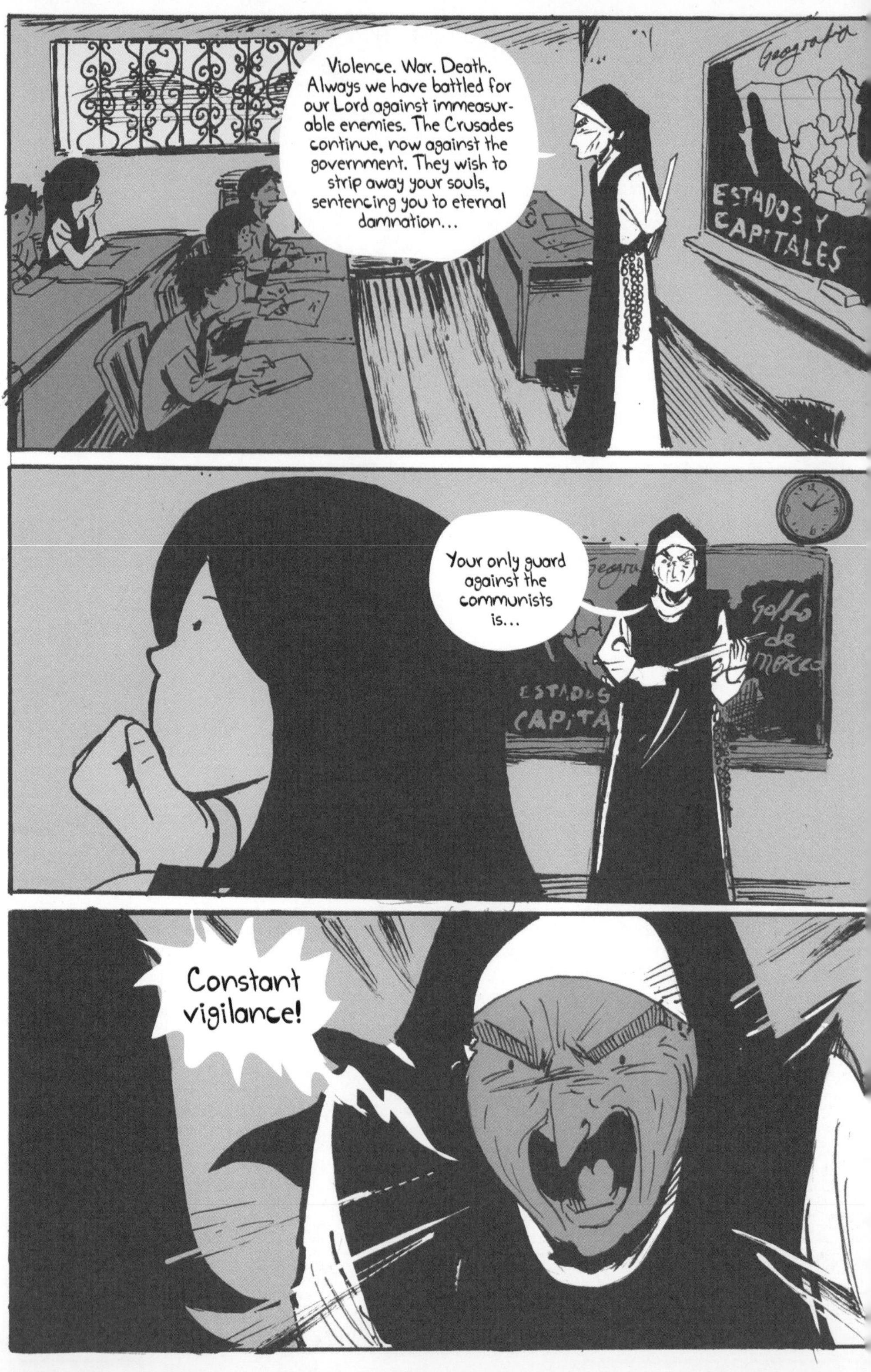
Violence. War. Death. Always we have battled for our Lord against immeasurable enemies. The Crusades continue, now against the government. They wish to strip away your souls, sentencing you to eternal damnation...
ESTADOS Y CAPITALES
Your only guard against the communists is...
Golfo de México
ESTADOS CAPITA
Constant vigilance!

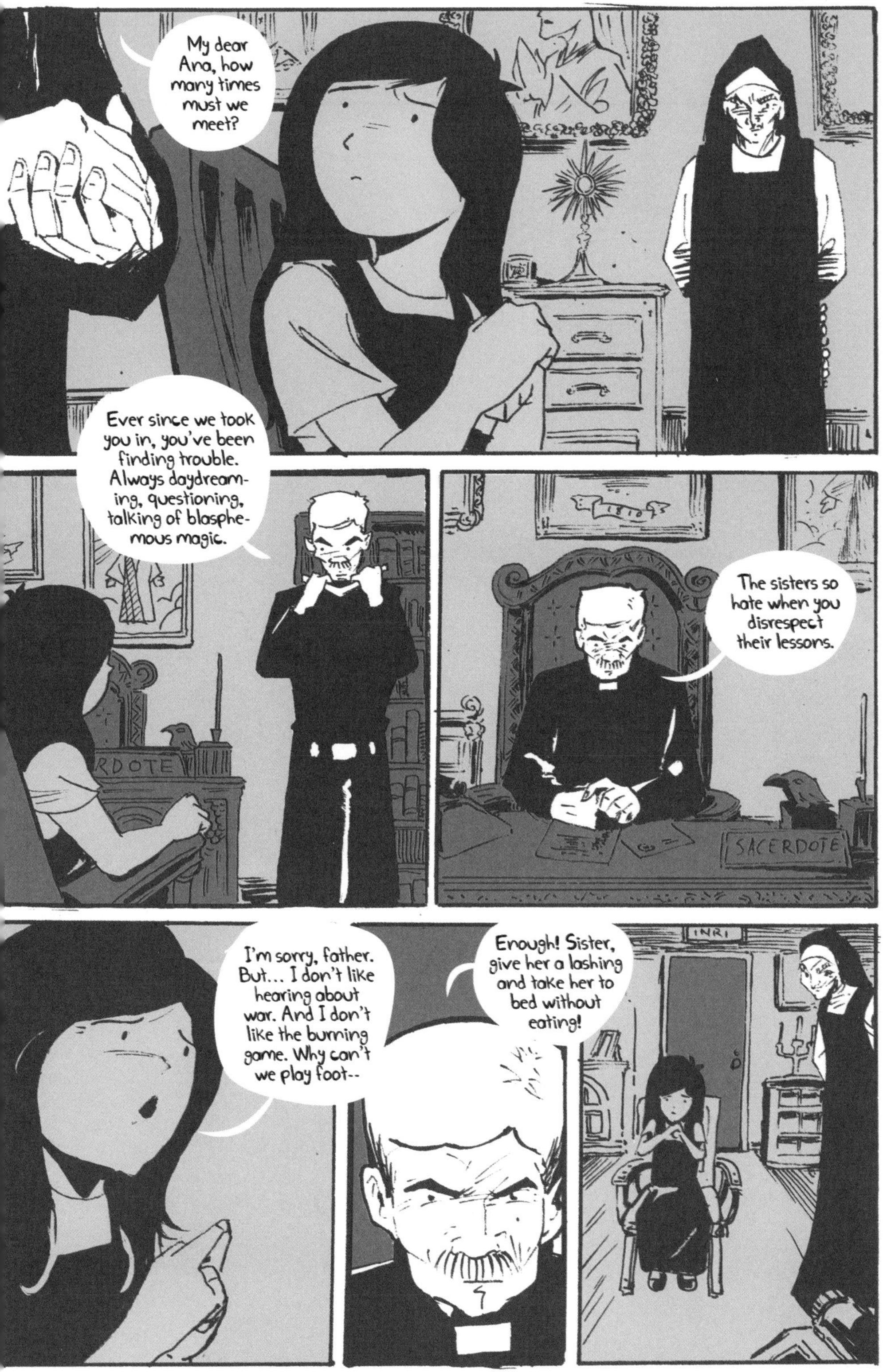
My dear Ana, how many times must we meet?
Ever since we took you in, you've been finding trouble. Always daydreaming, questioning, talking of blasphemous magic.
RDOTE
The sisters so hate when you disrespect their lessons.
SACERDOTE
I'm sorry, father. But... I don't like hearing about war. And I don't like the burning game. Why can't we play foot--
Enough! Sister, give her a lashing and take her to bed without eating!
INRI

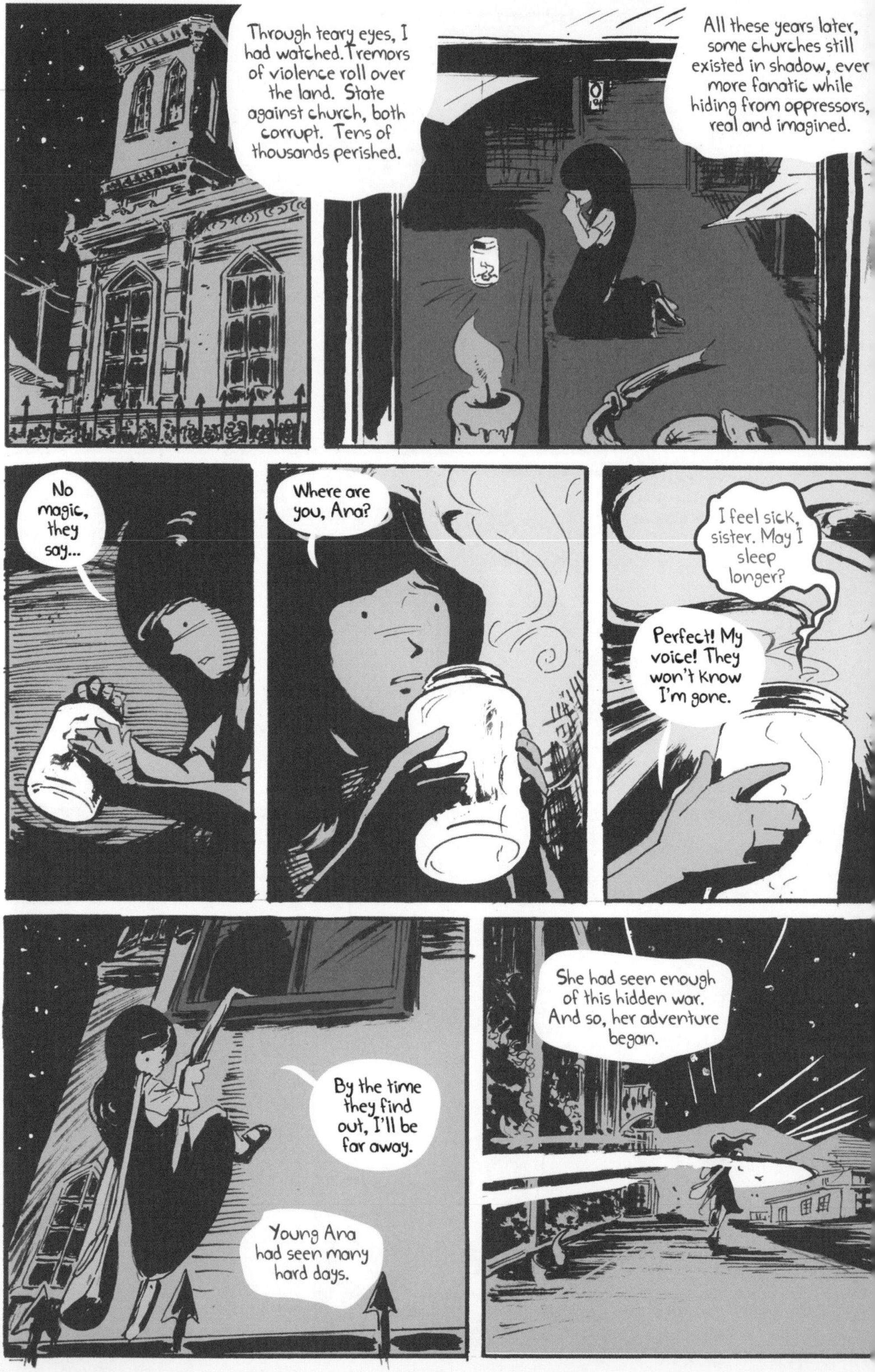

Through teary eyes, I had watched. Tremors of violence roll over the land. State against church, both corrupt. Tens of thousands perished.
All these years later, some churches still existed in shadow, ever more fanatic while hiding from oppressors, real and imagined.
No magic, they say...
Where are you, Ana?
I feel sick, sister. May I sleep longer?
Perfect! My voice! They won't know I'm gone.
By the time they find out, I'll be far away.
Young Ana had seen many hard days.
She had seen enough of this hidden war. And so, her adventure began.

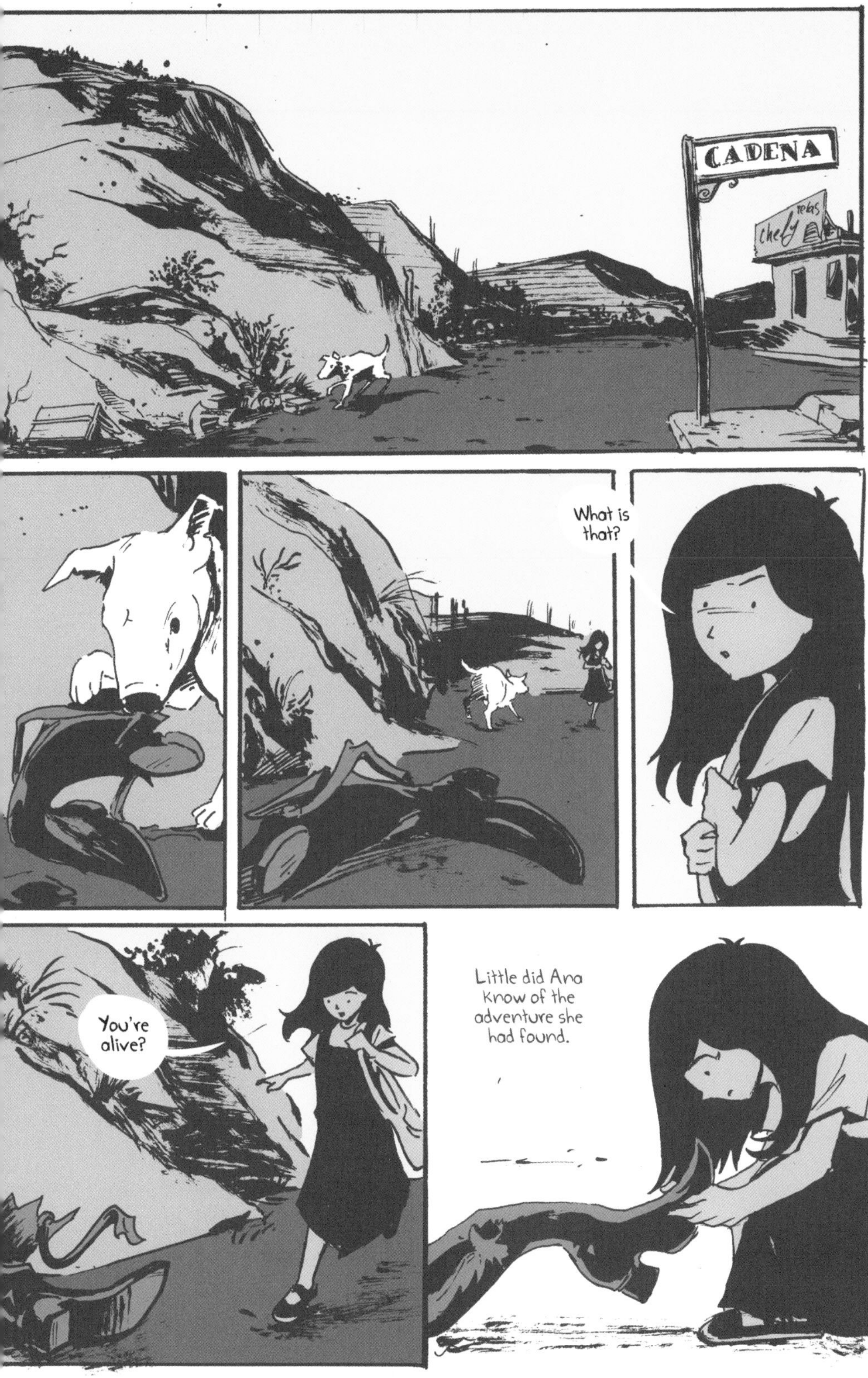
CADENA
What is that?
You're alive?
Little did Ana know of the adventure she had found.

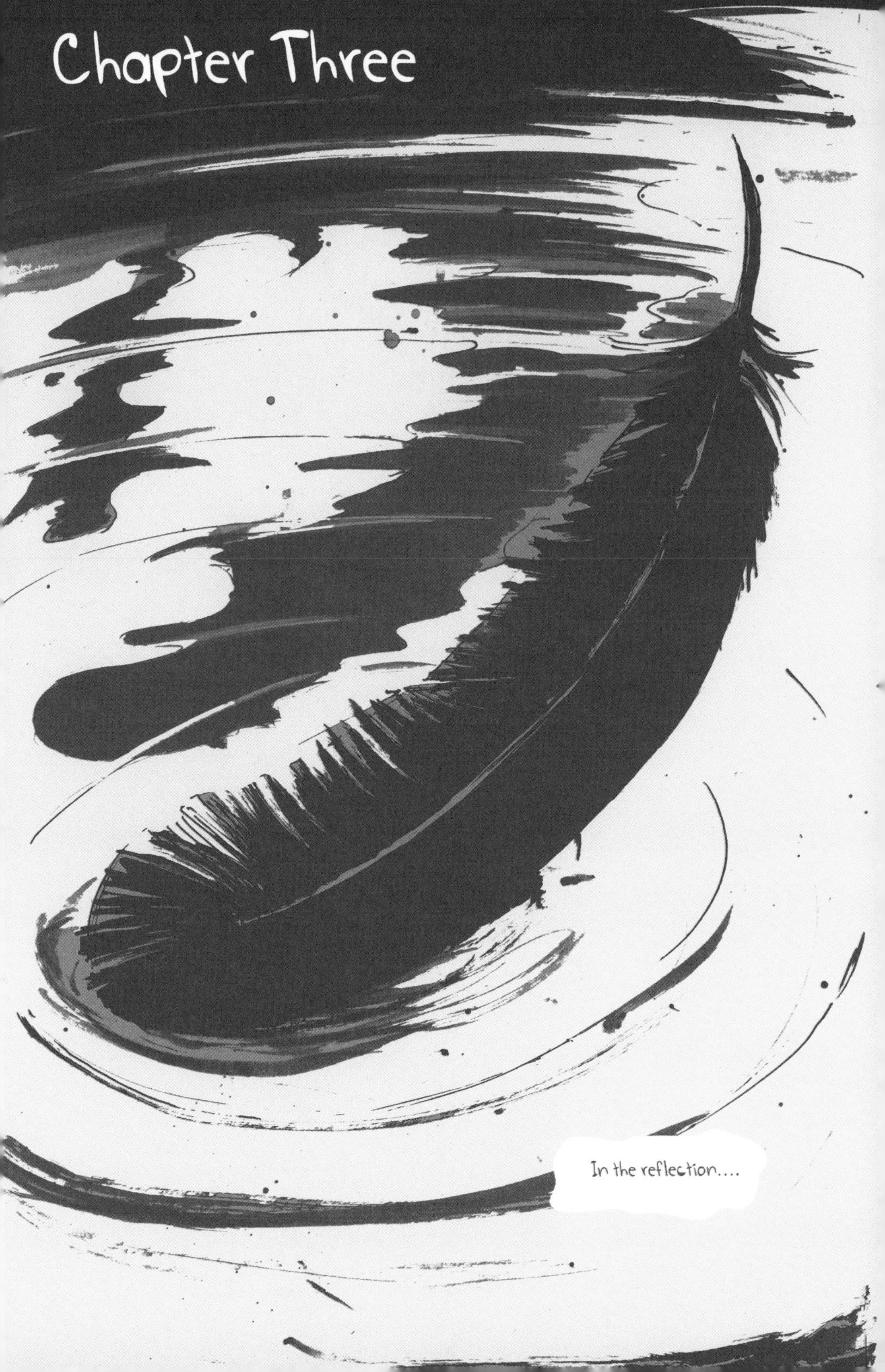
Chapter Three
In the reflection....

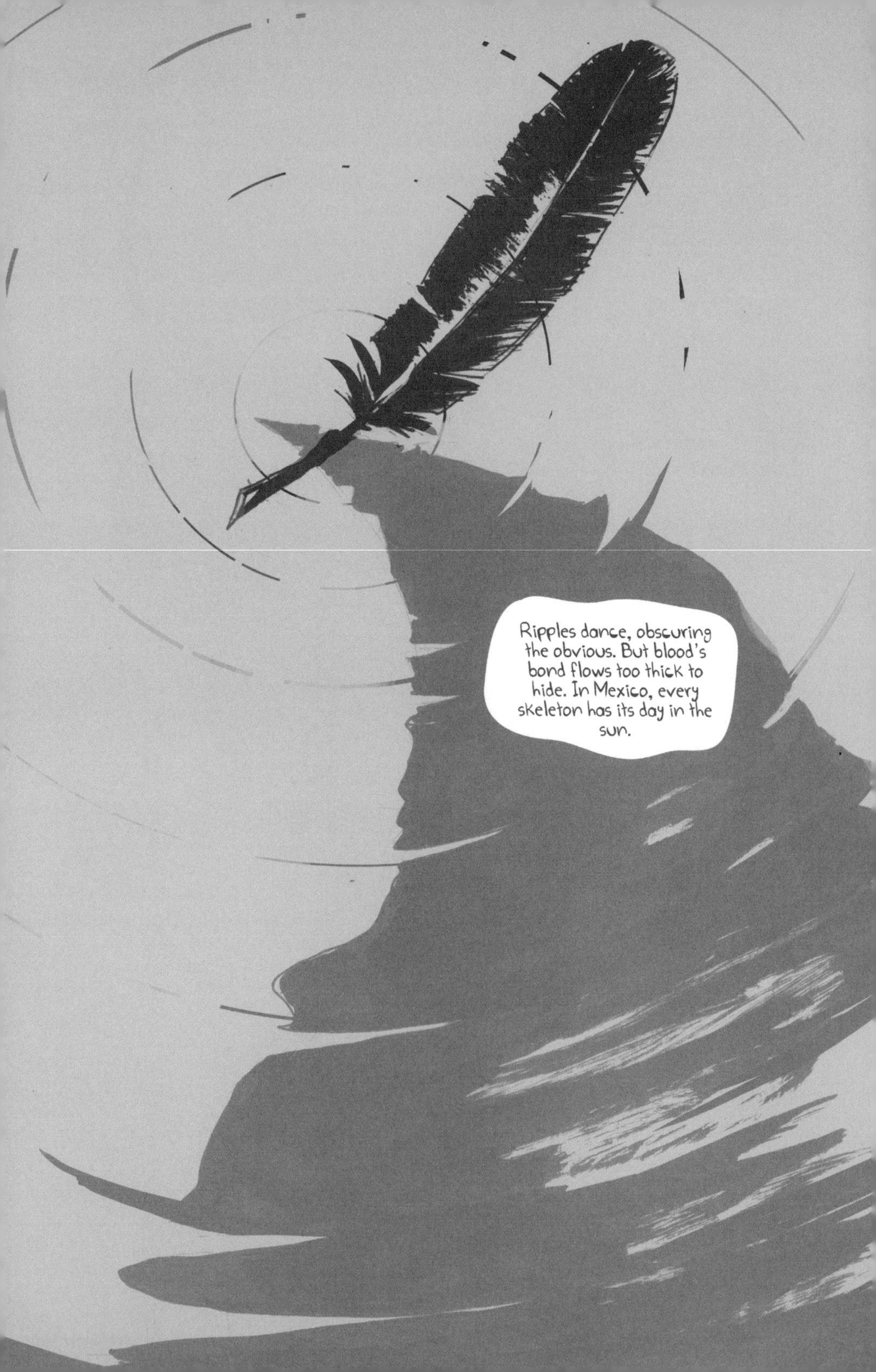
Ripples dance, obscuring the obvious. But blood's bond flows too thick to hide. In Mexico, every skeleton has its day in the sun.

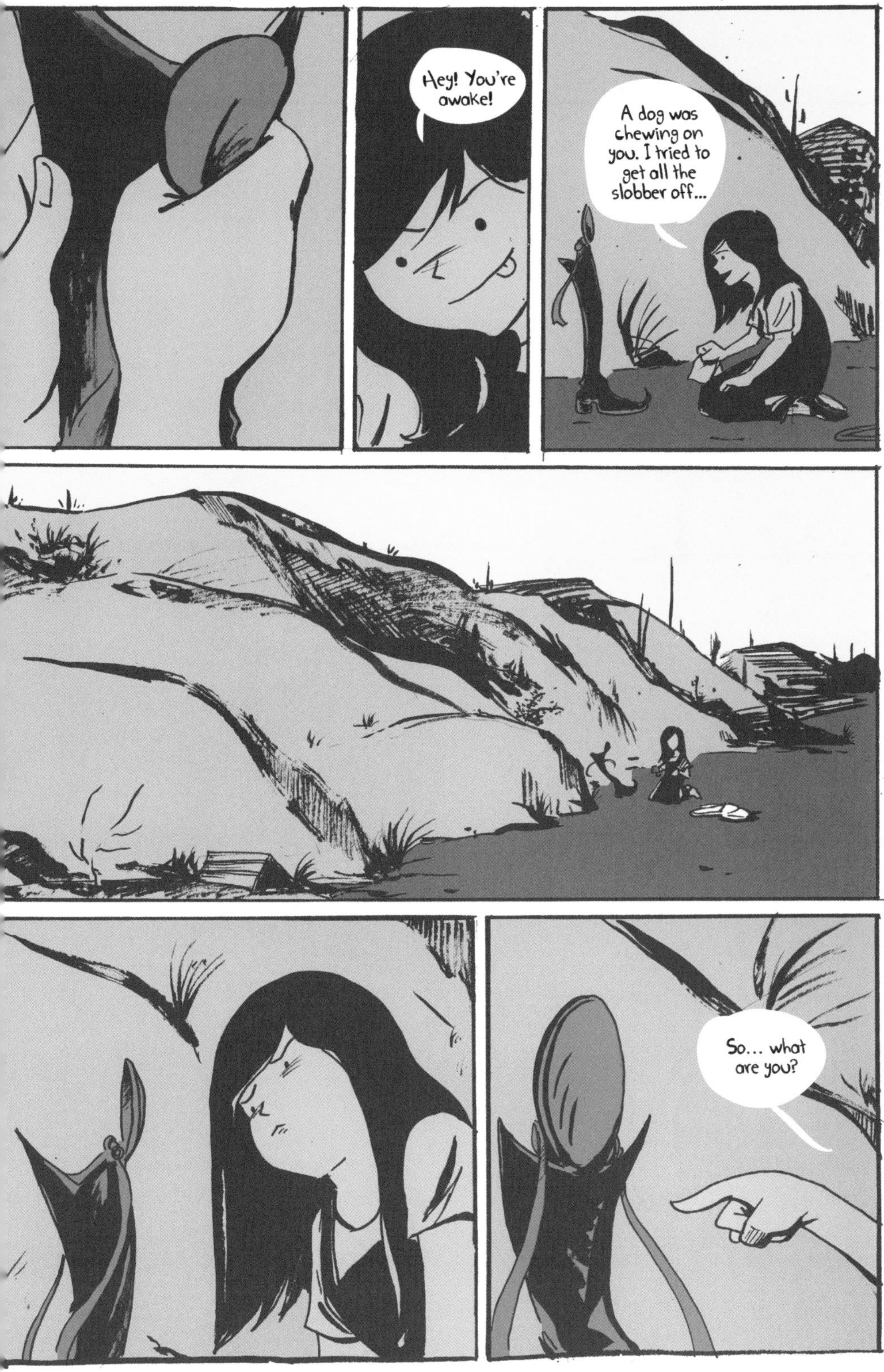
Hey! You're awake!
A dog was chewing on you. I tried to get all the slobber off...
So... what are you?

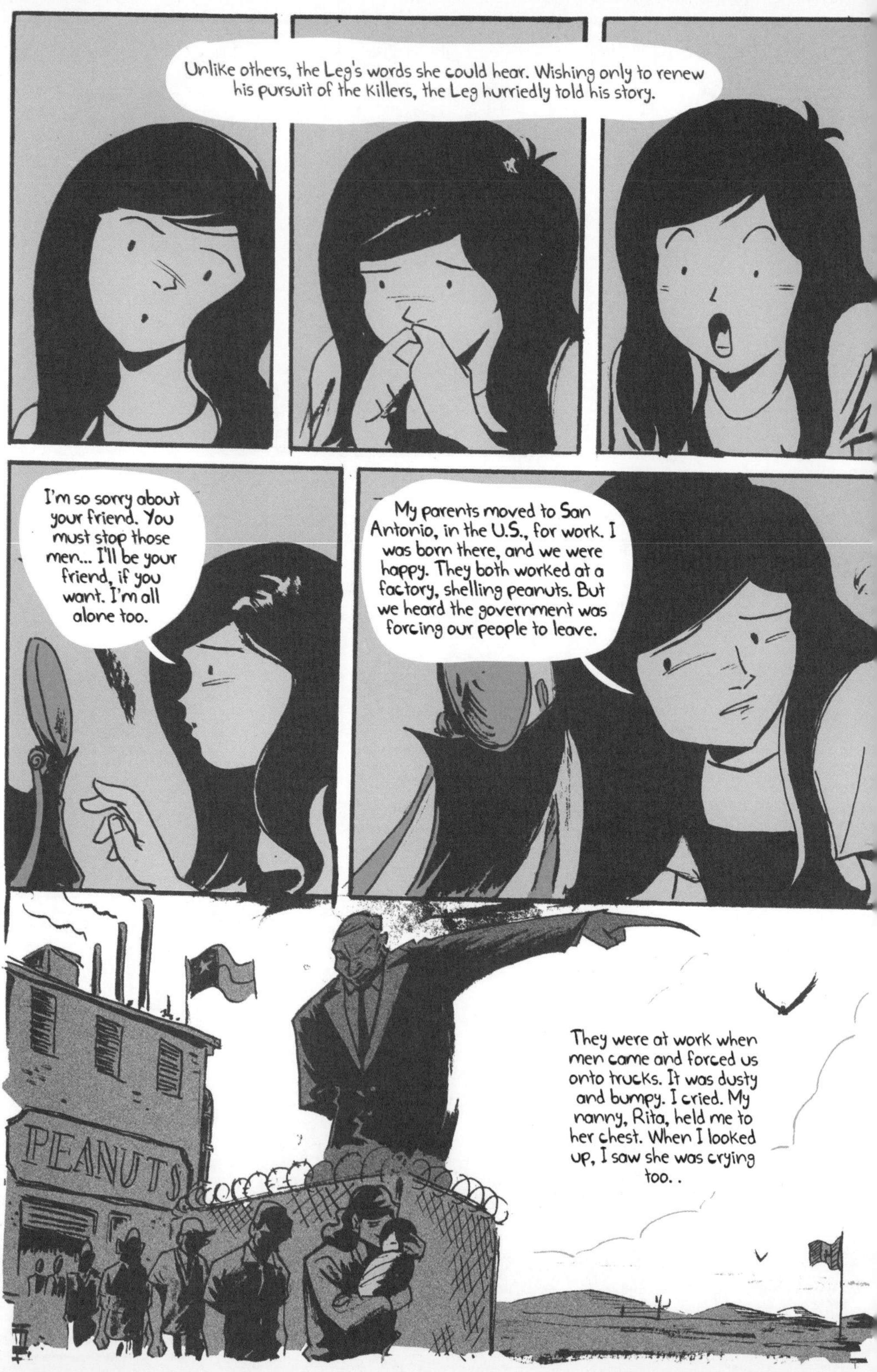
Unlike others, the Leg's words she could hear. Wishing only to renew his pursuit of the killers, the Leg hurriedly told his story.
I'm so sorry about your friend. You must stop those men... I'll be your friend, if you want. I'm all alone too.
My parents moved to San Antonio, in the U.S., for work. I was born there, and we were happy. They both worked at a factory, shelling peanuts. But we heard the government was forcing our people to leave.
PEANUTS
They were at work when men came and forced us onto trucks. It was dusty and bumpy. I cried. My nanny, Rita, held me to her chest. When I looked up, I saw she was crying too. .

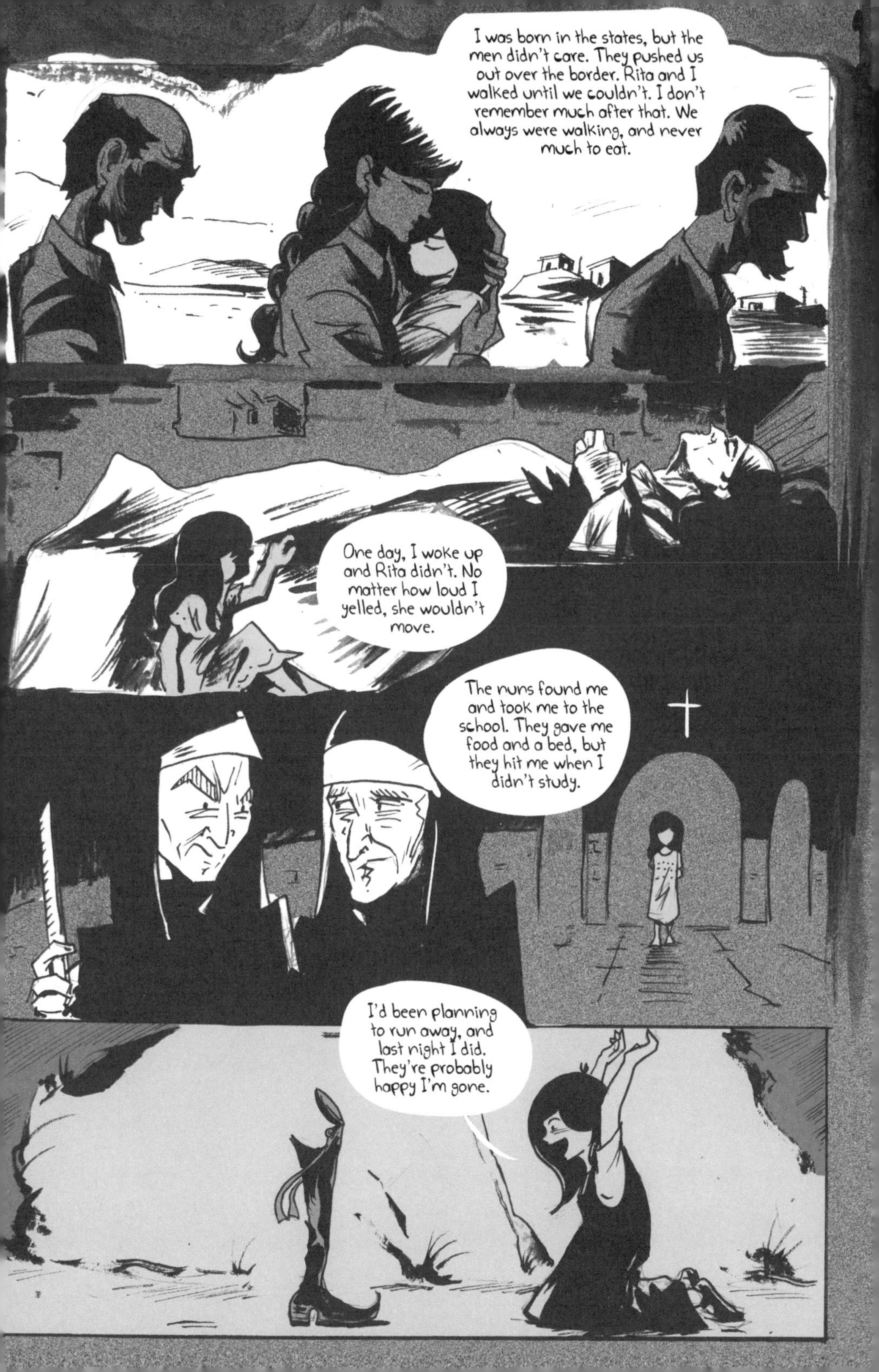
I was born in the states, but the men didn't care. They pushed us out over the border. Rita and I walked until we couldn't. I don't remember much after that. We always were walking, and never much to eat.
One day, I woke up and Rita didn't. No matter how loud I yelled, she wouldn't move.
The nuns found me and took me to the school. They gave me food and a bed, but they hit me when I didn't study.
I'd been planning to run away, and last night I did. They're probably happy I'm gone.

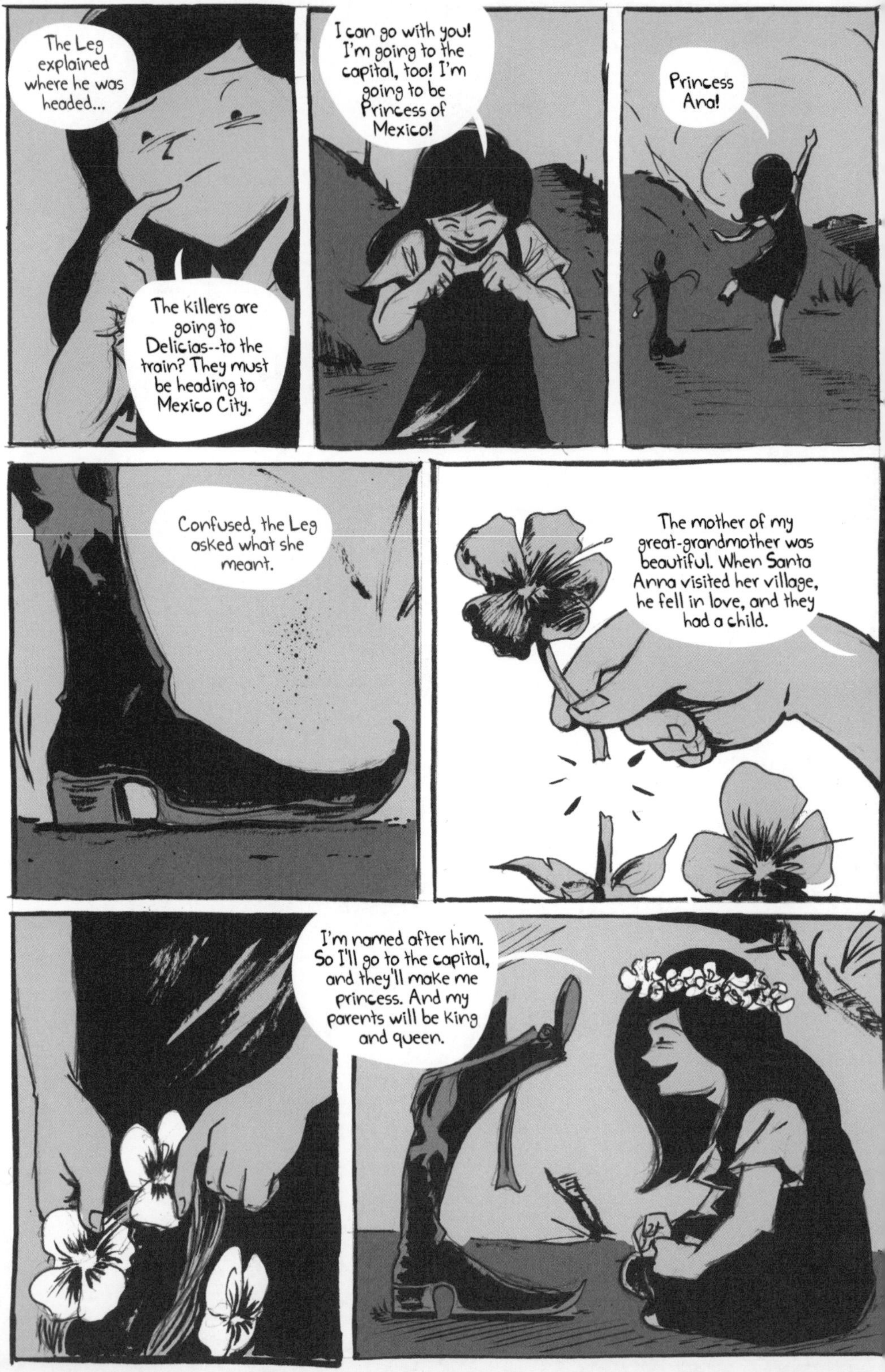
The Leg explained where he was headed...
The Killers are going to Delicias--to the train? They must be heading to Mexico City.
I can go with you! I'm going to the capital, too! I'm going to be Princess of Mexico!
Princess Ana!
Confused, the Leg asked what she meant.
The mother of my great-grandmother was beautiful. When Santa Anna visited her village, he fell in love, and they had a child.
I'm named after him. So I'll go to the capital, and they'll make me princess. And my parents will be King and queen.

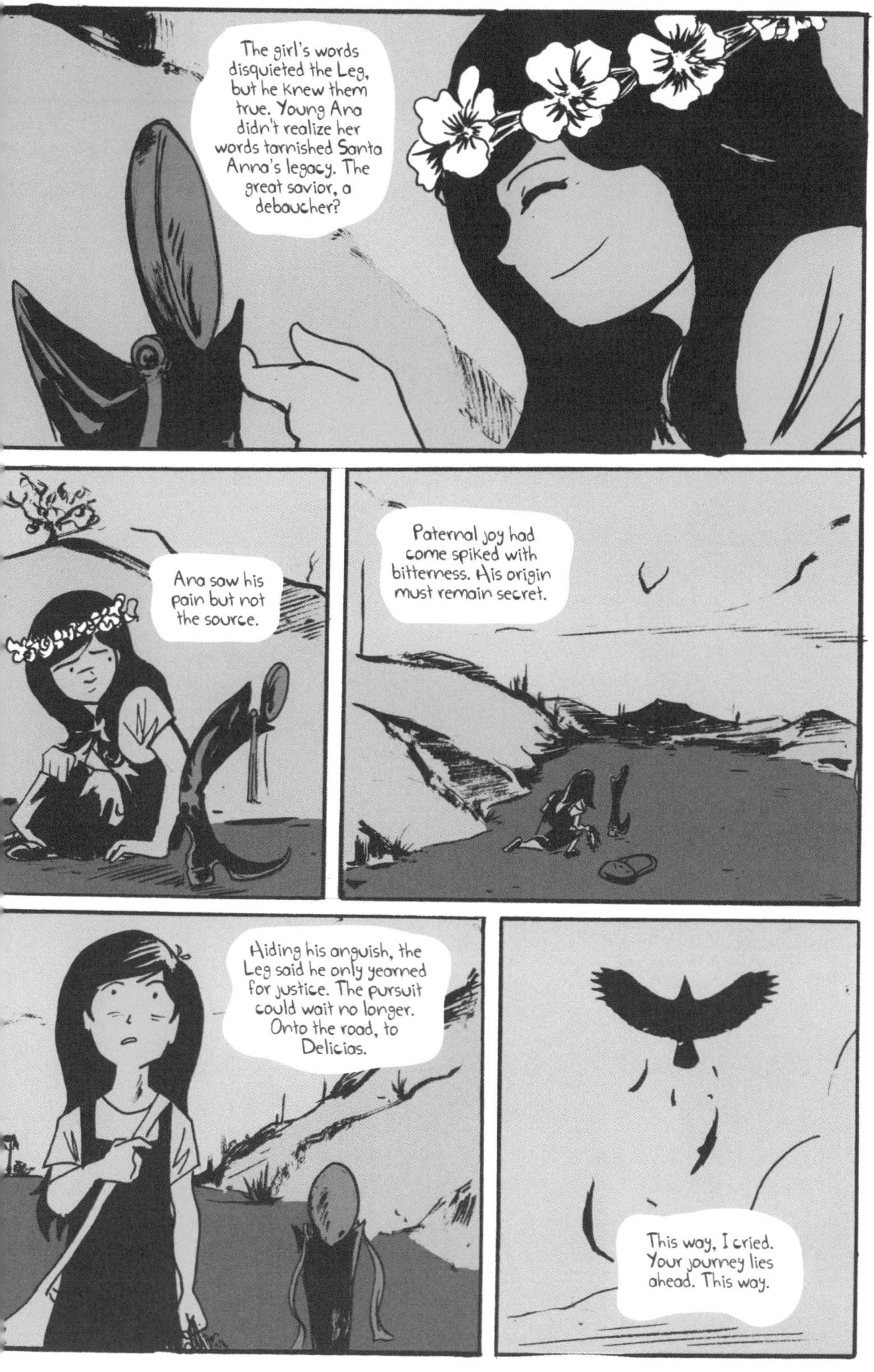
The girl's words disquieted the Leg, but he knew them true. Young Ana didn't realize her words tarnished Santa Anna's legacy. The great savior, a debaucher?
Ana saw his pain but not the source.
Paternal joy had come spiked with bitterness. His origin must remain secret.
Hiding his anguish, the Leg said he only yearned for justice. The pursuit could wait no longer. Onto the road, to Delicias.
This way, I cried. Your journey lies ahead. This way.

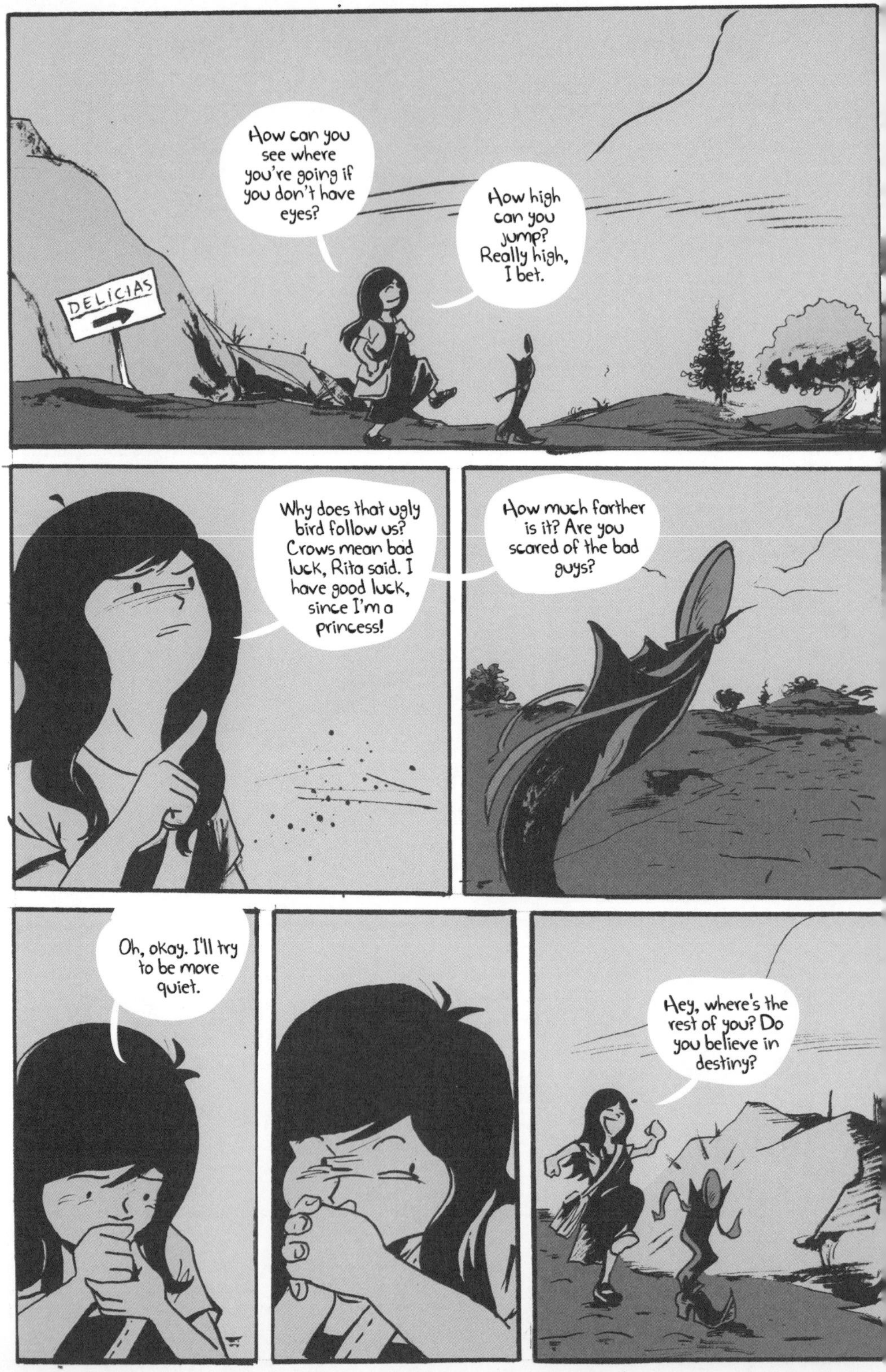
How can you see where you're going if you don't have eyes?
How high can you jump? Really high, I bet.
DELICIAS
Why does that ugly bird follow us? Crows mean bad luck, Rita said. I have good luck, since I'm a princess!
How much farther is it? Are you scared of the bad guys?
Oh, okay. I'll try to be more quiet.
Hey, where's the rest of you? Do you believe in destiny?

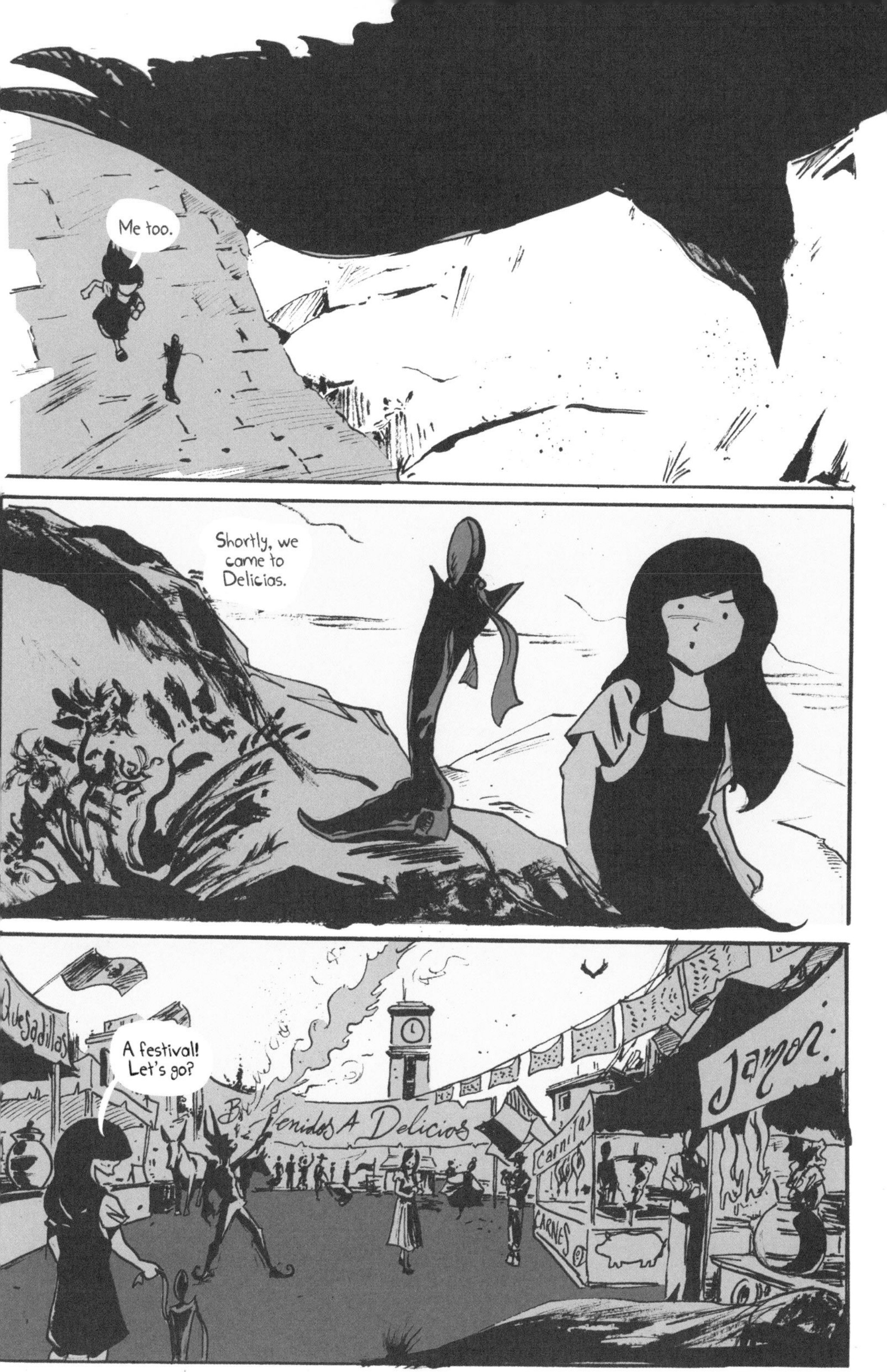
Me too.
Shortly, we came to Delicias.
Quesadillas
A festival! Let's go?
Jamon
Carnitas
Carnes

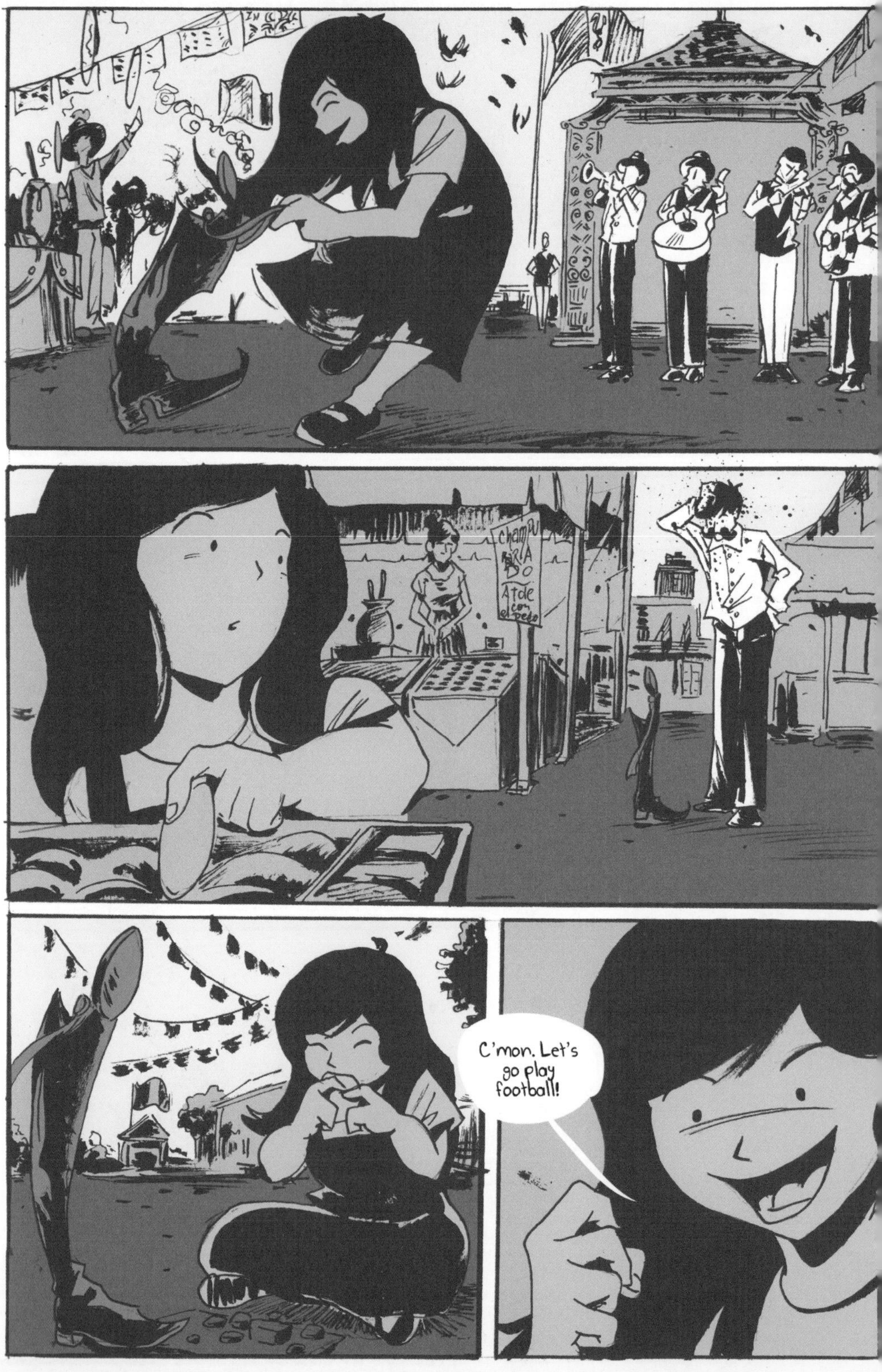
C'mon. Let's go play football!

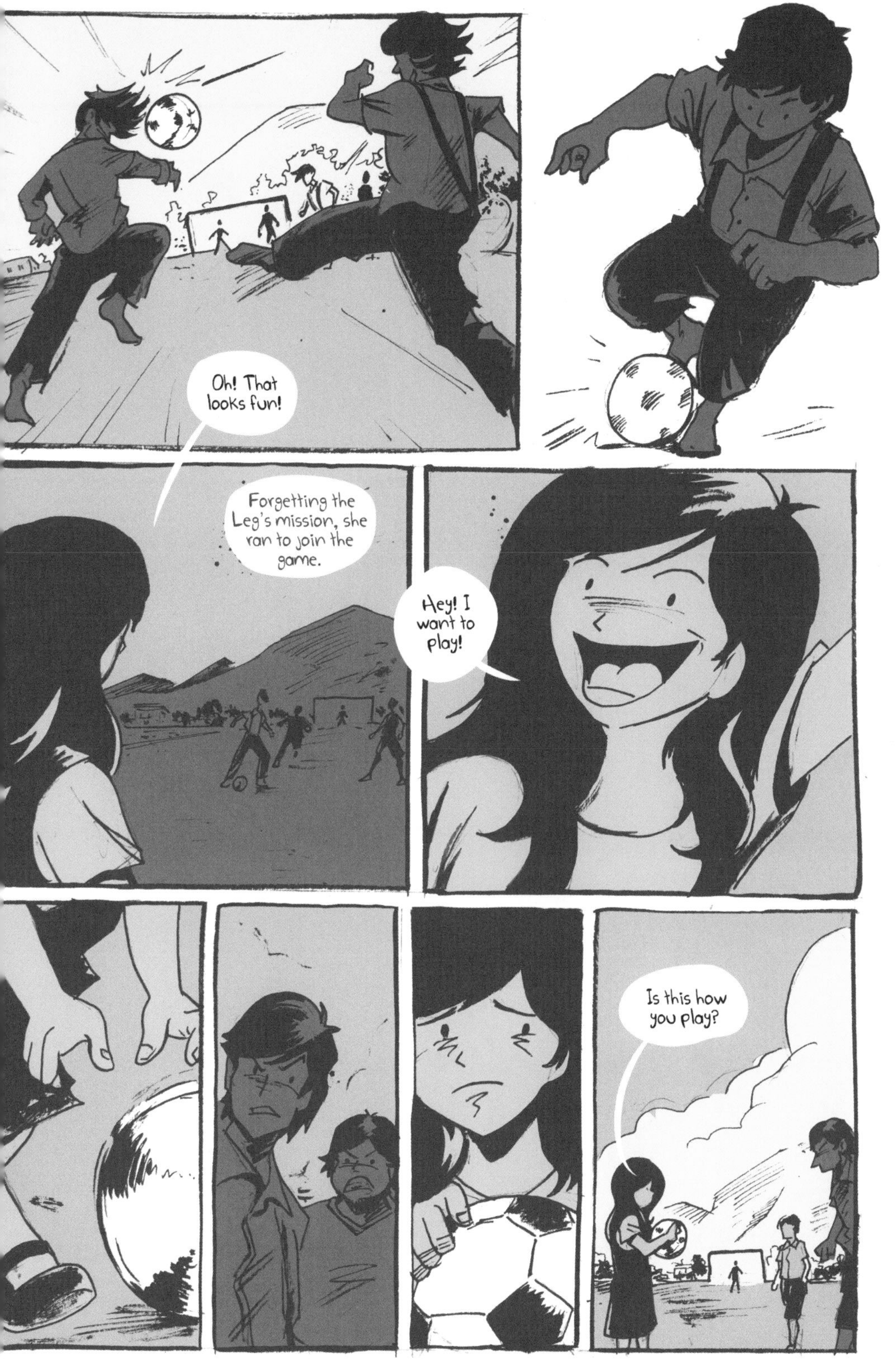
Oh! That looks fun!
Forgetting the Leg's mission, she ran to join the game.
Hey! I want to play!
Is this how you play?

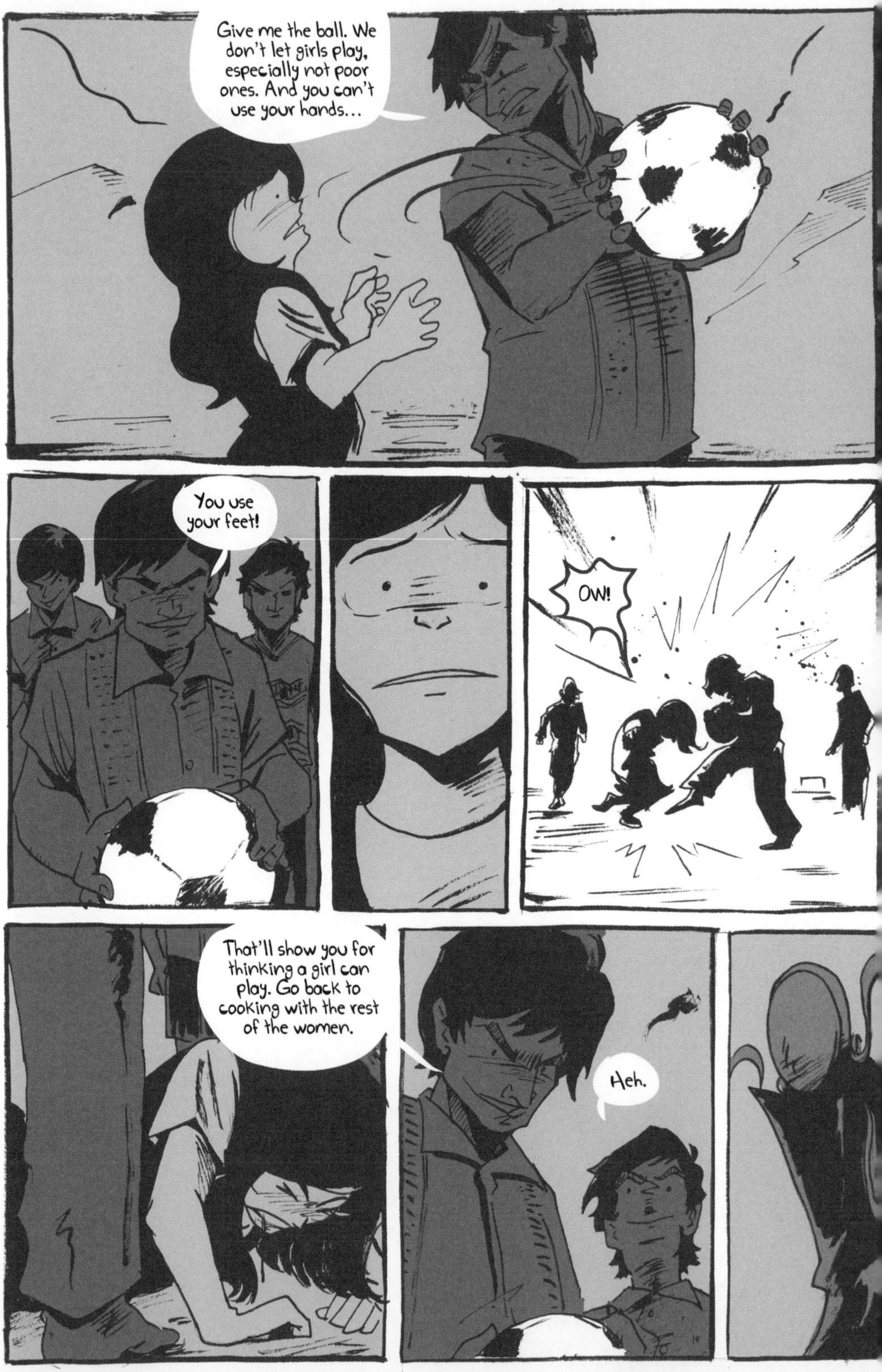
Give me the ball. We don't let girls play, especially not poor ones. And you can't use your hands...
You use your feet!
OW!
That'll show you for thinking a girl can play. Go back to cooking with the rest of the women.
Heh.

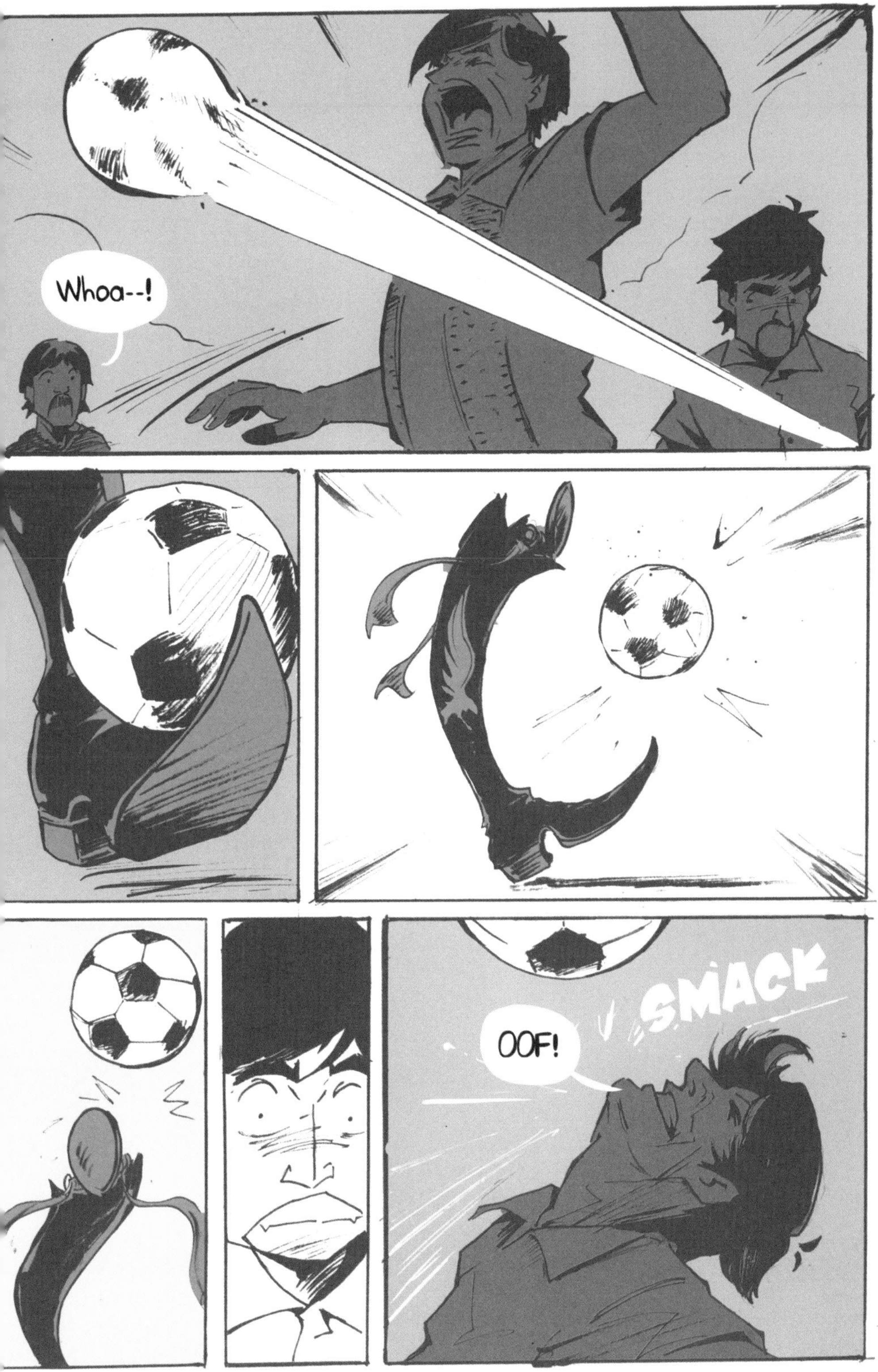
Whoa--!
SMACK
OOF!

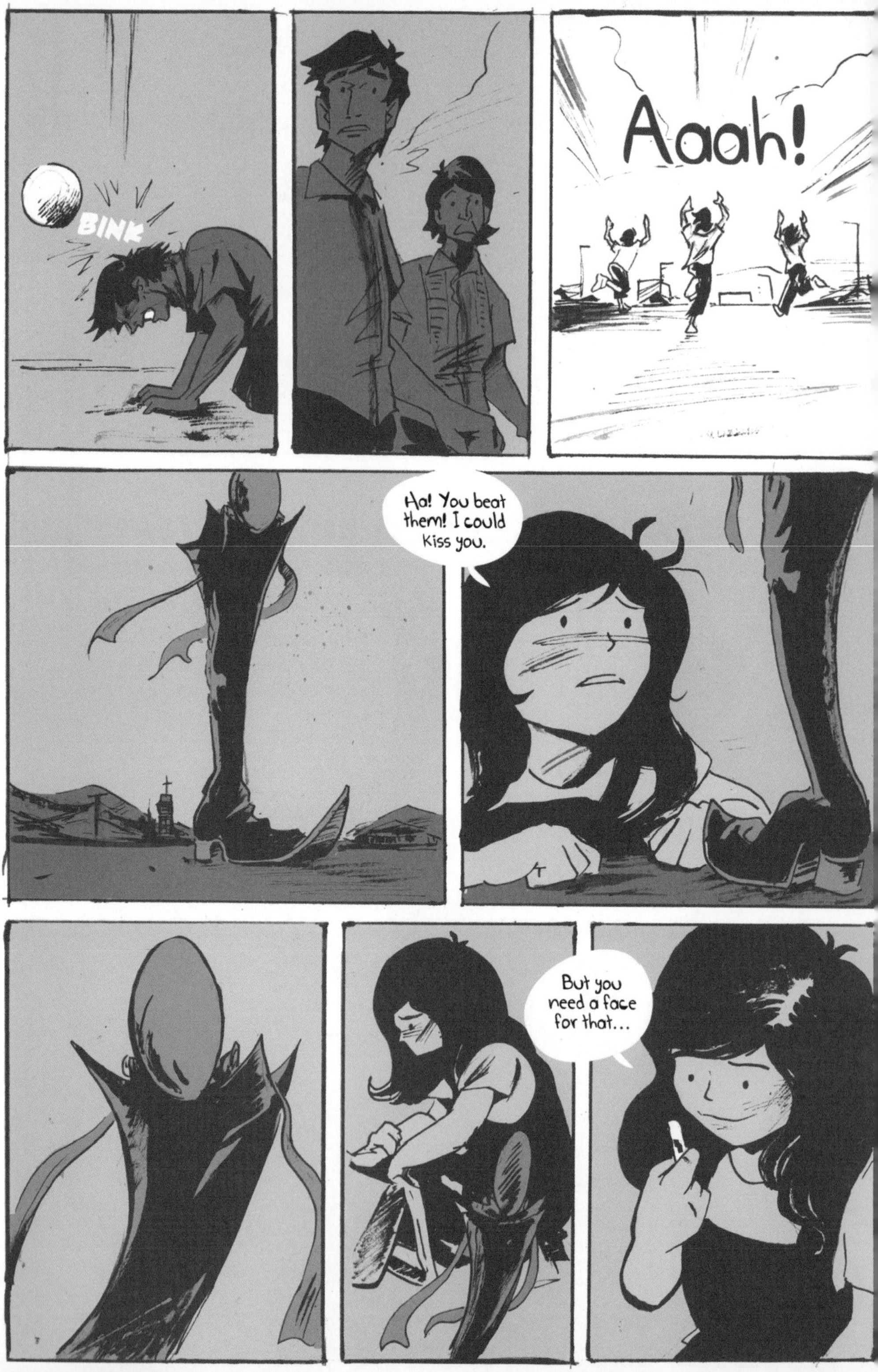
BINK
Aaah!
Ha! You beat them! I could kiss you.
But you need a face for that...

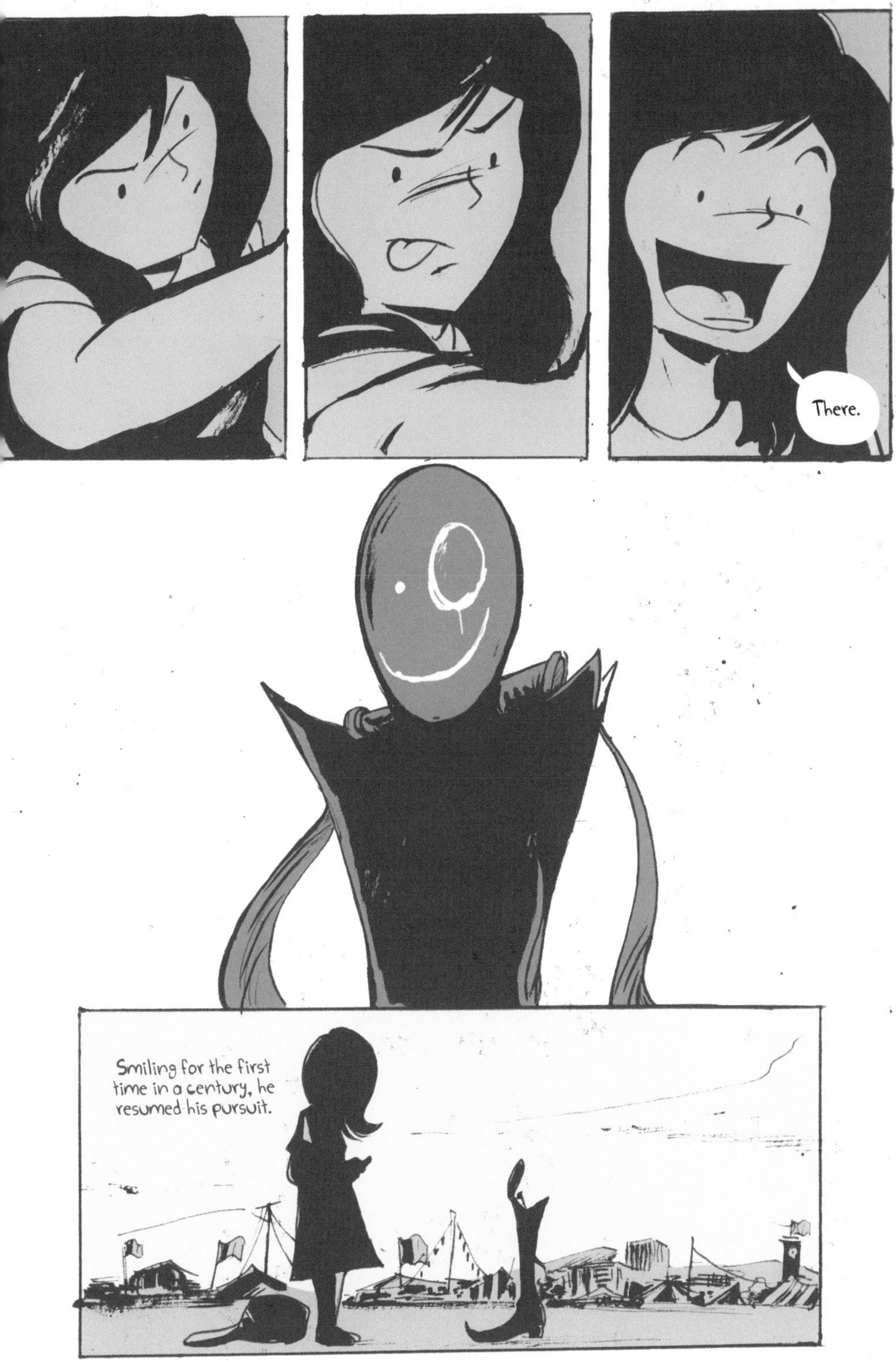
There.
Smiling for the first time in a century, he resumed his pursuit.

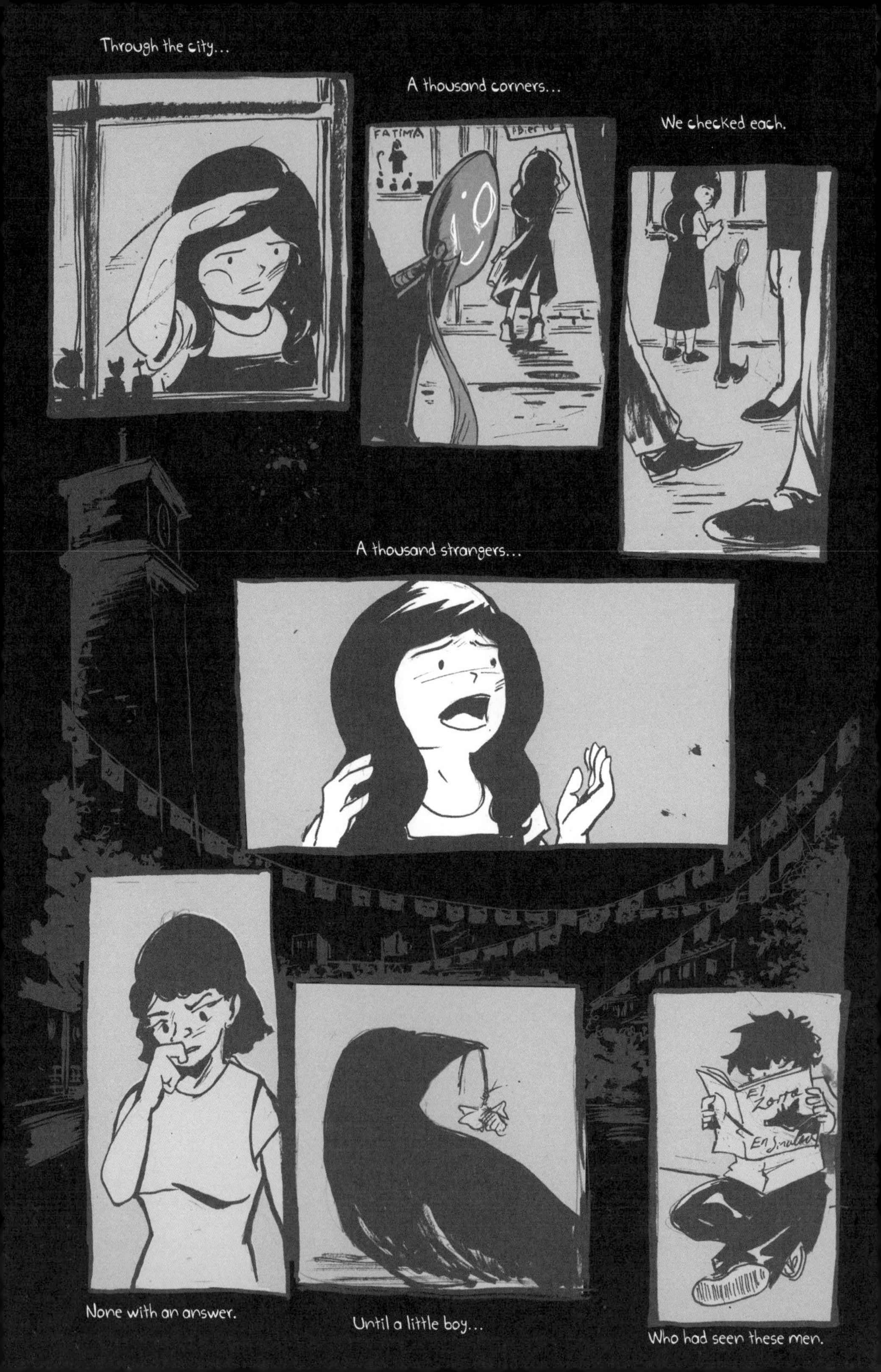

Through the city...
A thousand corners...
FATIMA
ABierto
We checked each.
A thousand strangers...
None with an answer.
Until a little boy...
El Zorro
En Sinaloa
Who had seen these men.

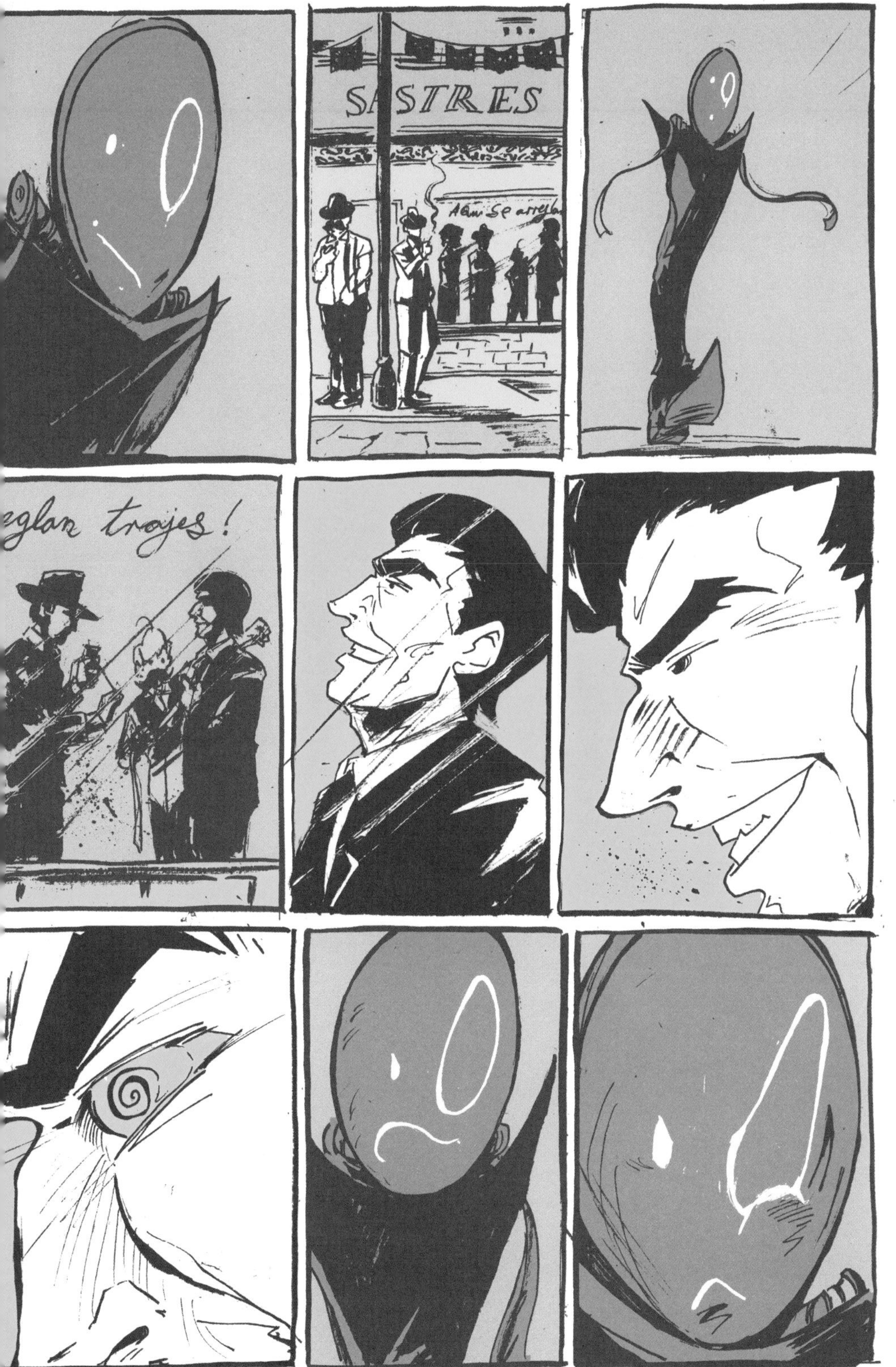
SASTRES
eglan trajes!

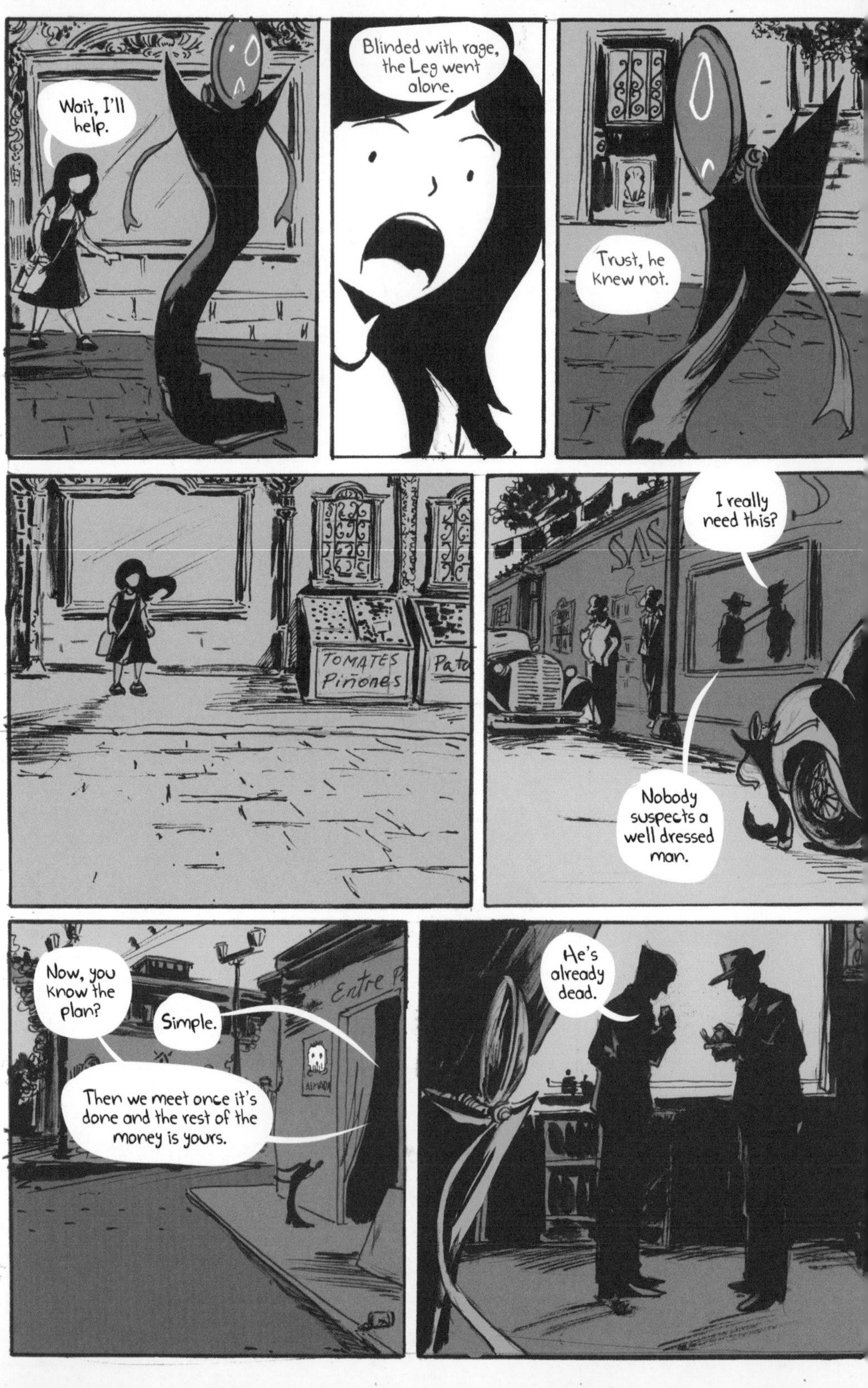
Wait, I'll help.
Blinded with rage, the Leg went alone.
Trust, he knew not.
TOMATES Piñones
I really need this?
Nobody suspects a well dressed man.
Now, you know the plan?
Simple.
Then we meet once it's done and the rest of the money is yours.
He's already dead.

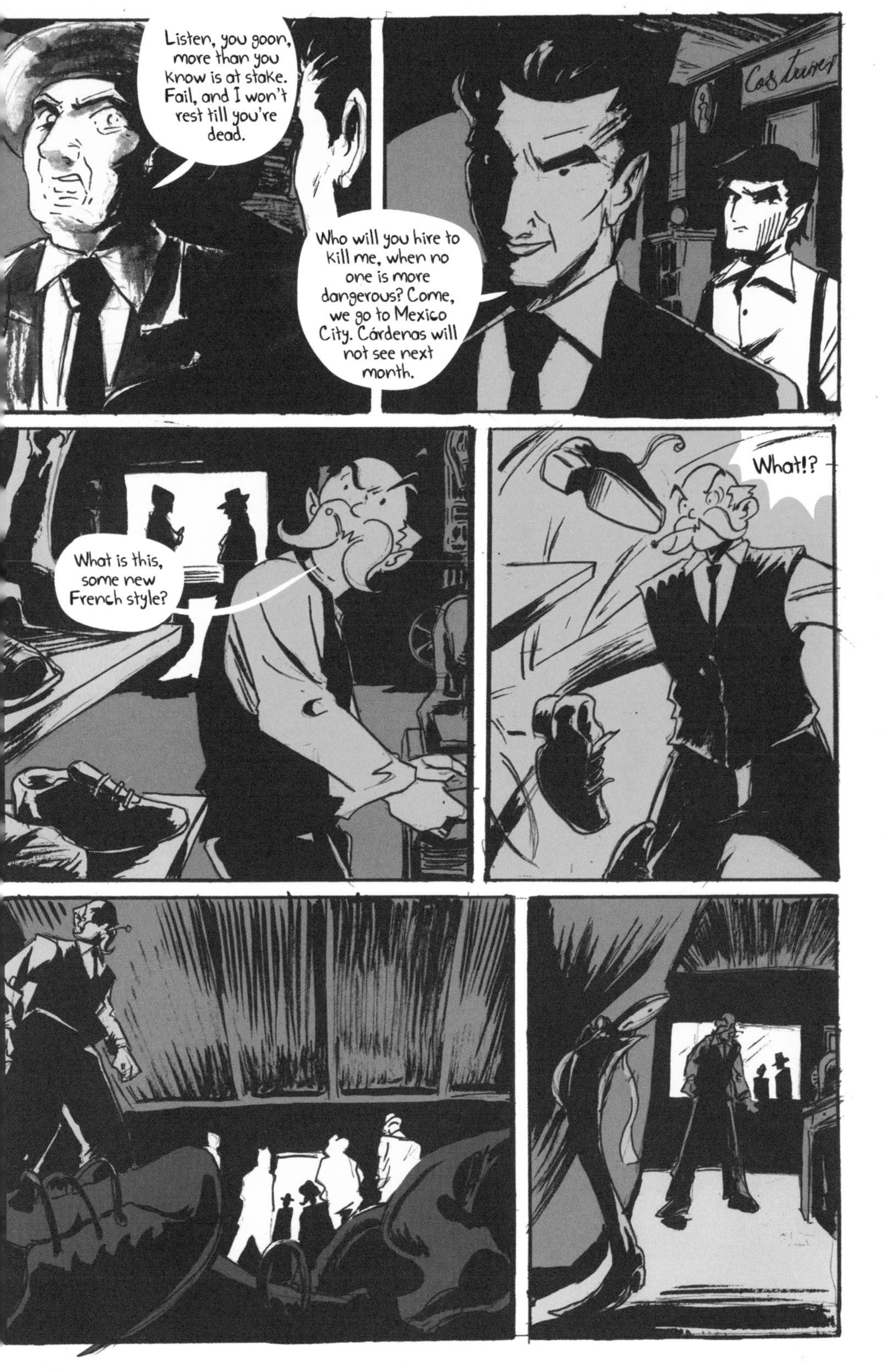
Listen, you goon, more than you know is at stake. Fail, and I won't rest till you're dead.
Who will you hire to kill me, when no one is more dangerous? Come, we go to Mexico City. Cárdenas will not see next month.
What is this, some new French style?
What!?

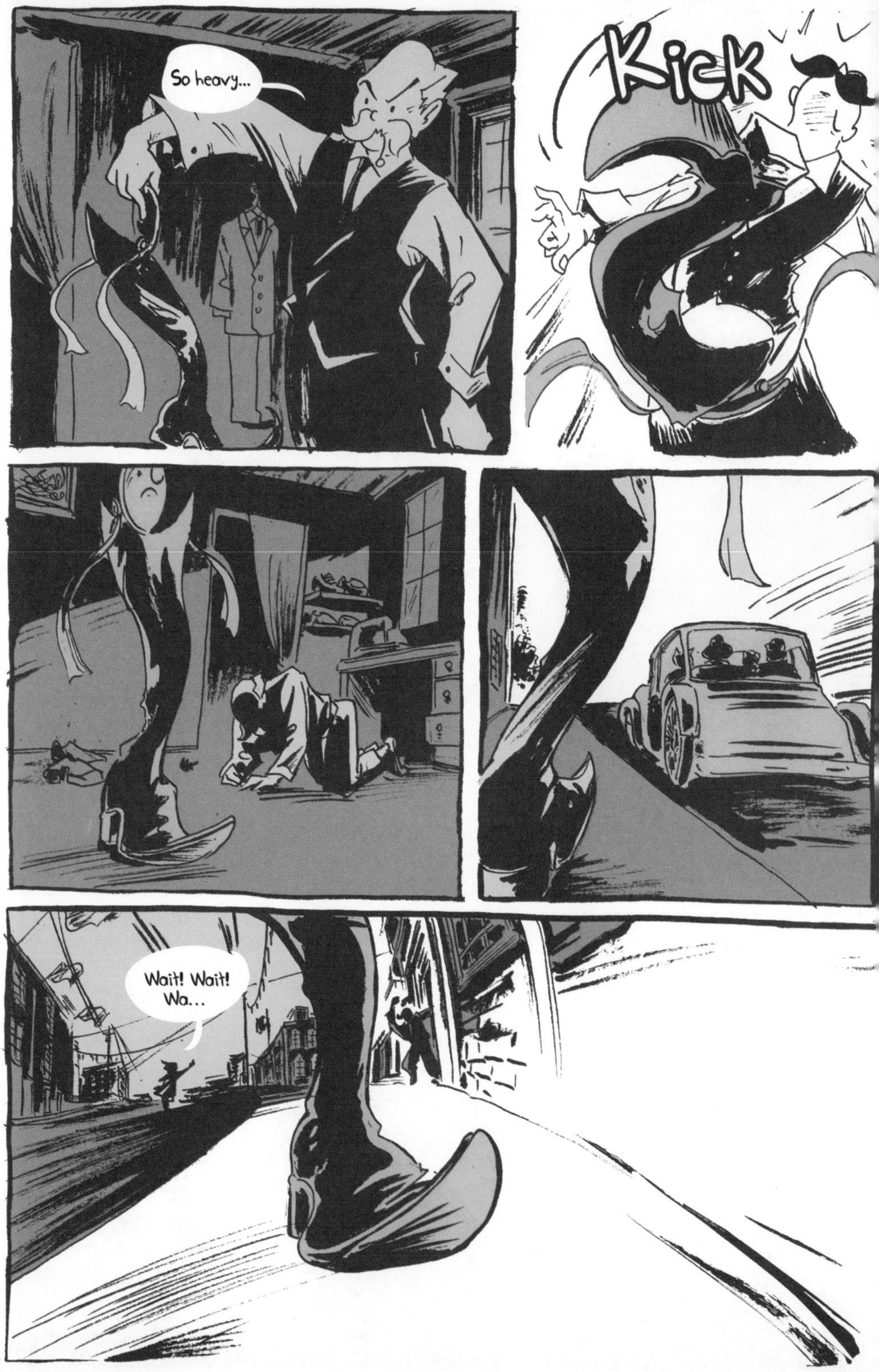
So heavy...
Kick
Wait! Wait! Wa...

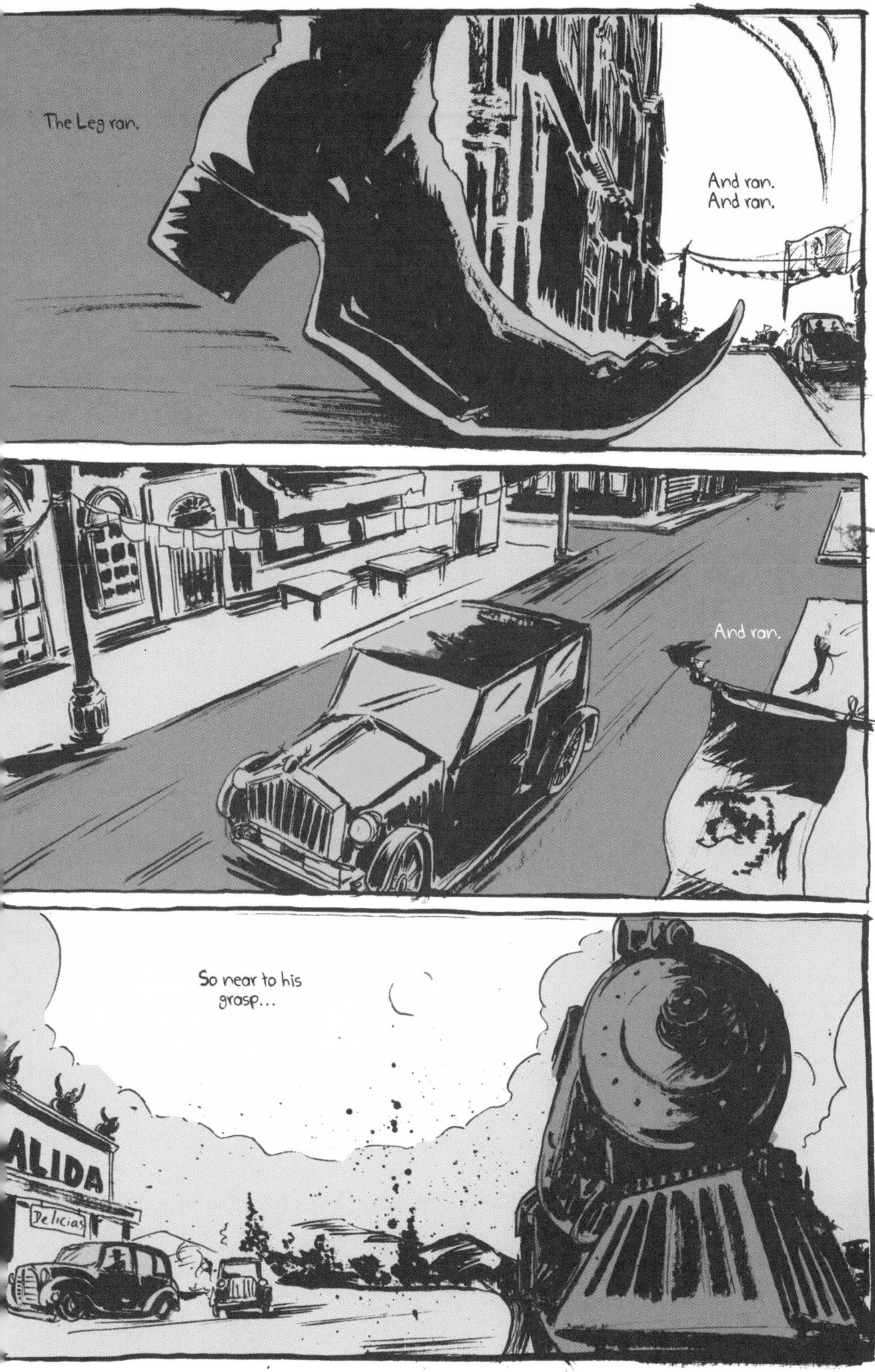
The Leg ran.
And ran.
And ran.
And ran.
So near to his grasp...
ALIDA
Delicias

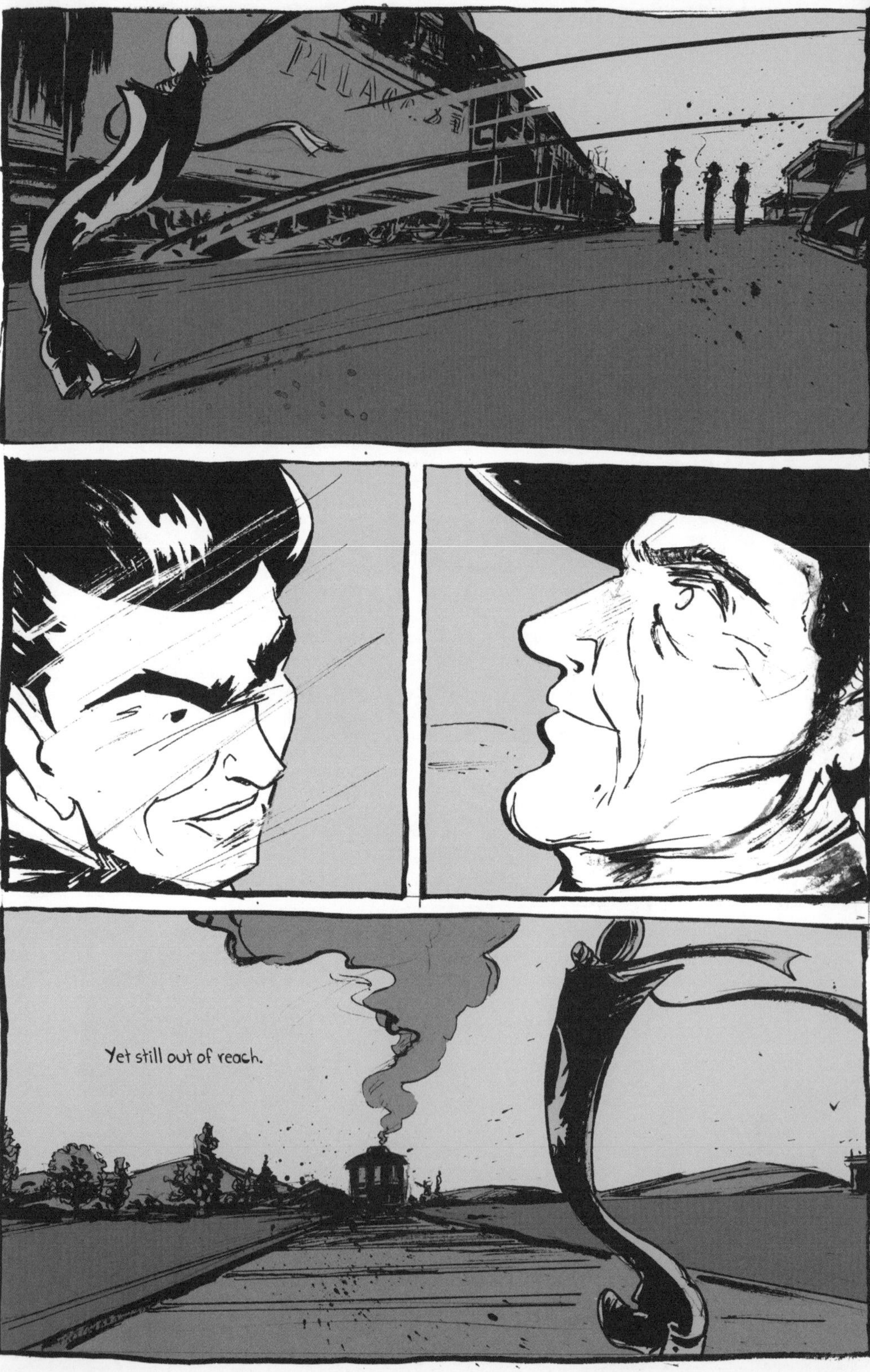
Yet still out of reach.

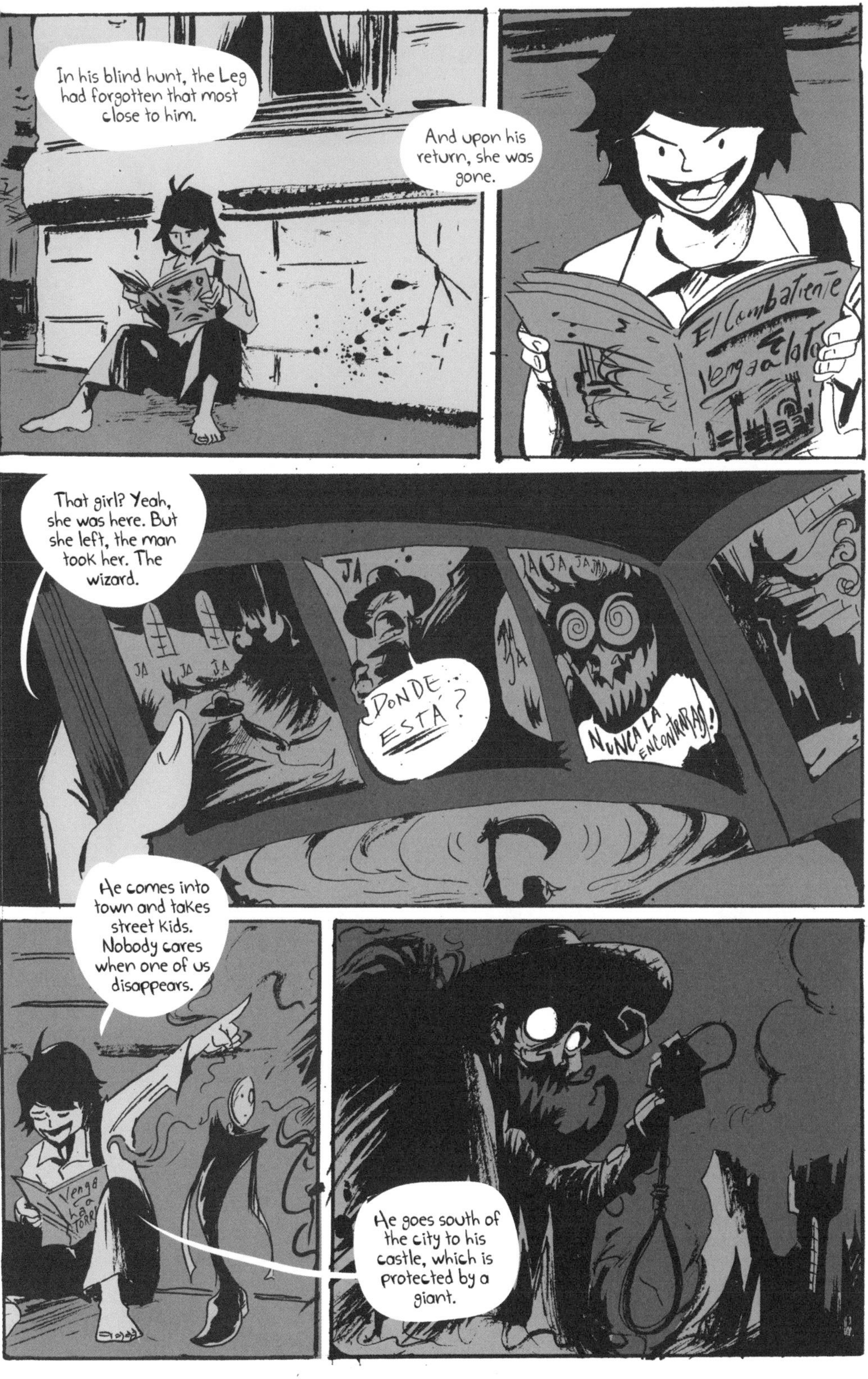
In his blind hunt, the Leg had forgotten that most close to him.
And upon his return, she was gone.
El Combatiente
Venga a la torre
That girl? Yeah, she was here. But she left, the man took her. The wizard.
JA JA JA
JA
JA JA JAJA
JA JA
DONDE ESTÁ?
NUNCA LA ENCONTRARAS!
He comes into town and takes street kids. Nobody cares when one of us disappears.
He goes south of the city to his castle, which is protected by a giant.

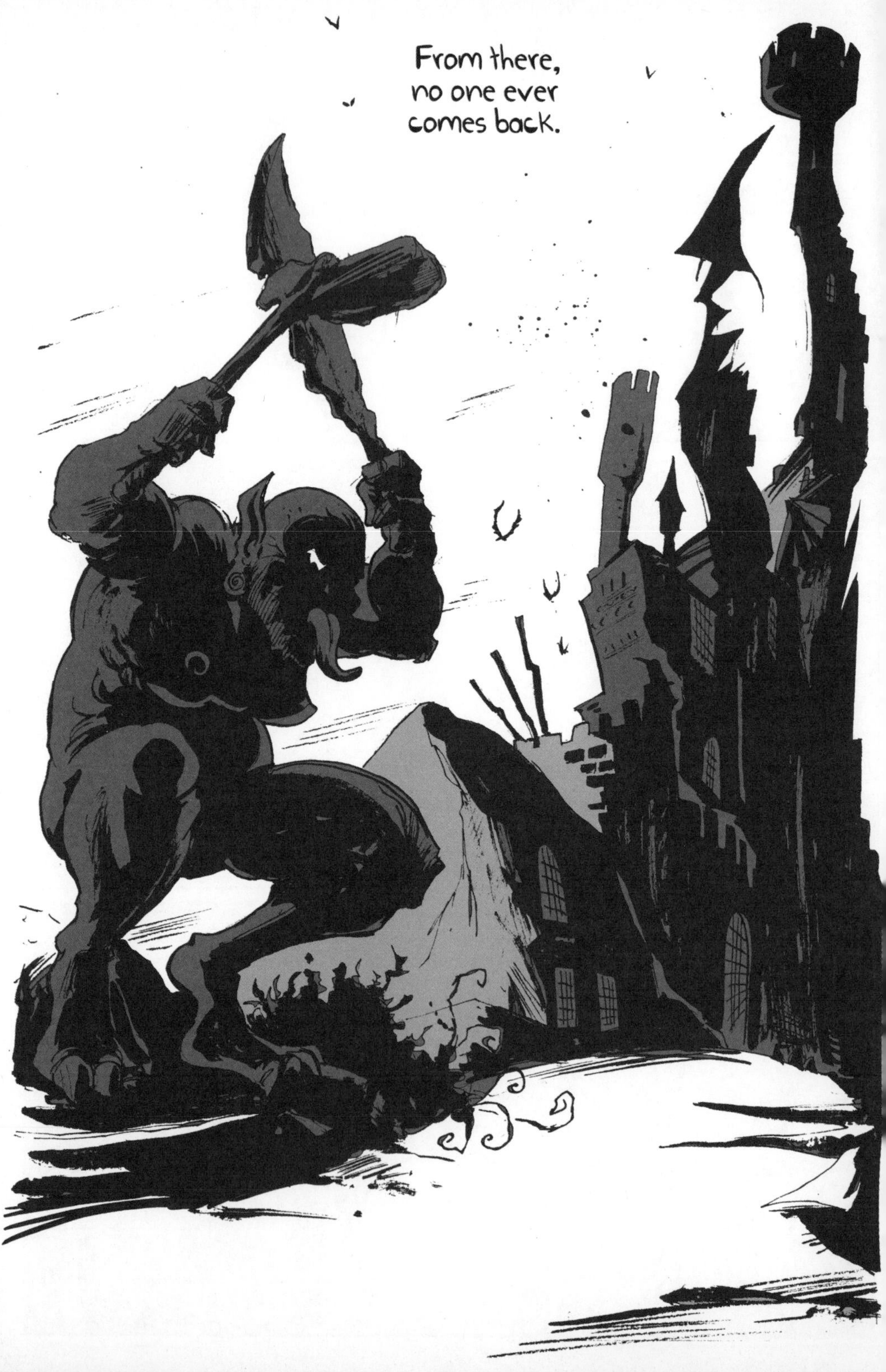
From there, no one ever comes back.

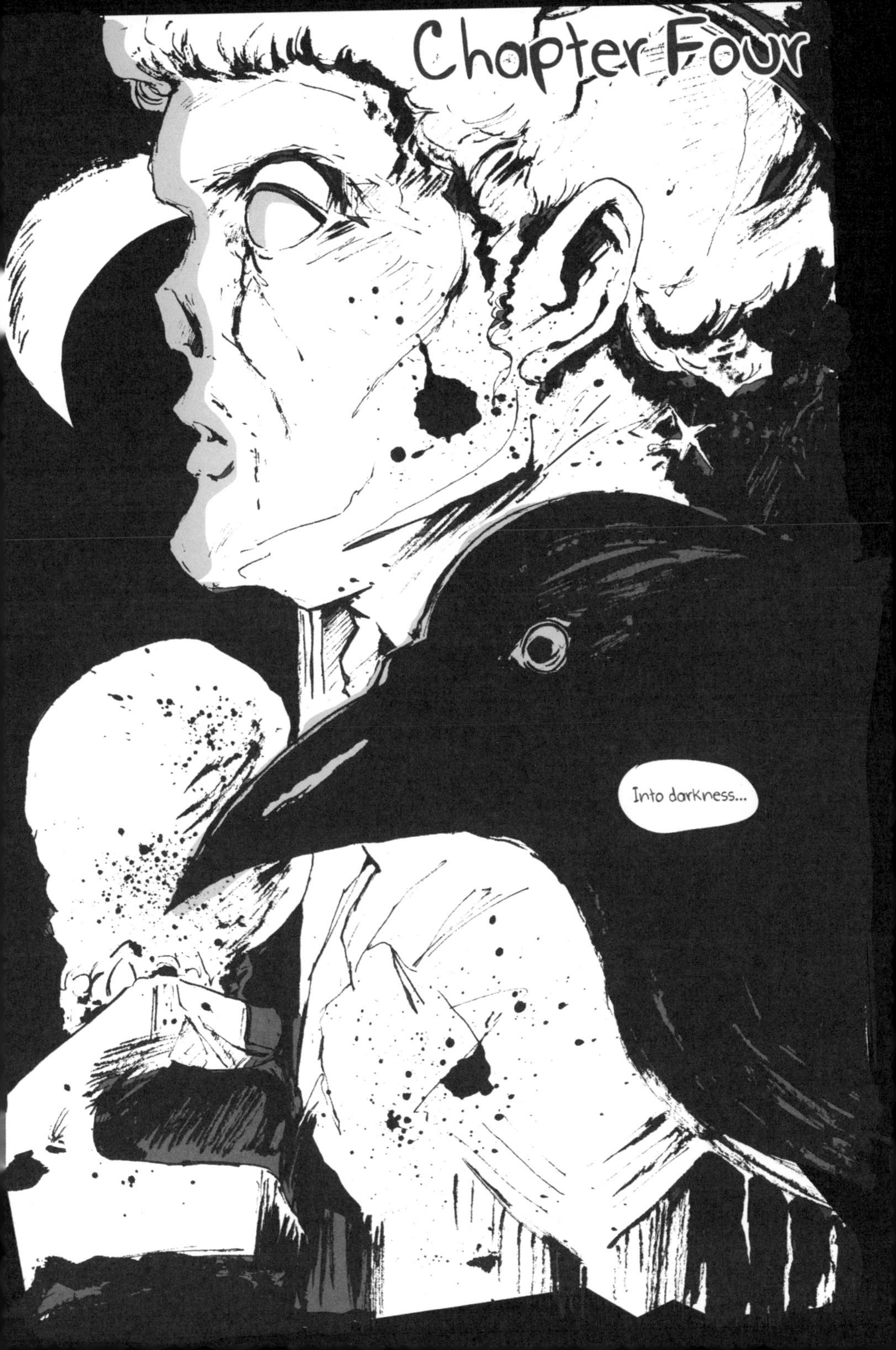
Chapter Four
Into darkness...

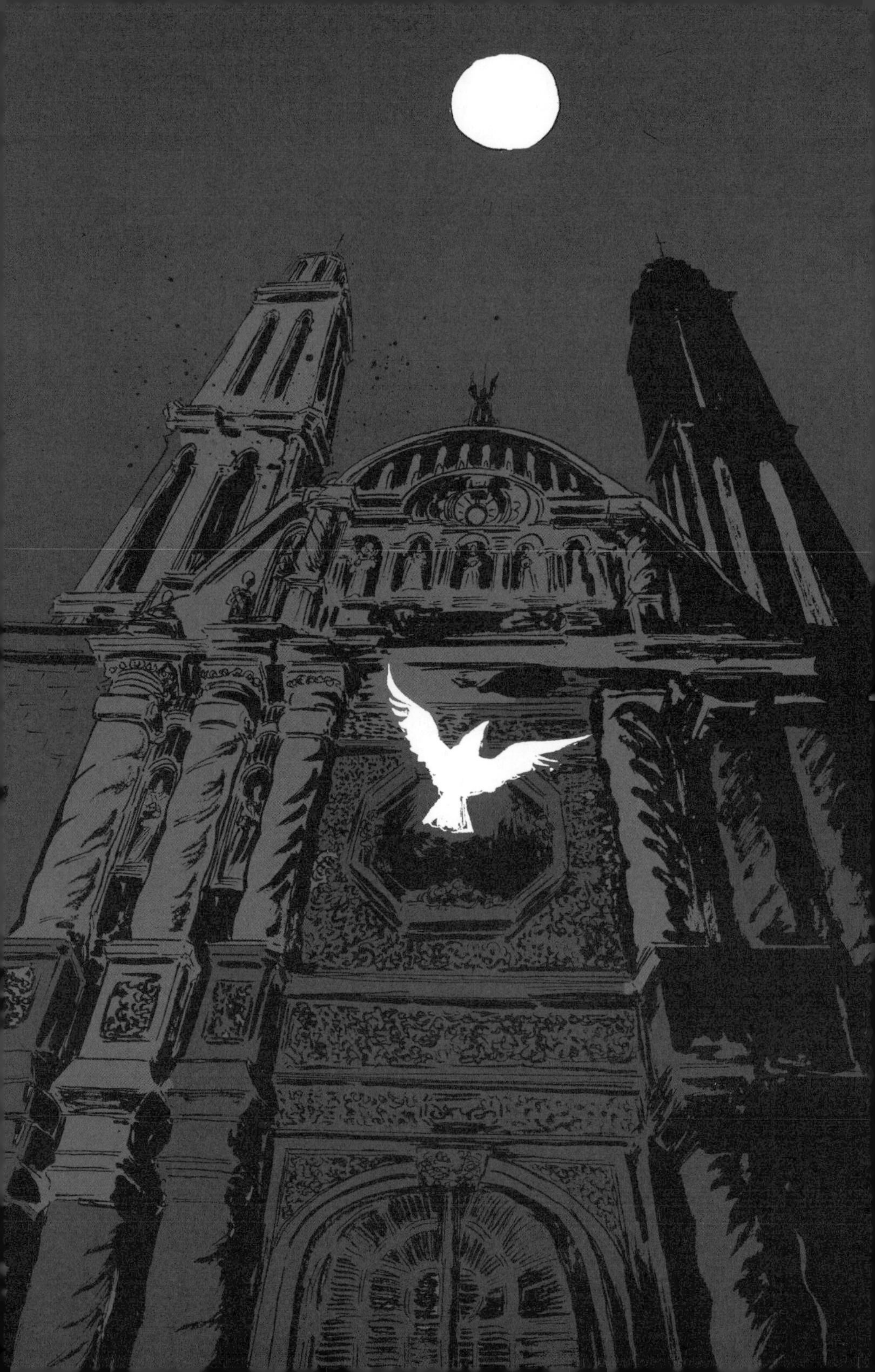

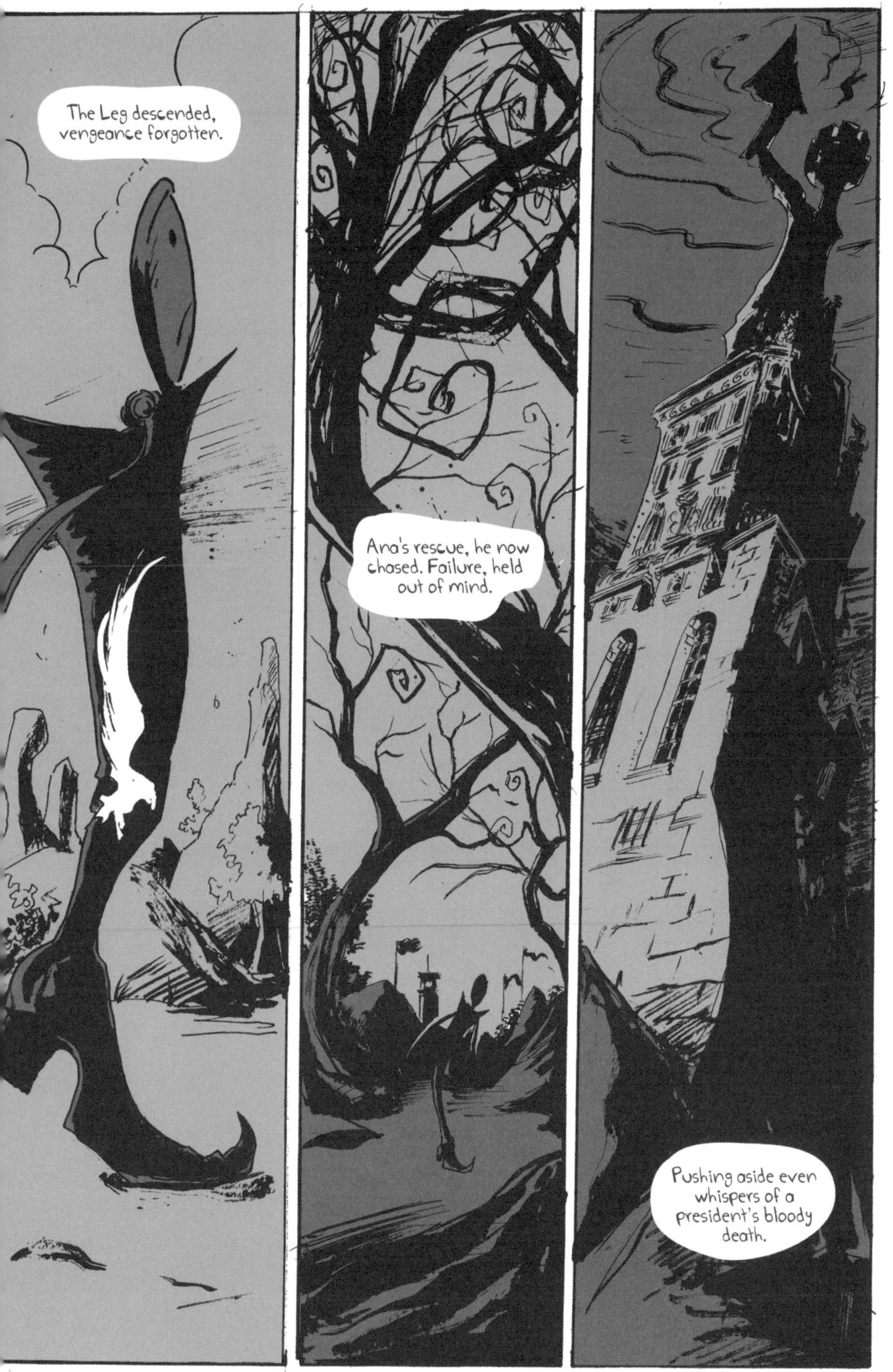
The Leg descended, vengeance forgotten.
Ana's rescue, he now chased. Failure, held out of mind.
Pushing aside even whispers of a president's bloody death.

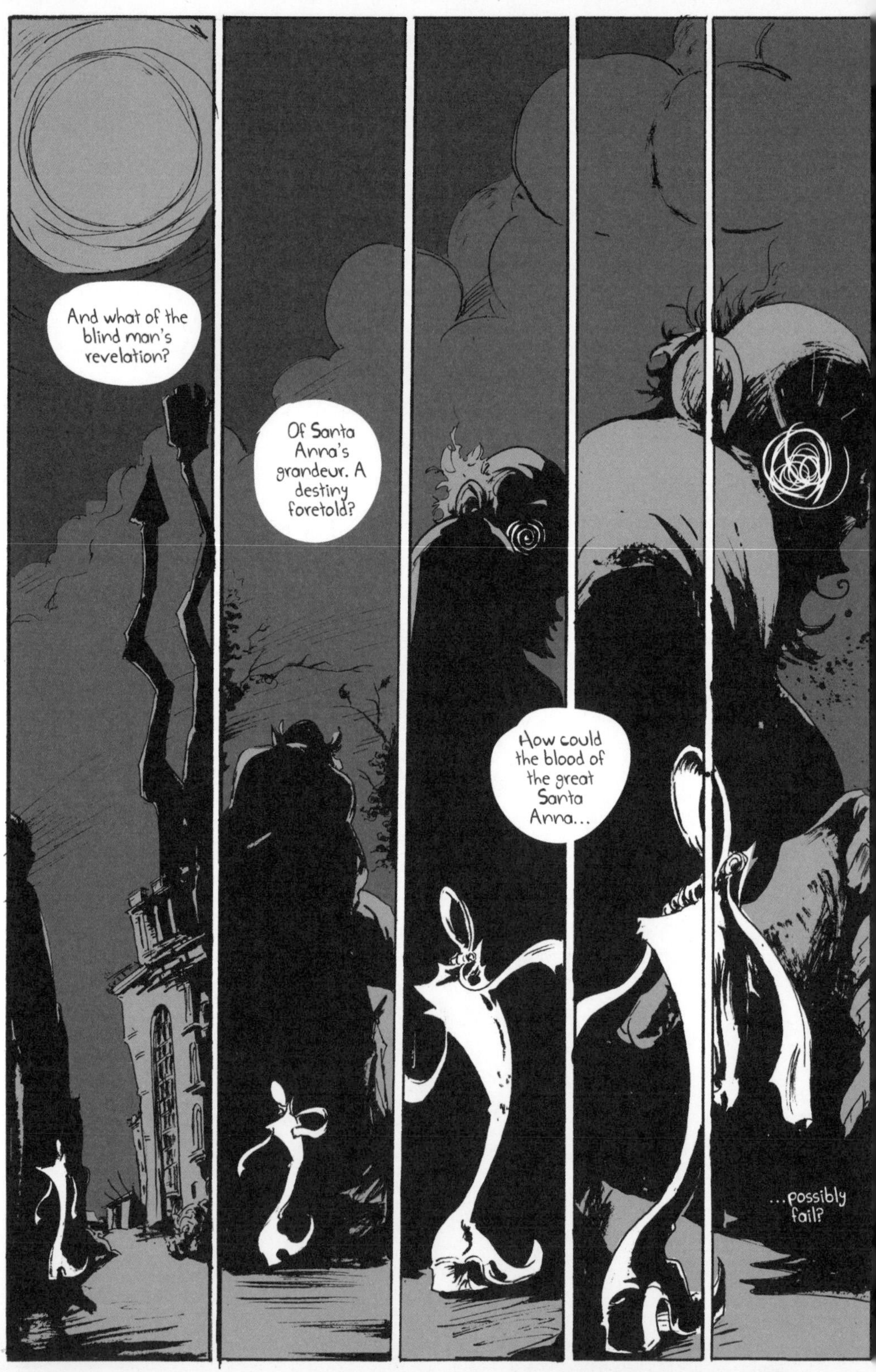
And what of the blind man's revelation?
Of Santa Anna's grandeur. A destiny foretold?
How could the blood of the great Santa Anna...
...possibly fail?

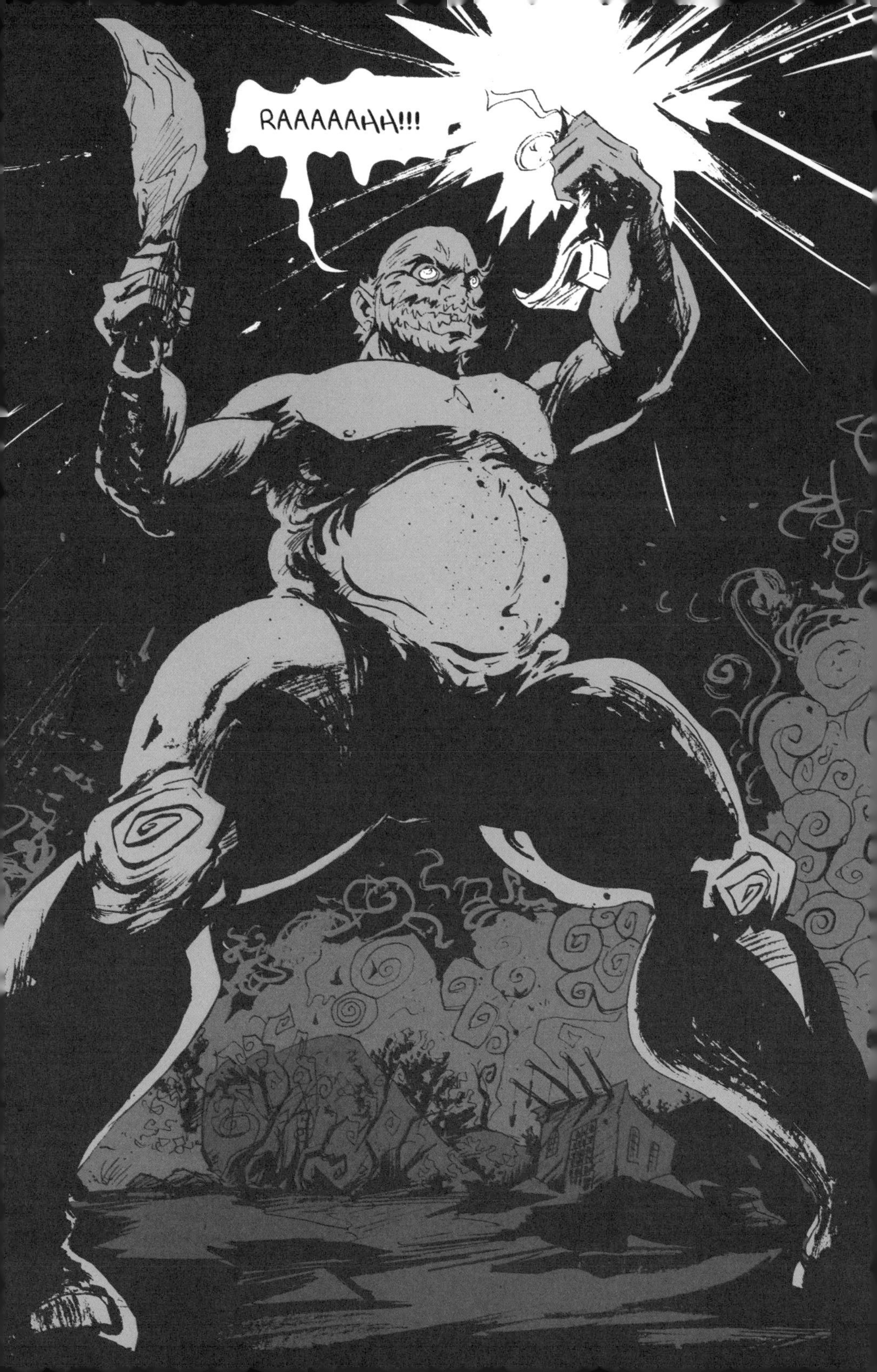
RAAAAAAH!!!

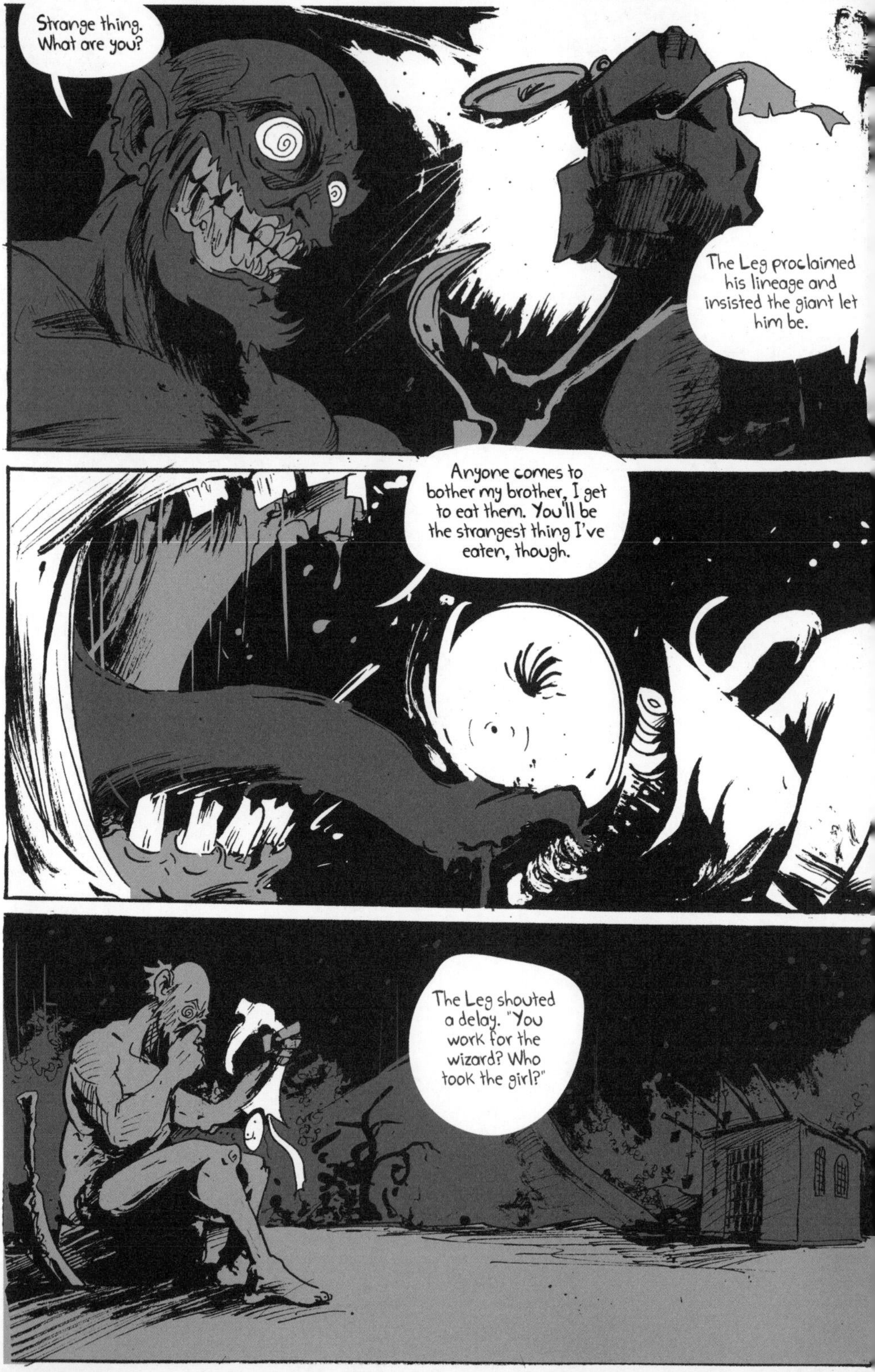
Strange thing. What are you?
The Leg proclaimed his lineage and insisted the giant let him be.
Anyone comes to bother my brother, I get to eat them. You'll be the strangest thing I've eaten, though.
The Leg shouted a delay. "You work for the wizard? Who took the girl?"

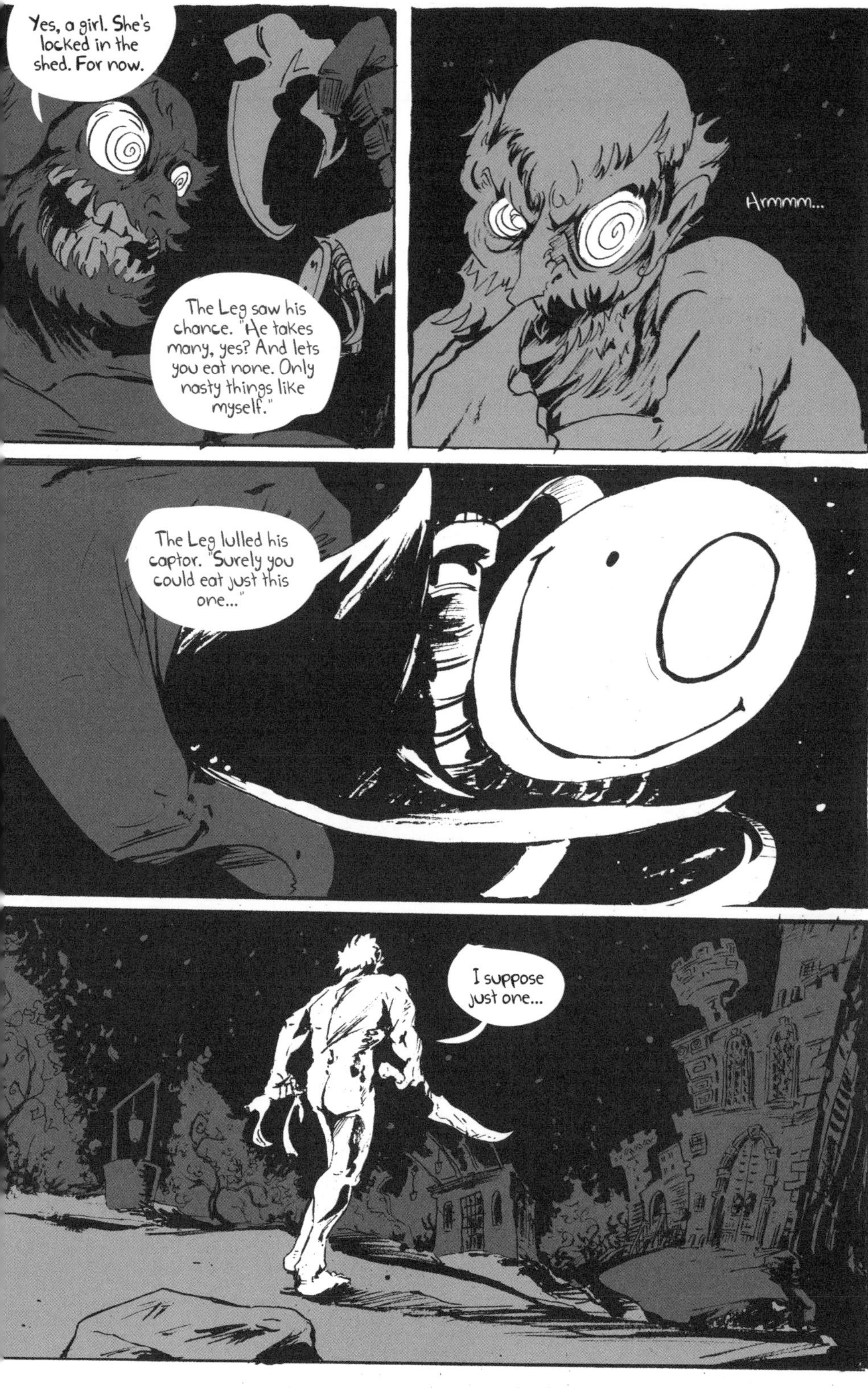
Yes, a girl. She's locked in the shed. For now.
The Leg saw his chance. "He takes many, yes? And lets you eat none. Only nasty things like myself."
Hrmmm...
The Leg lulled his captor. "Surely you could eat just this one..."
I suppose just one...

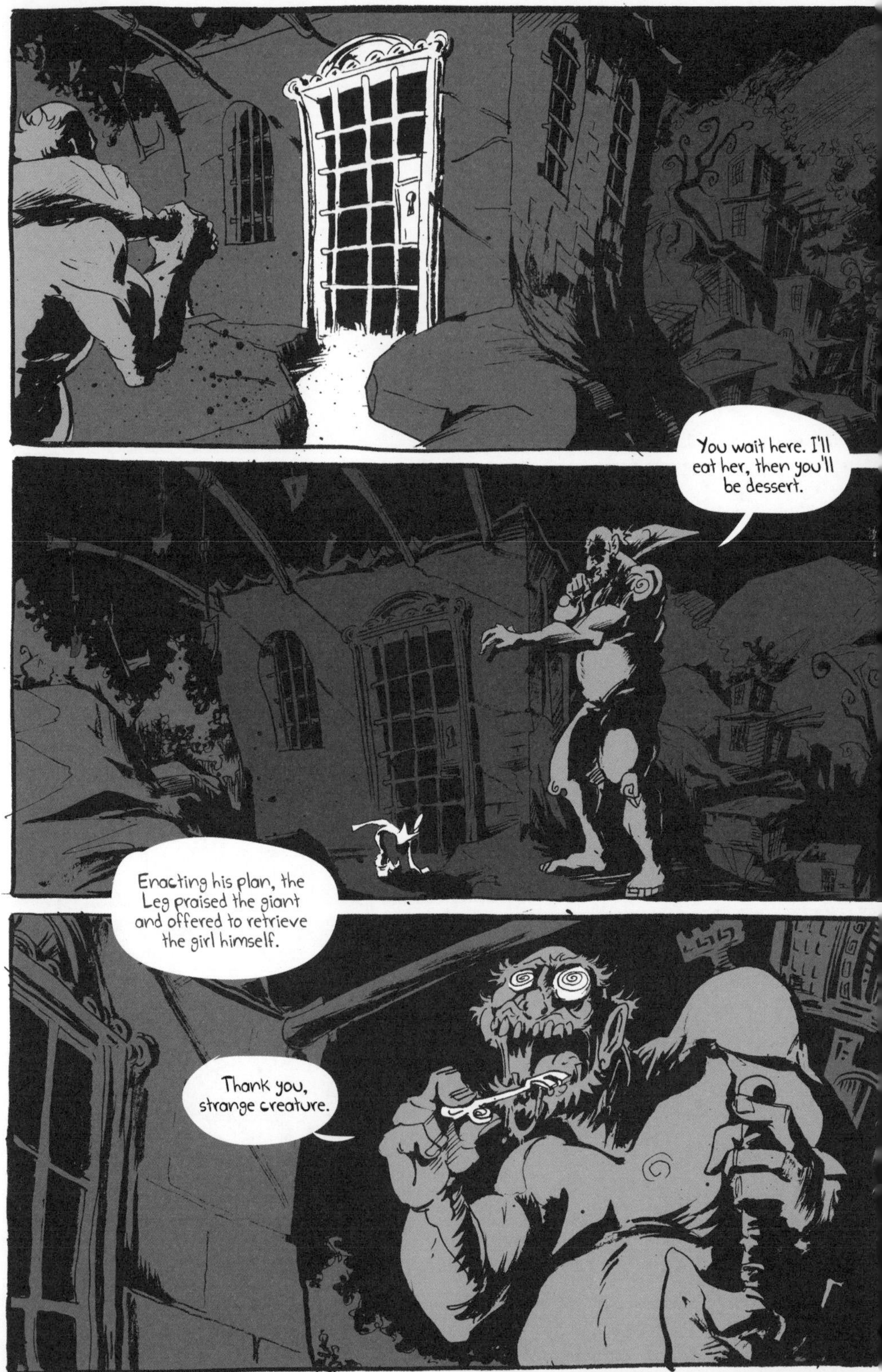
You wait here. I'll eat her, then you'll be dessert.
Enacting his plan, the Leg praised the giant and offered to retrieve the girl himself.
Thank you, strange creature.

What happened? Where is the girl? You promised...

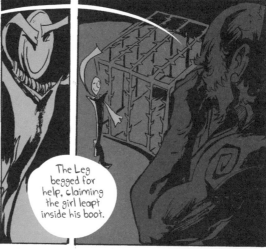

The Leg begged for help, claiming the girl leapt inside his boot.

"Come closer," the Leg pleaded. "Wrench out the wretch."

"Closer..."

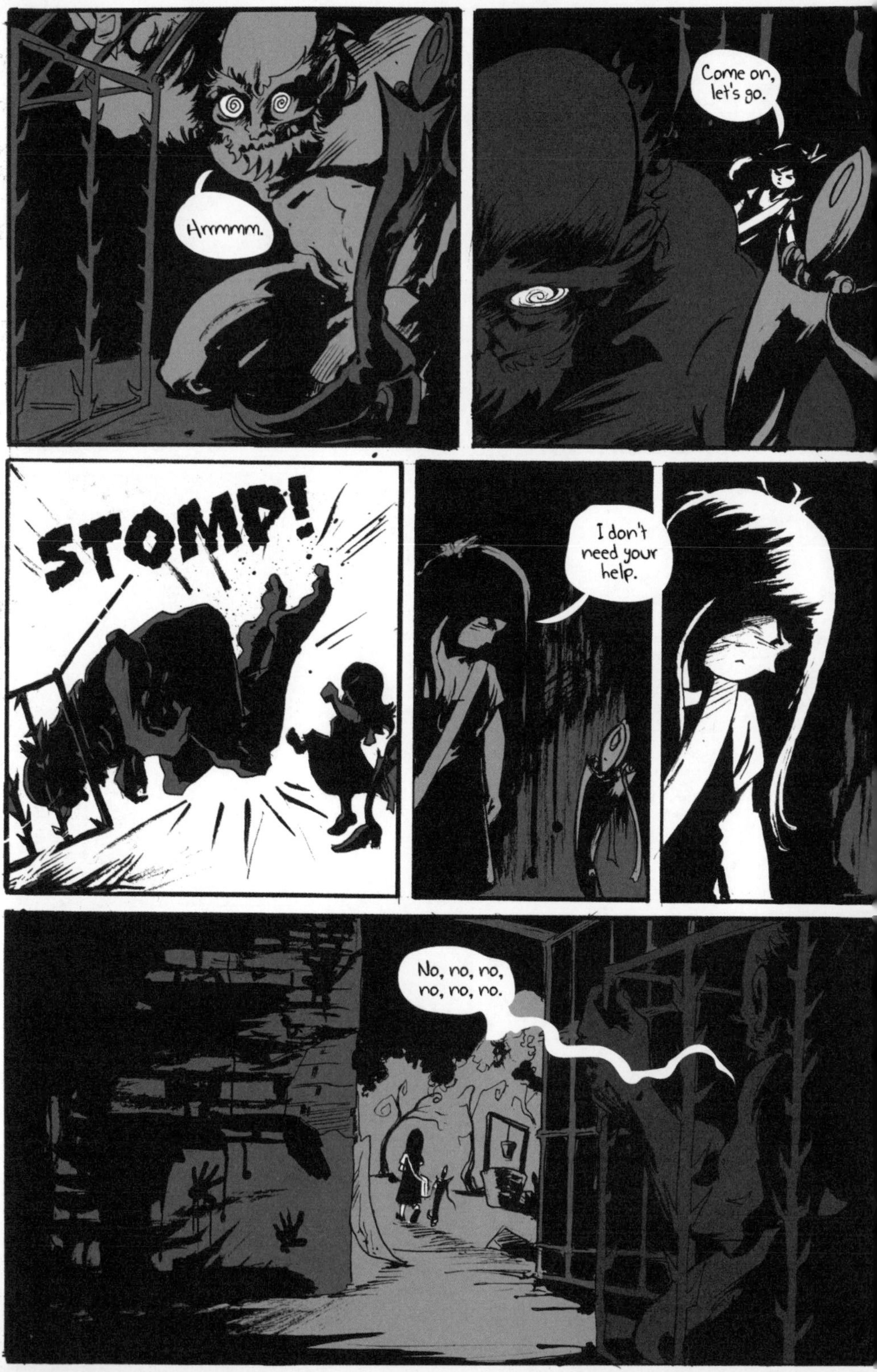
Hrmmm.
Come on, let's go.
STOMP!
I don't need your help.
No, no, no, no, no, no.

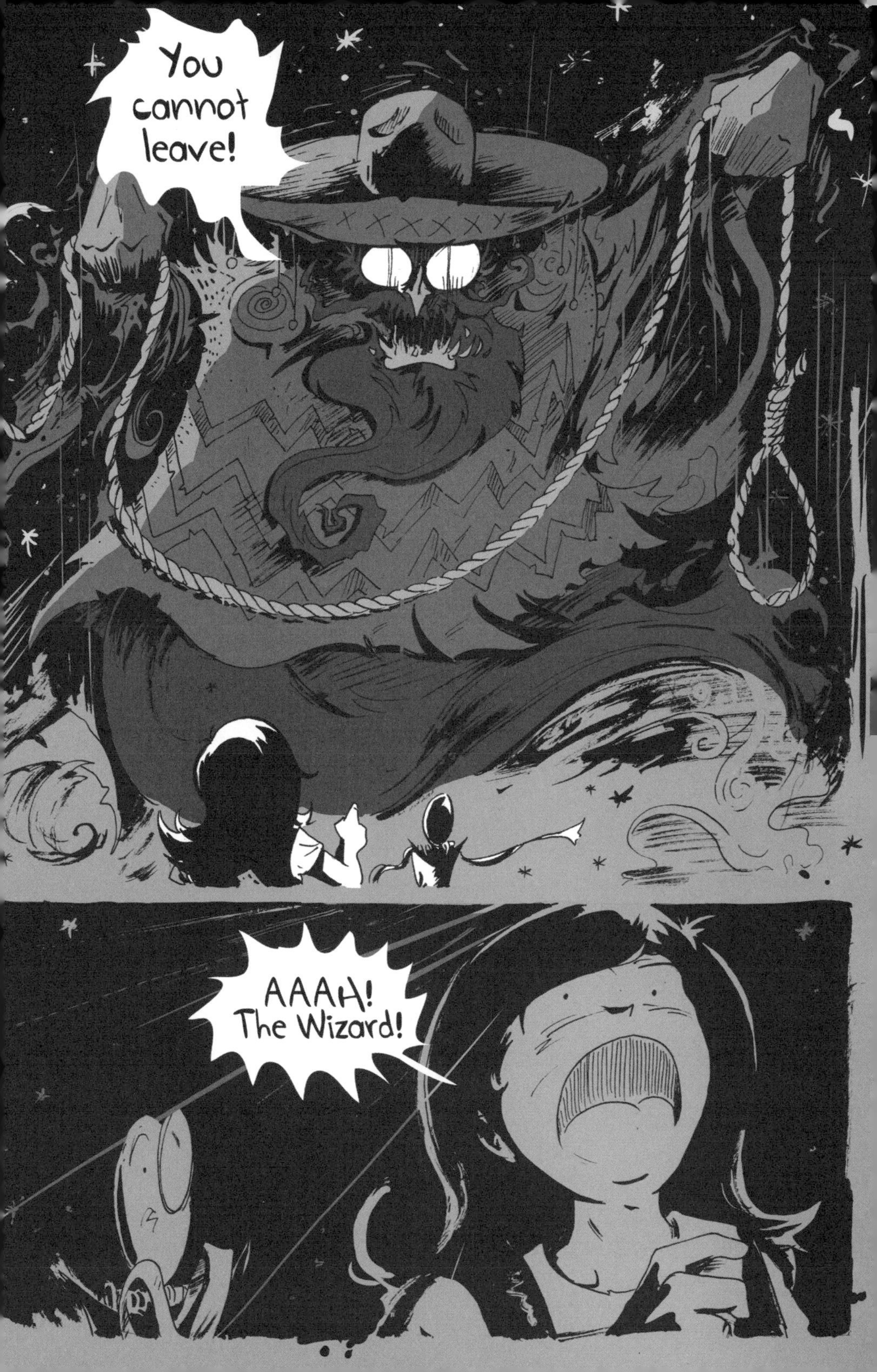
You cannot leave!
AAAH! The Wizard!

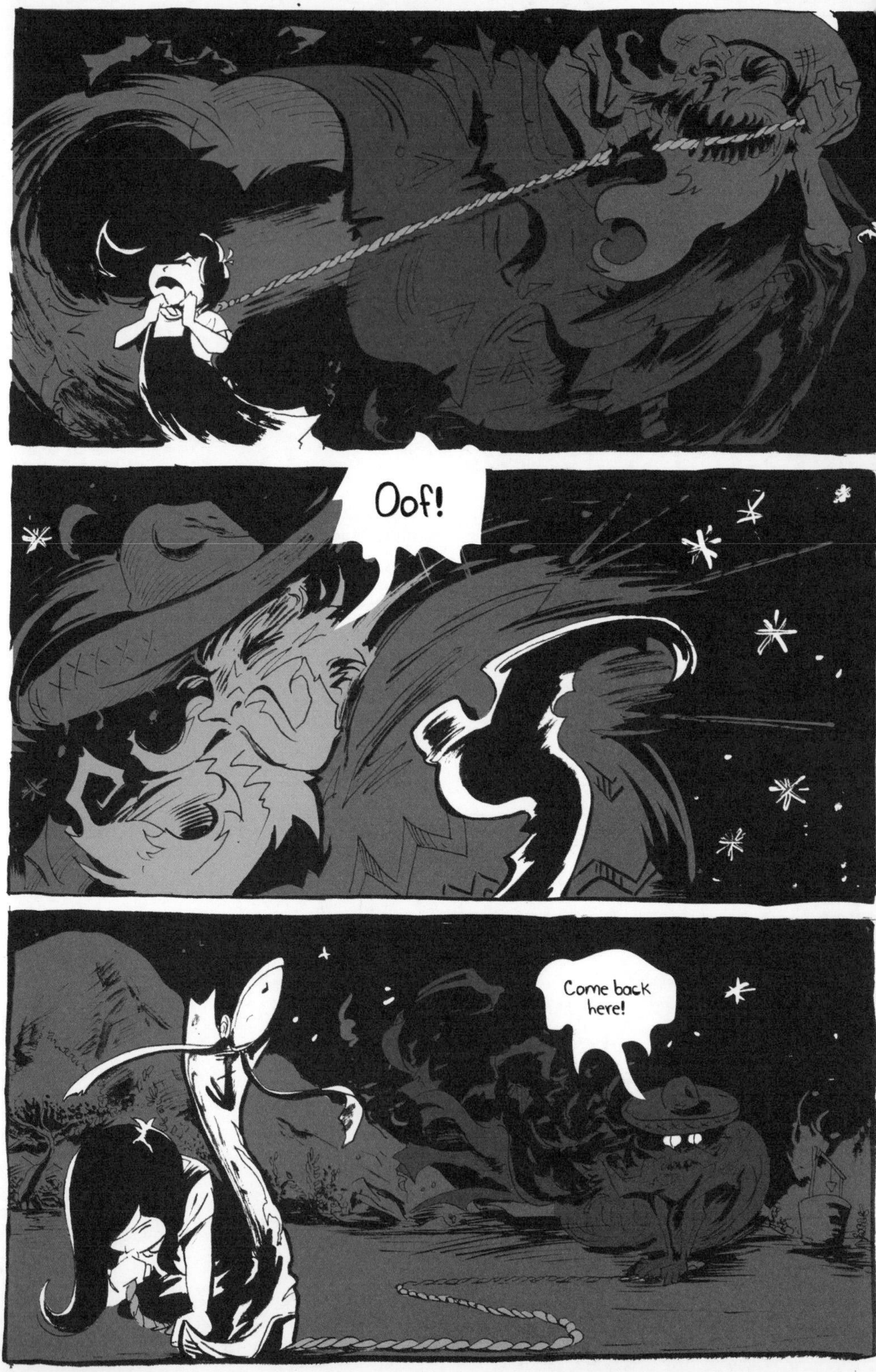
Oof!
Come back here!

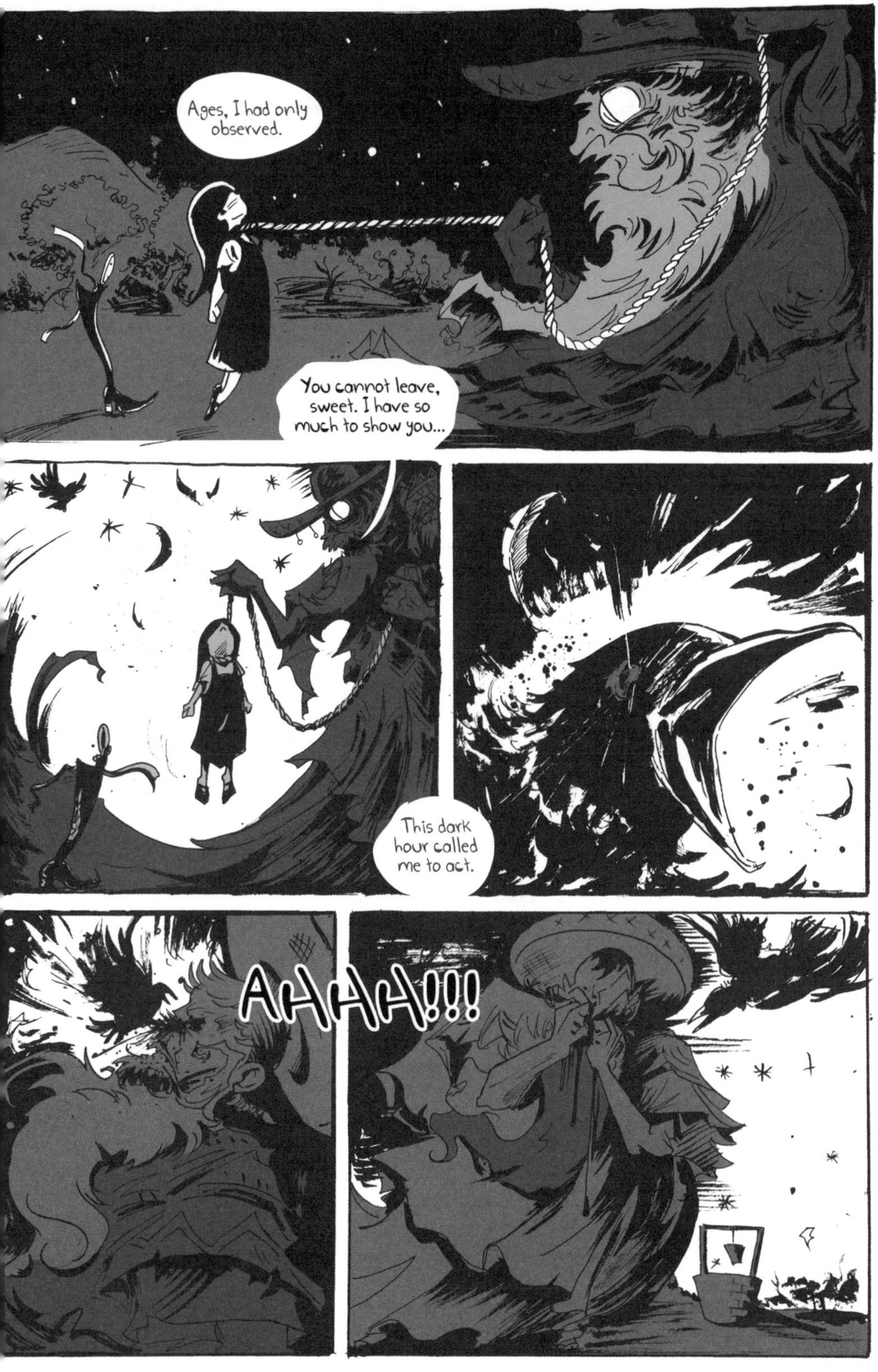
Ages, I had only observed.
You cannot leave, sweet. I have so much to show you...
This dark hour called me to act.
AHHH!!!

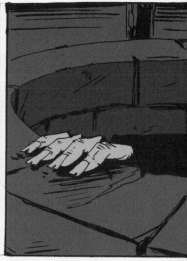

The... The ugly bird... It saved me.

The bird saved me, not you.

Oh, my stomach hurts

The water he gave me tasted weird.

It tasted like...

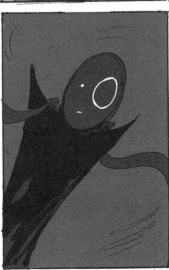

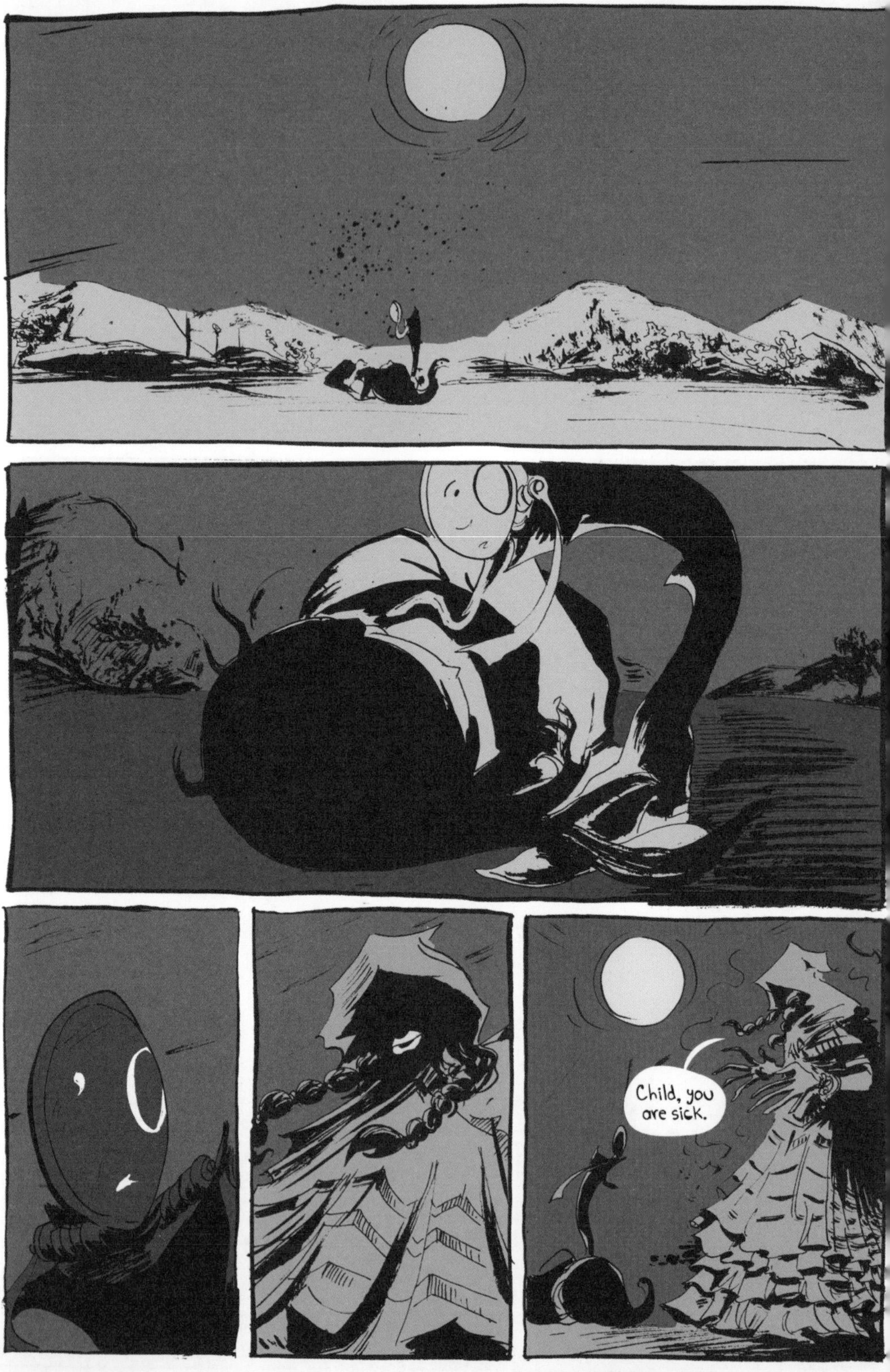
Child, you are sick.

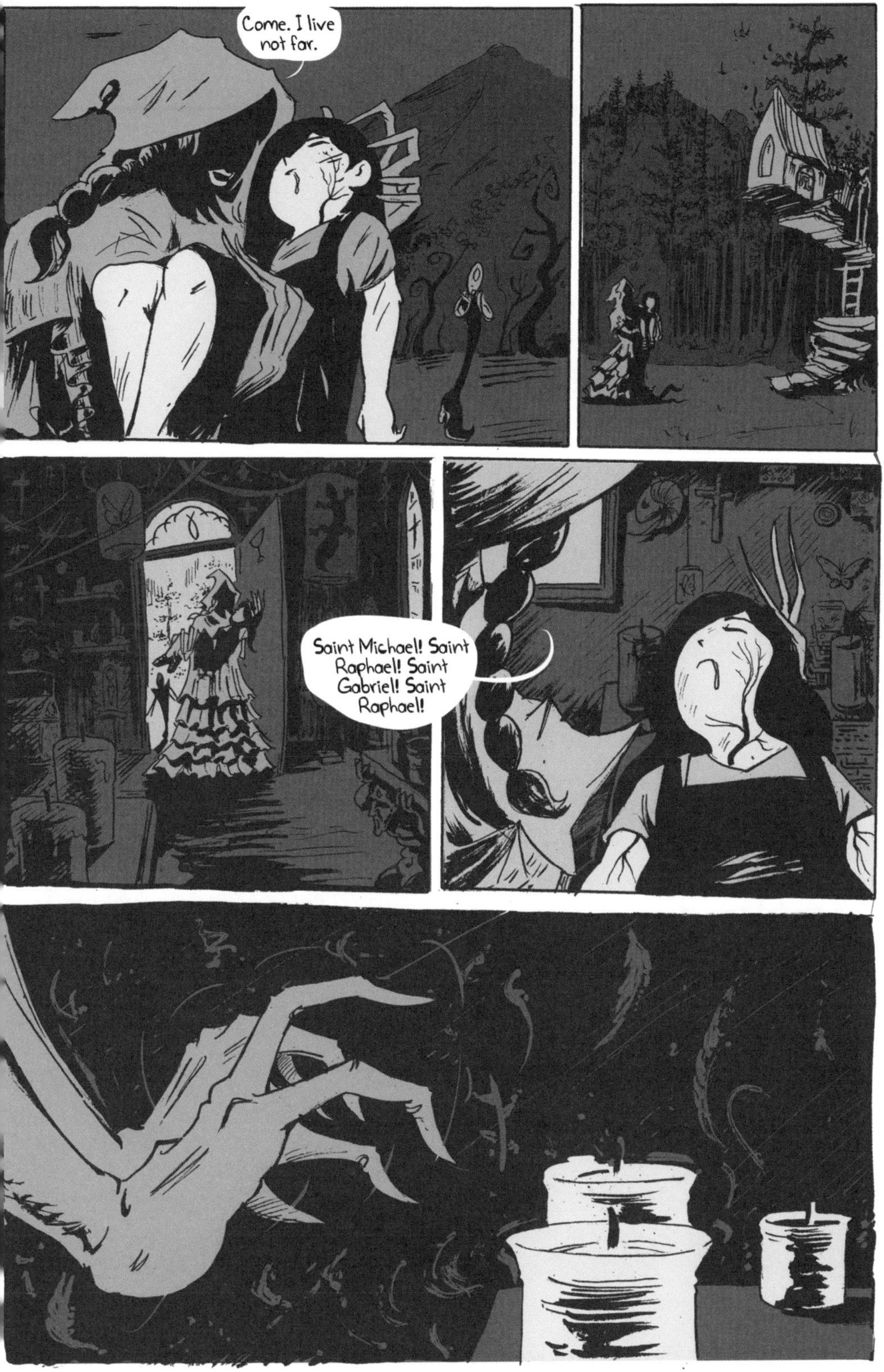
Come. I live not far.
Saint Michael! Saint Raphael! Saint Gabriel! Saint Raphael!

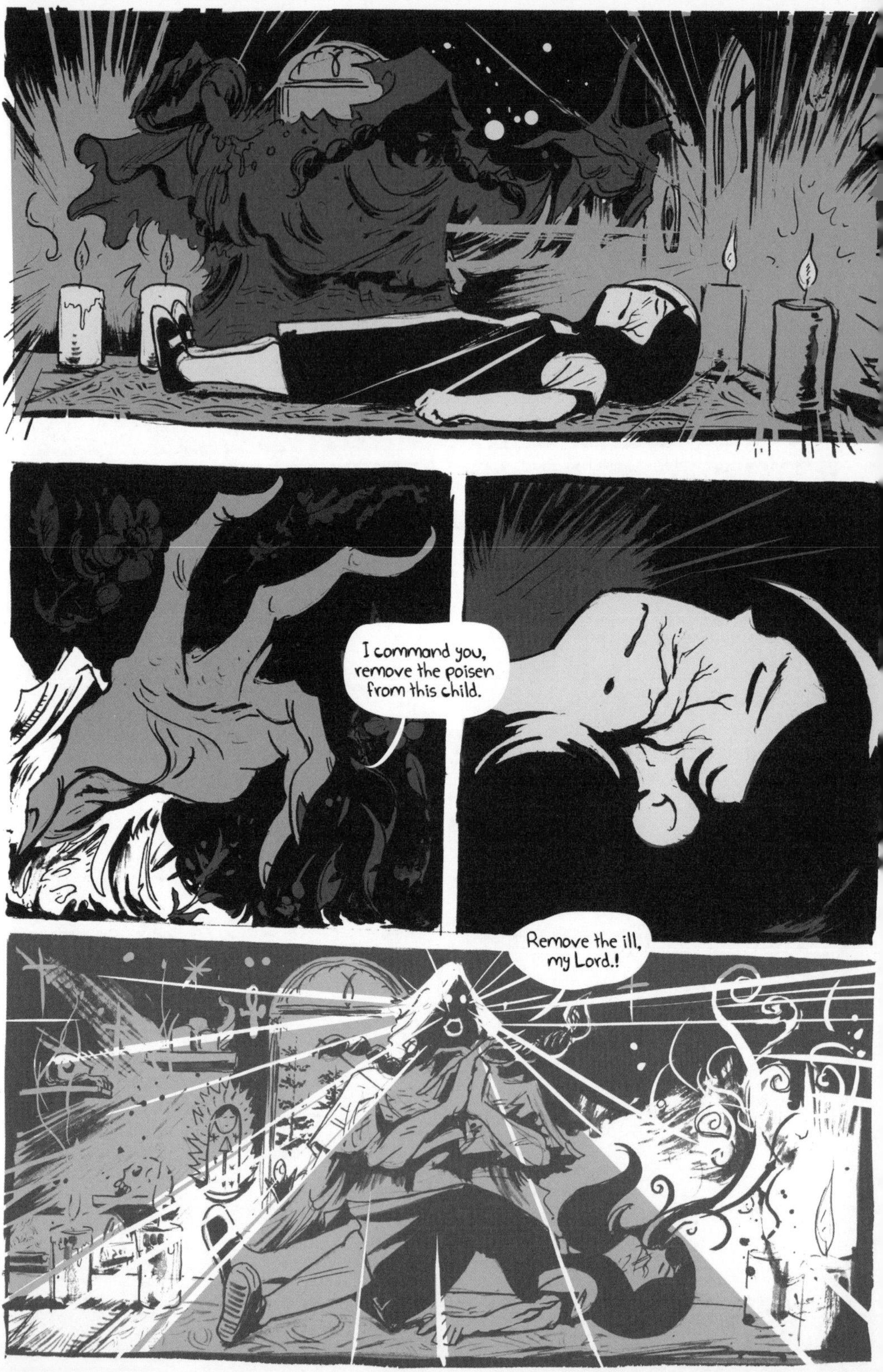
I command you, remove the poisen from this child.
Remove the ill, my Lord.!

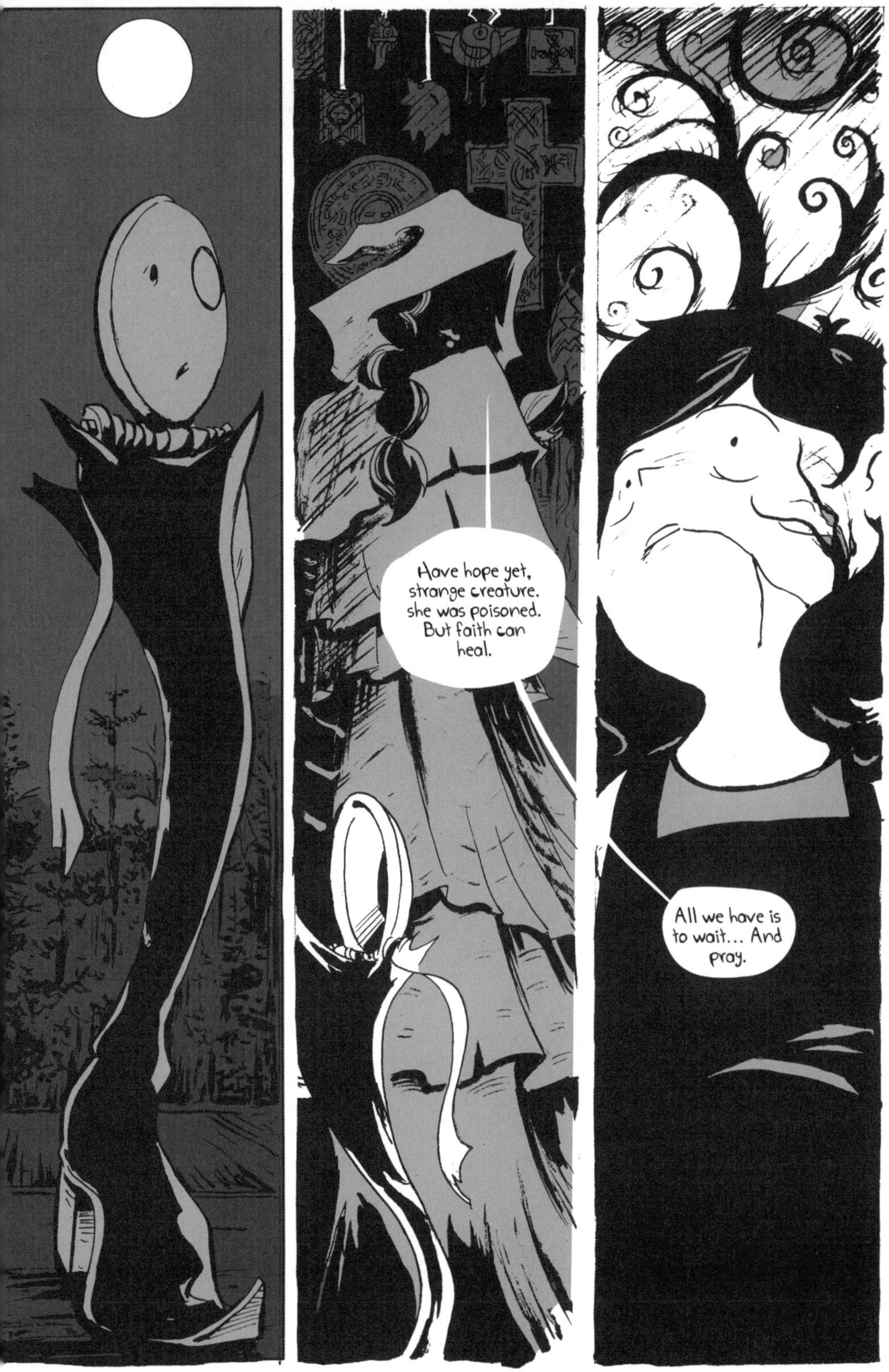
Have hope yet, strange creature. she was poisoned. But faith can heal.
All we have is to wait... And pray.

Elsewhere

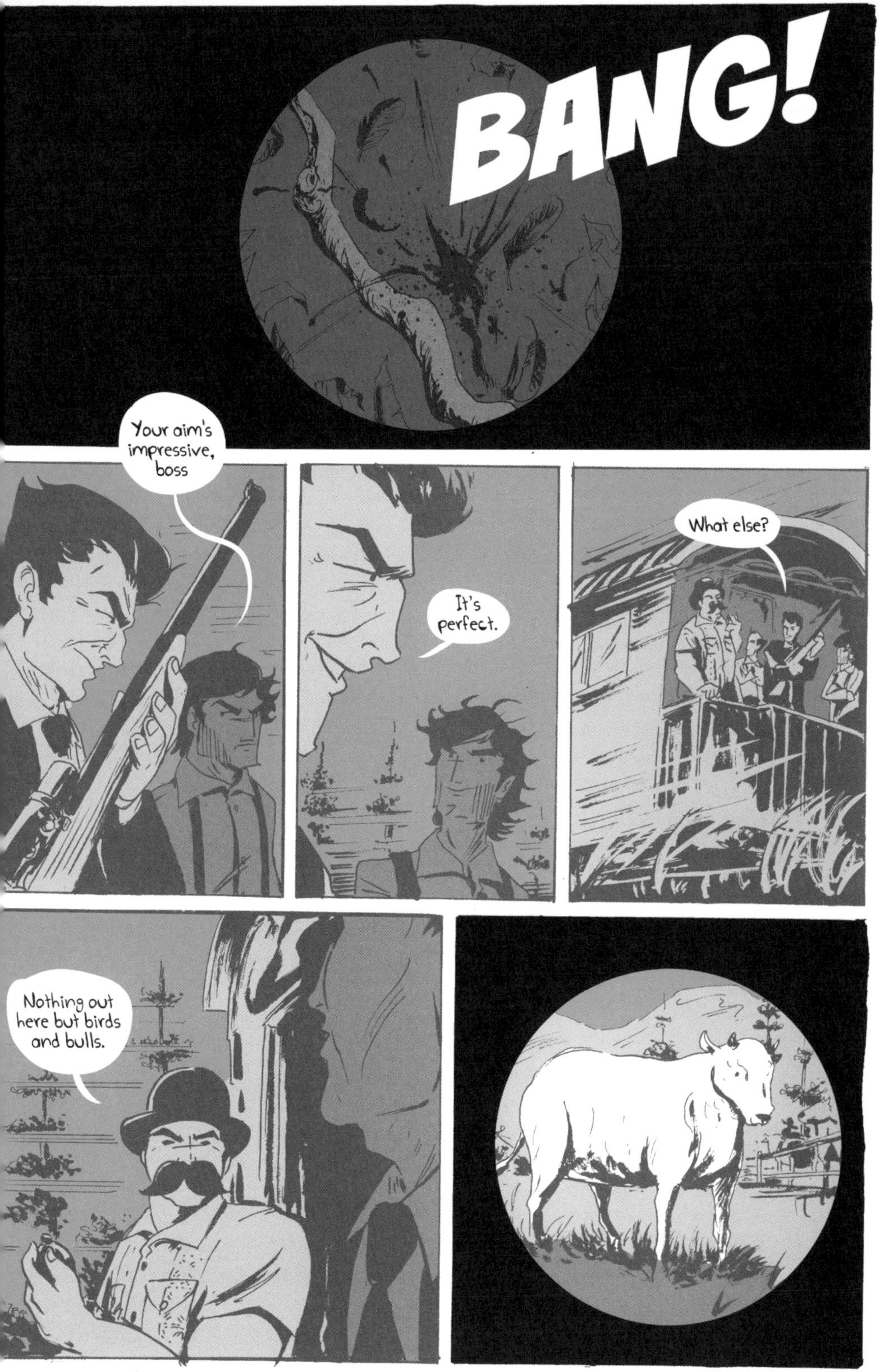
BANG!
Your aim's impressive, boss
It's perfect.
What else?
Nothing out here but birds and bulls.

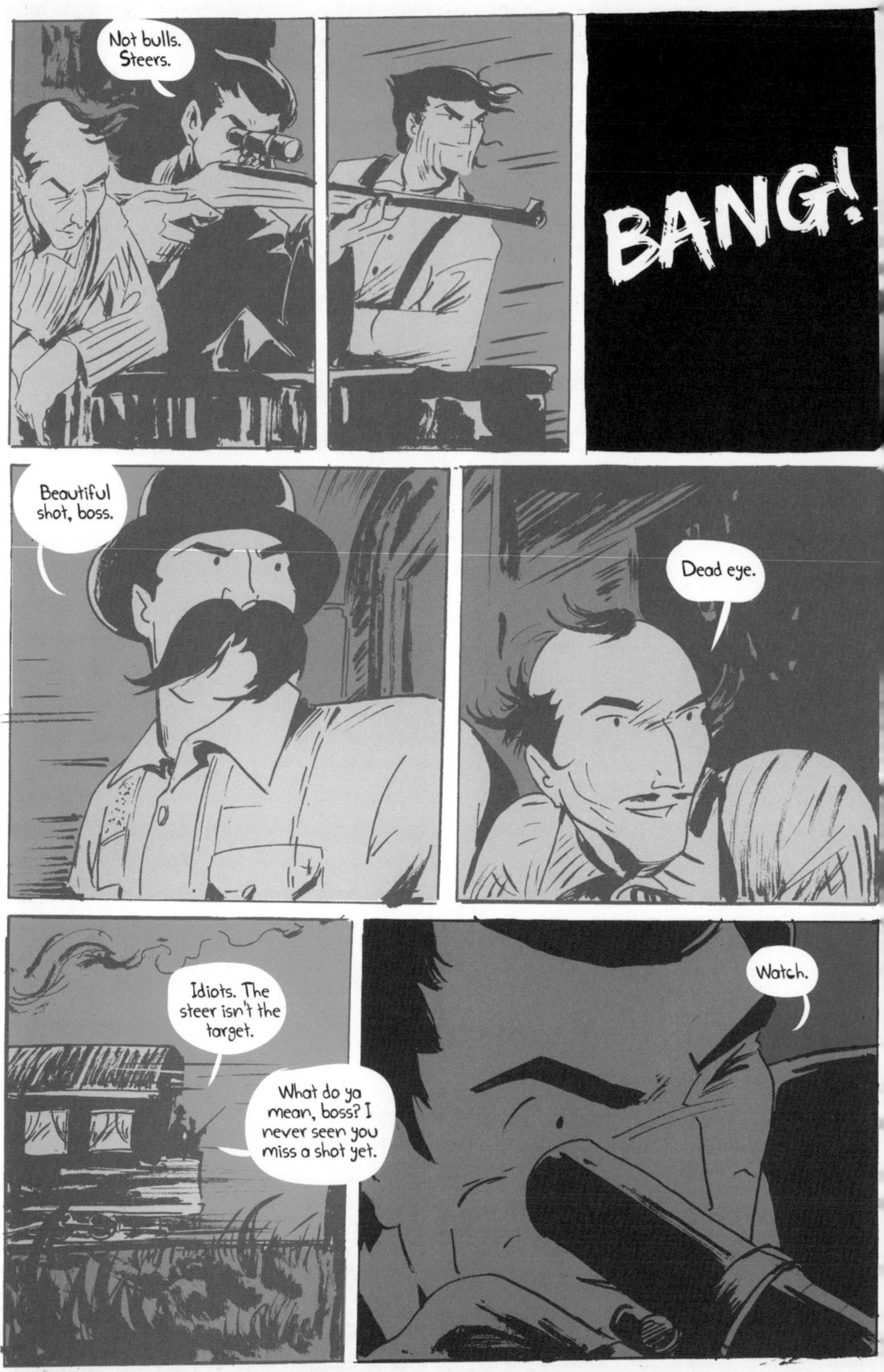

Not bulls. Steers.
BANG!
Beautiful shot, boss.
Dead eye.
Idiots. The steer isn't the target.
What do ya mean, boss? I never seen you miss a shot yet.
Watch.

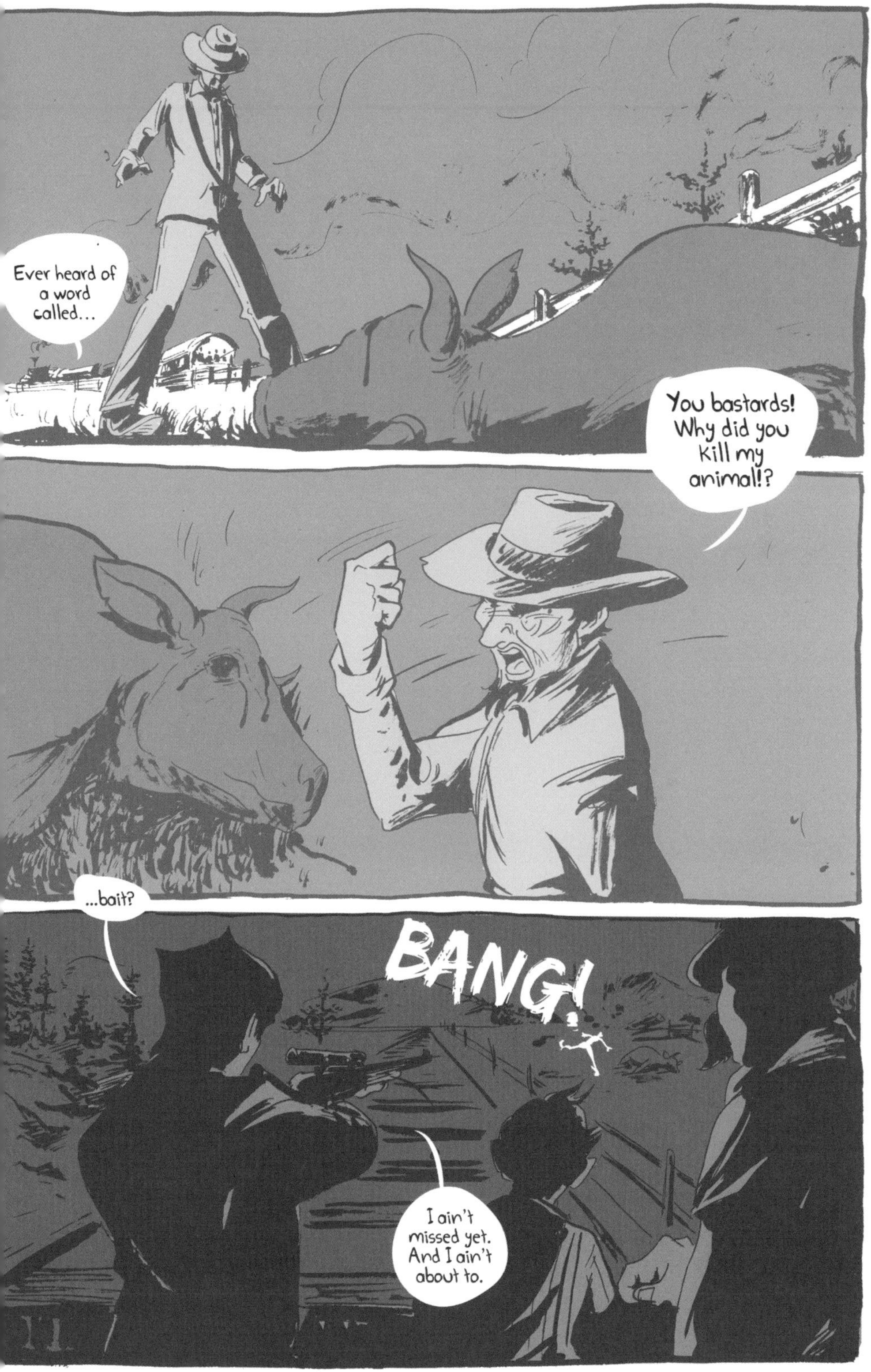
Ever heard of a word called...
You bastards! Why did you kill my animal!?
...bait?
BANG!
I ain't missed yet. And I ain't about to.

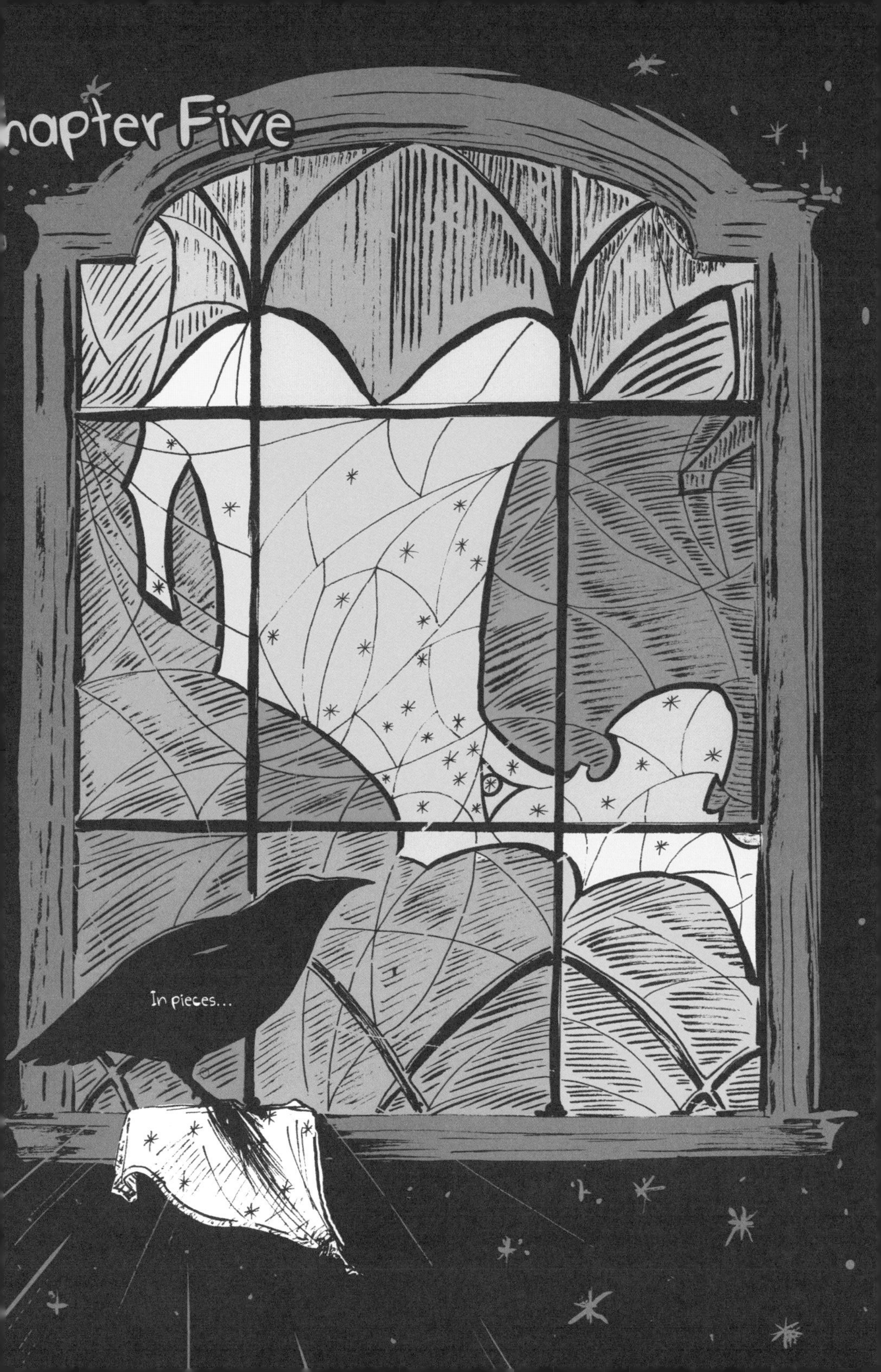
hapter Five
In pieces...

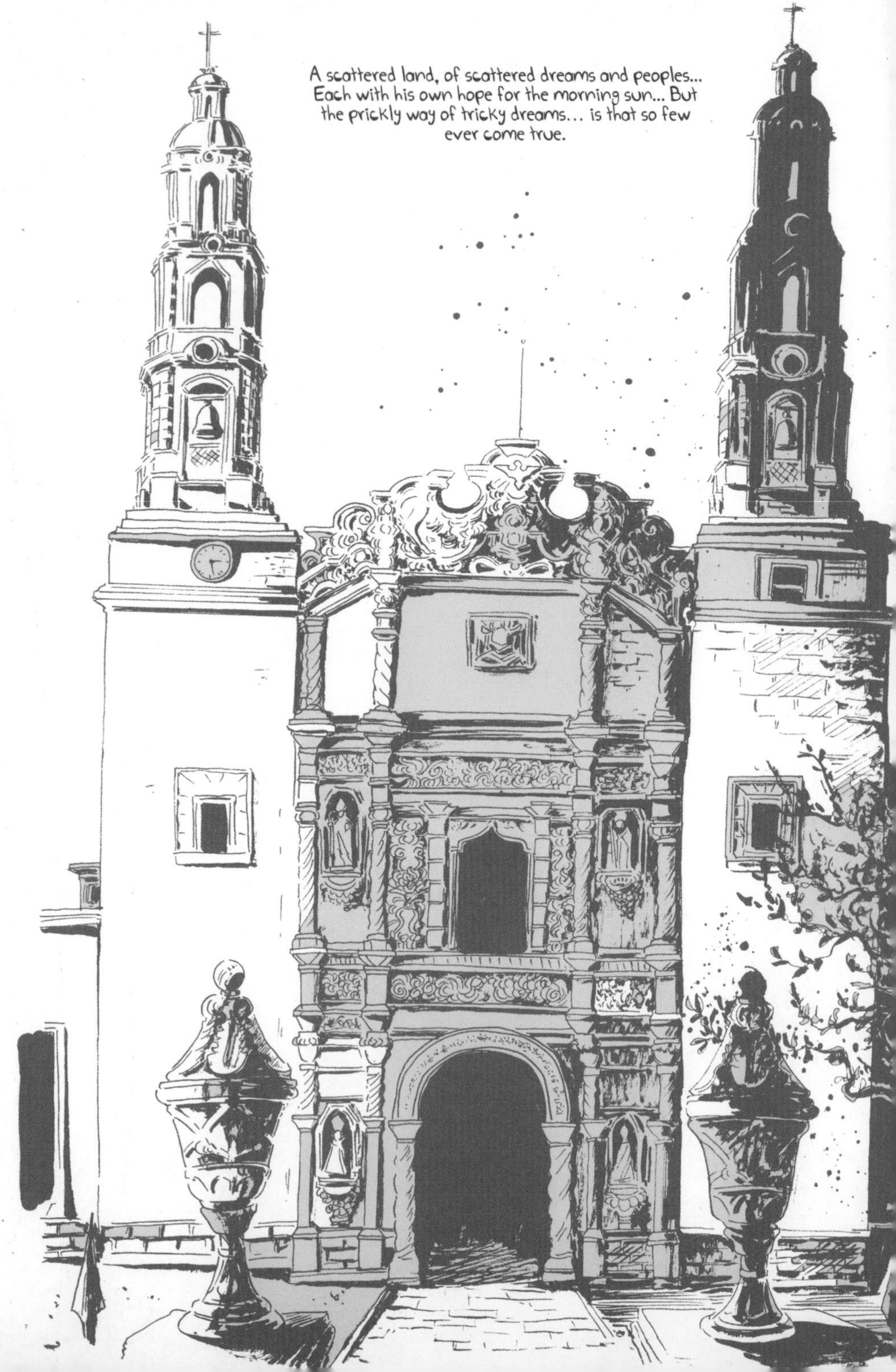
A scattered land, of scattered dreams and peoples... Each with his own hope for the morning sun... But the prickly way of tricky dreams... is that so few ever come true.

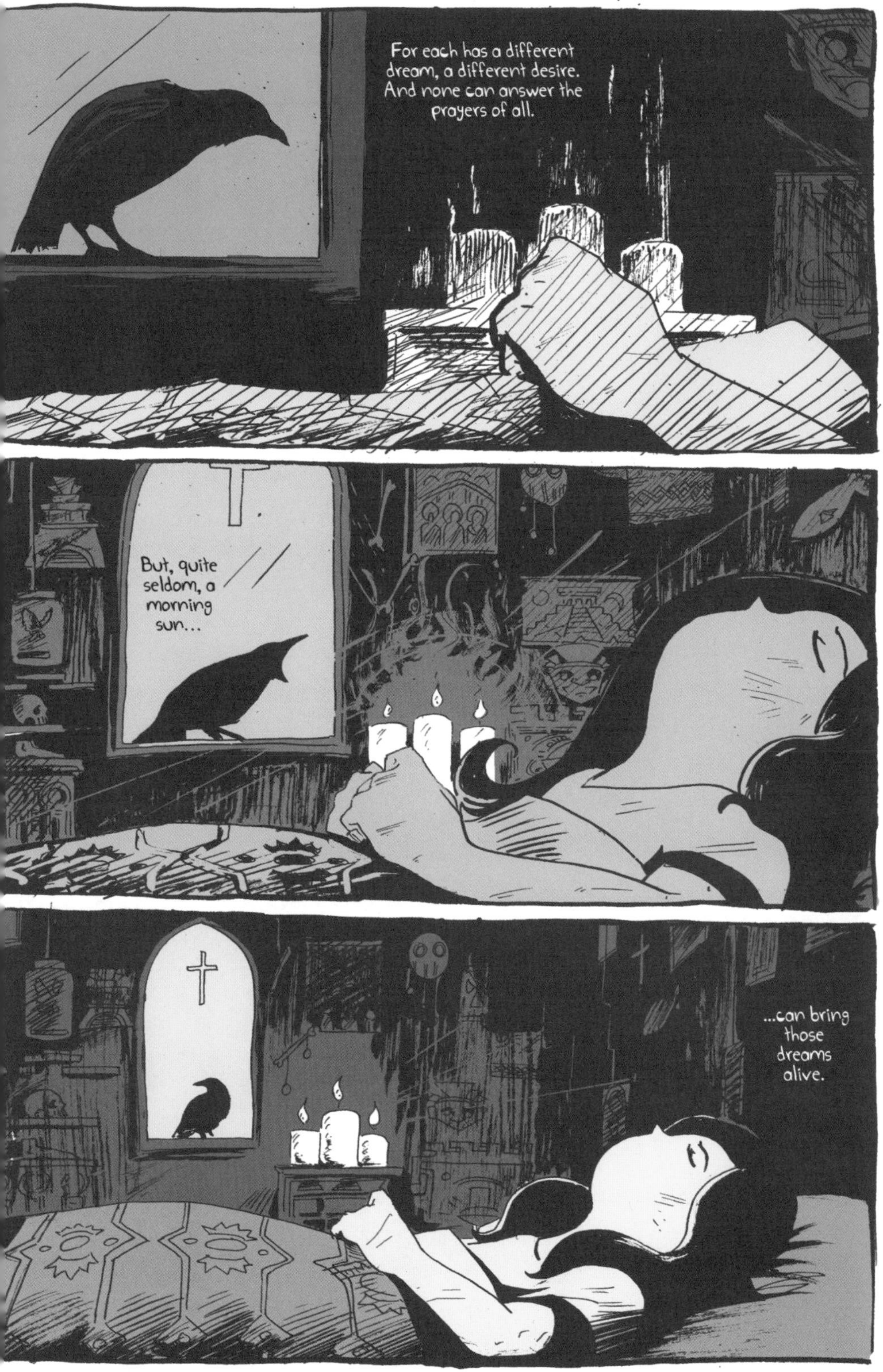
For each has a different dream, a different desire. And none can answer the prayers of all.
But, quite seldom, a morning sun...
...can bring those dreams alive.

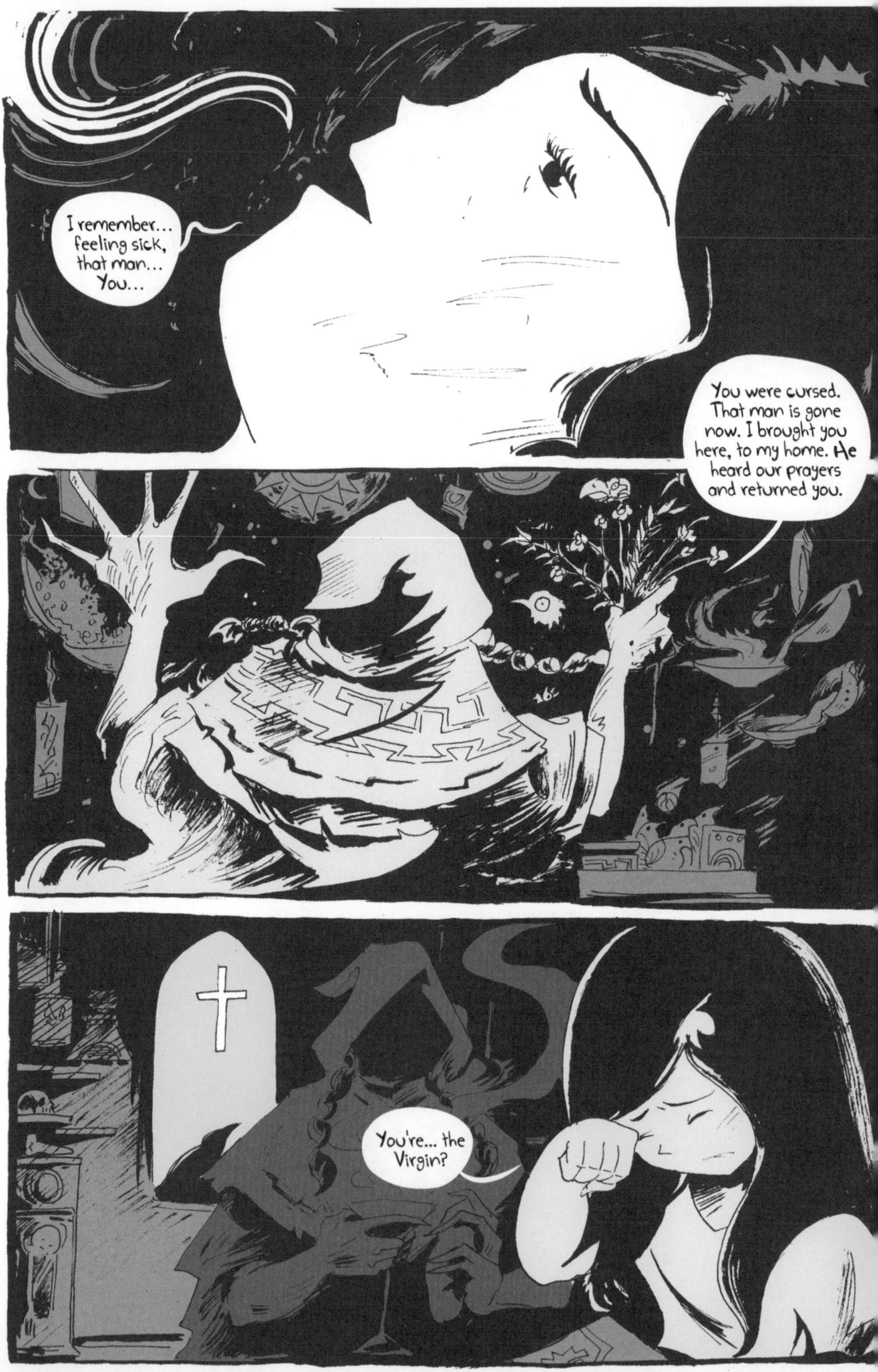
I remember... feeling sick, that man... You...
You were cursed. That man is gone now. I brought you here, to my home. He heard our prayers and returned you.
You're... the Virgin?

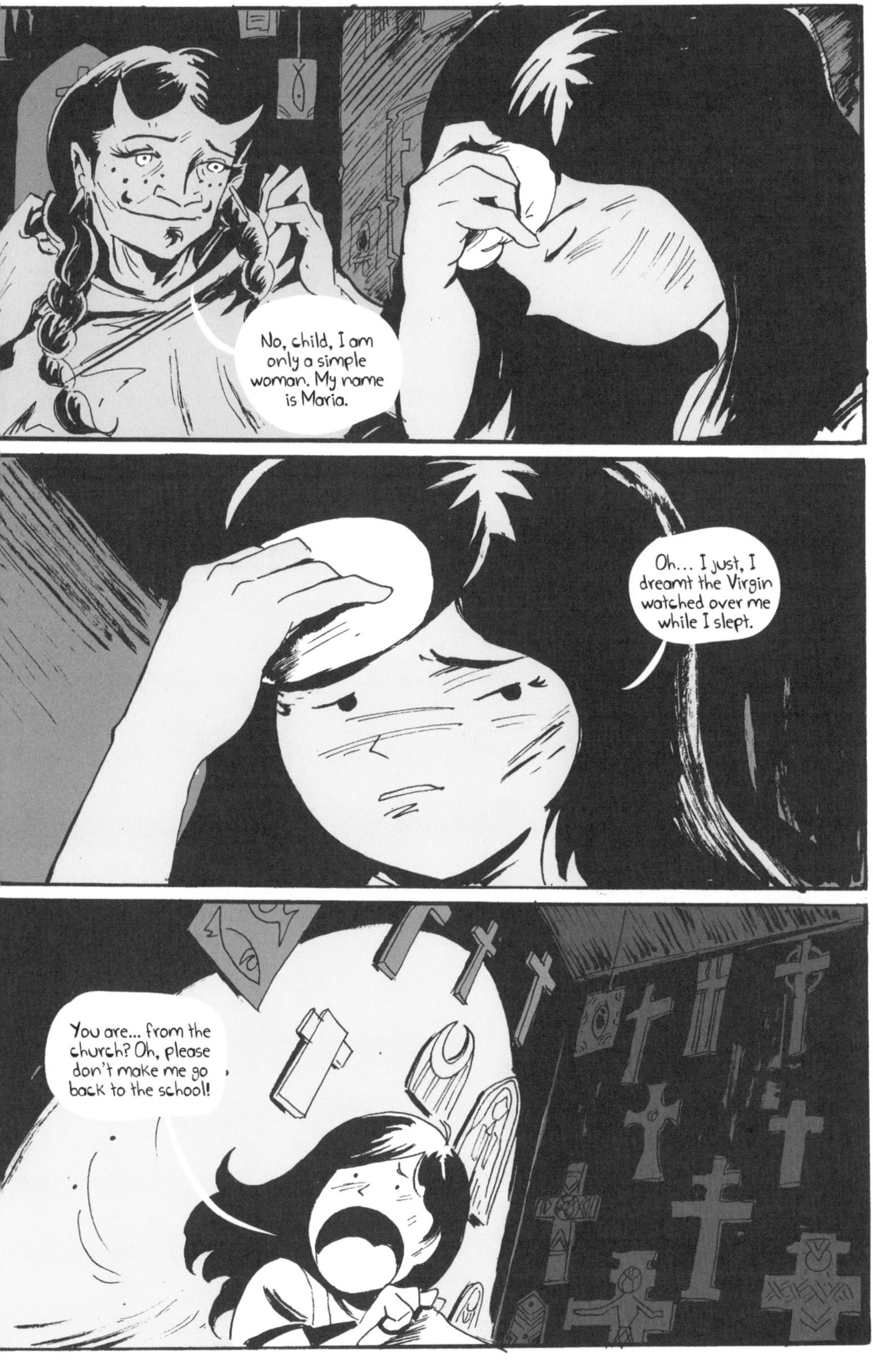
No, child, I am only a simple woman. My name is Maria.
Oh... I just, I dreamt the Virgin watched over me while I slept.
You are... from the church? Oh, please don't make me go back to the school!

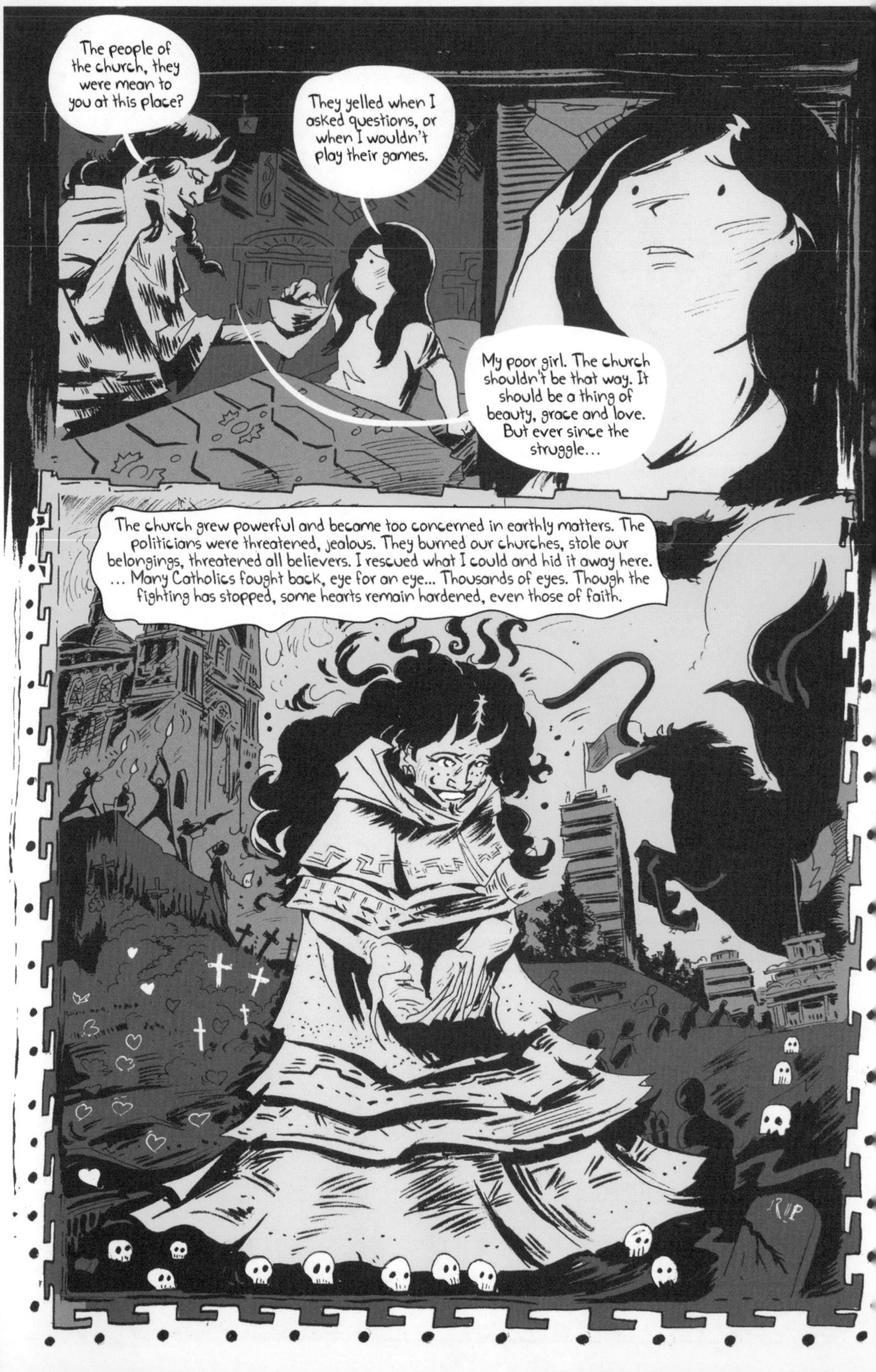
The people of the church, they were mean to you at this place?
They yelled when I asked questions, or when I wouldn't play their games.
My poor girl. The church shouldn't be that way. It should be a thing of beauty, grace and love. But ever since the struggle...
The church grew powerful and became too concerned in earthly matters. The politicians were threatened, jealous. They burned our churches, stole our belongings, threatened all believers. I rescued what I could and hid it away here. ... Many Catholics fought back, eye for an eye... Thousands of eyes. Though the fighting has stopped, some hearts remain hardened, even those of faith.
RIP

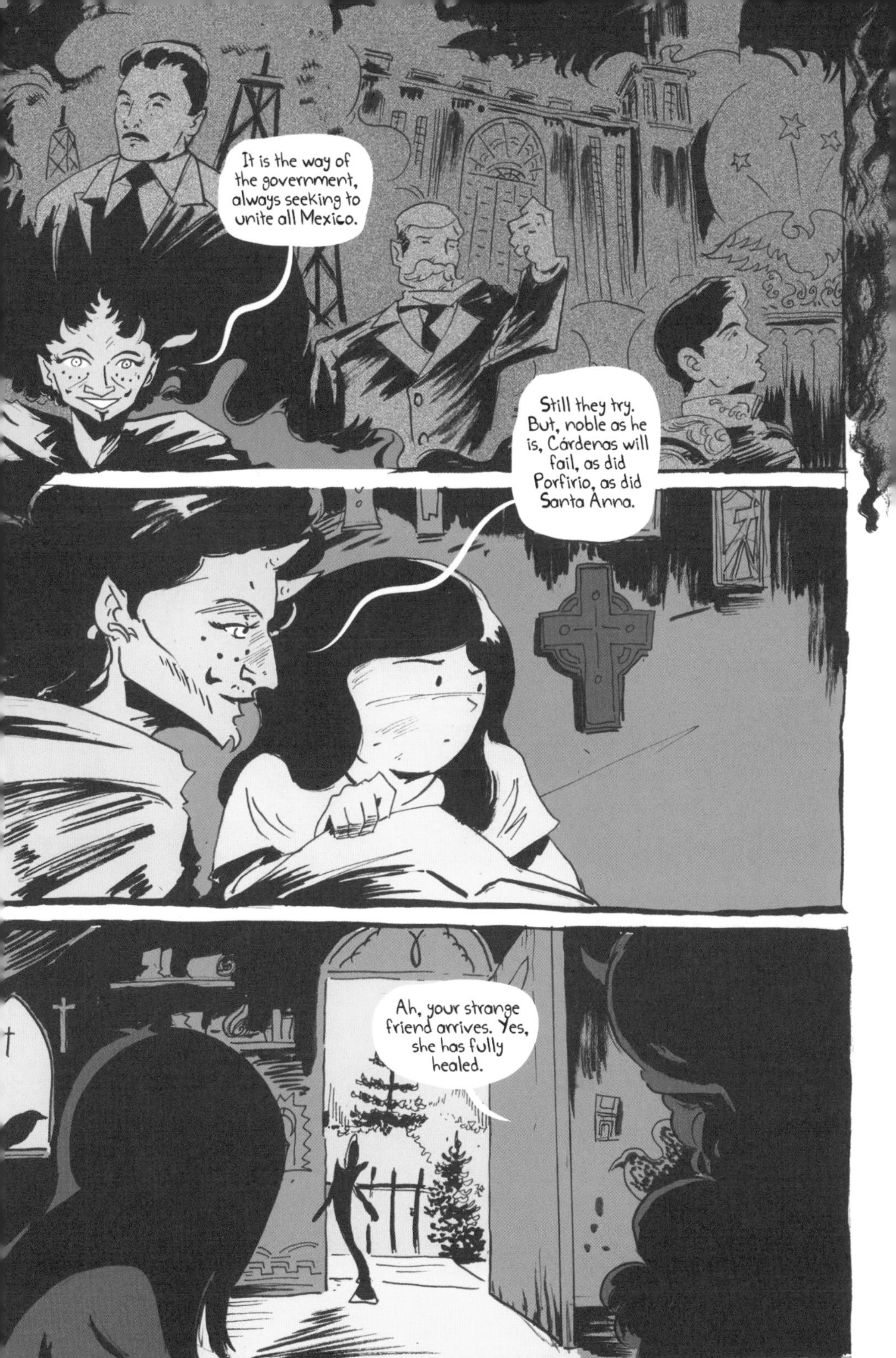
It is the way of the government, always seeking to unite all Mexico.
Still they try. But, noble as he is, Cárdenas will fail, as did Porfirio, as did Santa Anna.
Ah, your strange friend arrives. Yes, she has fully healed.

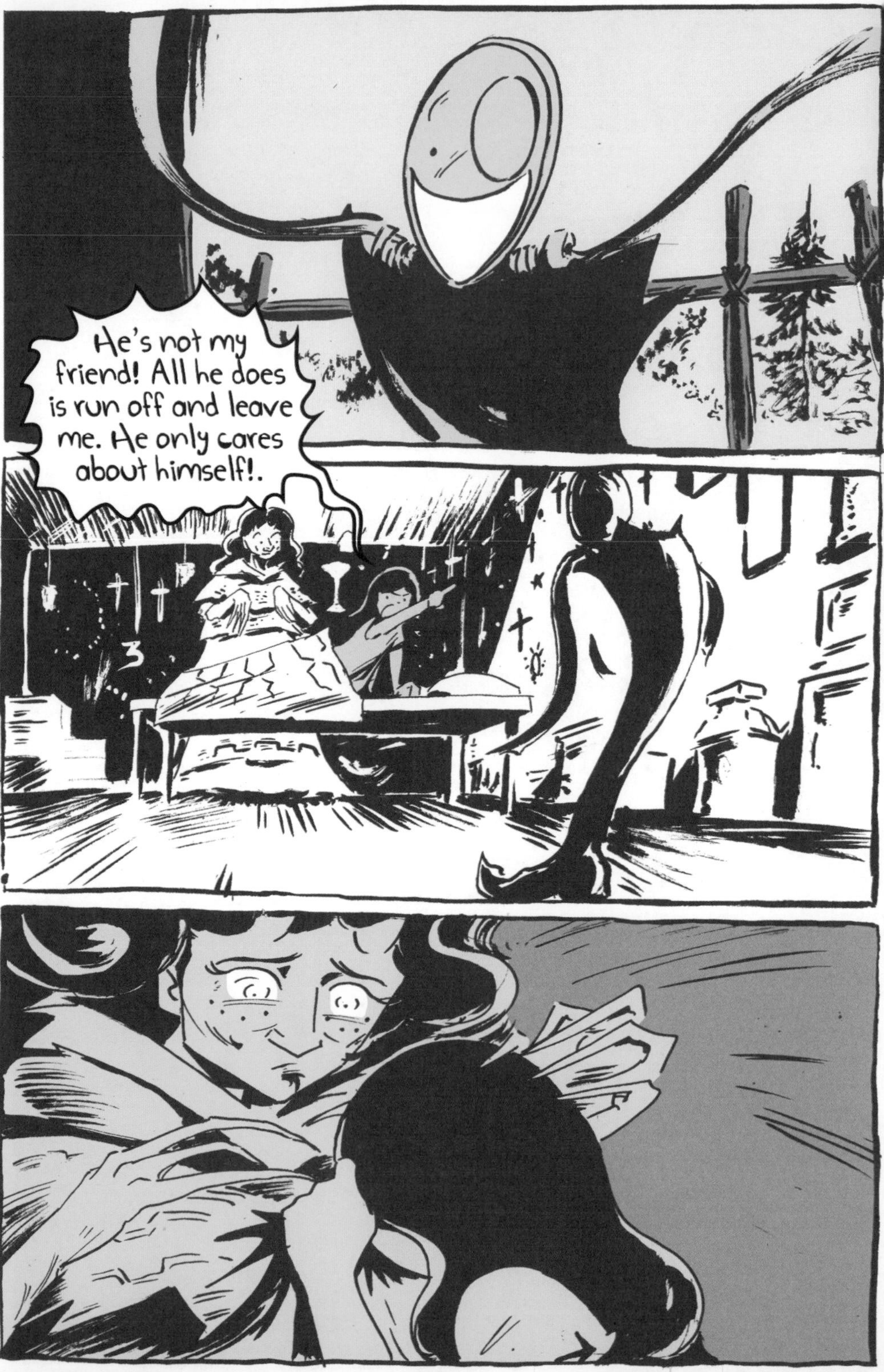
He's not my friend! All he does is run off and leave me. He only cares about himself!.

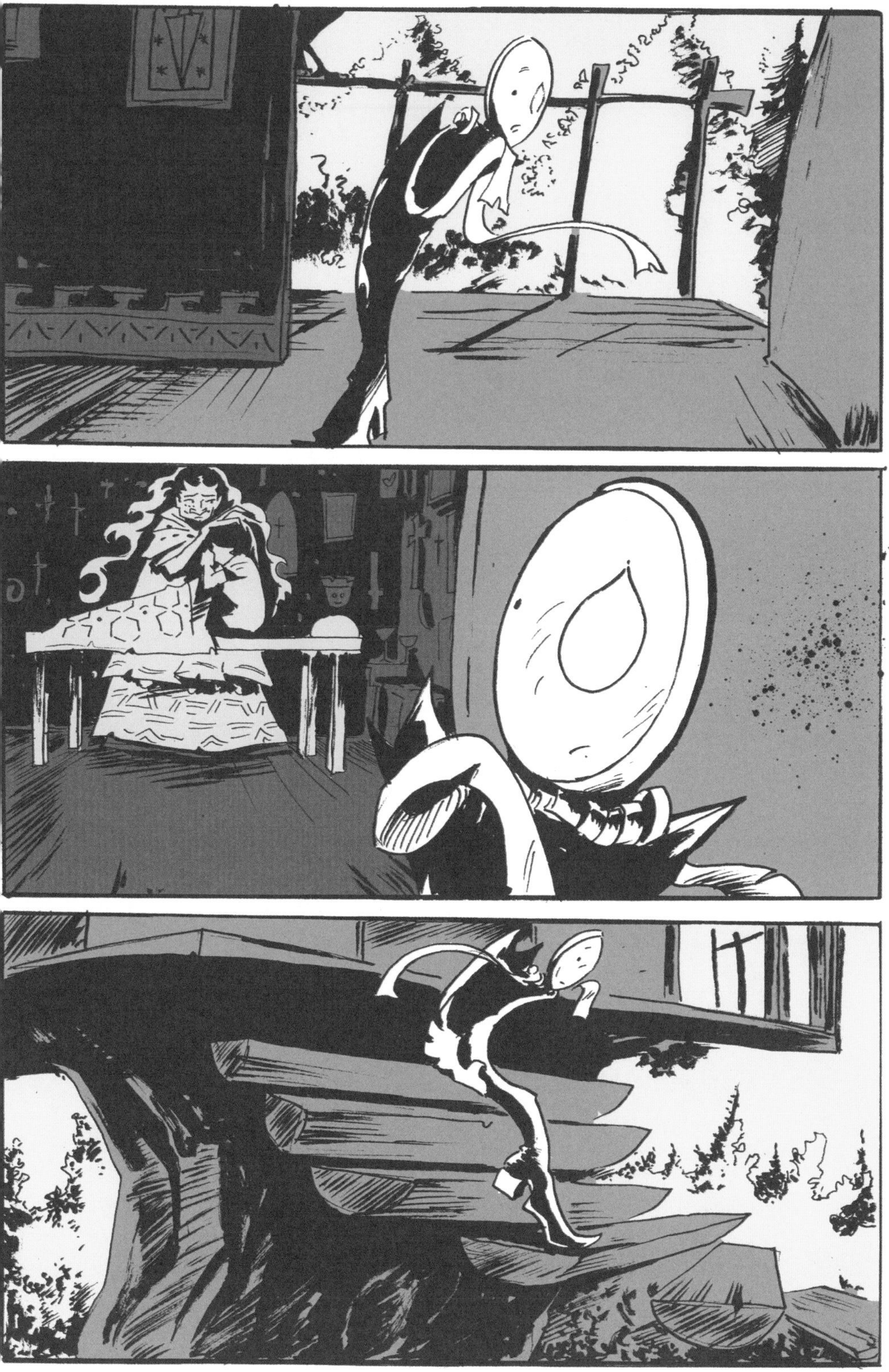

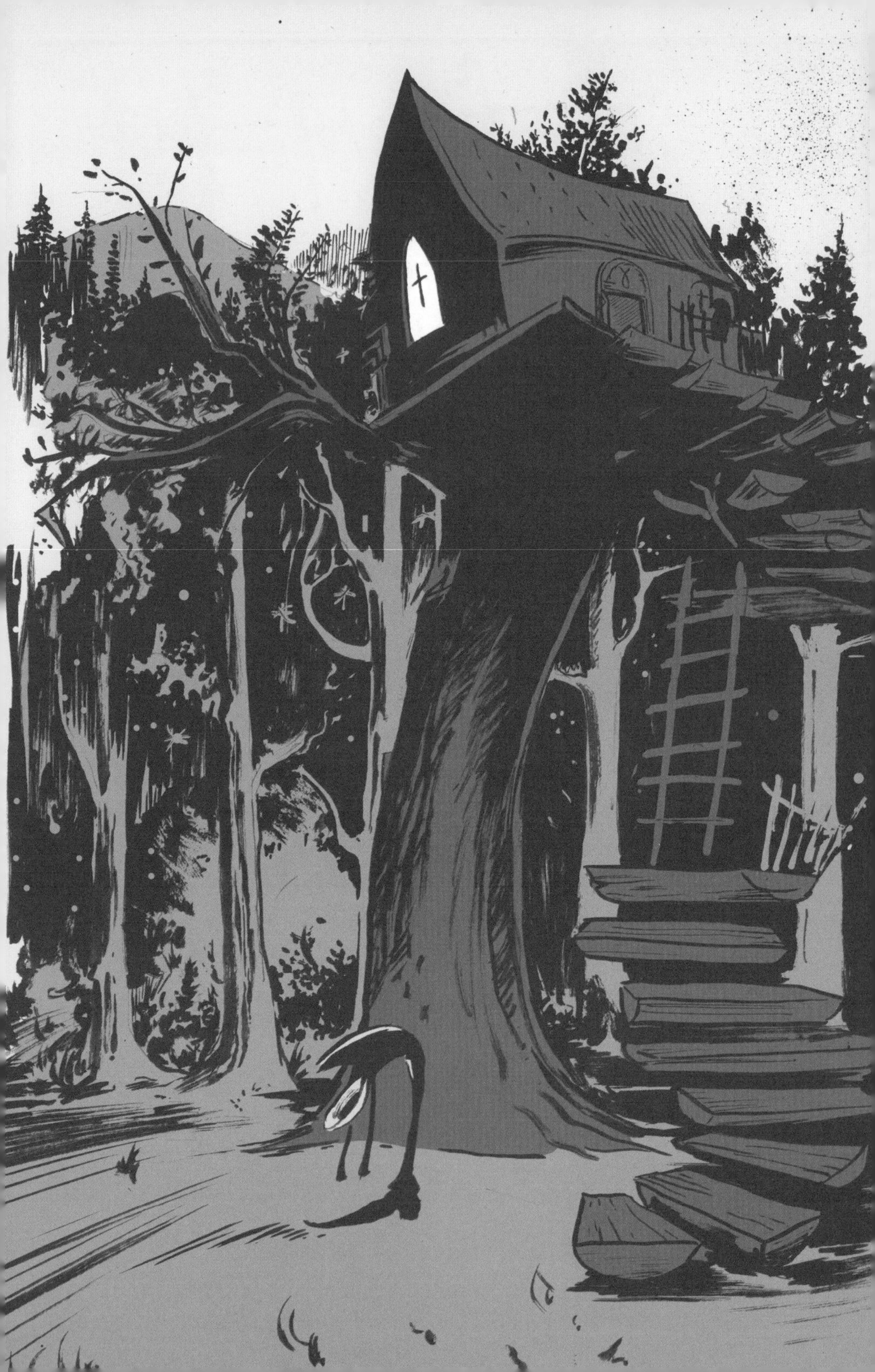

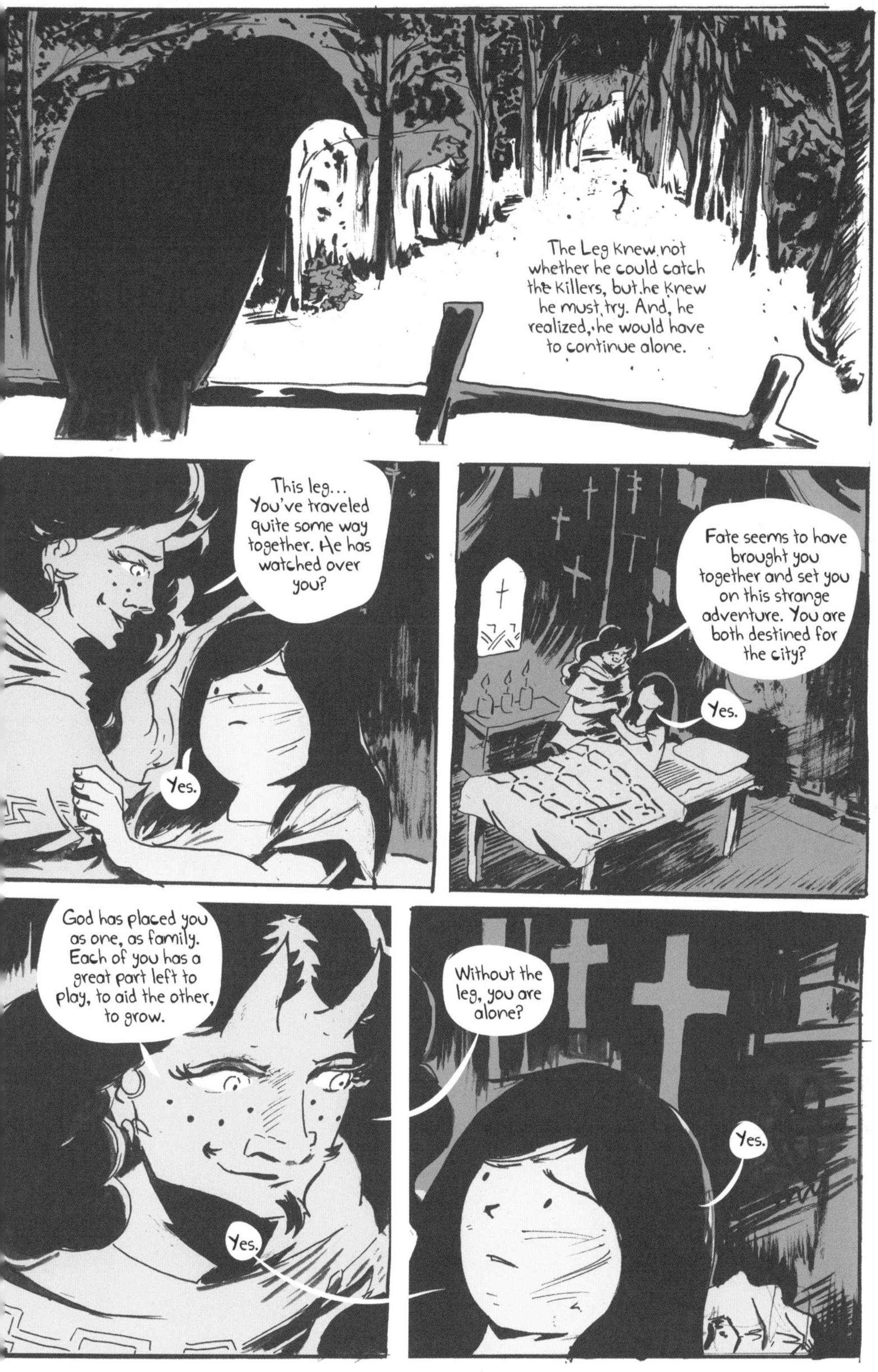
The Leg knew not whether he could catch the killers, but he knew he must try. And, he realized, he would have to continue alone.
This leg... You've traveled quite some way together. He has watched over you?
Yes.
Fate seems to have brought you together and set you on this strange adventure. You are both destined for the city?
Yes.
God has placed you as one, as family. Each of you has a great part left to play, to aid the other, to grow.
Yes.
Without the leg, you are alone?
Yes.

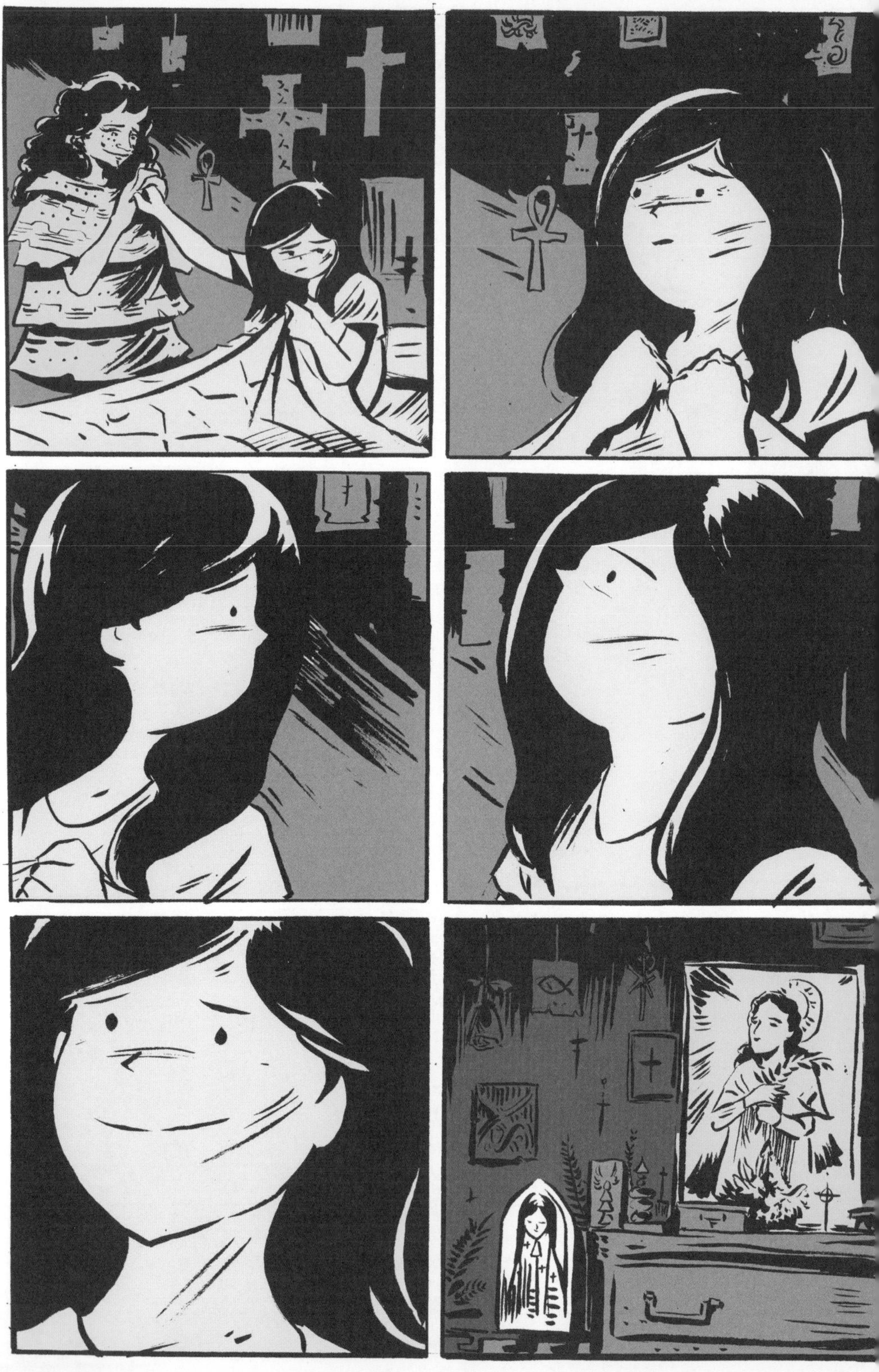

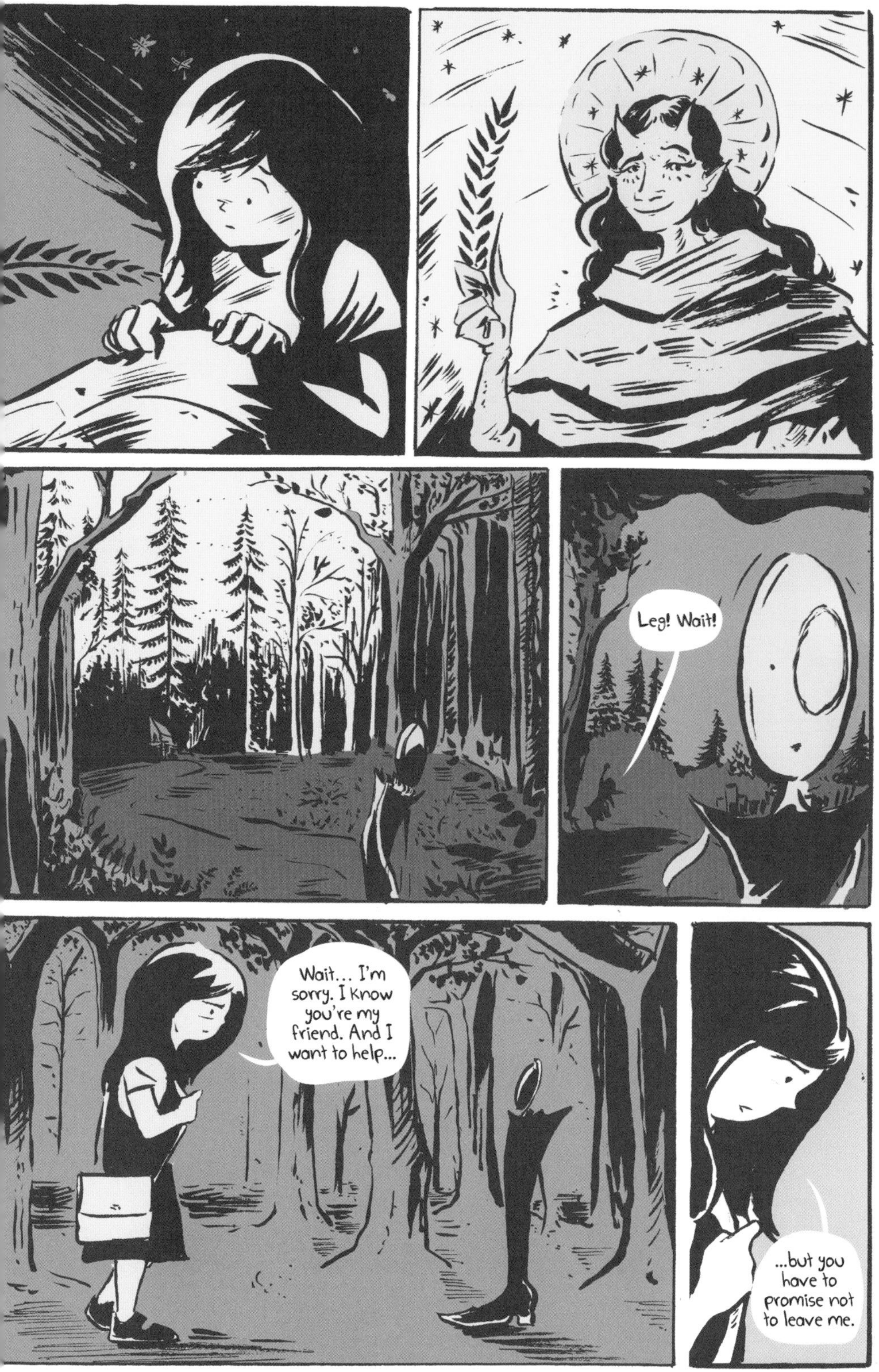
Leg! Wait!
Wait... I'm sorry. I know you're my friend. And I want to help...
...but you have to promise not to leave me.

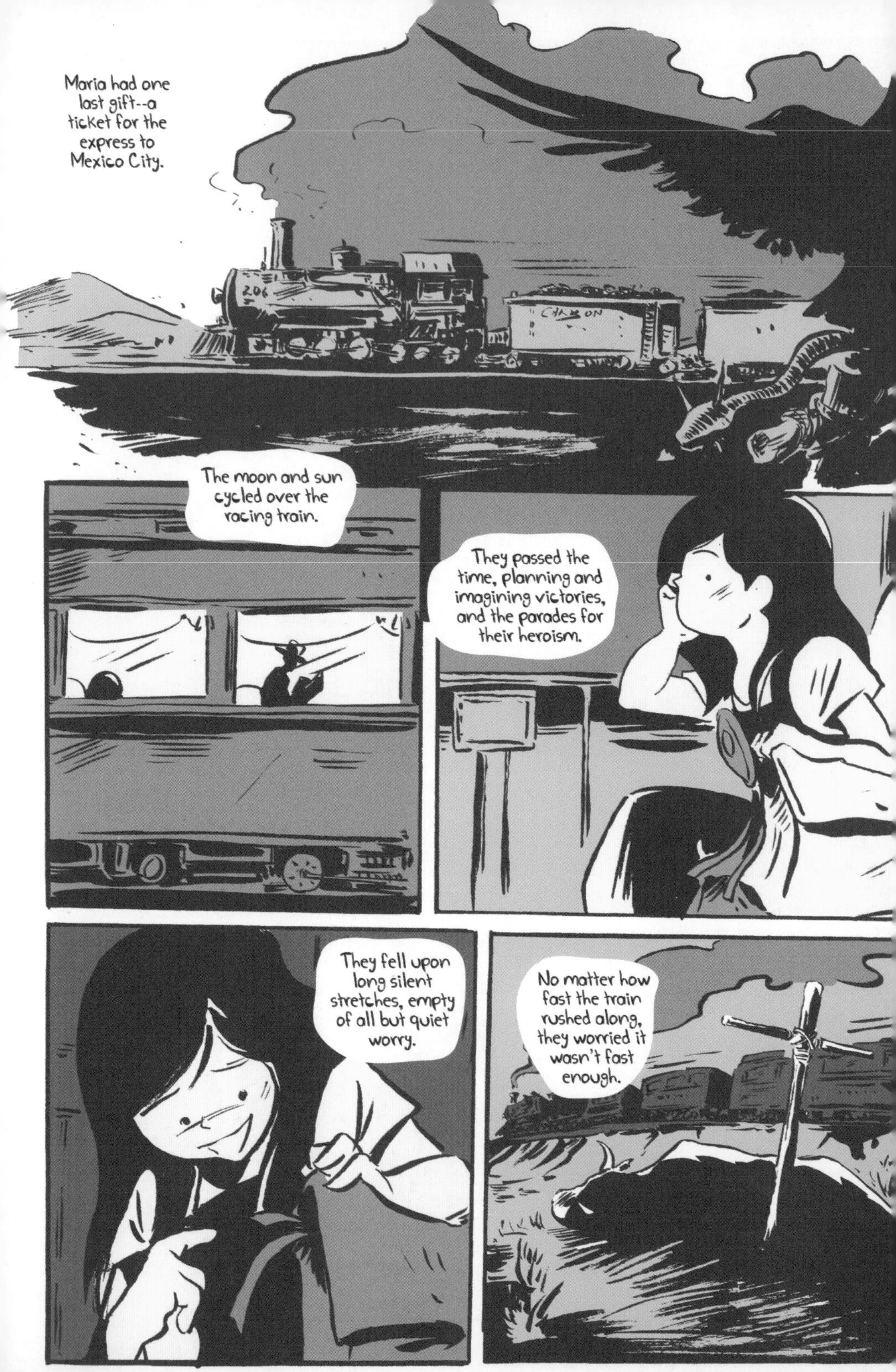
Maria had one last gift--a ticket for the express to Mexico City.
The moon and sun cycled over the racing train.
They passed the time, planning and imagining victories, and the parades for their heroism.
They fell upon long silent stretches, empty of all but quiet worry.
No matter how fast the train rushed along, they worried it wasn't fast enough.

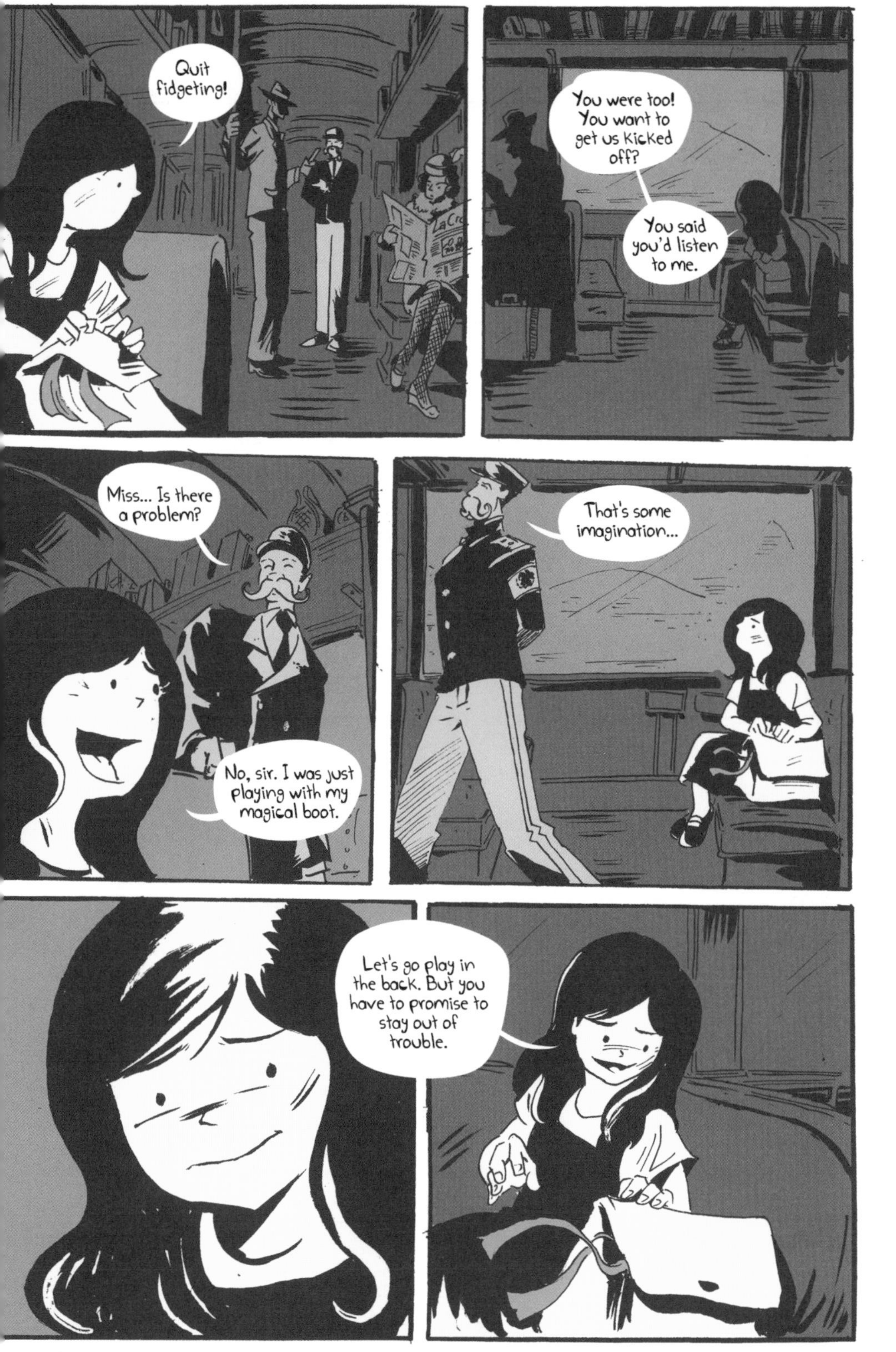
Quit fidgeting!
You were too! You want to get us kicked off?
You said you'd listen to me.
Miss... Is there a problem?
No, sir. I was just playing with my magical boot.
That's some imagination...
Let's go play in the back. But you have to promise to stay out of trouble.

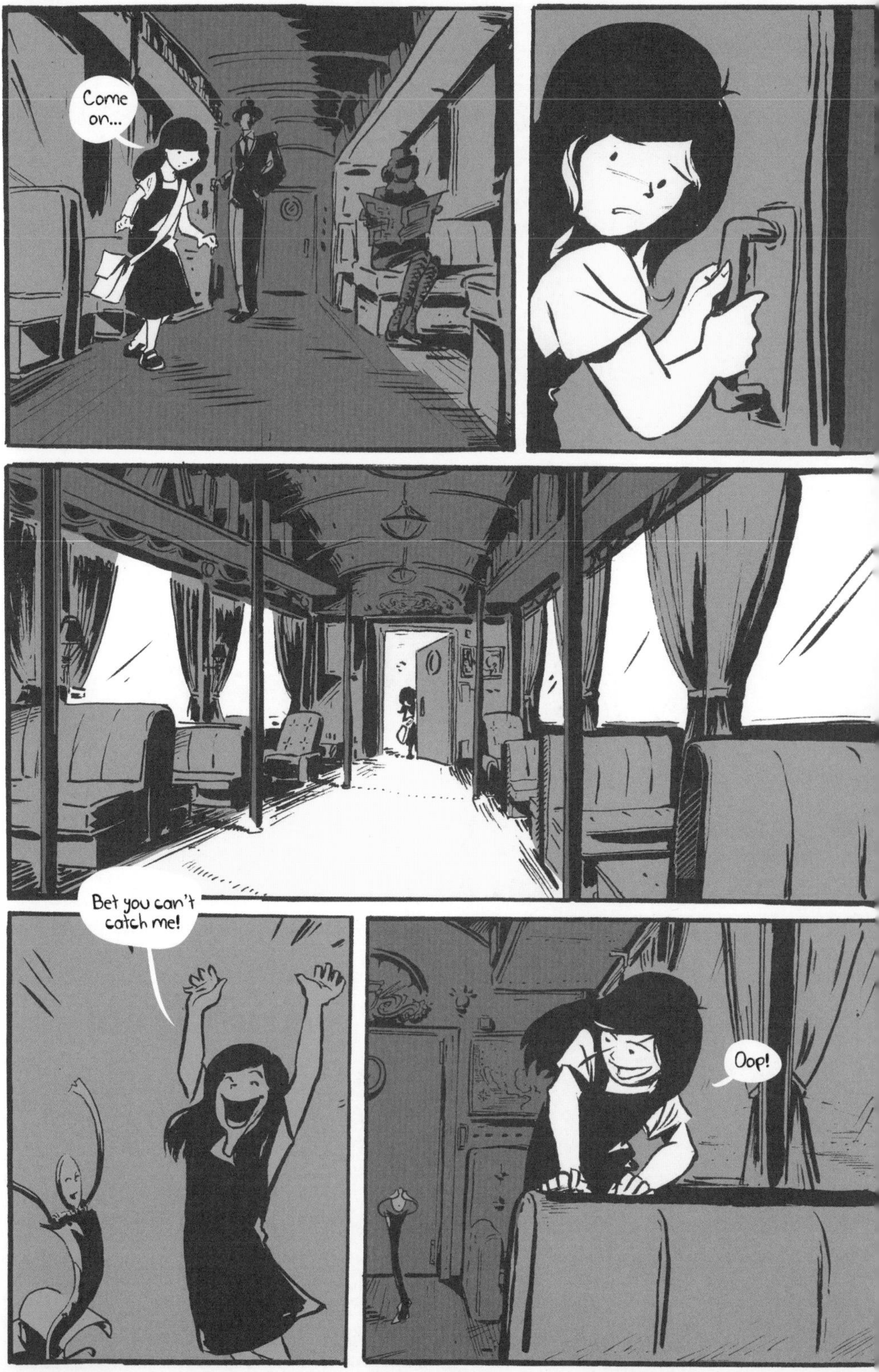
Come on...
Bet you can't catch me!
Oop!

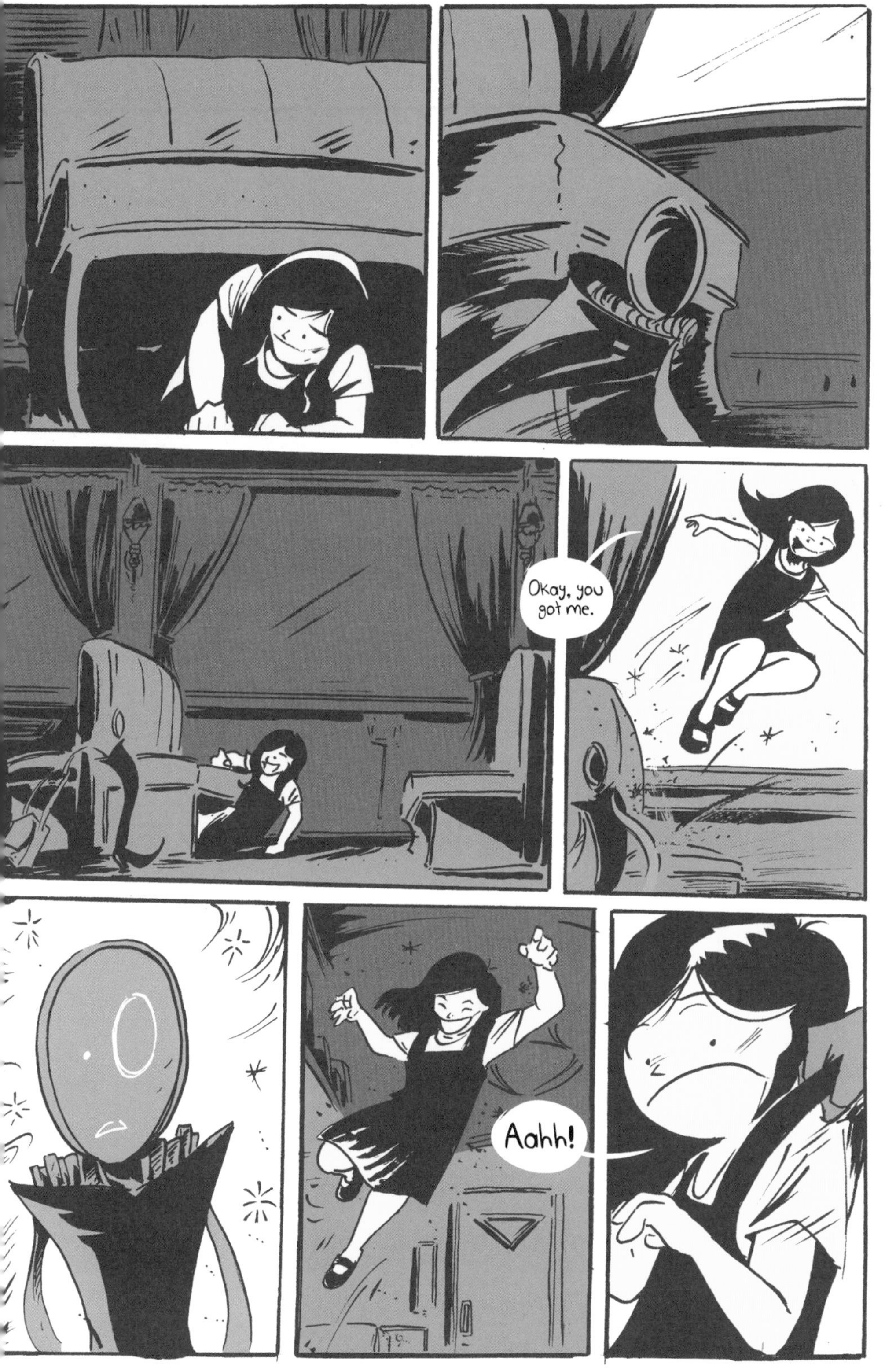
Okay, you got me.
Aahh!

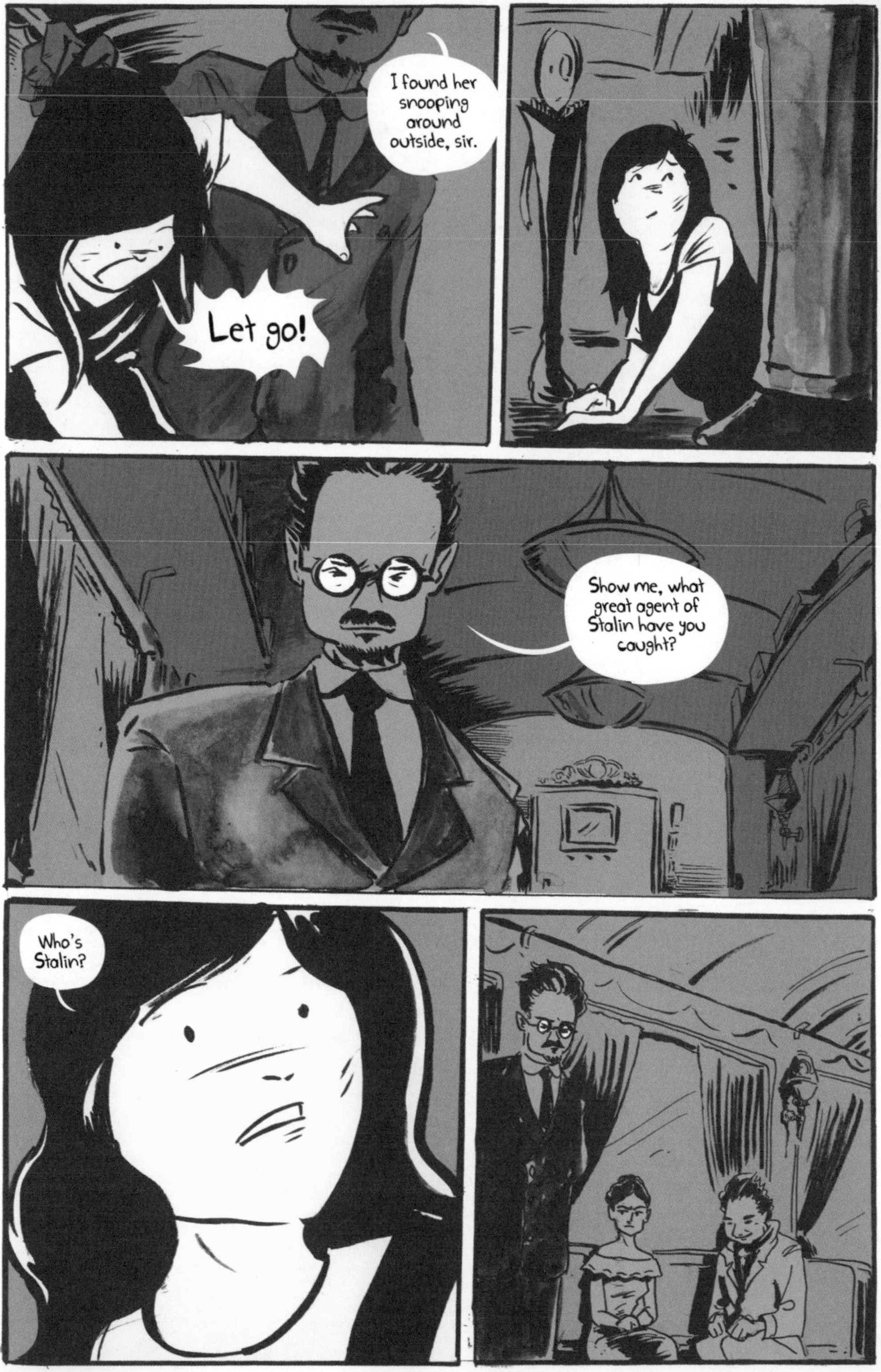
I found her snooping around outside, sir.
Let go!
Show me, what great agent of Stalin have you caught?
Who's Stalin?

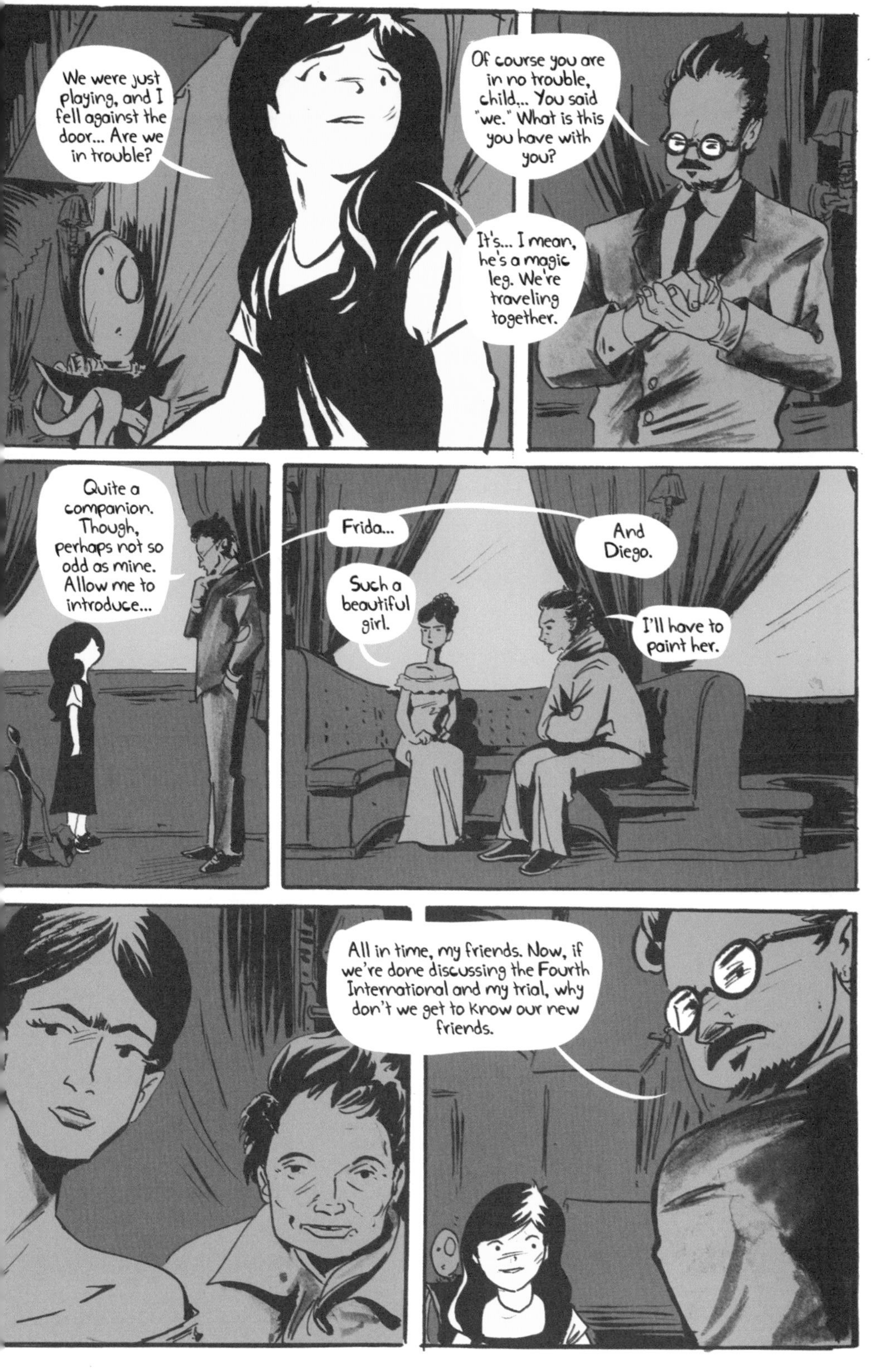
We were just playing, and I fell against the door... Are we in trouble?
Of course you are in no trouble, child... You said "we." What is this you have with you?
It's... I mean, he's a magic leg. We're traveling together.
Quite a companion. Though, perhaps not so odd as mine. Allow me to introduce...
Frida...
And Diego.
Such a beautiful girl.
I'll have to paint her.
All in time, my friends. Now, if we're done discussing the Fourth International and my trial, why don't we get to know our new friends.

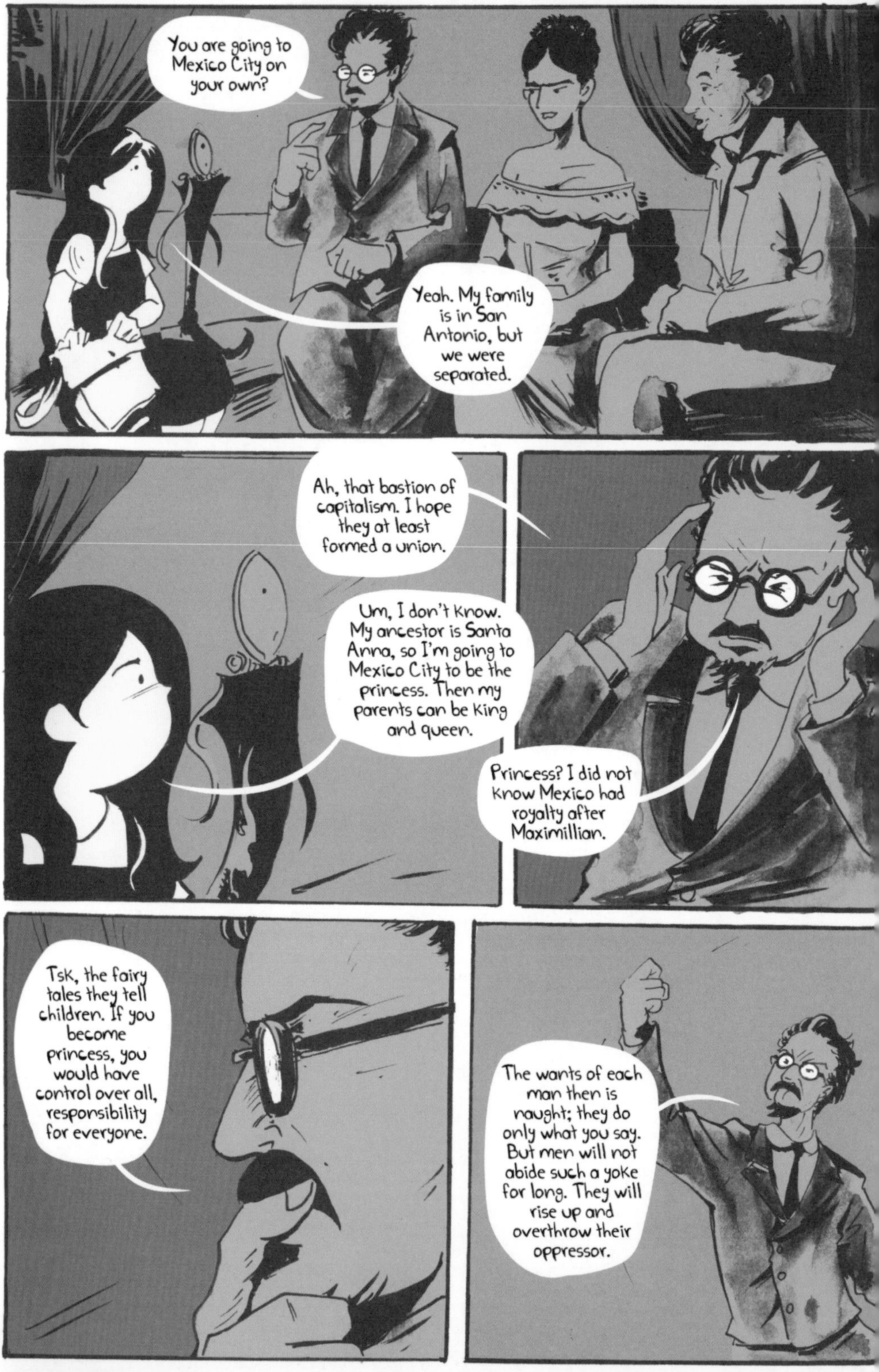
You are going to Mexico City on your own?
Yeah. My family is in San Antonio, but we were separated.
Ah, that bastion of capitalism. I hope they at least formed a union.
Um, I don't know. My ancestor is Santa Anna, so I'm going to Mexico City to be the princess. Then my parents can be king and queen.
Princess? I did not know Mexico had royalty after Maximillian.
Tsk, the fairy tales they tell children. If you become princess, you would have control over all, responsibility for everyone.
The wants of each man then is naught; they do only what you say. But men will not abide such a yoke for long. They will rise up and overthrow their oppressor.

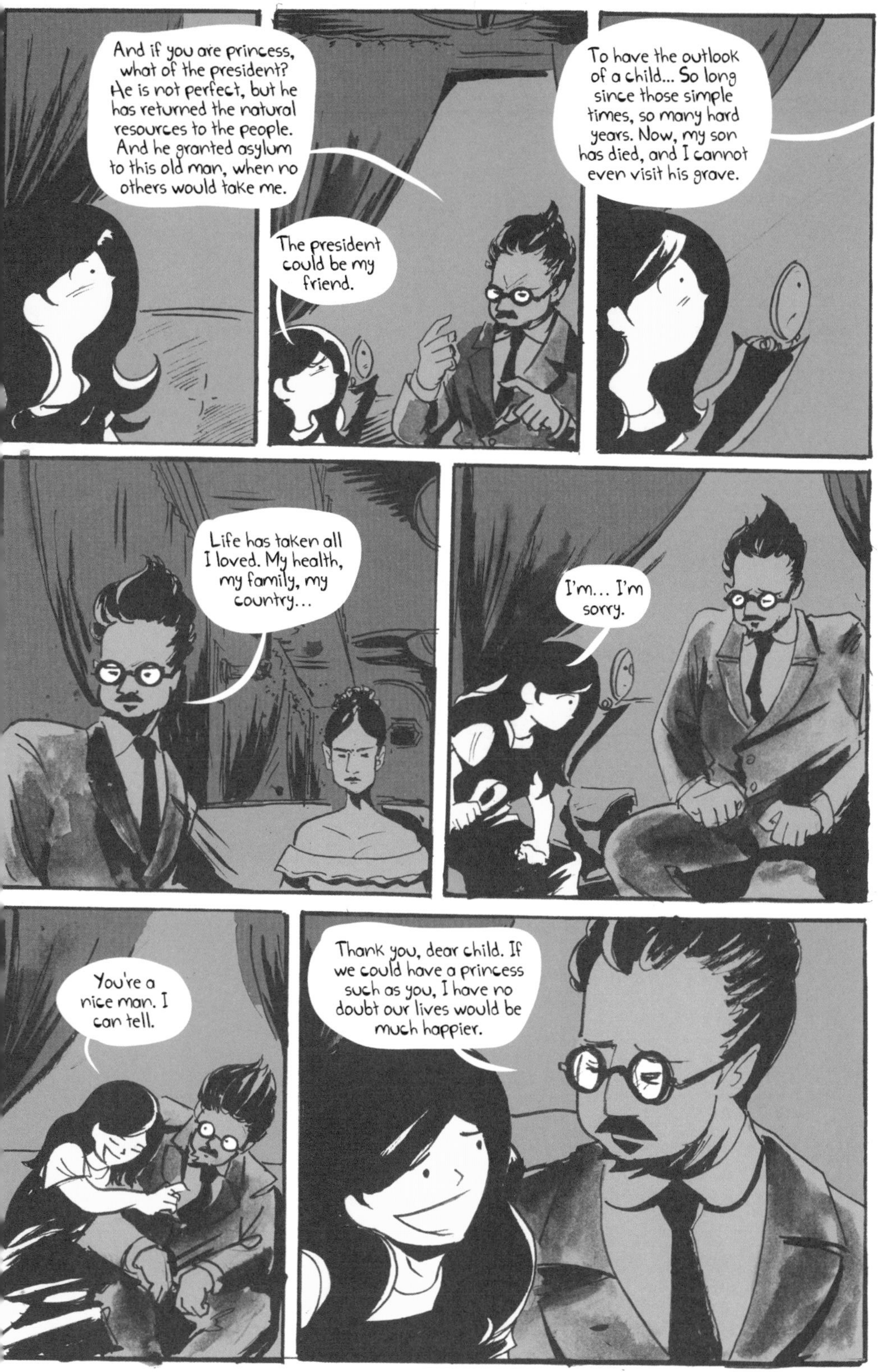
And if you are princess, what of the president? He is not perfect, but he has returned the natural resources to the people. And he granted asylum to this old man, when no others would take me.
The president could be my friend.
To have the outlook of a child... So long since those simple times, so many hard years. Now, my son has died, and I cannot even visit his grave.
Life has taken all I loved. My health, my family, my country...
I'm... I'm sorry.
You're a nice man. I can tell.
Thank you, dear child. If we could have a princess such as you, I have no doubt our lives would be much happier.

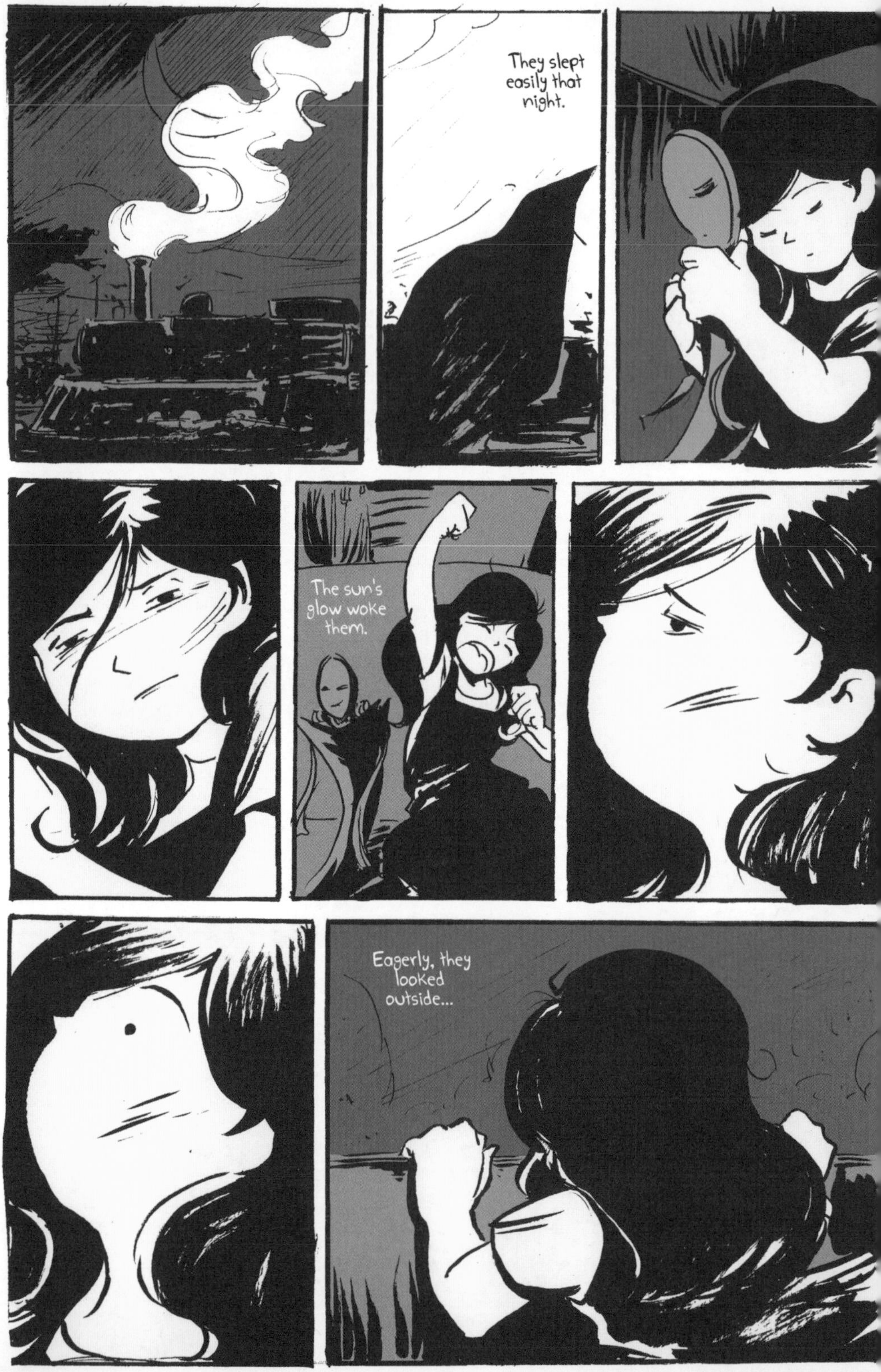
They slept easily that night.
The sun's glow woke them.
Eagerly, they looked outside...

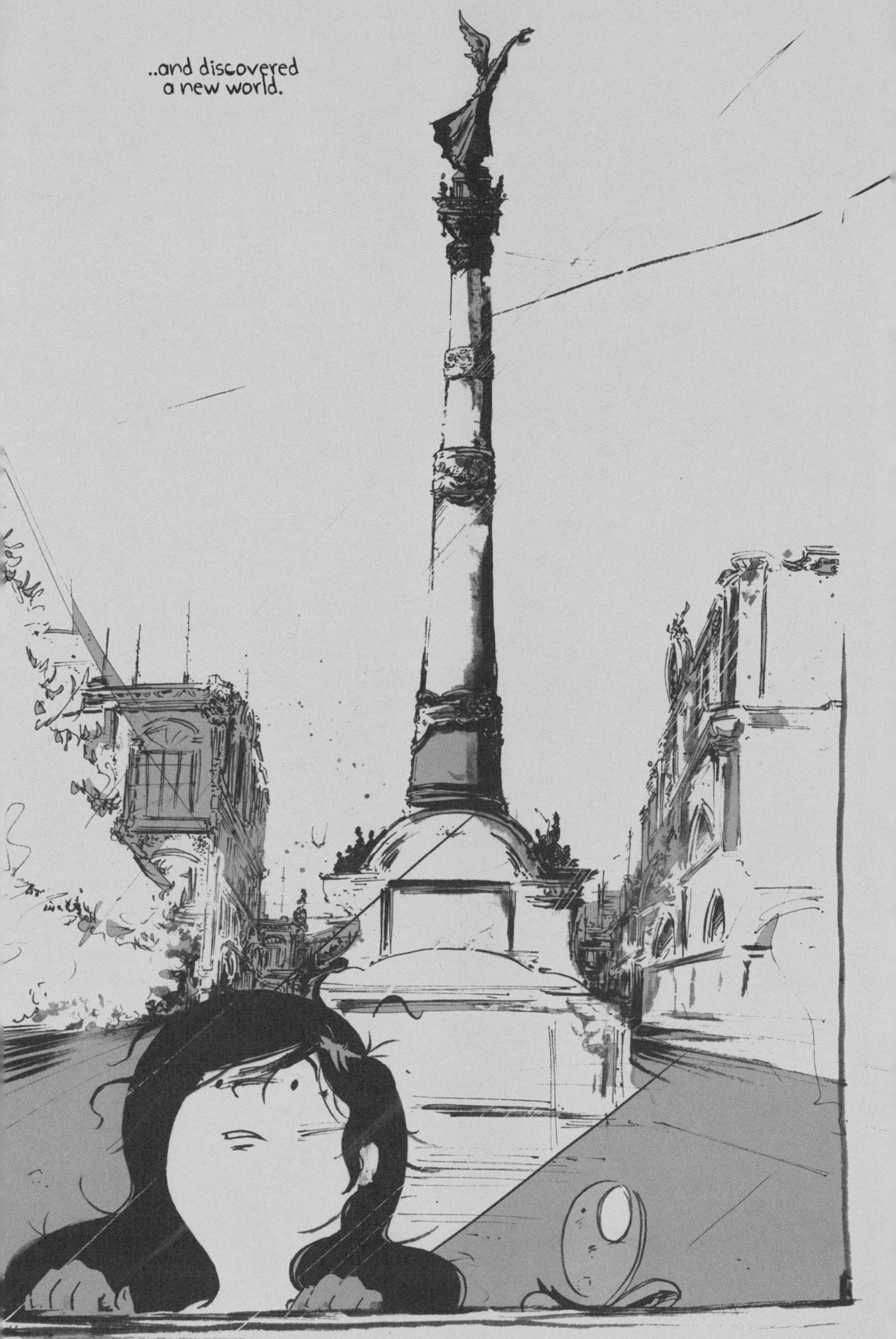
..and discovered a new world.

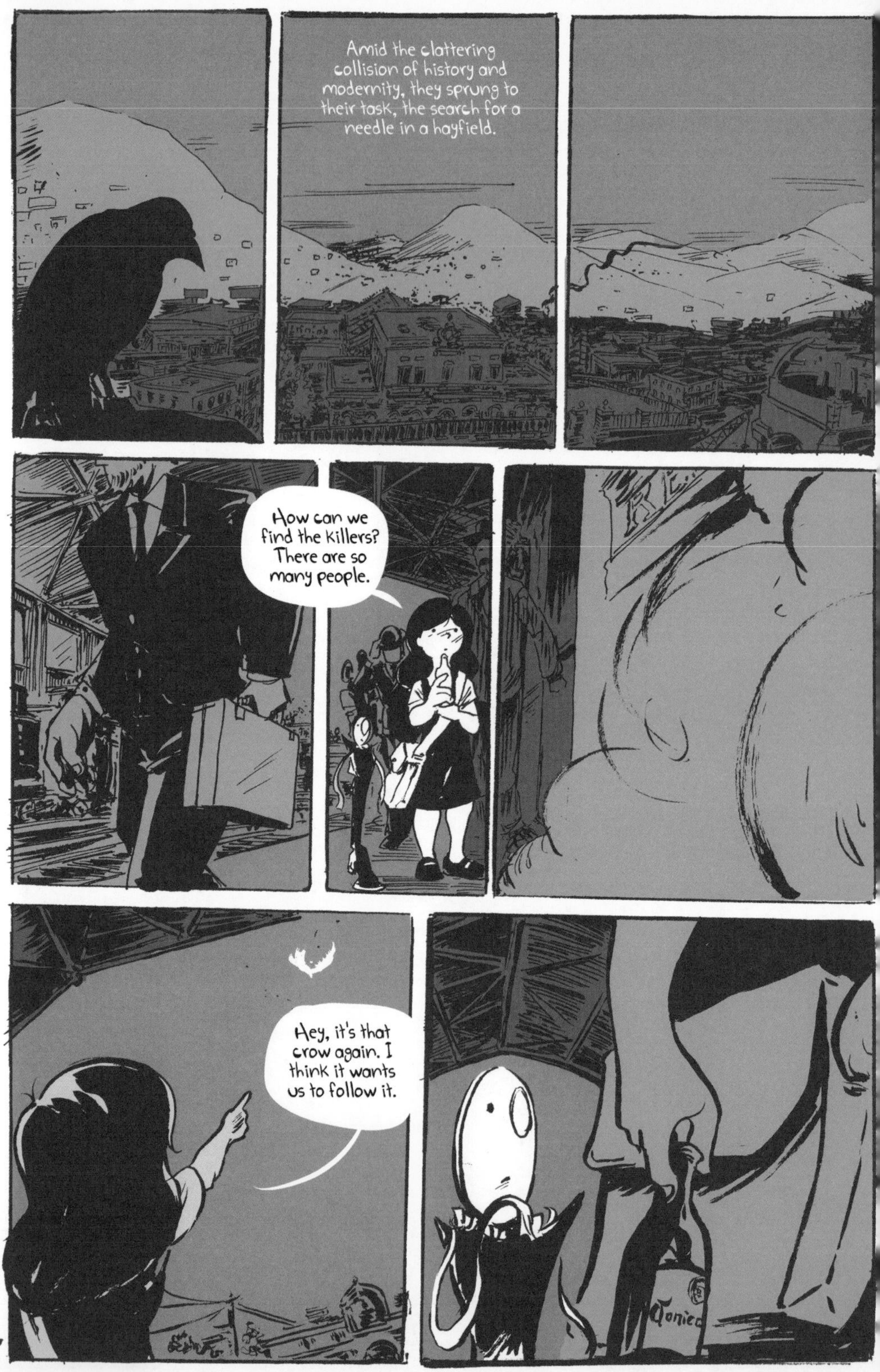
Amid the clattering collision of history and modernity, they sprung to their task, the search for a needle in a hayfield.
How can we find the killers? There are so many people.
Hey, it's that crow again. I think it wants us to follow it.
Tonica

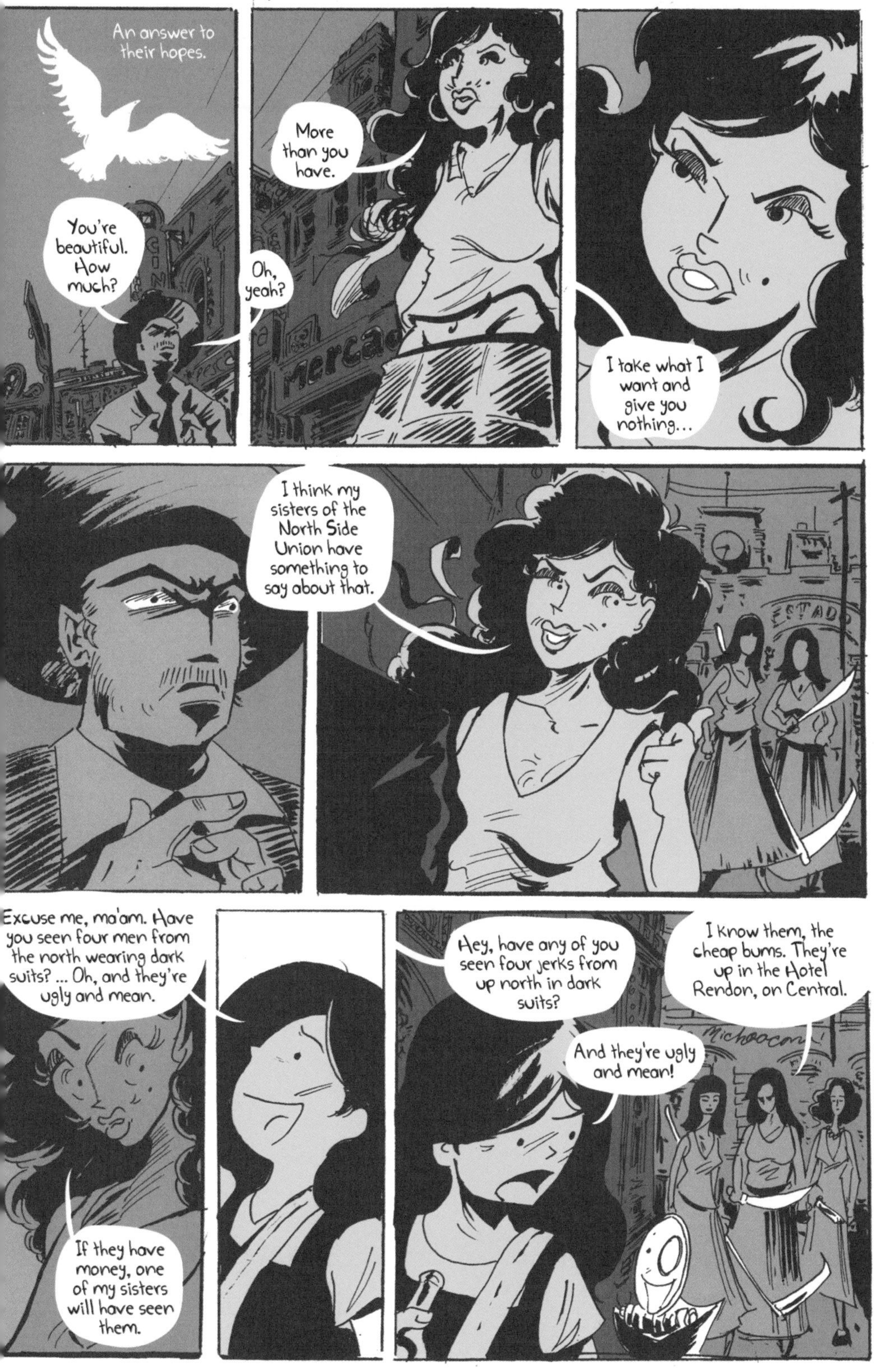

An answer to their hopes.
You're beautiful. How much?
Oh, yeah?
More than you have.
I take what I want and give you nothing...
I think my sisters of the North Side Union have something to say about that.
Excuse me, ma'am. Have you seen four men from the north wearing dark suits? ... Oh, and they're ugly and mean.
If they have money, one of my sisters will have seen them.
Hey, have any of you seen four jerks from up north in dark suits?
And they're ugly and mean!
I know them, the cheap bums. They're up in the Hotel Rendon, on Central.

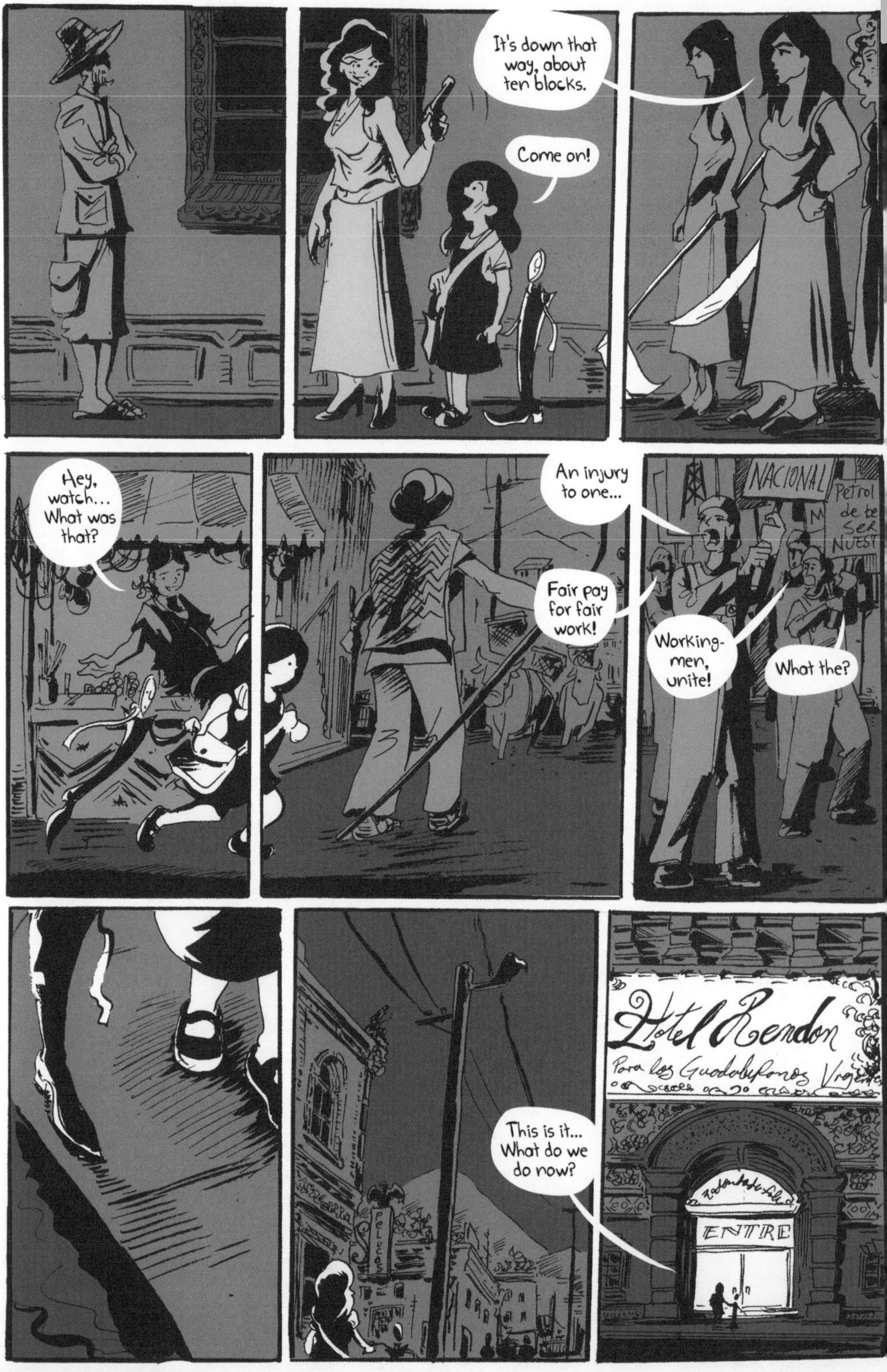
It's down that way, about ten blocks.
Come on!
Hey, watch... What was that?
An injury to one...
Fair pay for fair work!
NACIONAL
Workingmen, unite!
What the?
Hotel Rendon
This is it... What do we do now?
ENTRE

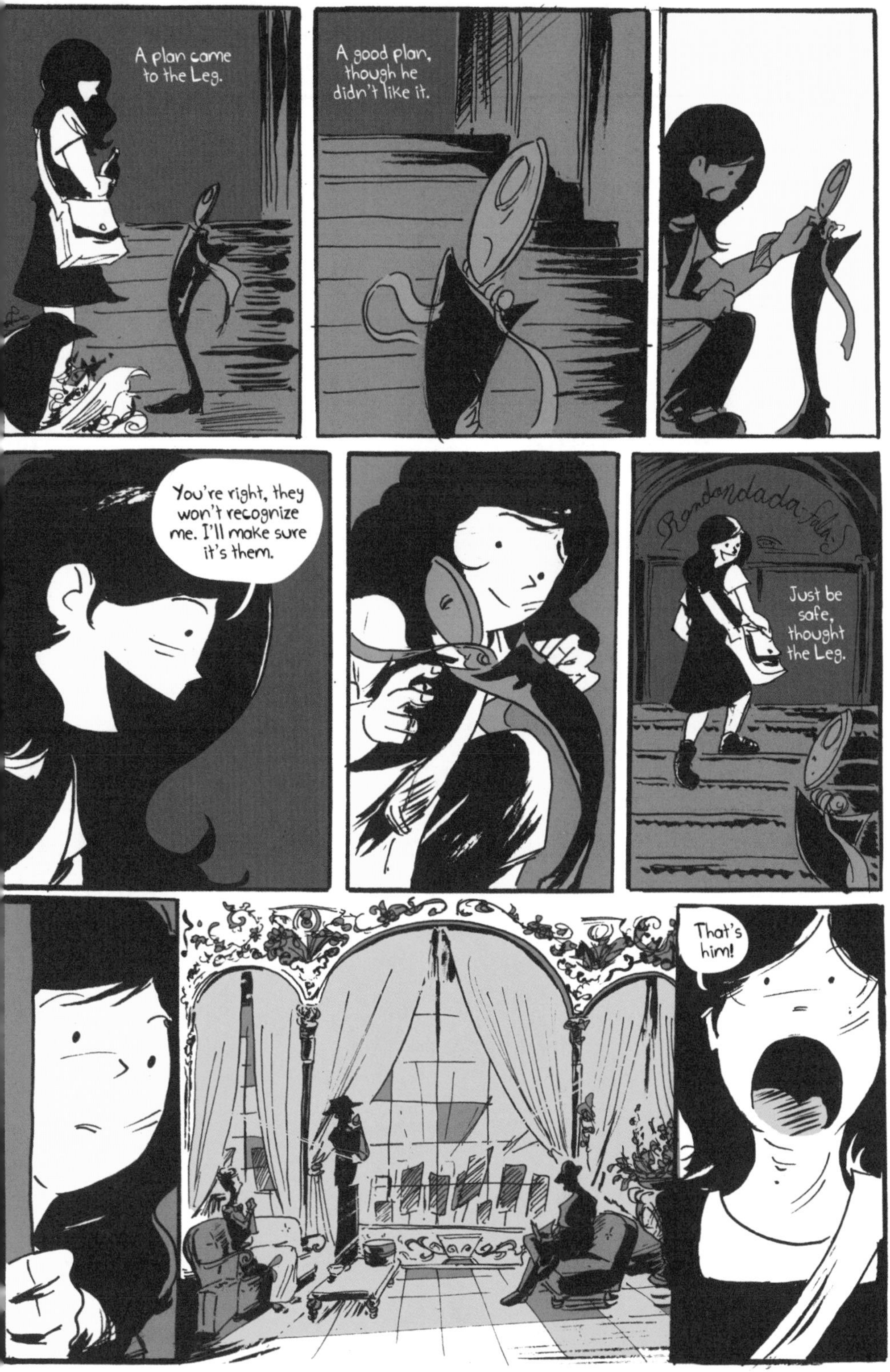
A plan came to the Leg.
A good plan, though he didn't like it.
You're right, they won't recognize me. I'll make sure it's them.
Just be safe, thought the Leg.
That's him!

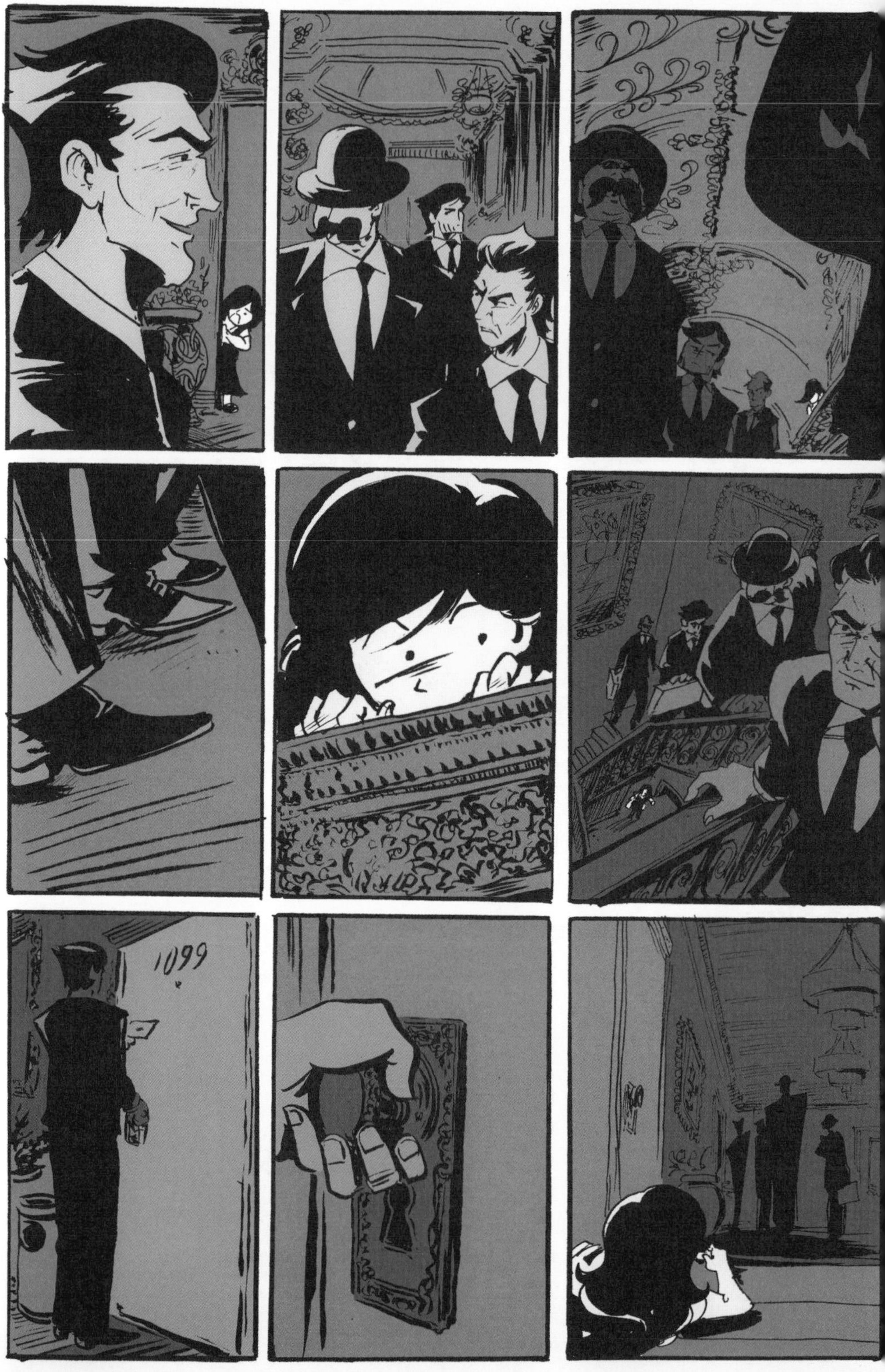
1099

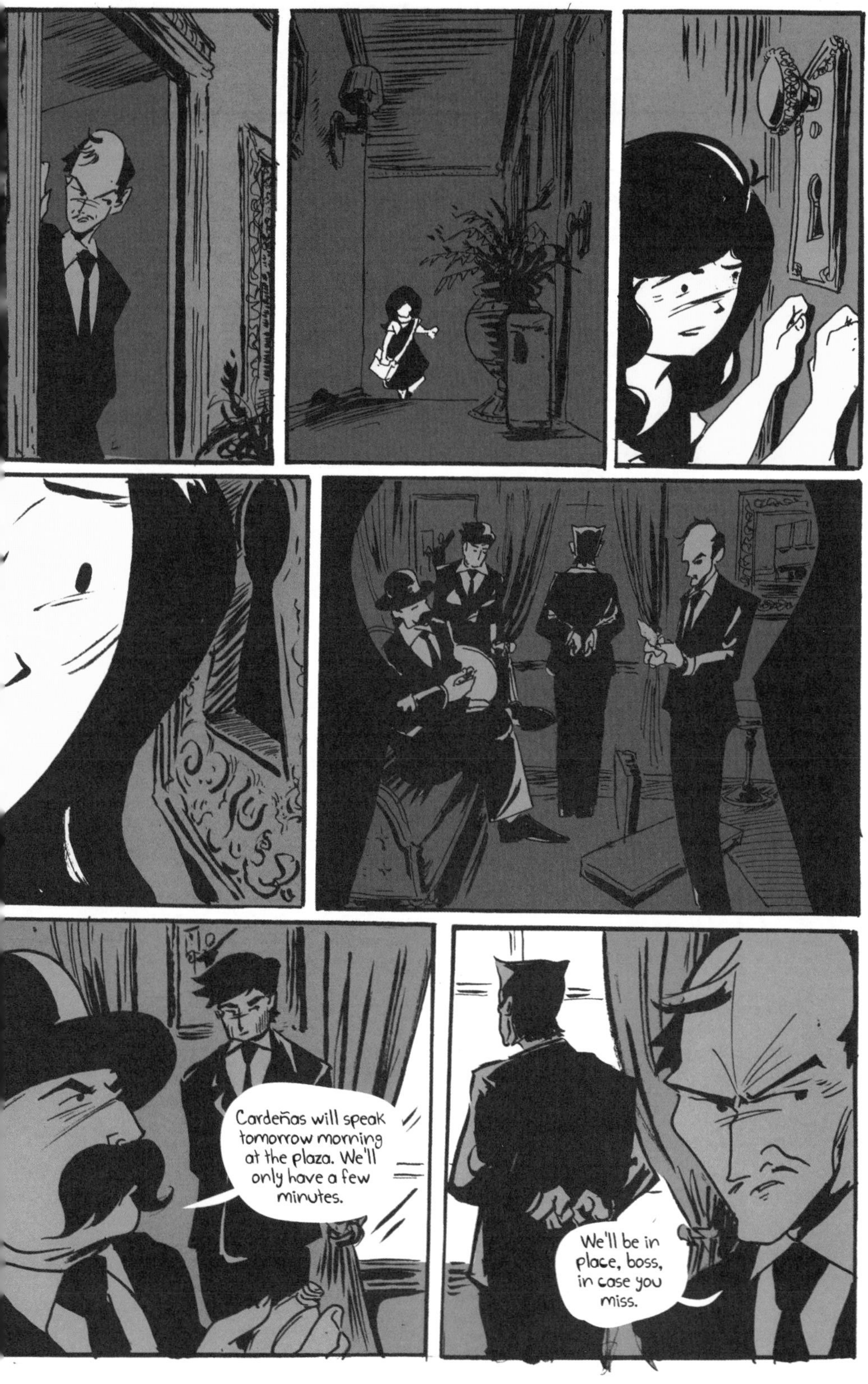
Cardeñas will speak tomorrow morning at the plaza. We'll only have a few minutes.
We'll be in place, boss, in case you miss.

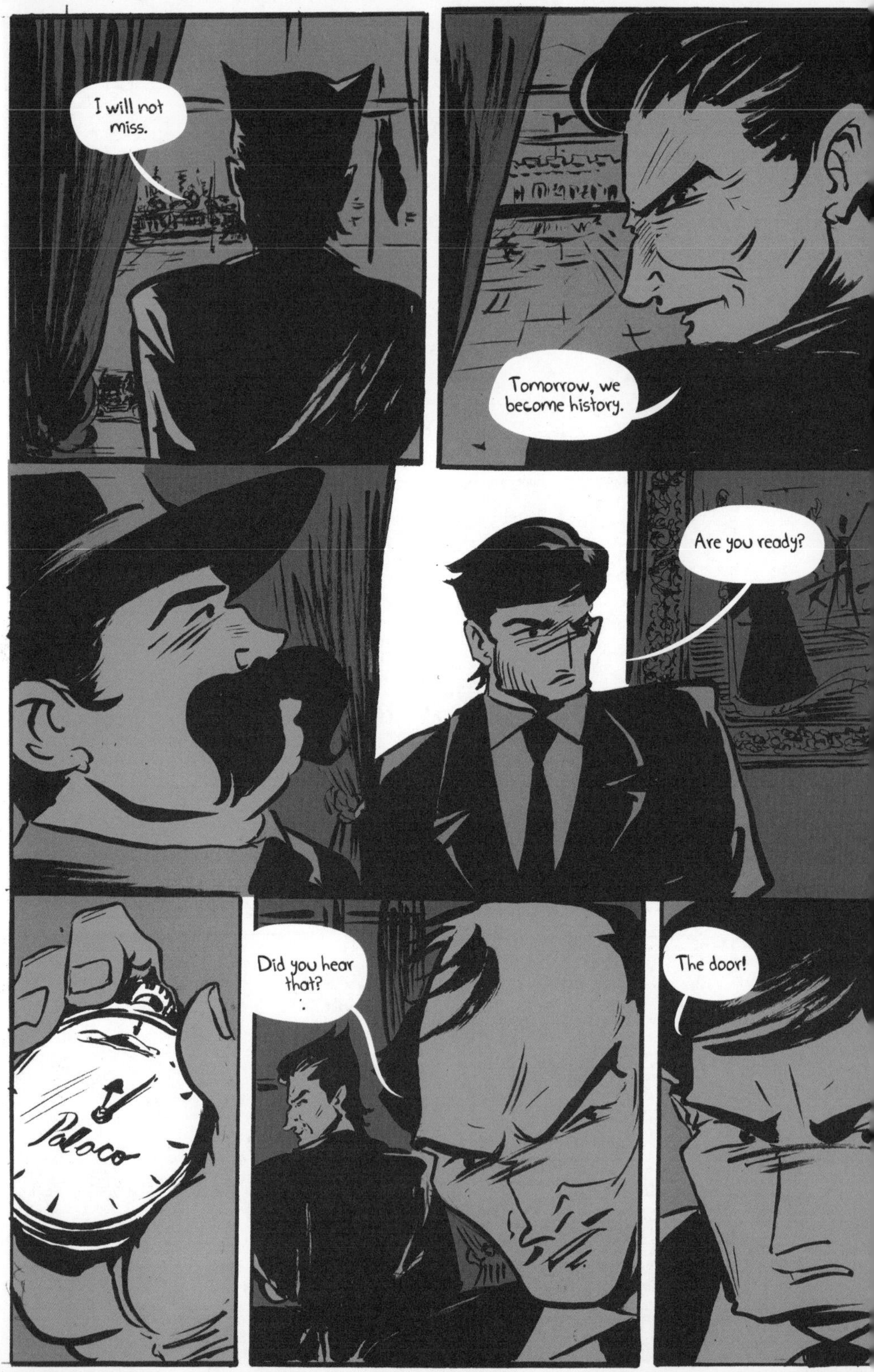
I will not miss.
Tomorrow, we become history.
Are you ready?
Did you hear that?
The door!

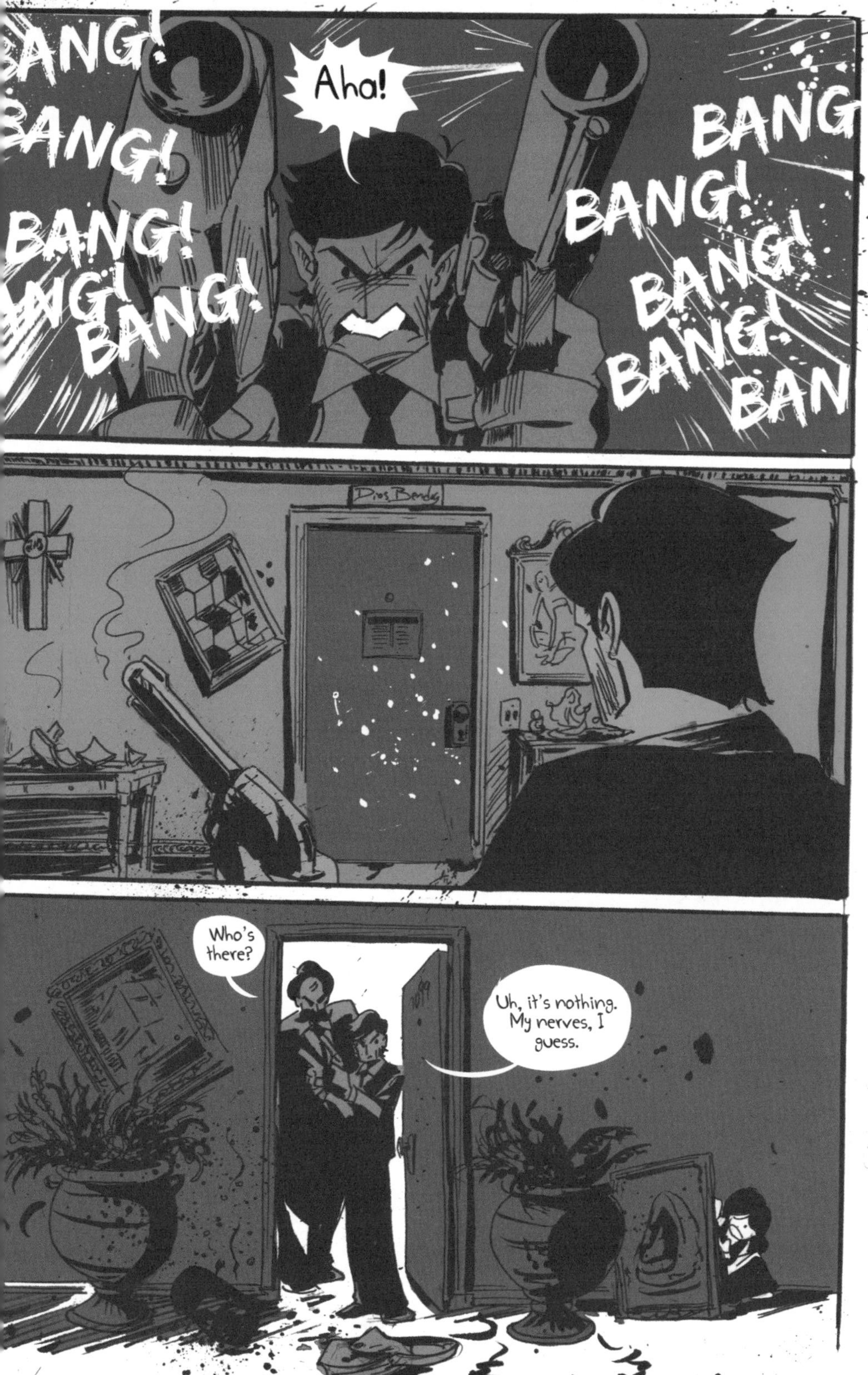
BANG!
BANG!
BANG!
BANG!
BANG!
Aha!
BANG
BANG!
BANG!
BANG!
BAN
Dios Bendiga
Who's there?
Uh, it's nothing. My nerves, I guess.

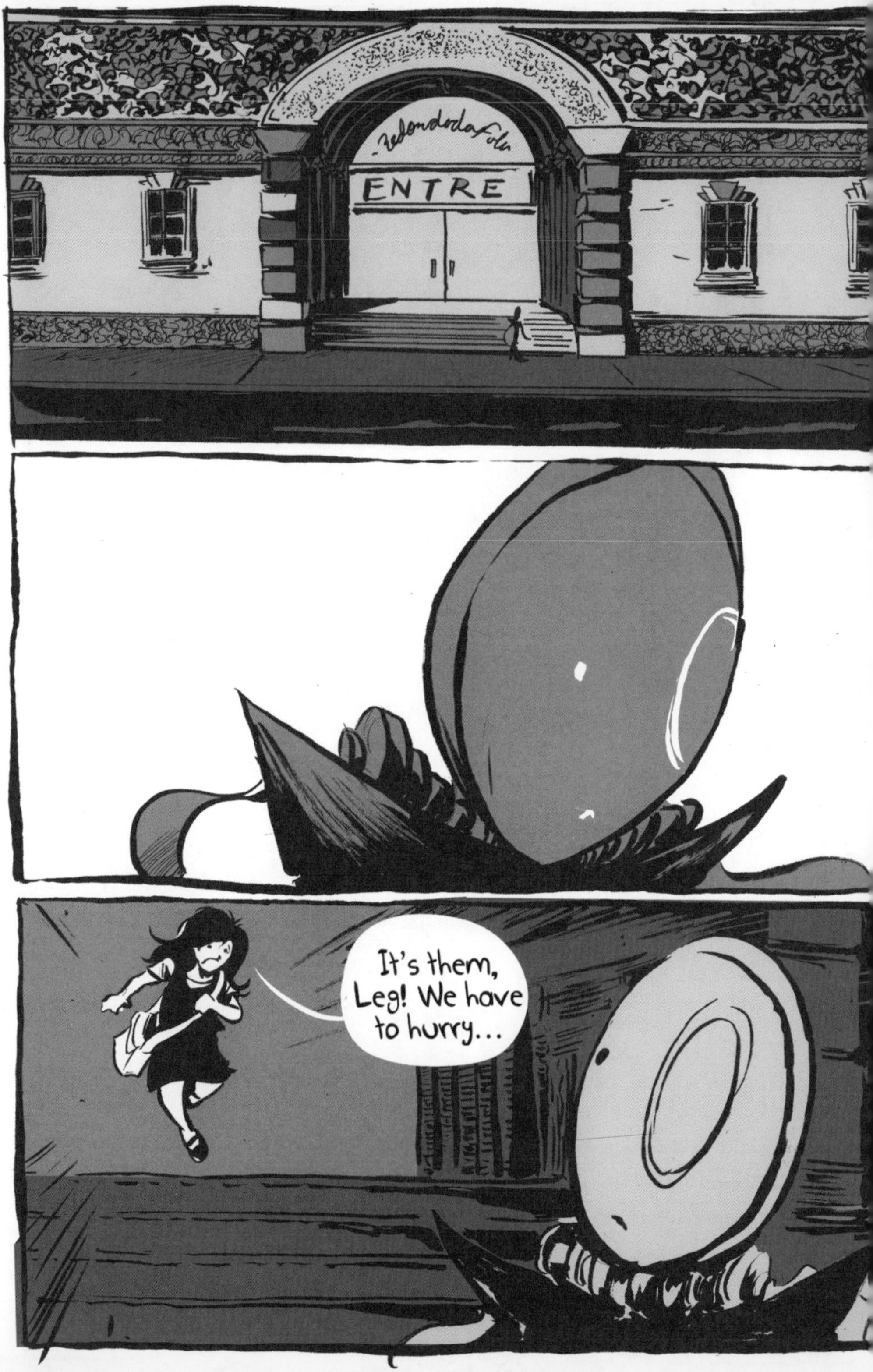
ENTRE
It's them, Leg! We have to hurry...

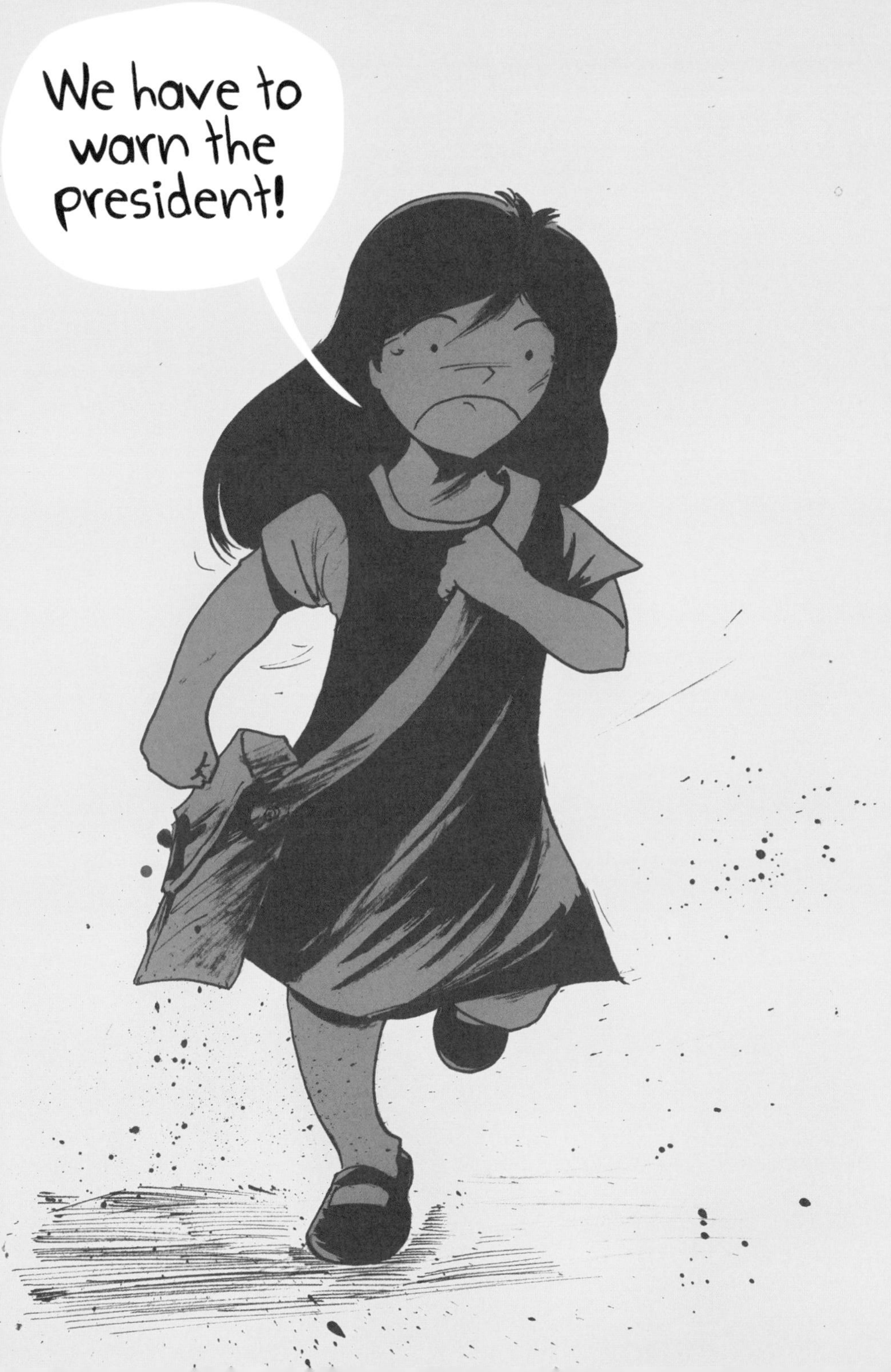
We have to warn the president!

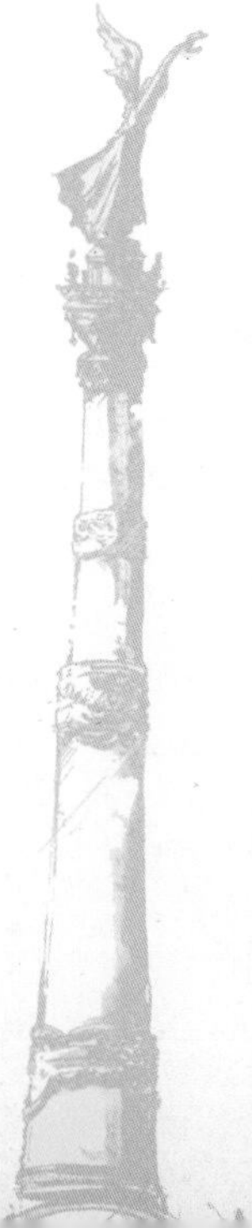

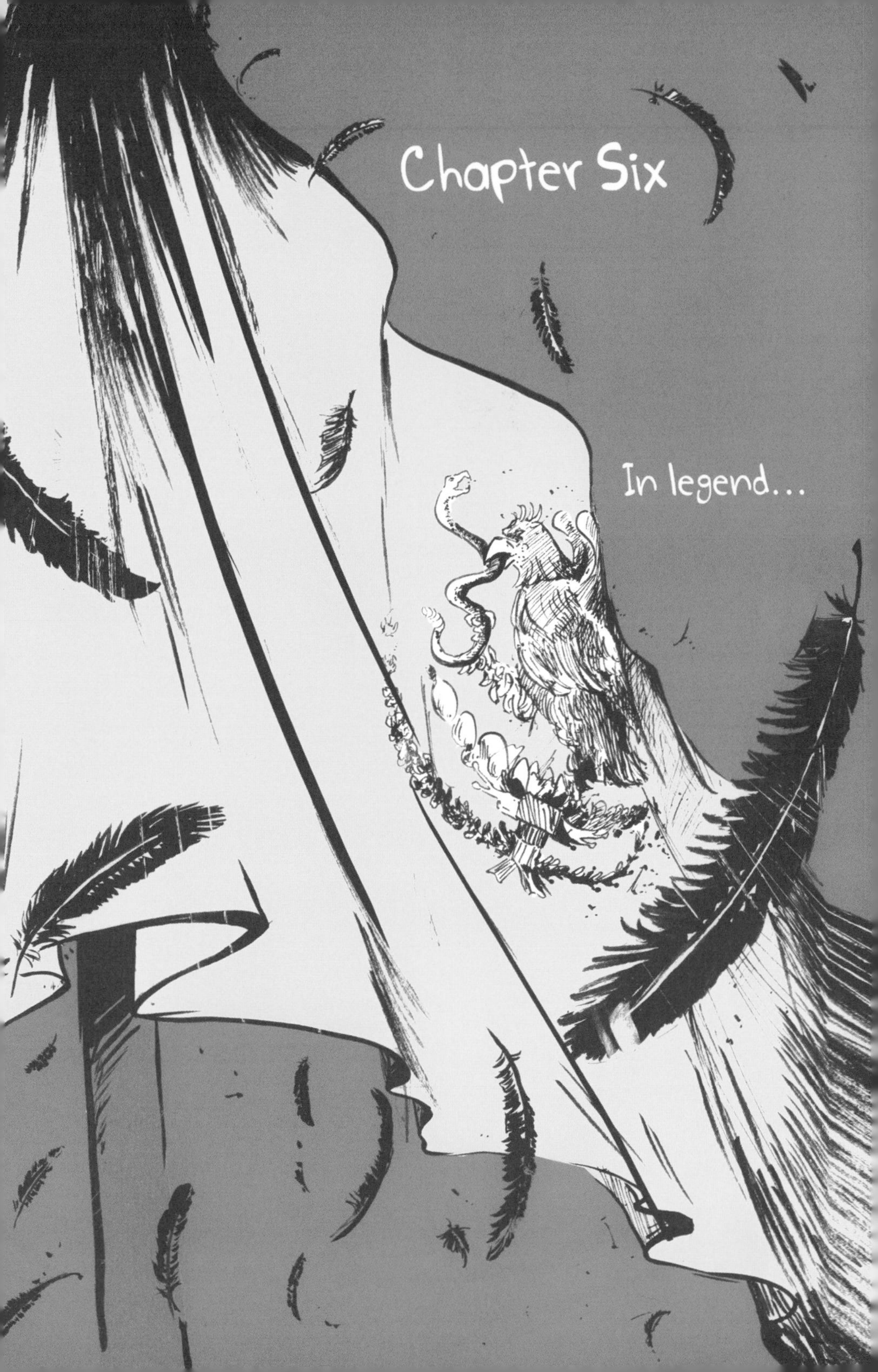
Chapter Six
In legend...

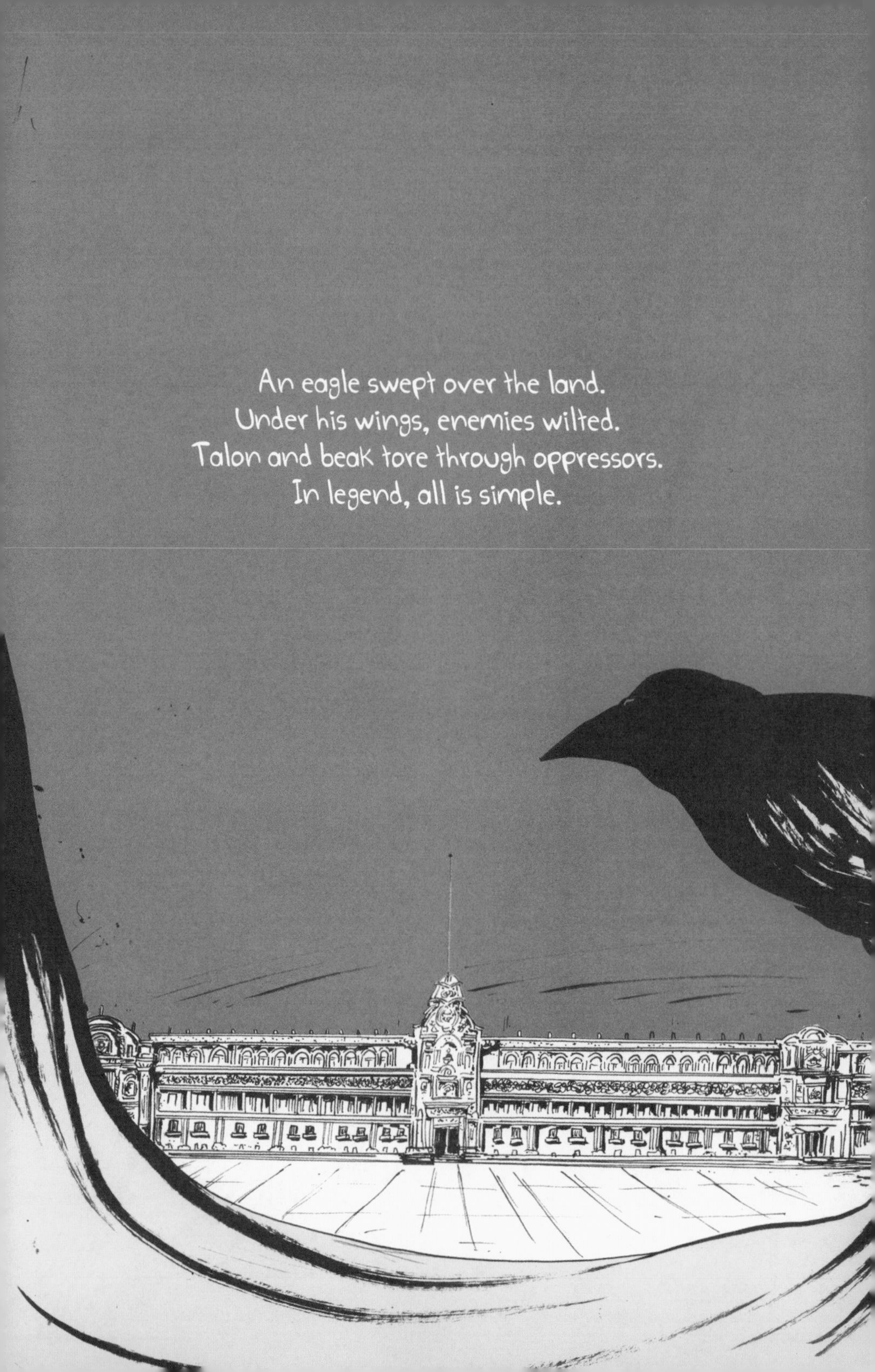
An eagle swept over the land.
Under his wings, enemies wilted.
Talon and beak tore through oppressors.
In legend, all is simple.

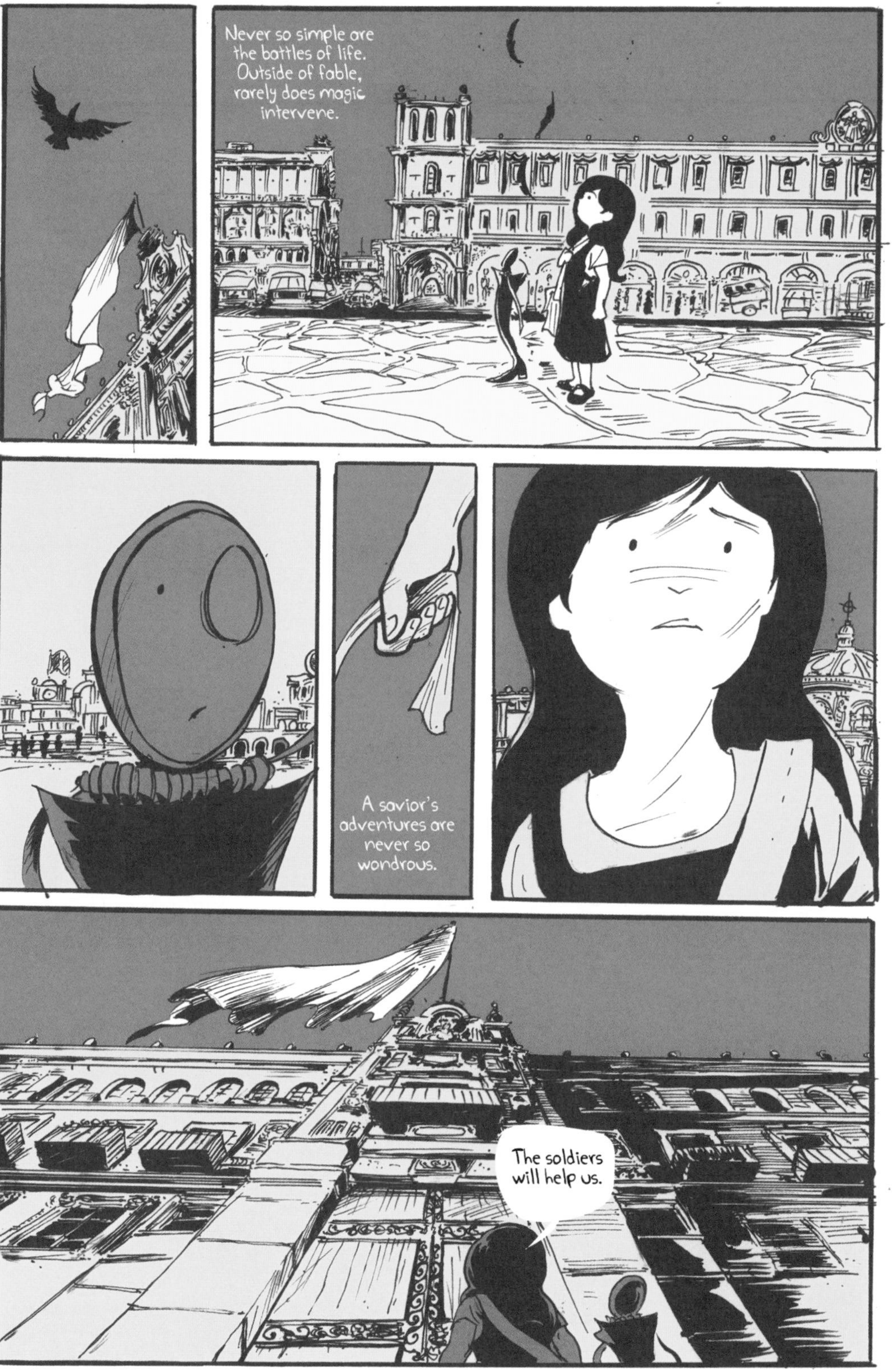
Never so simple are the battles of life. Outside of fable, rarely does magic intervene.
A savior's adventures are never so wondrous.
The soldiers will help us.

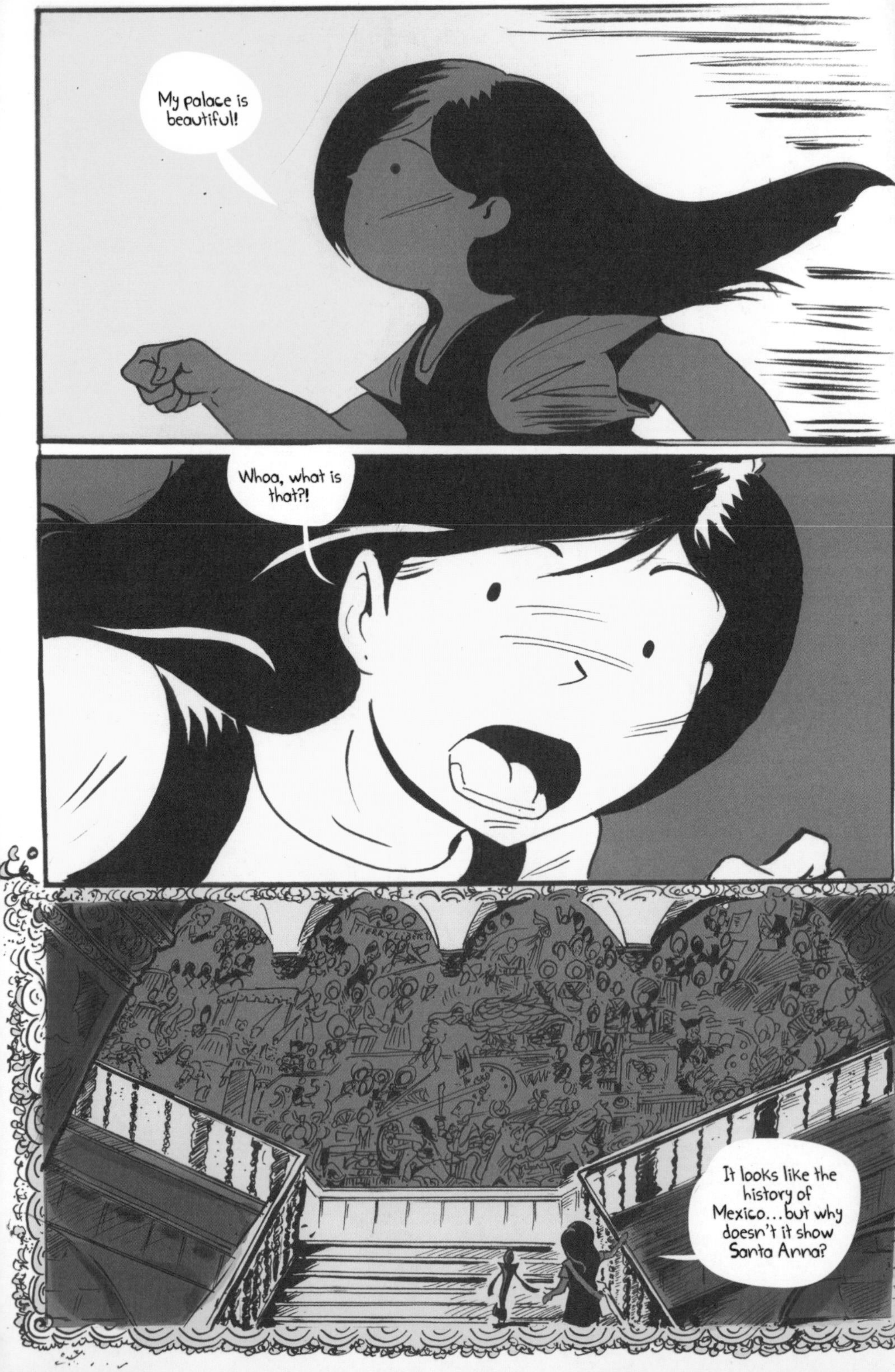
My palace is beautiful!
Whoa, what is that?!
It looks like the history of Mexico... but why doesn't it show Santa Anna?

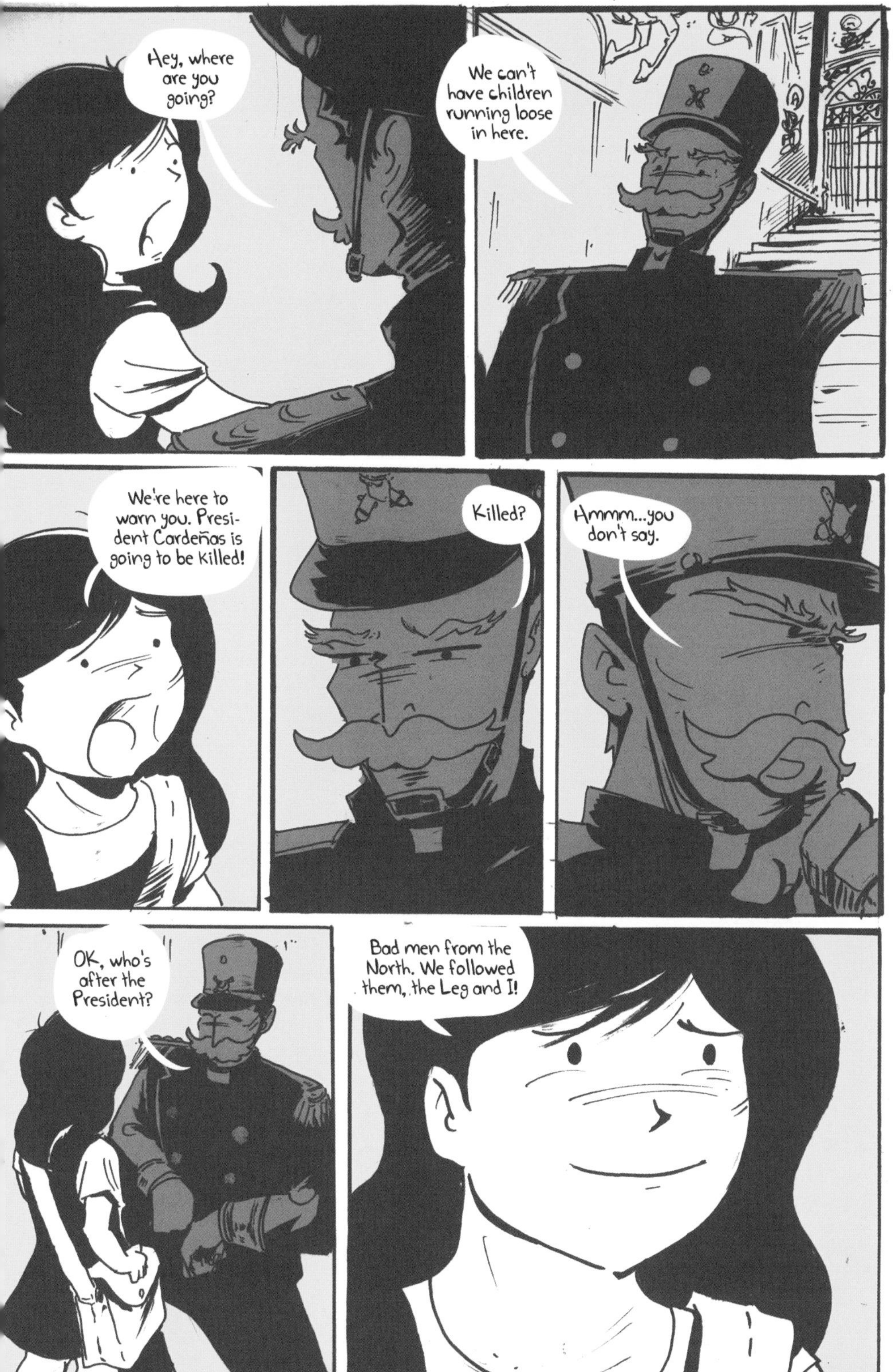
Hey, where are you going?
We can't have children running loose in here.
We're here to warn you. President Cardeñas is going to be killed!
Killed?
Hmmm...you don't say.
OK, who's after the President?
Bad men from the North. We followed them, the Leg and I!

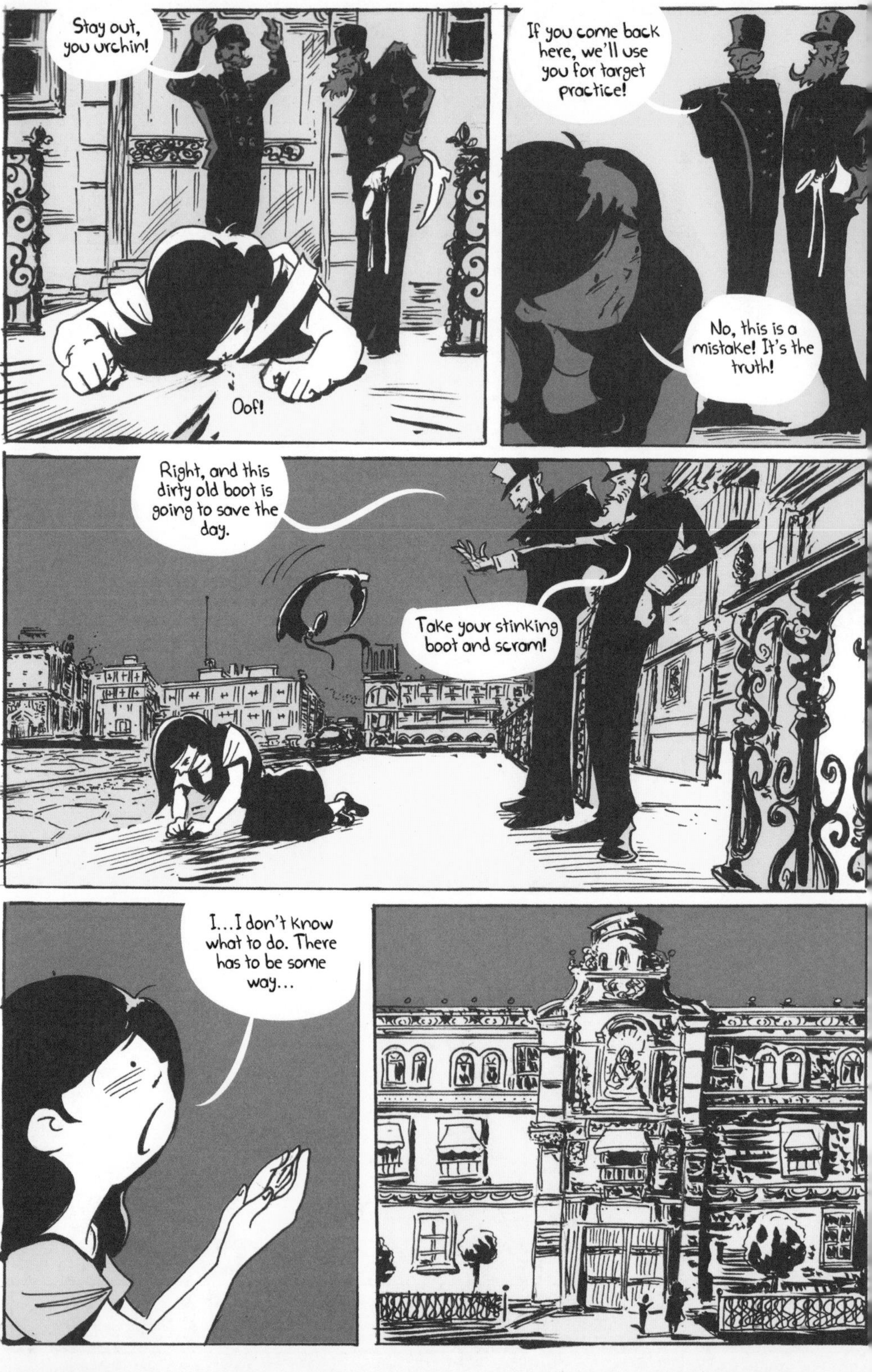
Stay out, you urchin!
Oof!
If you come back here, we'll use you for target practice!
No, this is a mistake! It's the truth!
Right, and this dirty old boot is going to save the day.
Take your stinking boot and scram!
I...I don't know what to do. There has to be some way...

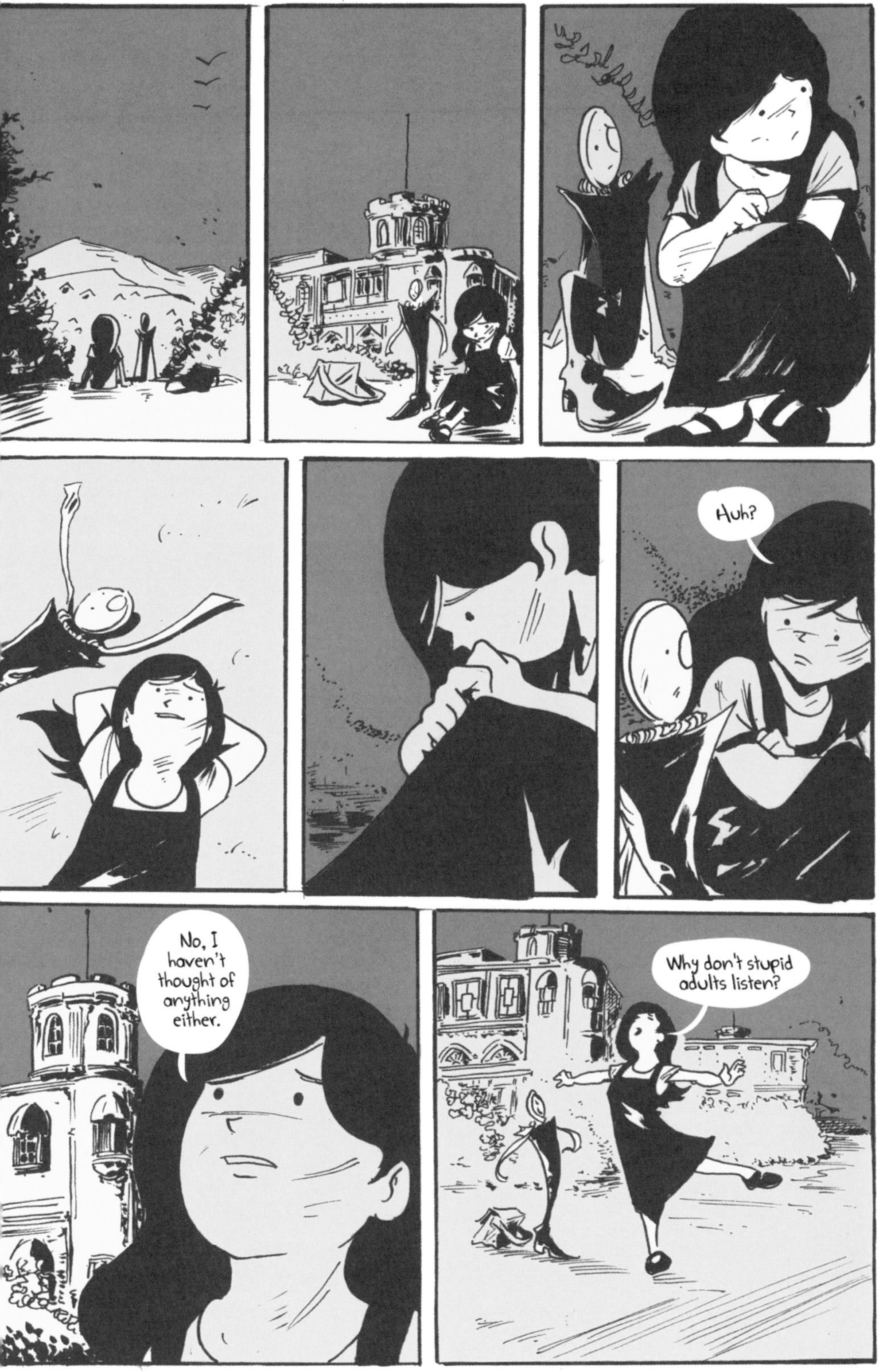
Huh?
No, I haven't thought of anything either.
Why don't stupid adults listen?

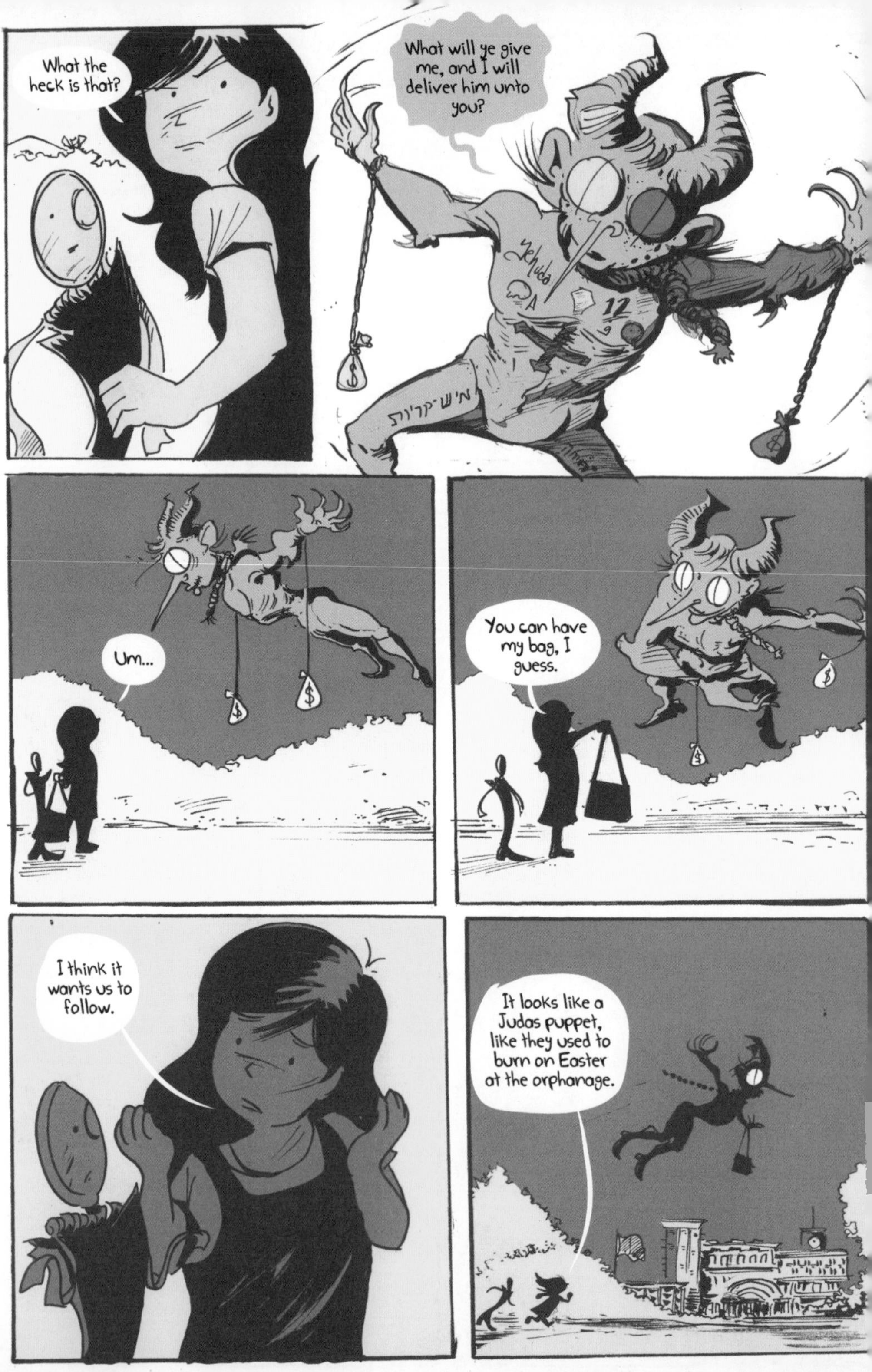
What the heck is that?
What will ye give me, and I will deliver him unto you?
Yehuda
Um...
You can have my bag, I guess.
I think it wants us to follow.
It looks like a Judas puppet, like they used to burn on Easter at the orphanage.

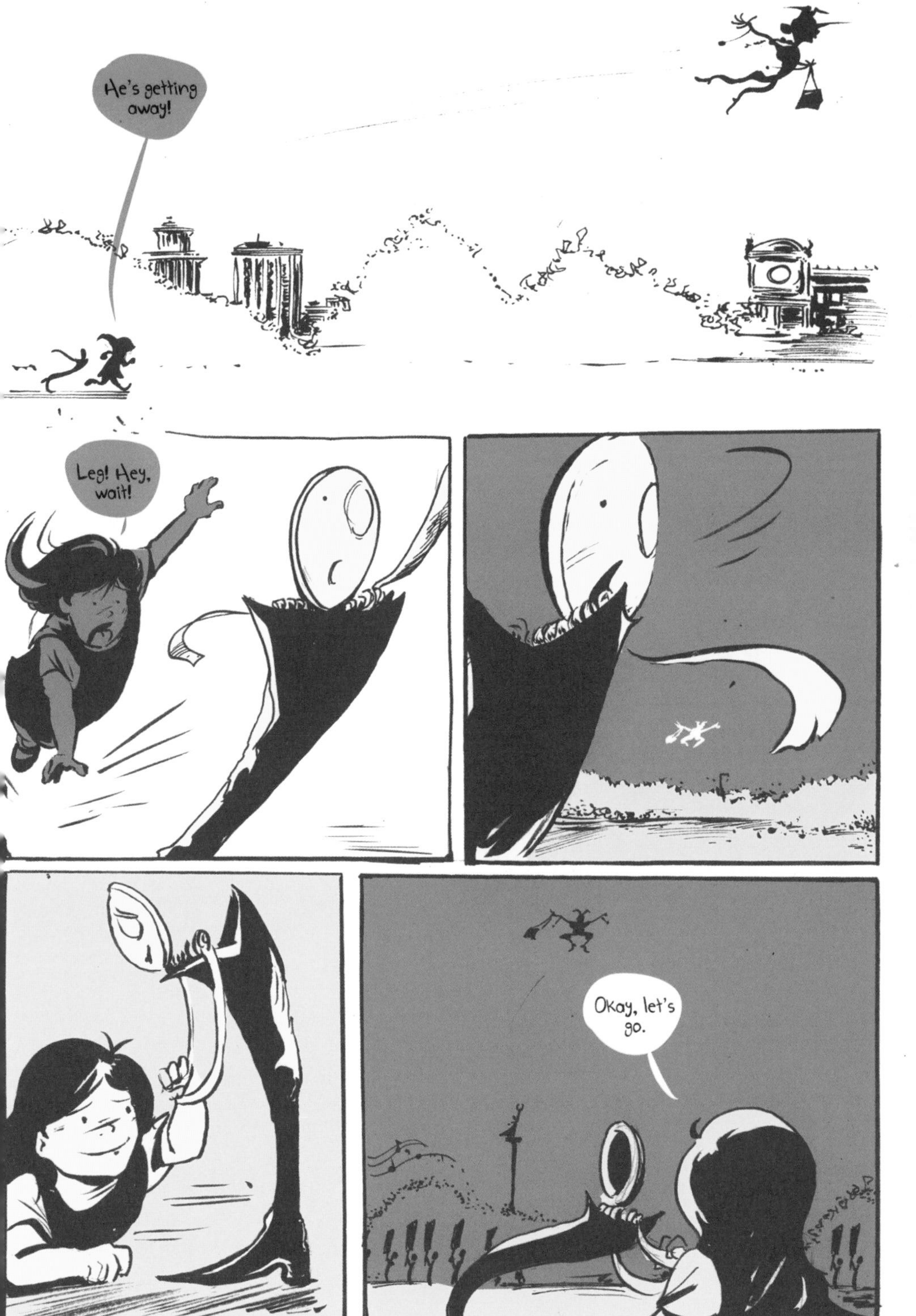
He's getting away!
Leg! Hey, wait!
Okay, let's go.

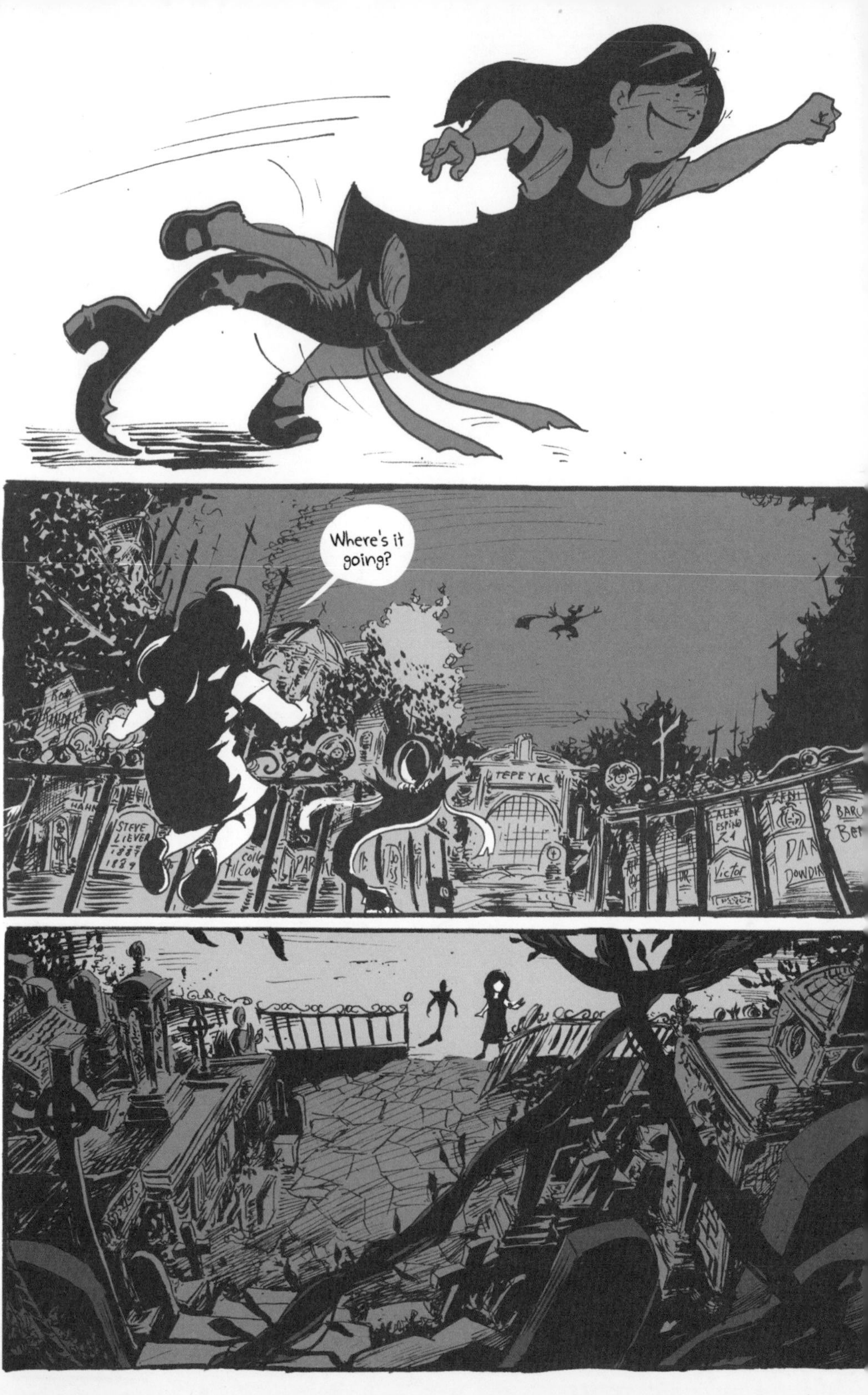
Where's it going?
STEVE LIEVER
TEPEYAC
Victor

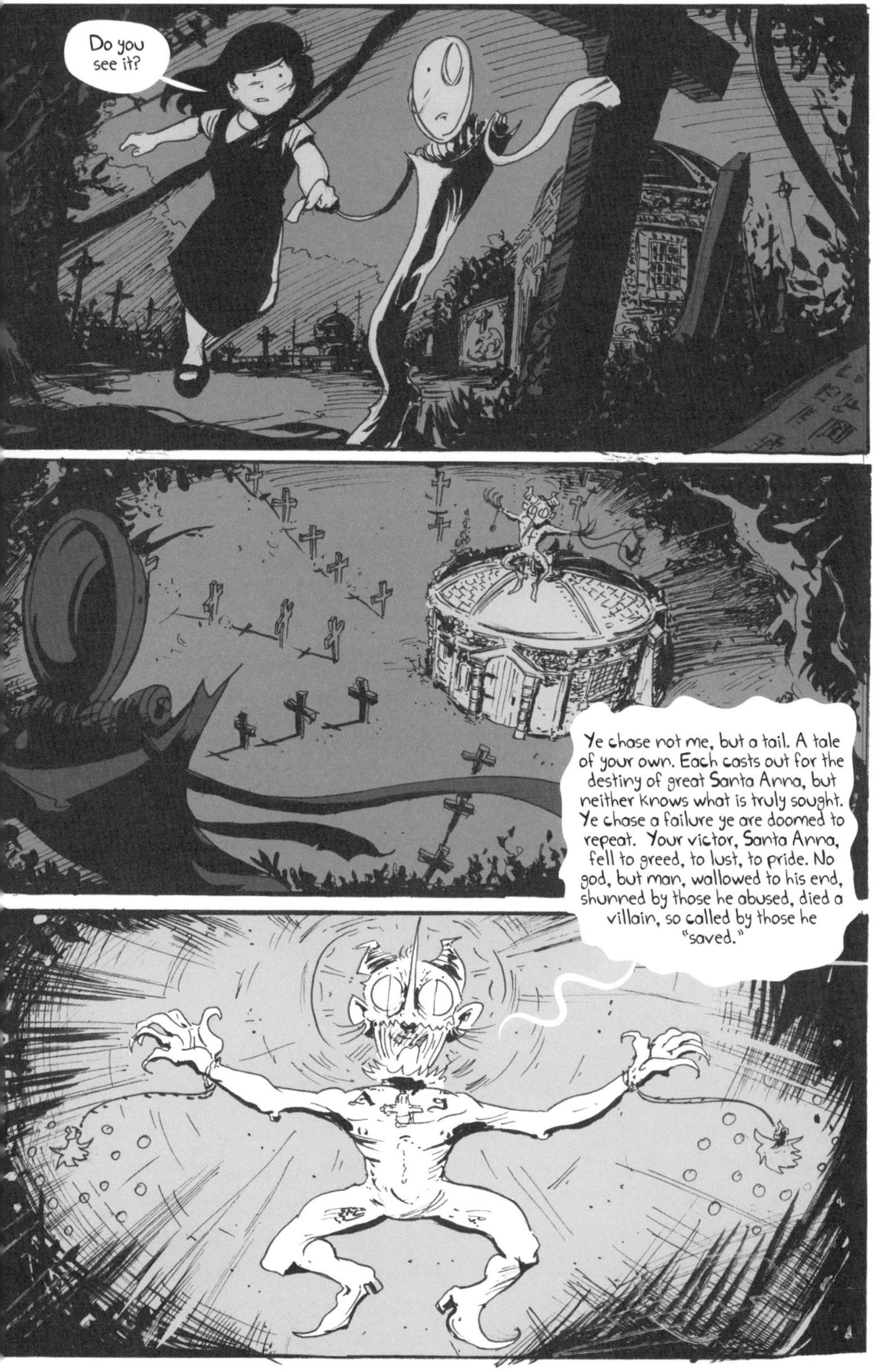
Do you see it?
Ye chase not me, but a tail. A tale of your own. Each casts out for the destiny of great Santa Anna, but neither knows what is truly sought. Ye chase a failure ye are doomed to repeat. Your victor, Santa Anna, fell to greed, to lust, to pride. No god, but man, wallowed to his end, shunned by those he abused, died a villain, so called by those he "saved."

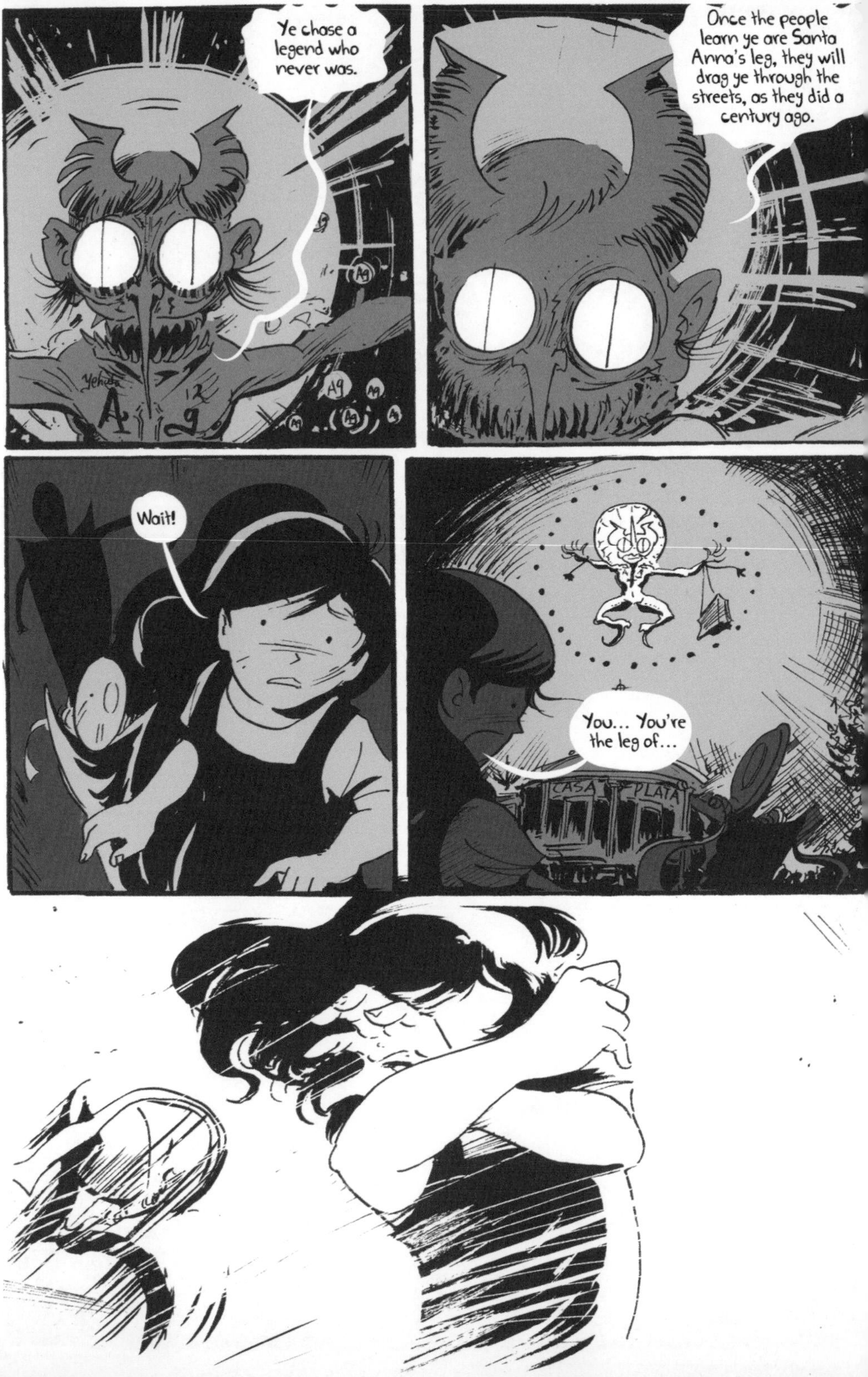
Ye chose a legend who never was.
Once the people learn ye are Santa Anna's leg, they will drag ye through the streets, as they did a century ago.
Wait!
You... You're the leg of...
CASA PLATA

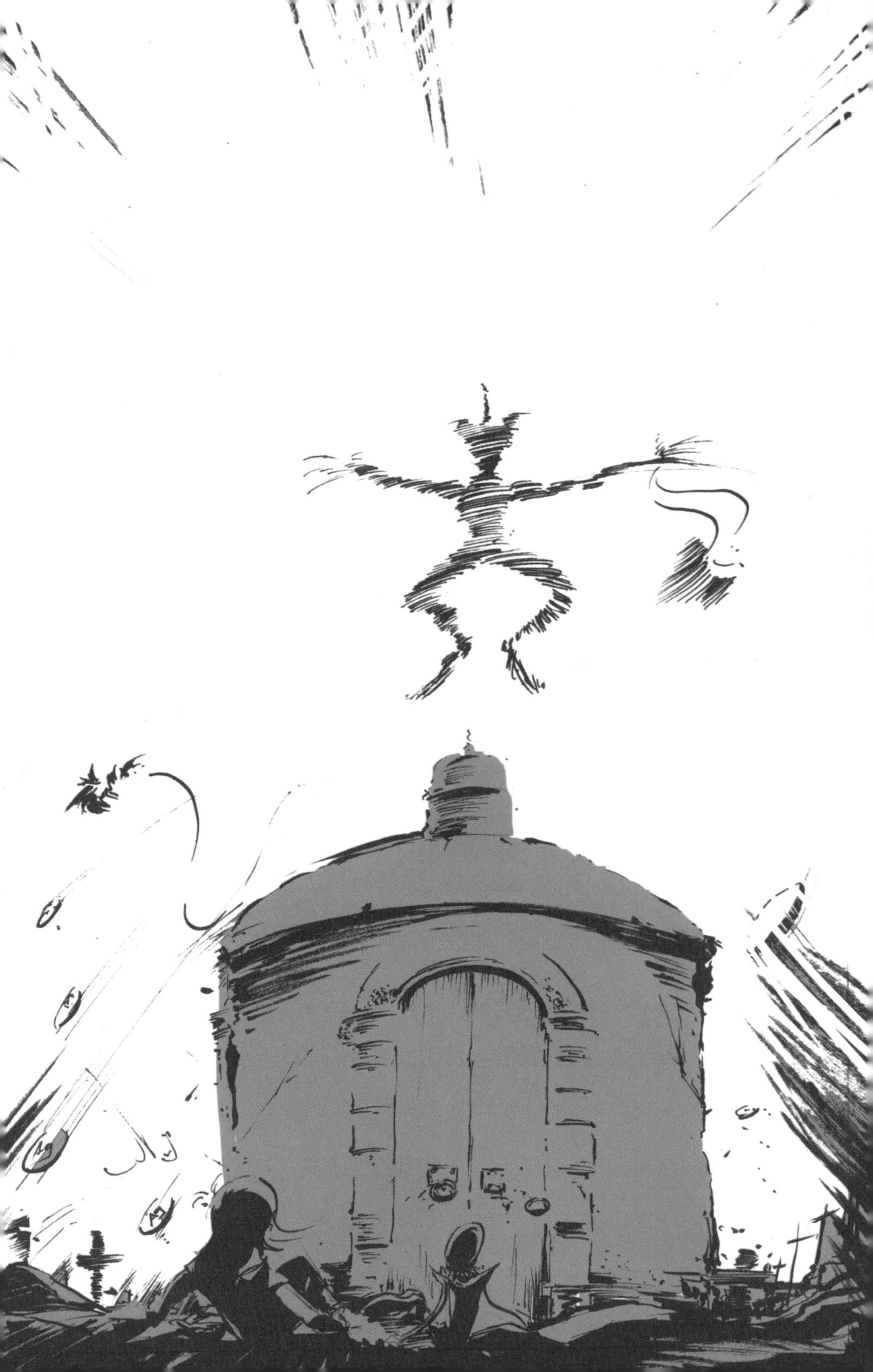

This whole time... You knew all along.

Why didn't you...

Why...

Leg!

Santa Anna... He was a, a bad man?

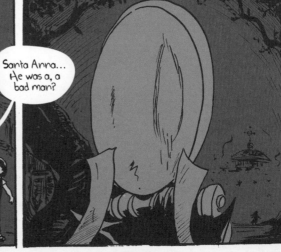

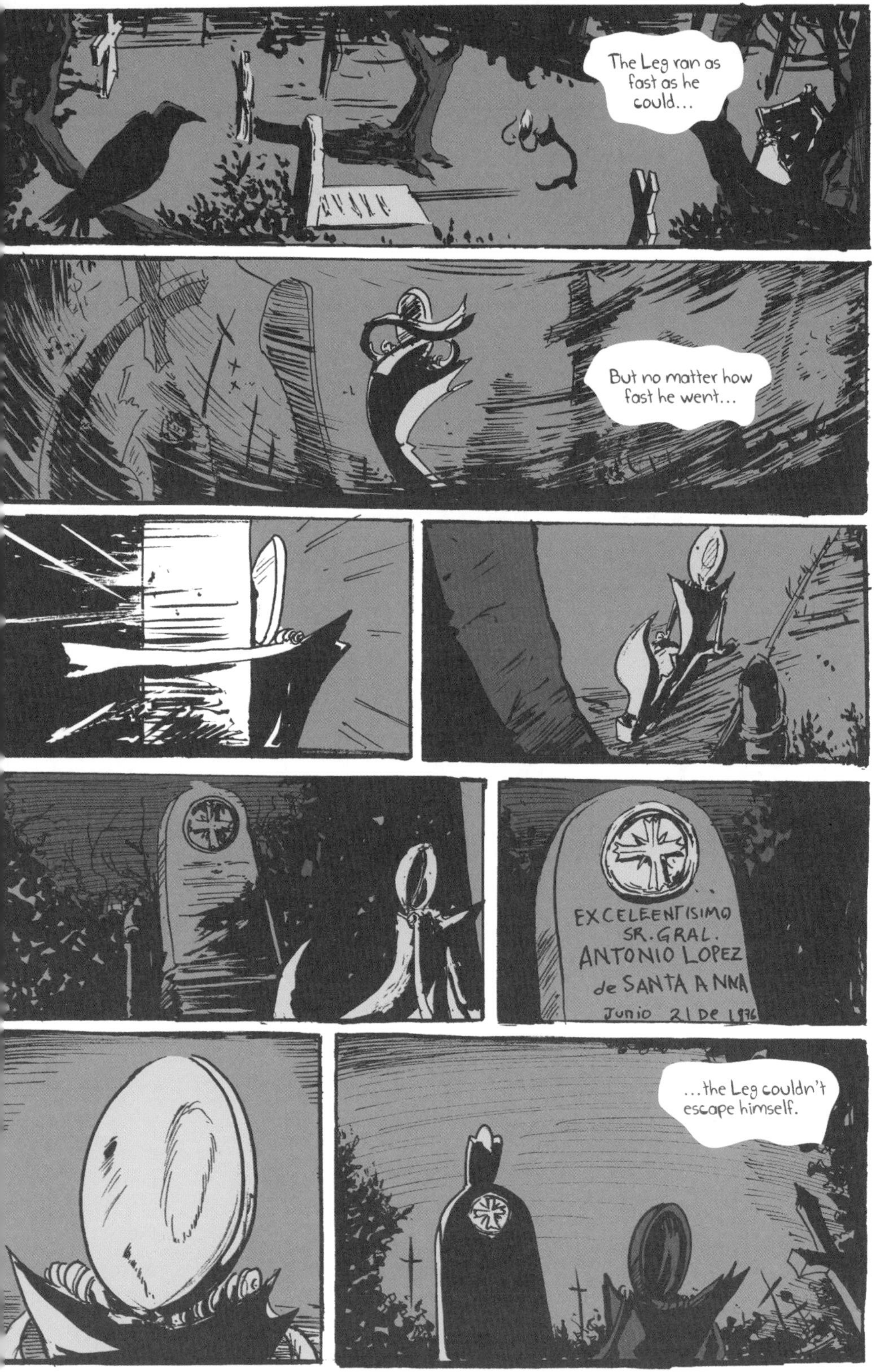
The Leg ran as fast as he could...
But no matter how fast he went...
EXCELEENTISIMO SR. GRAL. ANTONIO LOPEZ de SANTA ANNA JUNIO 21 DE 1876
...the Leg couldn't escape himself.

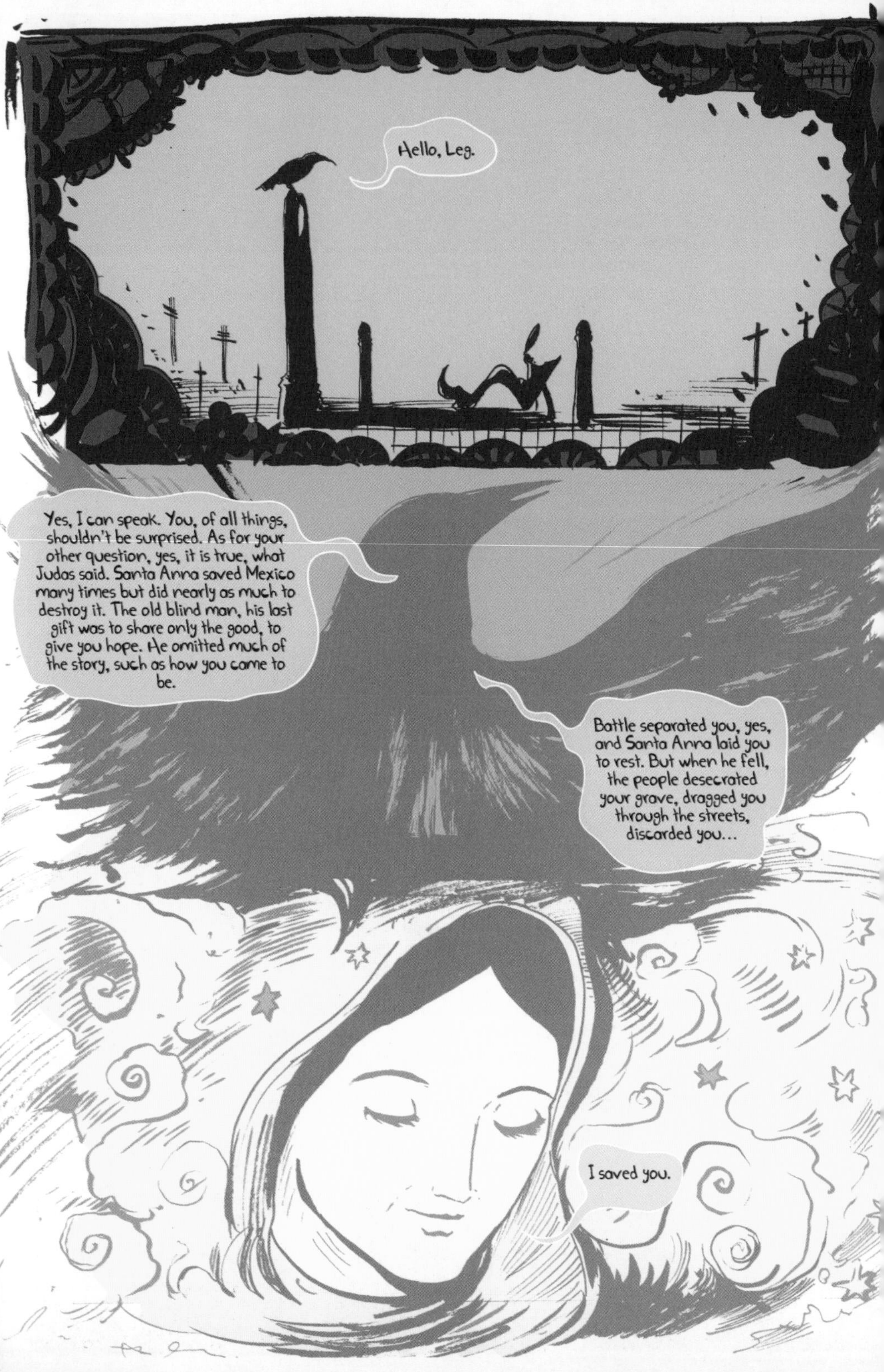
Hello, Leg.
Yes, I can speak. You, of all things, shouldn't be surprised. As for your other question, yes, it is true, what Judas said. Santa Anna saved Mexico many times but did nearly as much to destroy it. The old blind man, his last gift was to share only the good, to give you hope. He omitted much of the story, such as how you came to be.
Battle separated you, yes, and Santa Anna laid you to rest. But when he fell, the people desecrated your grave, dragged you through the streets, discarded you...
I saved you.

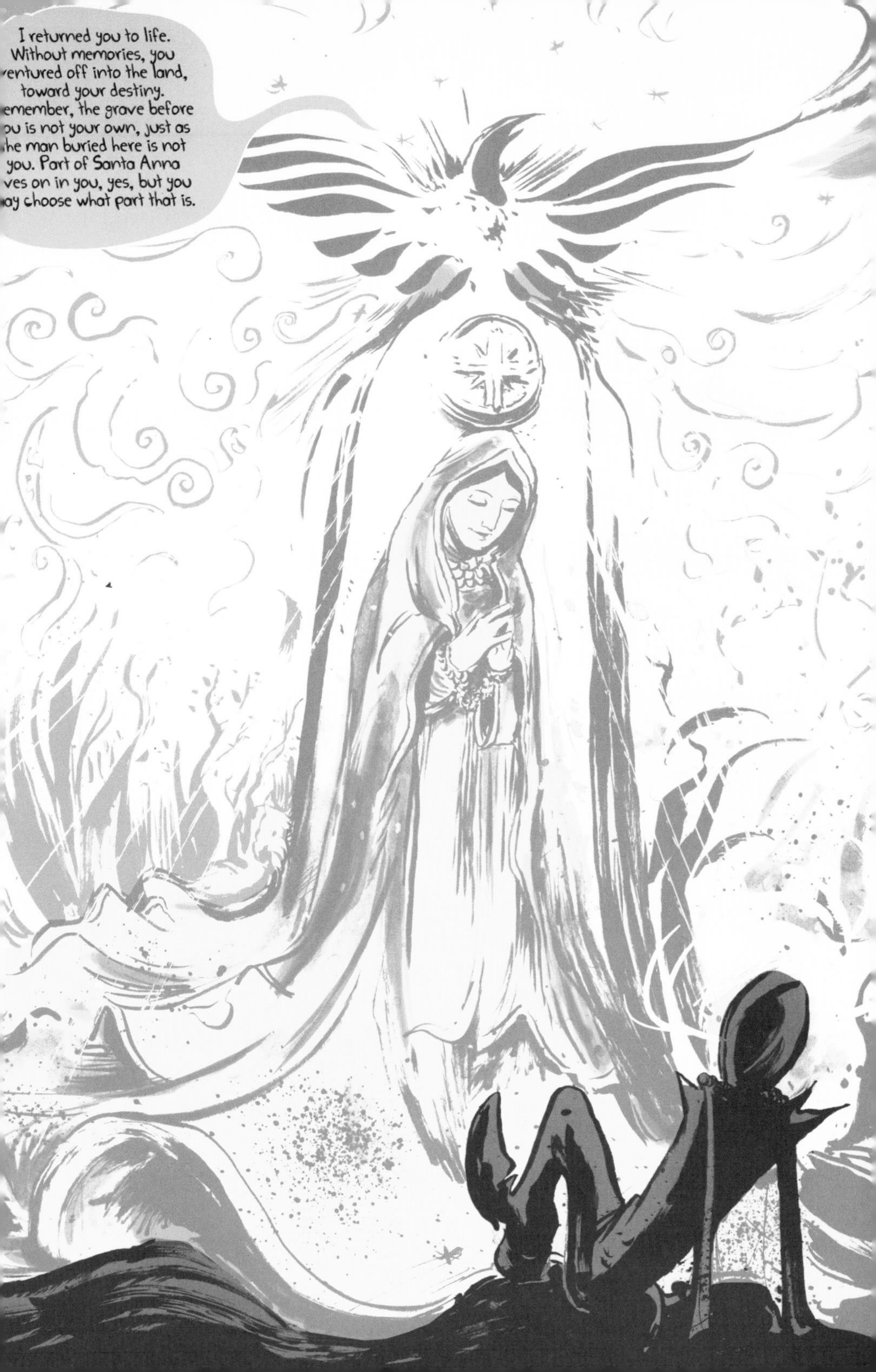
I returned you to life. Without memories, you ventured off into the land, toward your destiny. emember, the grave before ou is not your own, just as he man buried here is not you. Part of Santa Anna ves on in you, yes, but you ay choose what part that is.

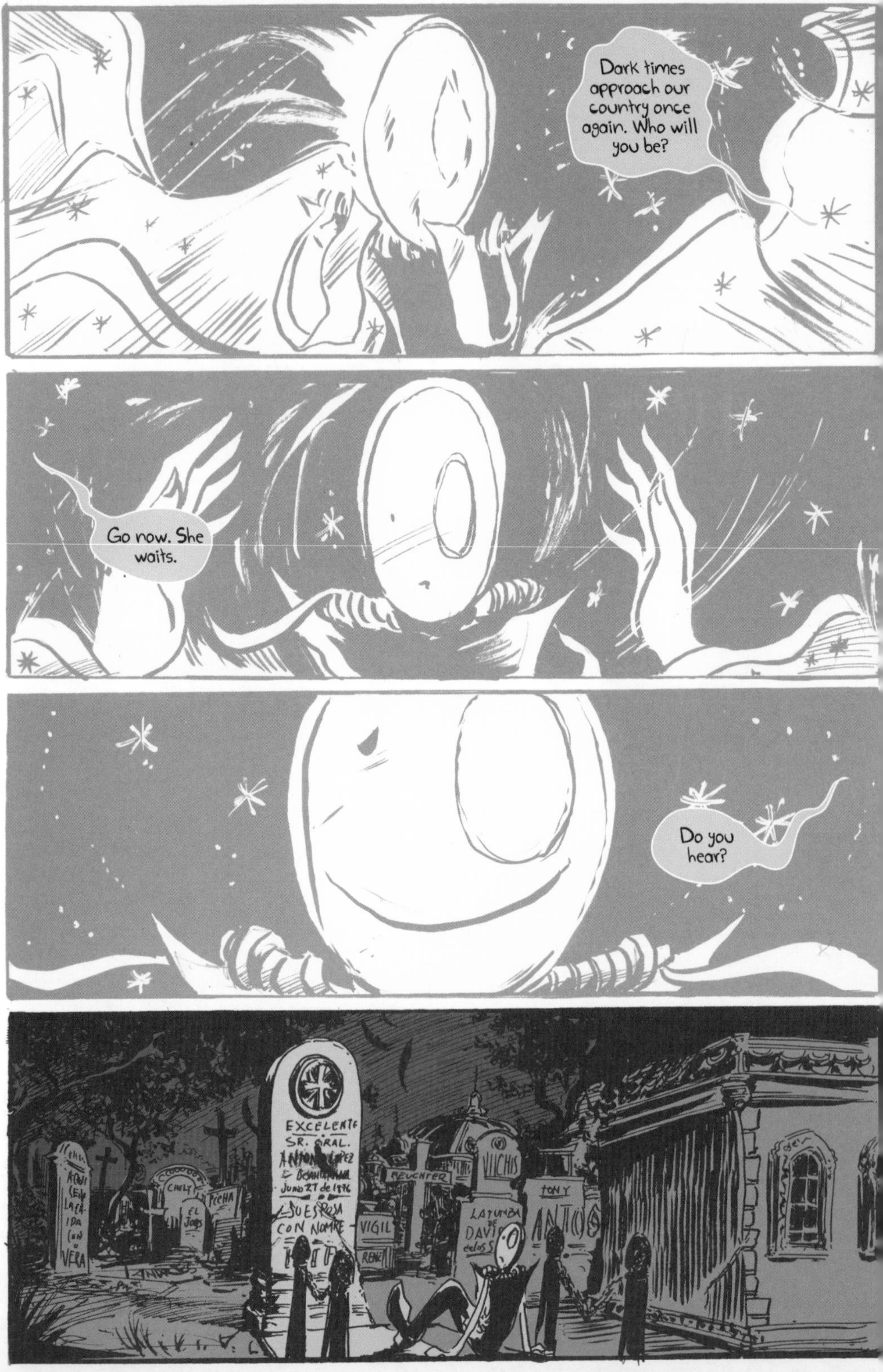
Dark times approach our country once again. Who will you be?
Go now. She waits.
Do you hear?
EXCELENTE
SR. GIRAL.
Junio 27 de 1876
CON NOMRE
VIGIL
VILCHIS
TONY
REUCHTER
CARLY
VERA

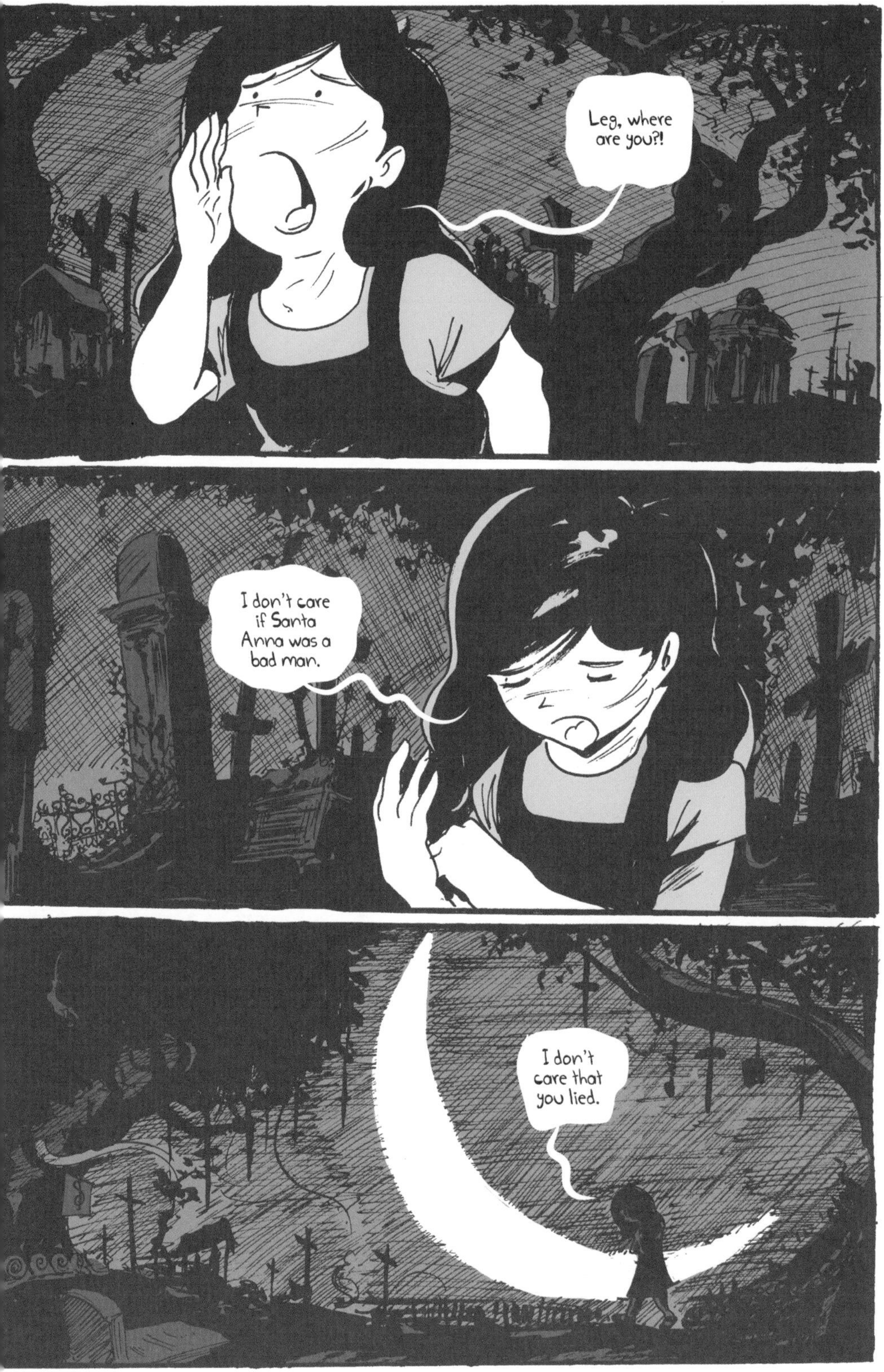
Leg, where are you?!
I don't care if Santa Anna was a bad man.
I don't care that you lied.

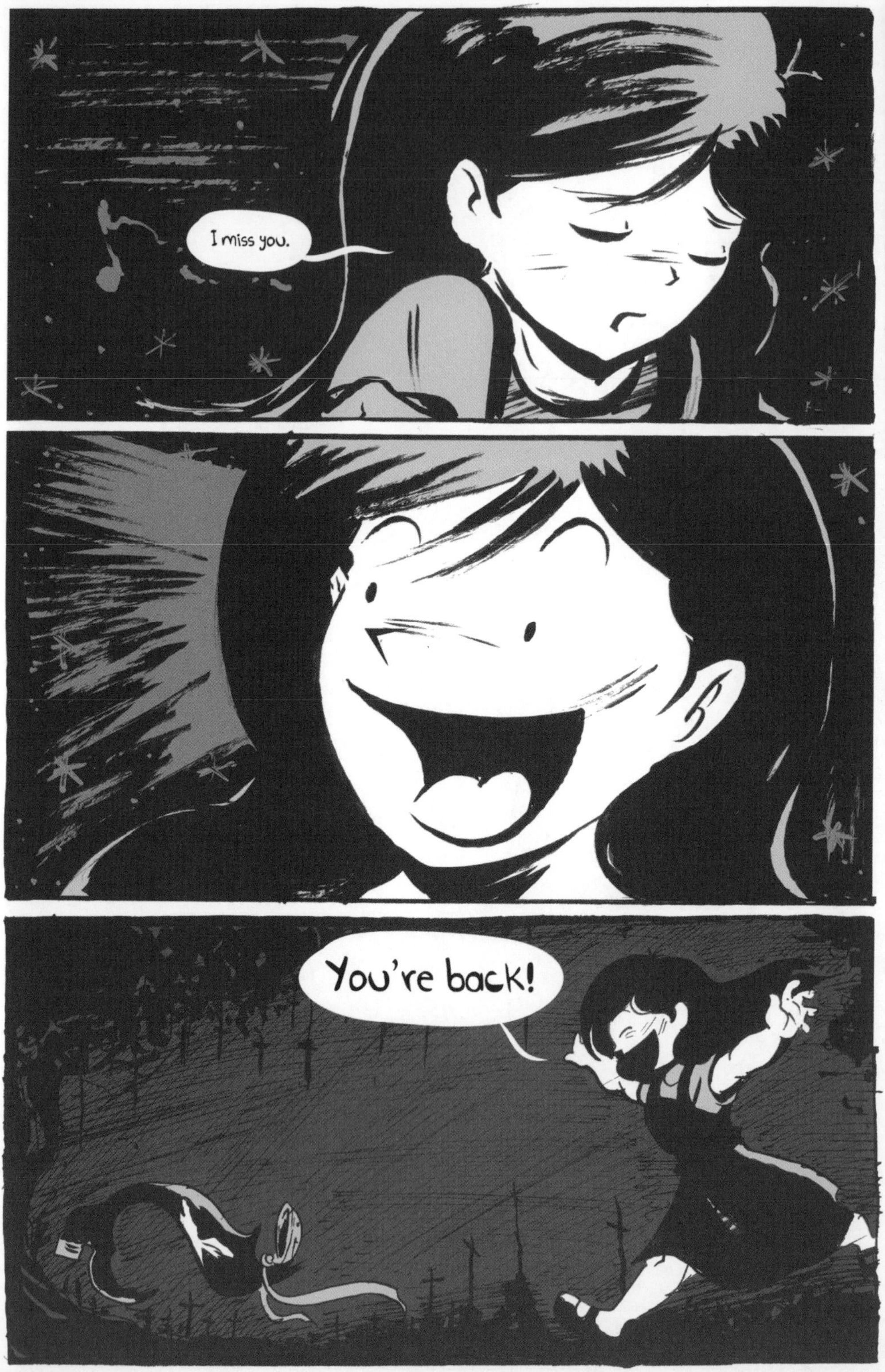
I miss you.
You're back!

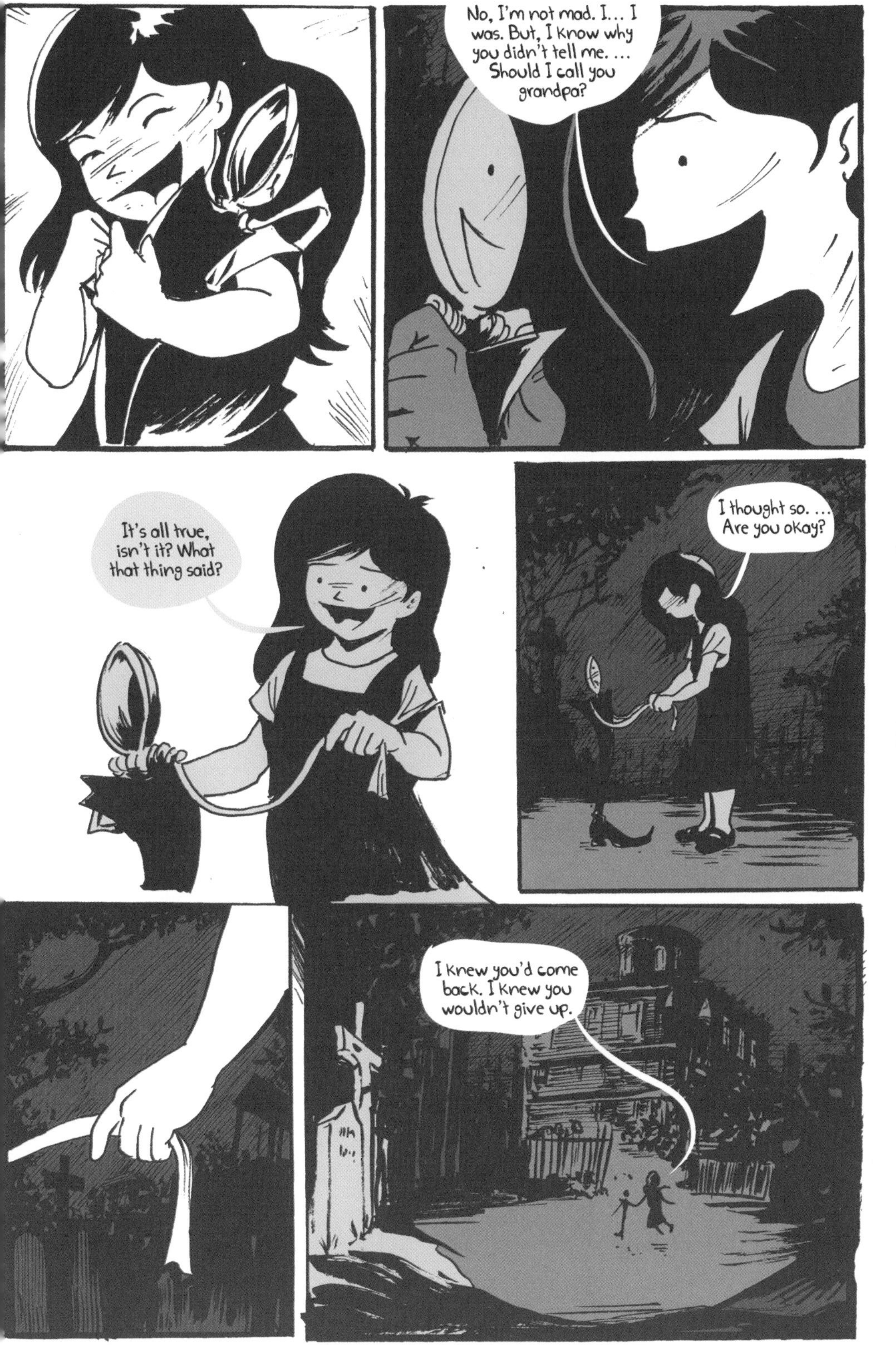
No, I'm not mad. I... I was. But, I know why you didn't tell me. ... Should I call you grandpa?
It's all true, isn't it? What that thing said?
I thought so. ... Are you okay?
I knew you'd come back. I knew you wouldn't give up.

Chapter Seven

Into history…

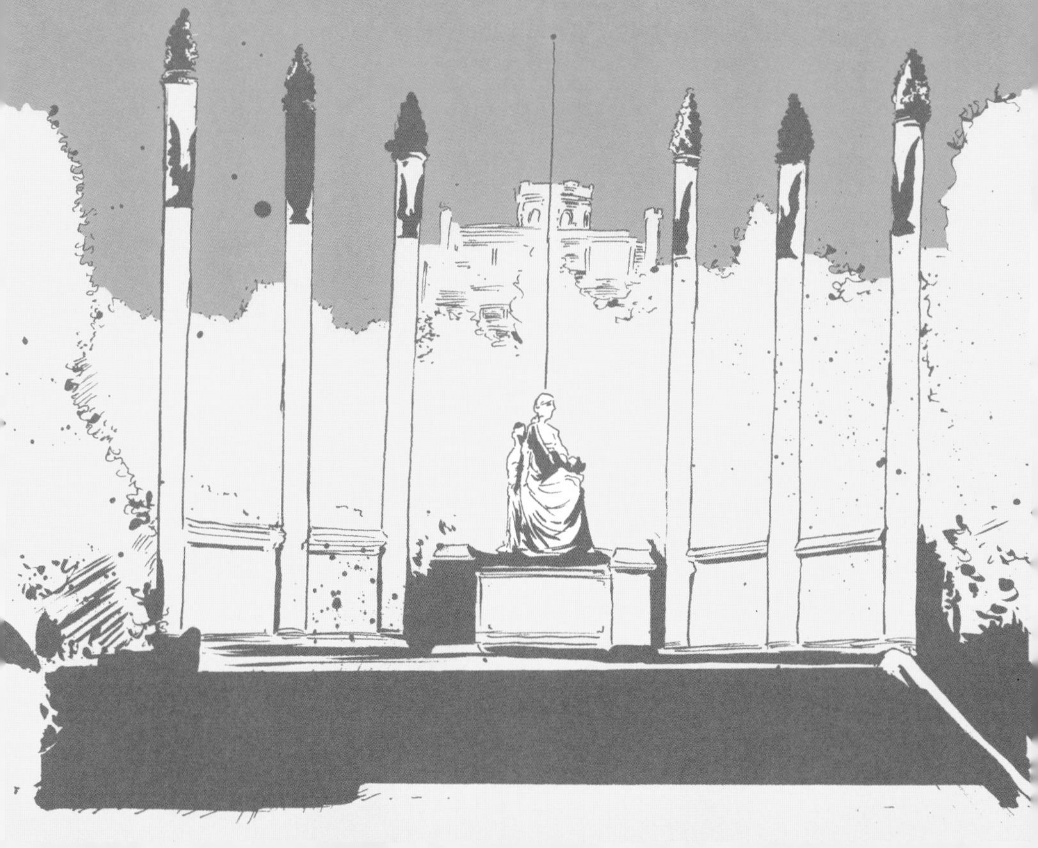

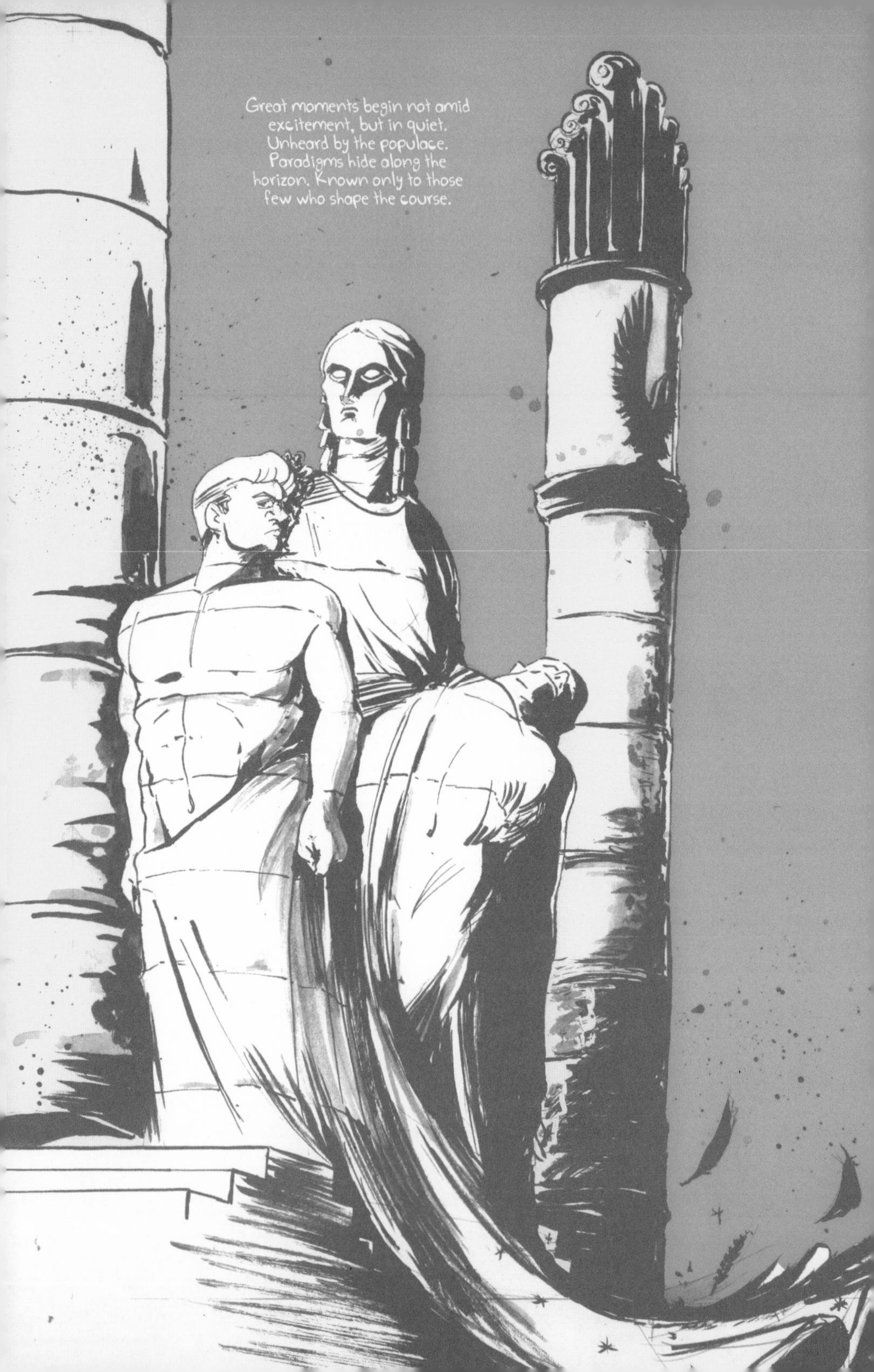
Great moments begin not amid excitement, but in quiet. Unheard by the populace. Paradigms hide along the horizon. Known only to those few who shape the course.

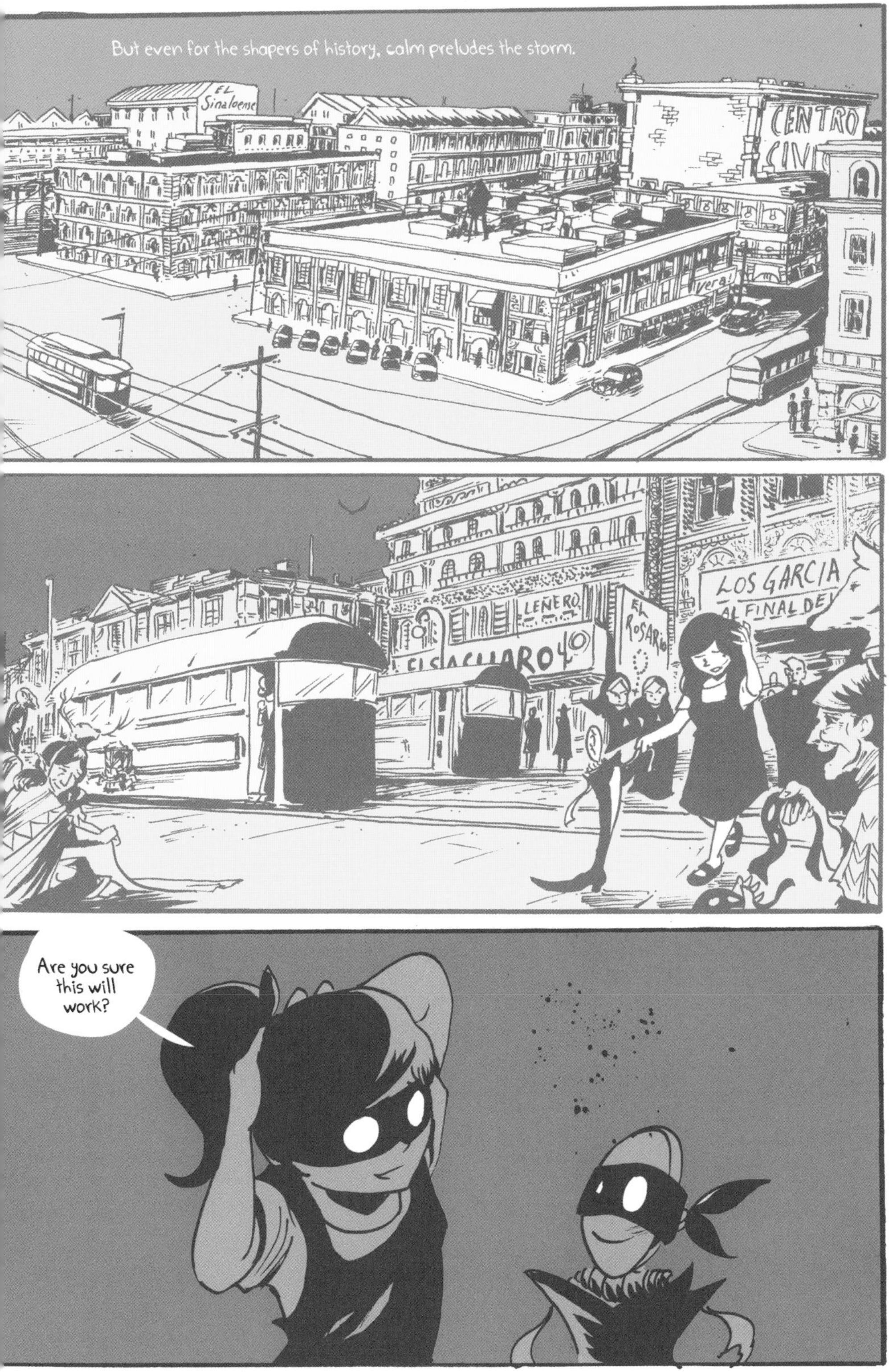
But even for the shapers of history, calm preludes the storm.
EL Sinaloense
CENTRO
LOS GARCIA
AL FINAL DE
LEÑERO
EL ROSARIO
Are you sure this will work?

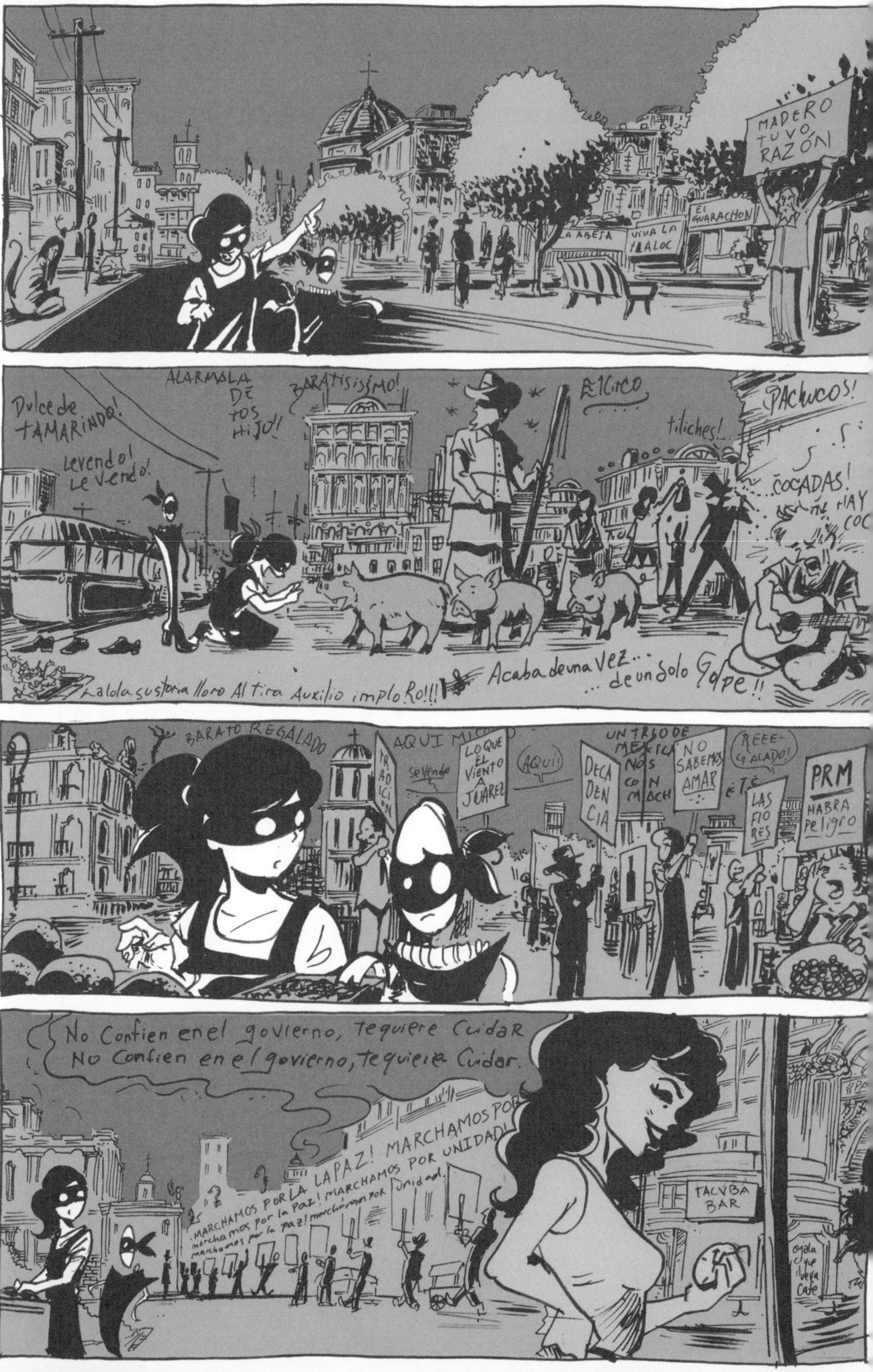
MADERO TUVO RAZÓN
LA ABEJA
VIVA LA TLALOC
EL GUARACHON
Dulce de TAMARINDO!
ALARMALA DE TOS HIJO!
BARATISISIMO!
¡PACHUCOS!
tiliches!
Le vendo! Le vendo!
COCADAS!
Lalola sustoria lloro Al tira Auxilio imploRo!!!
Acaba de una vez... de un solo Golpe!!
BARATO REGALADO
TRADICION
se vendo
LO QUE EL VIENTO A JUAREZ
AQUI
DECADENCIA
NO SABEMOS AMAR
REEE-GALADO!
LAS FLORES
PRM HABRA peligro
No Confien enel govierno, tequiere Cuidar
No Confien enel govierno, tequiere Cuidar.
MARCHAMOS POR LA PAZ! MARCHAMOS POR UNIDAD!
marchamos por la paz! marchamos por unidad.
TACUBA BAR
ojala que llueva cafe

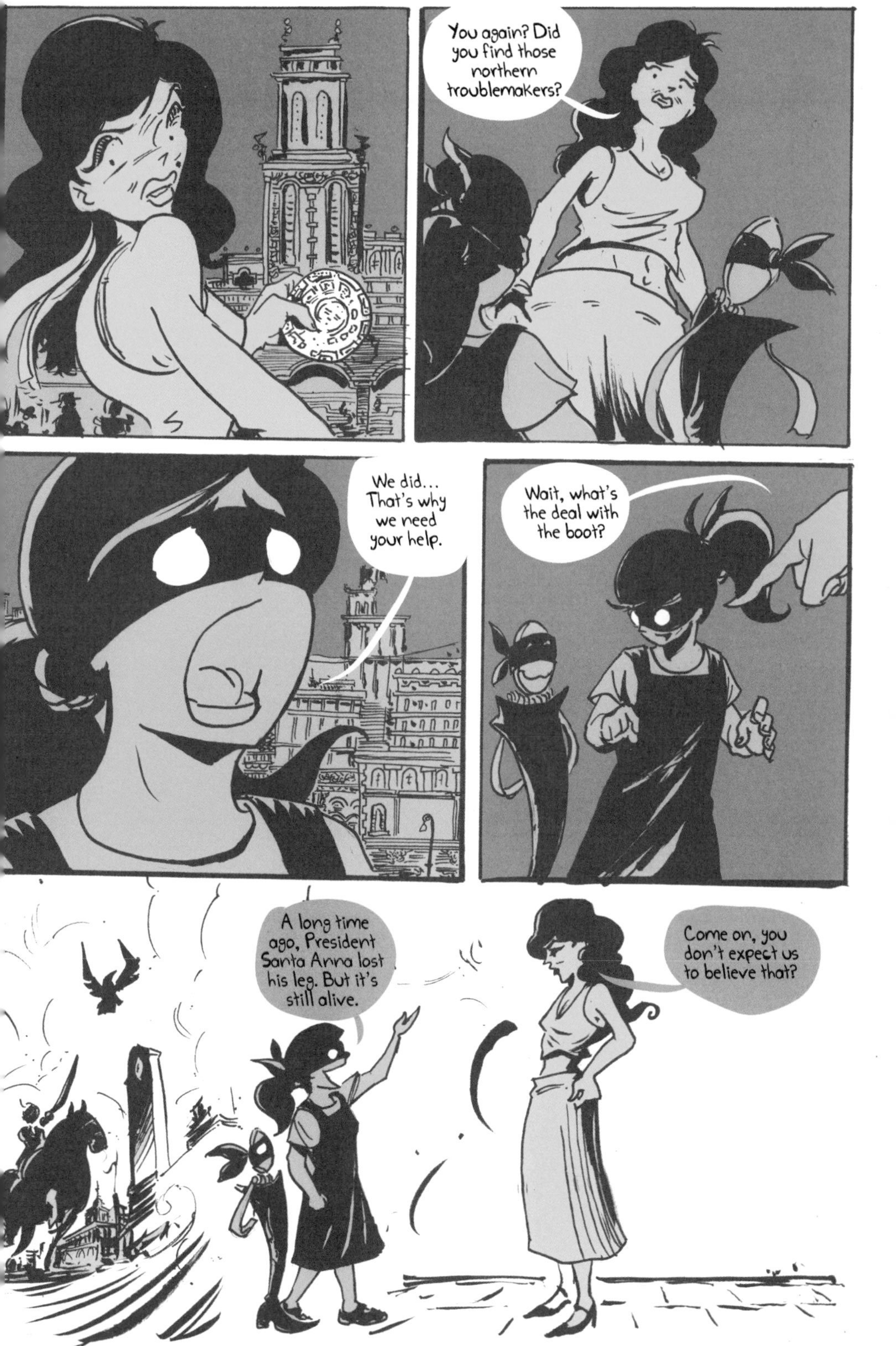
You again? Did you find those northern troublemakers?
We did... That's why we need your help.
Wait, what's the deal with the boot?
A long time ago, President Santa Anna lost his leg. But it's still alive.
Come on, you don't expect us to believe that?

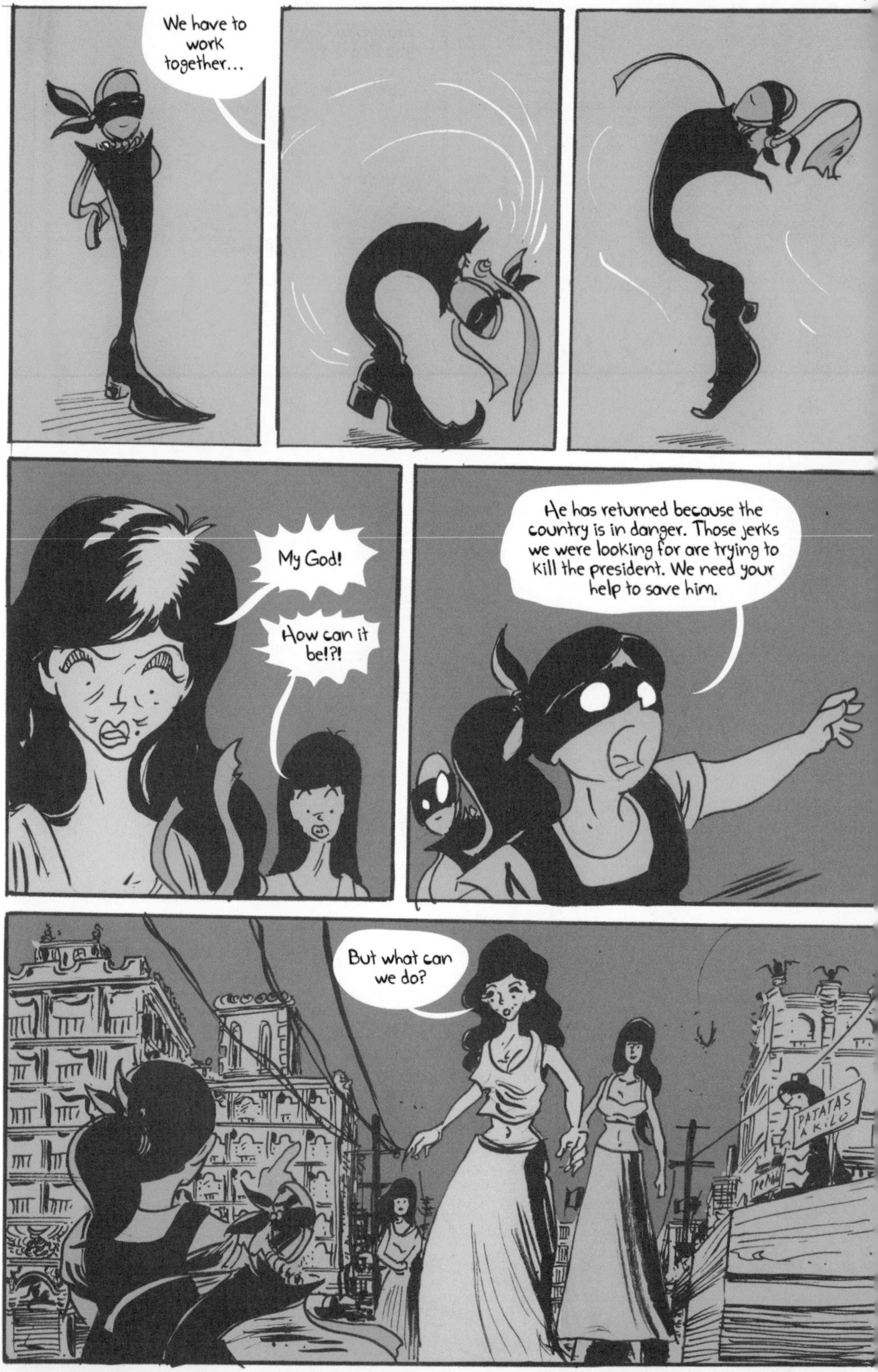
We have to work together...
My God!
How can it be!?!
He has returned because the country is in danger. Those jerks we were looking for are trying to kill the president. We need your help to save him.
But what can we do?
PATATAS A KILO

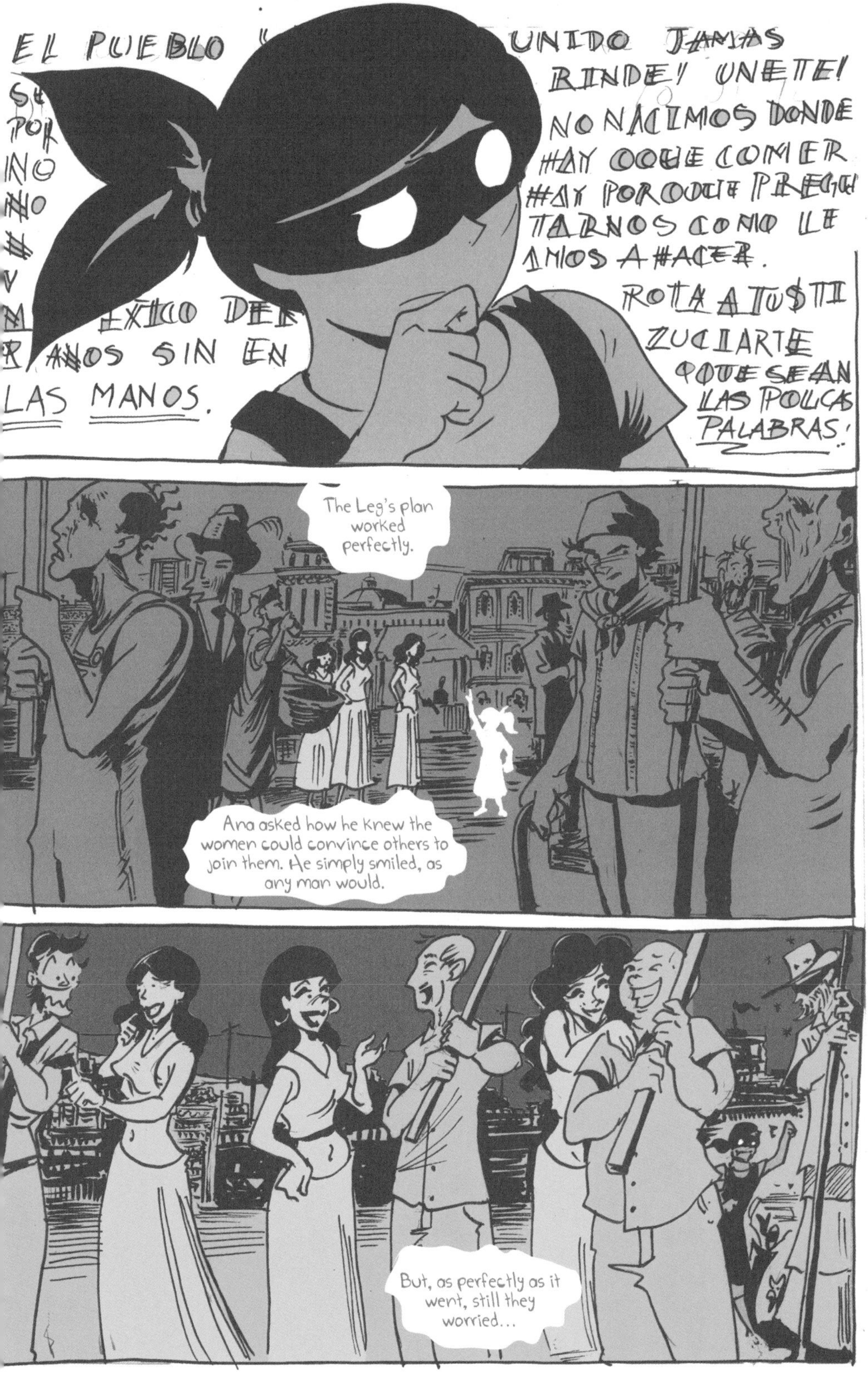
EL PUEBLO
UNIDO JAMAS RINDE! UNETE!
NO NACIMOS DONDE
LAS MANOS.
PALABRAS!
The Leg's plan worked perfectly.
Ana asked how he knew the women could convince others to join them. He simply smiled, as any man would.
But, as perfectly as it went, still they worried...

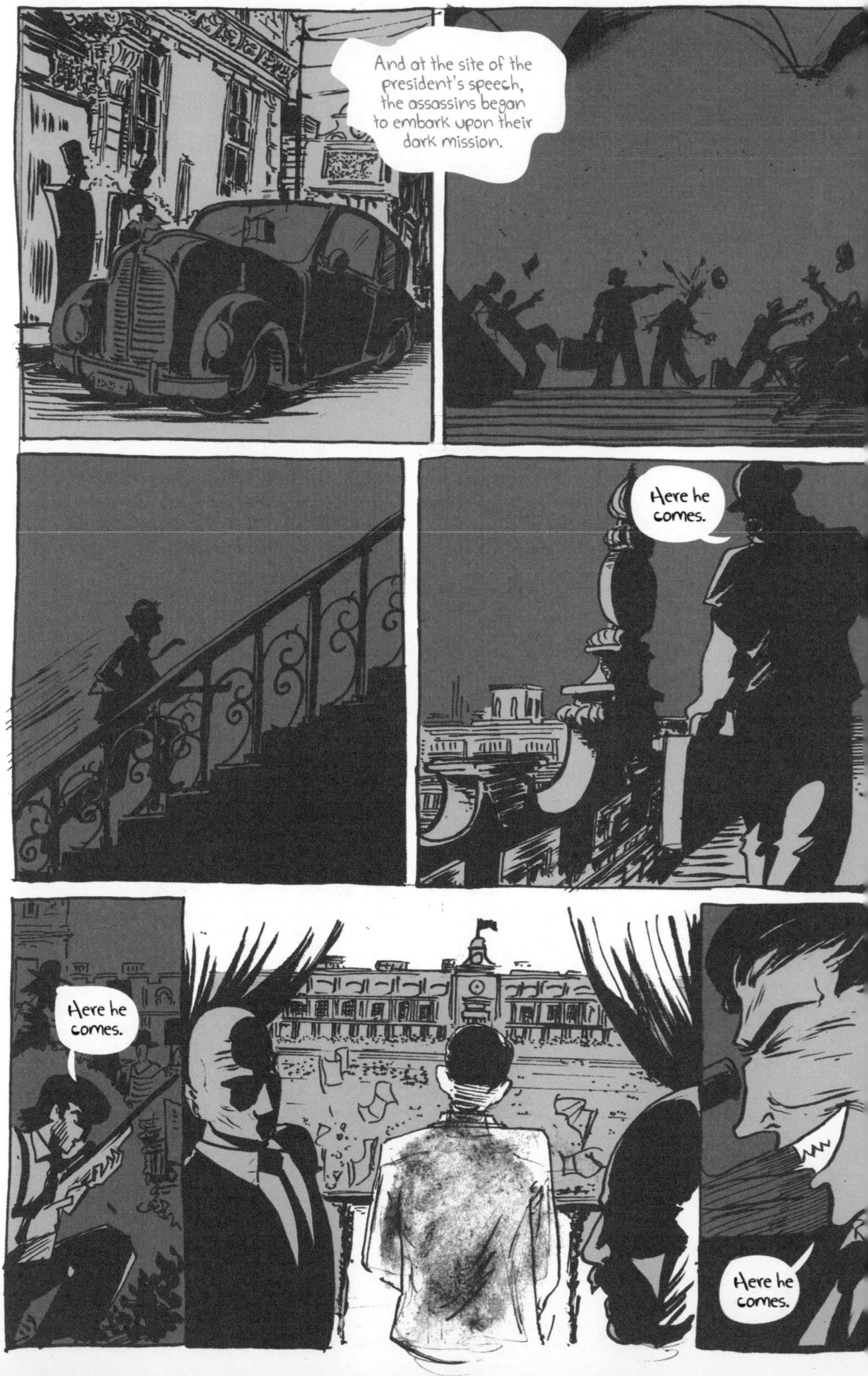
And at the site of the president's speech, the assassins began to embark upon their dark mission.
Here he comes.
Here he comes.
Here he comes.

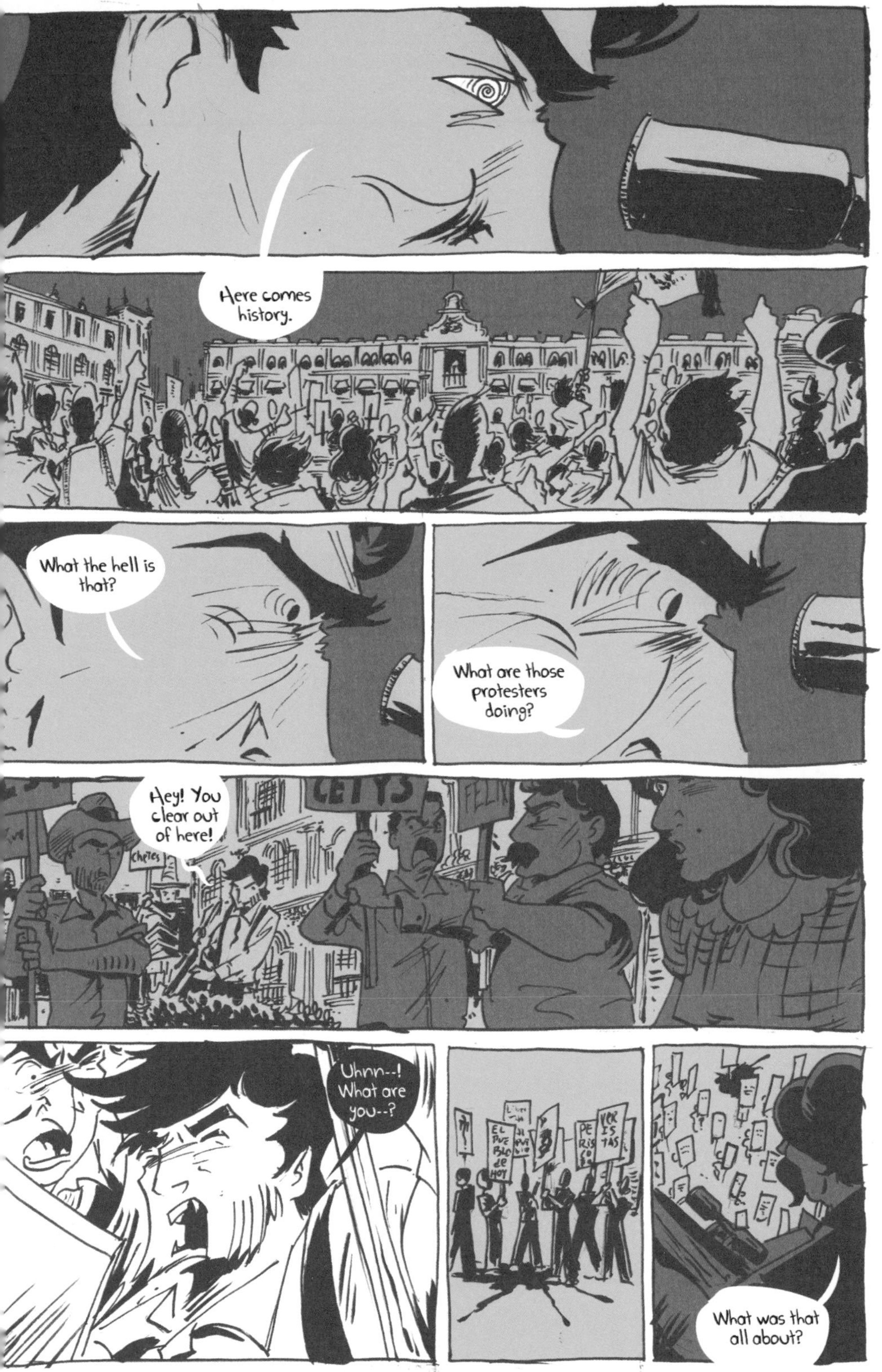
Here comes history.
What the hell is that?
What are those protesters doing?
CETYS
Hey! You clear out of here!
Uhnn--! What are you--?
EL PUEBLO de HOY
PERIODISTAS
What was that all about?

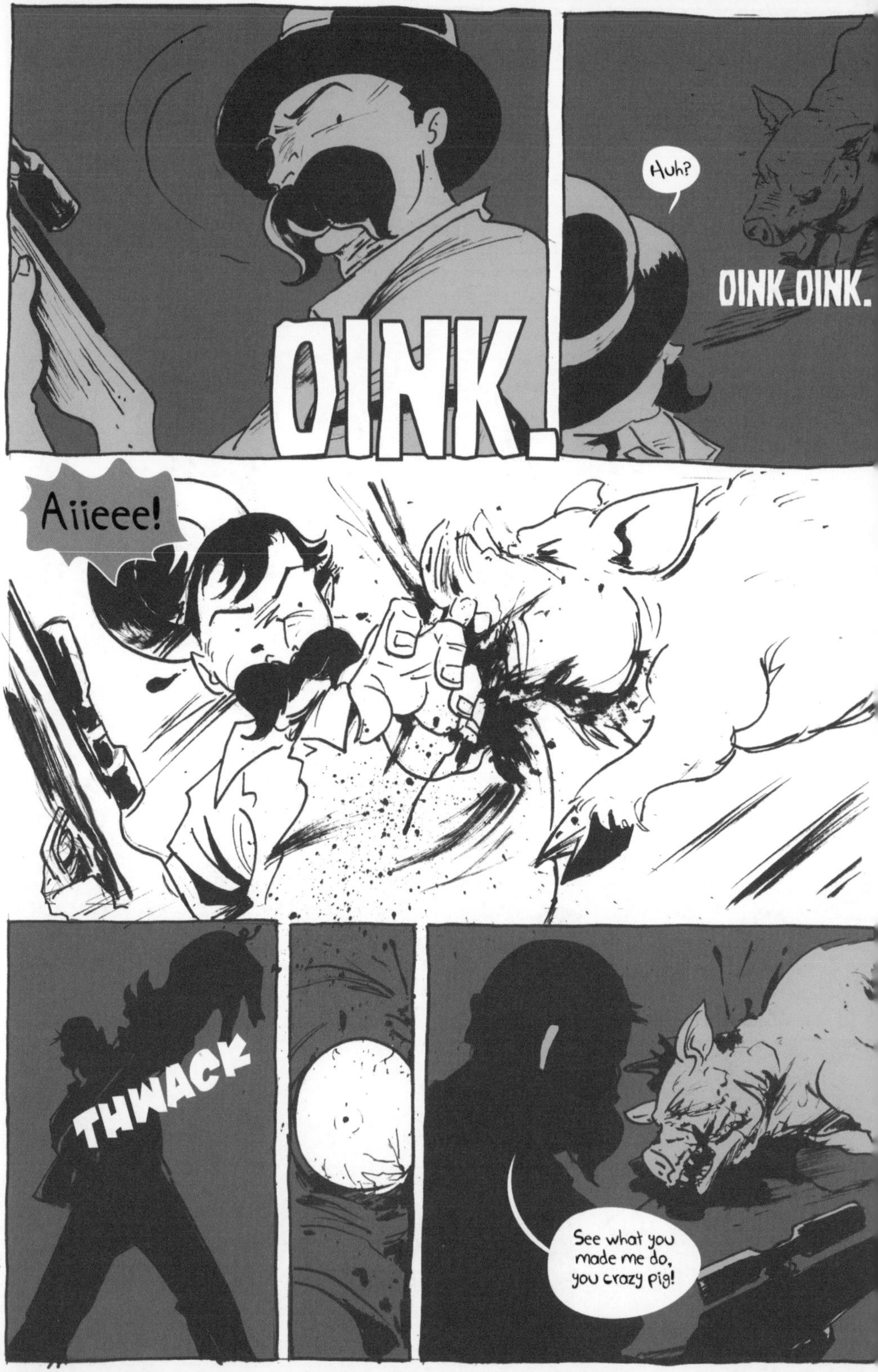
OINK.
Huh?
OINK.OINK.
Aiieee!
THWACK
See what you made me do, you crazy pig!

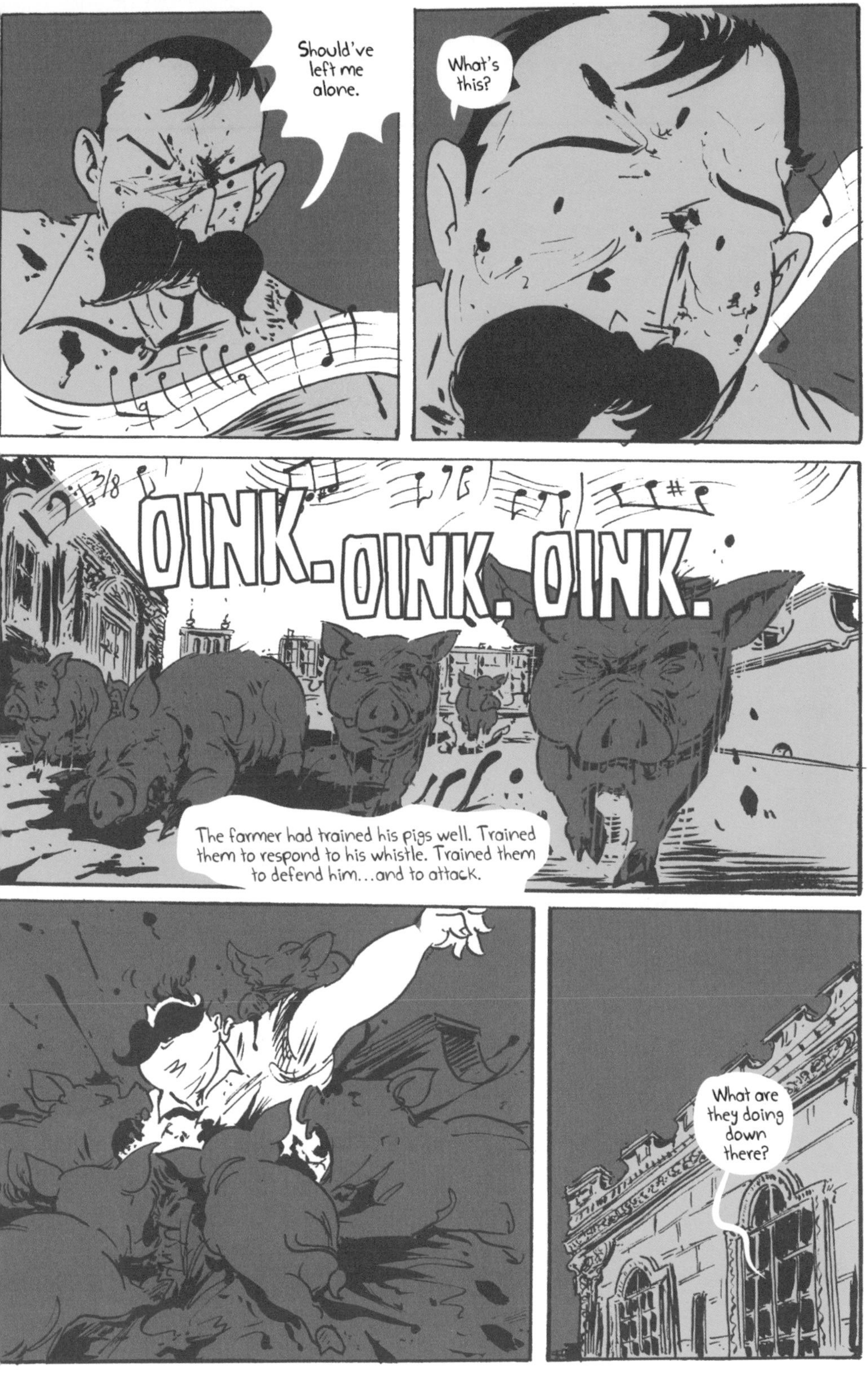
Should've left me alone.
What's this?
3/8
OINK. OINK. OINK.
The farmer had trained his pigs well. Trained them to respond to his whistle. Trained them to defend him...and to attack.
What are they doing down there?

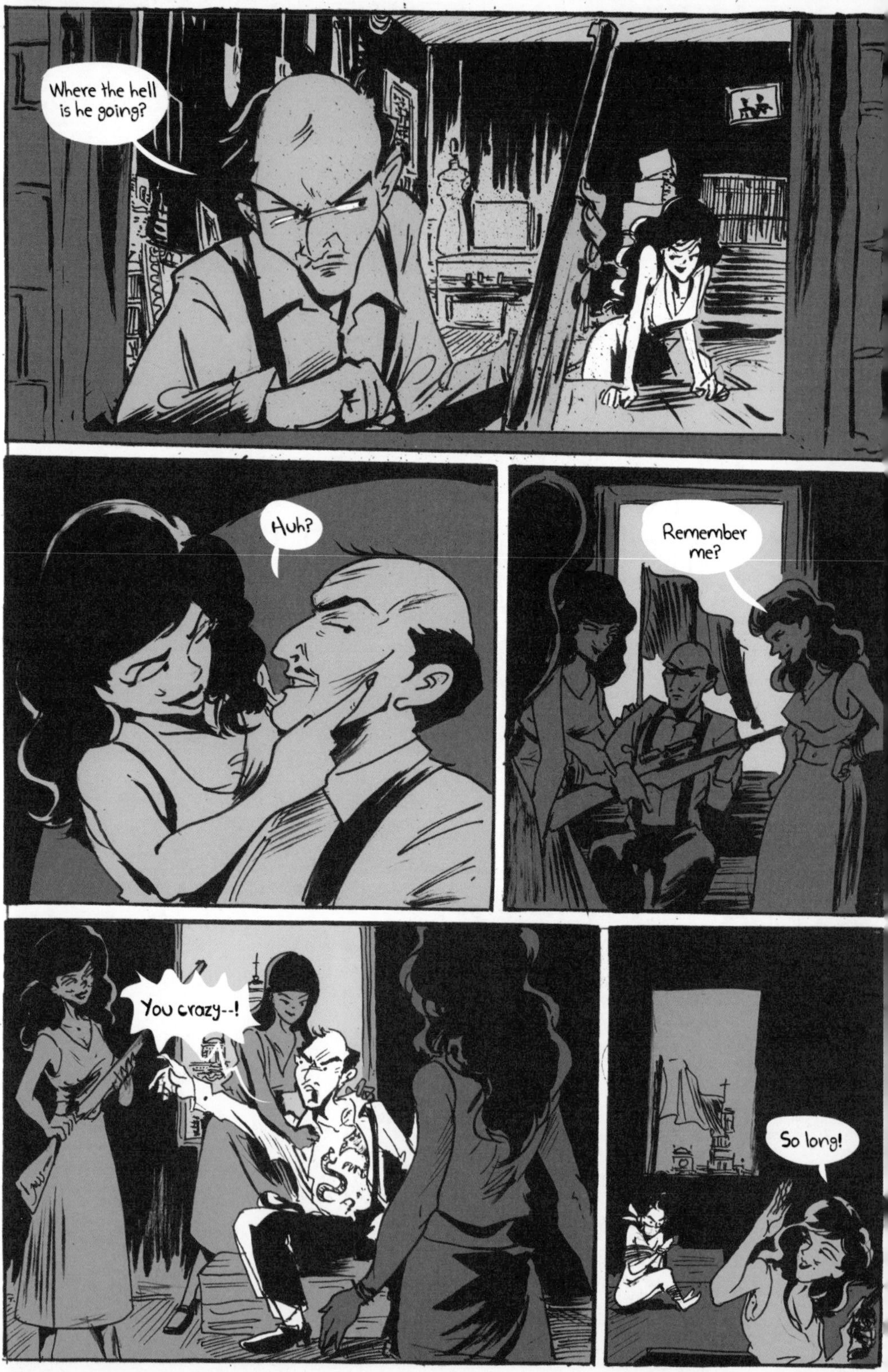
Where the hell is he going?
Huh?
Remember me?
You crazy--!
So long!

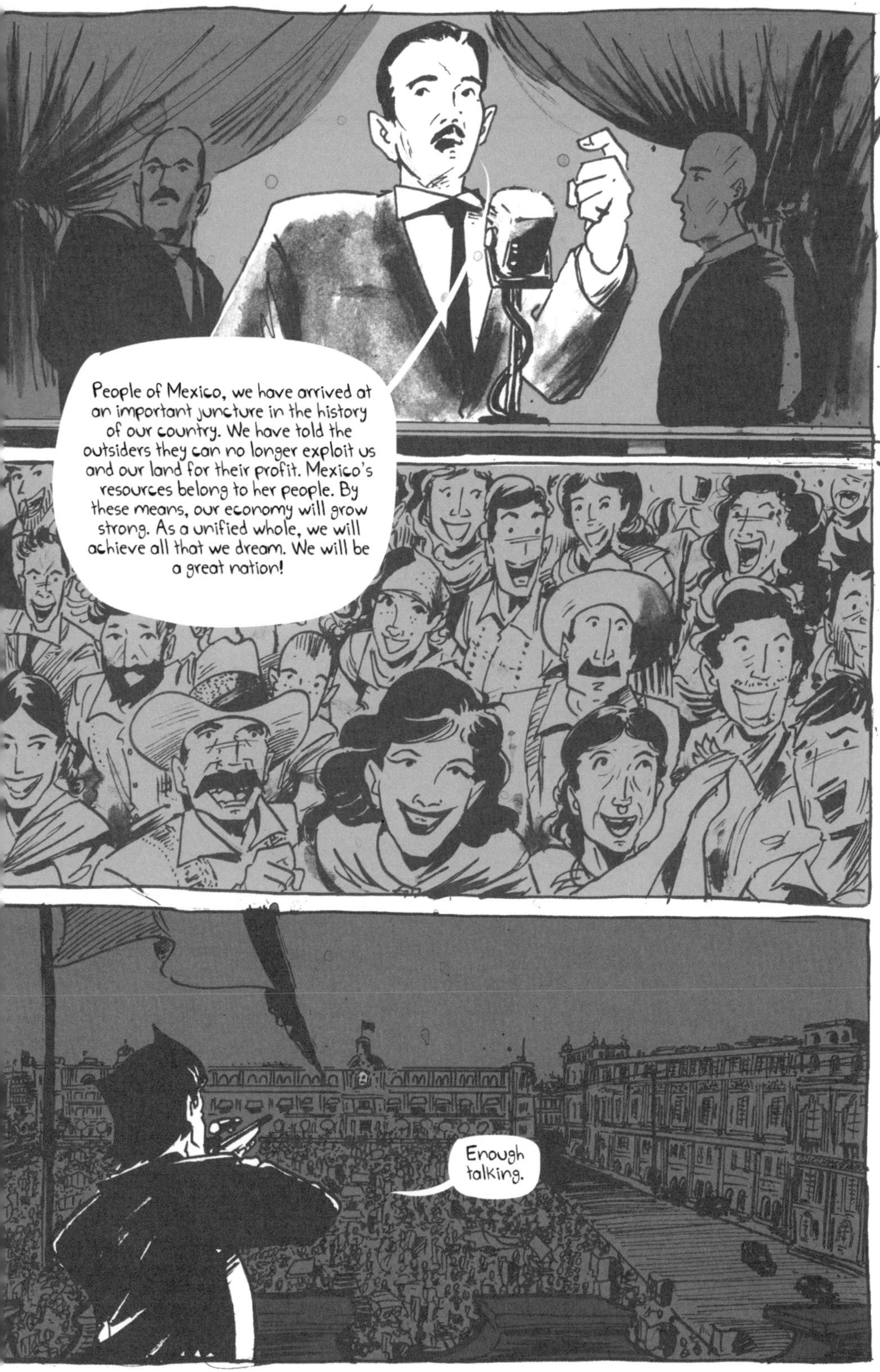
People of Mexico, we have arrived at an important juncture in the history of our country. We have told the outsiders they can no longer exploit us and our land for their profit. Mexico's resources belong to her people. By these means, our economy will grow strong. As a unified whole, we will achieve all that we dream. We will be a great nation!
Enough talking.

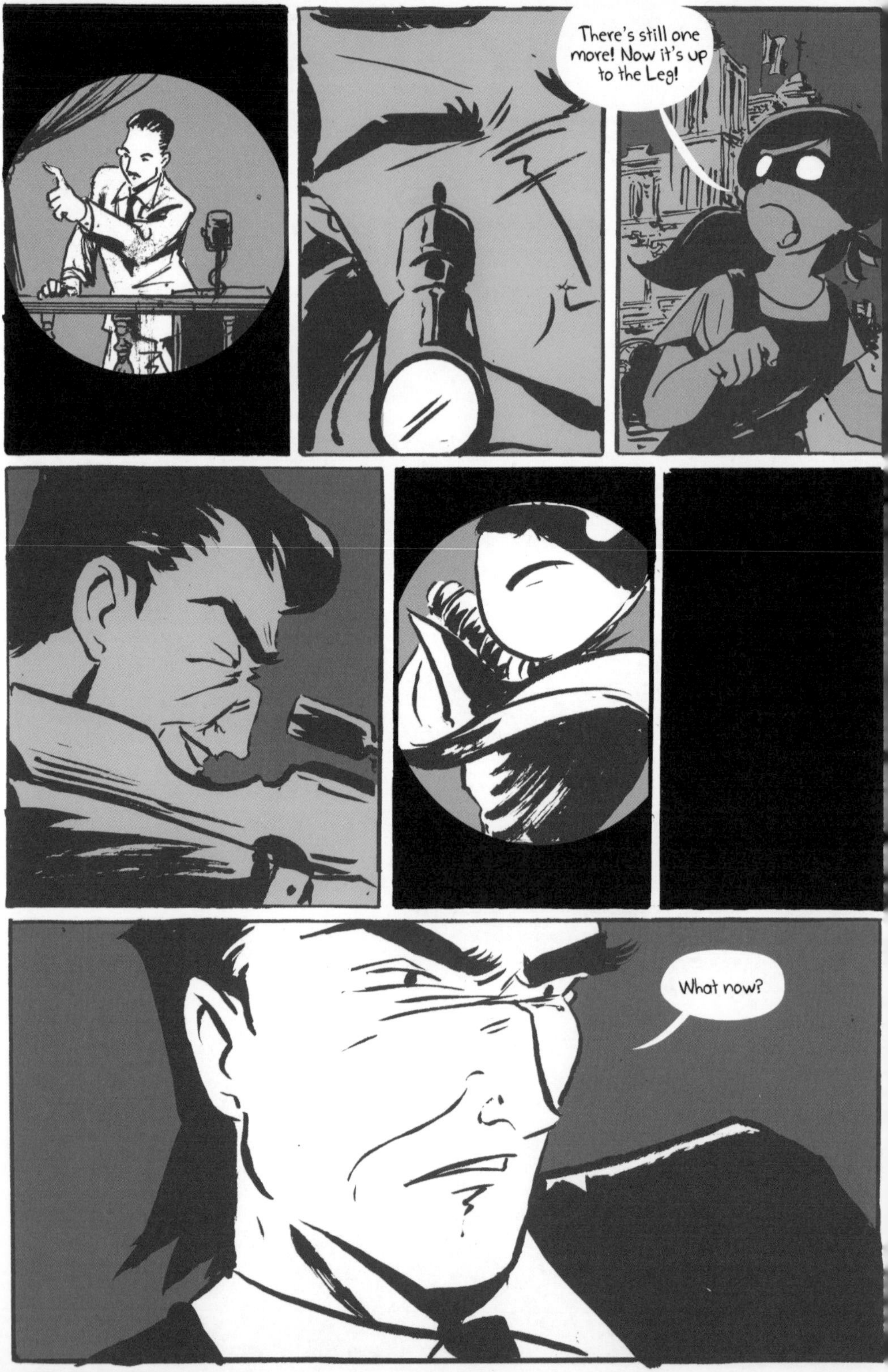
There's still one more! Now it's up to the Leg!
What now?

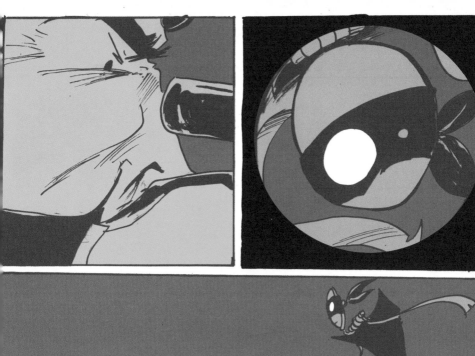

You again.

...that old man.

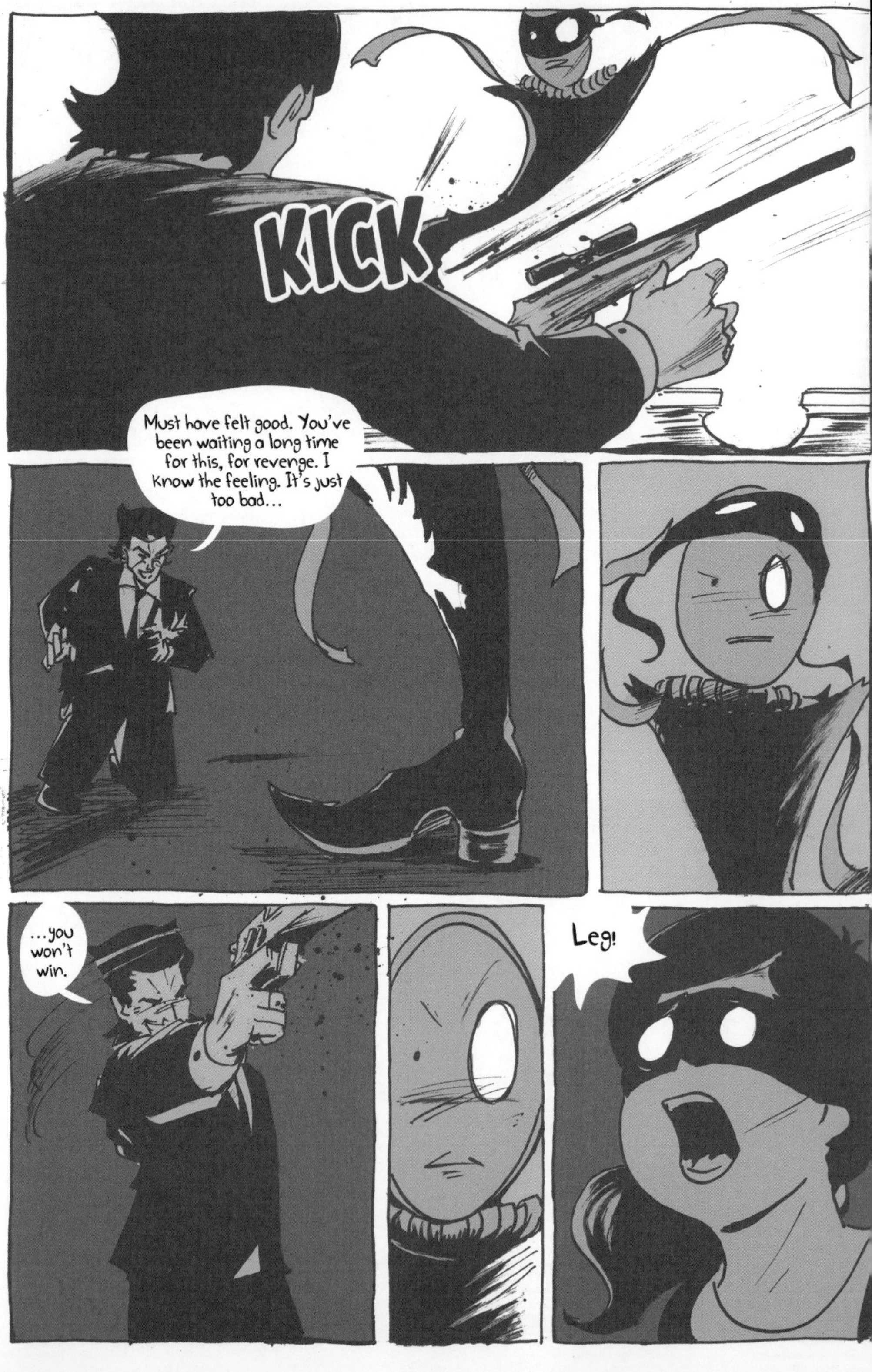
KICK
Must have felt good. You've been waiting a long time for this, for revenge. I know the feeling. It's just too bad...
...you won't win.
Leg!

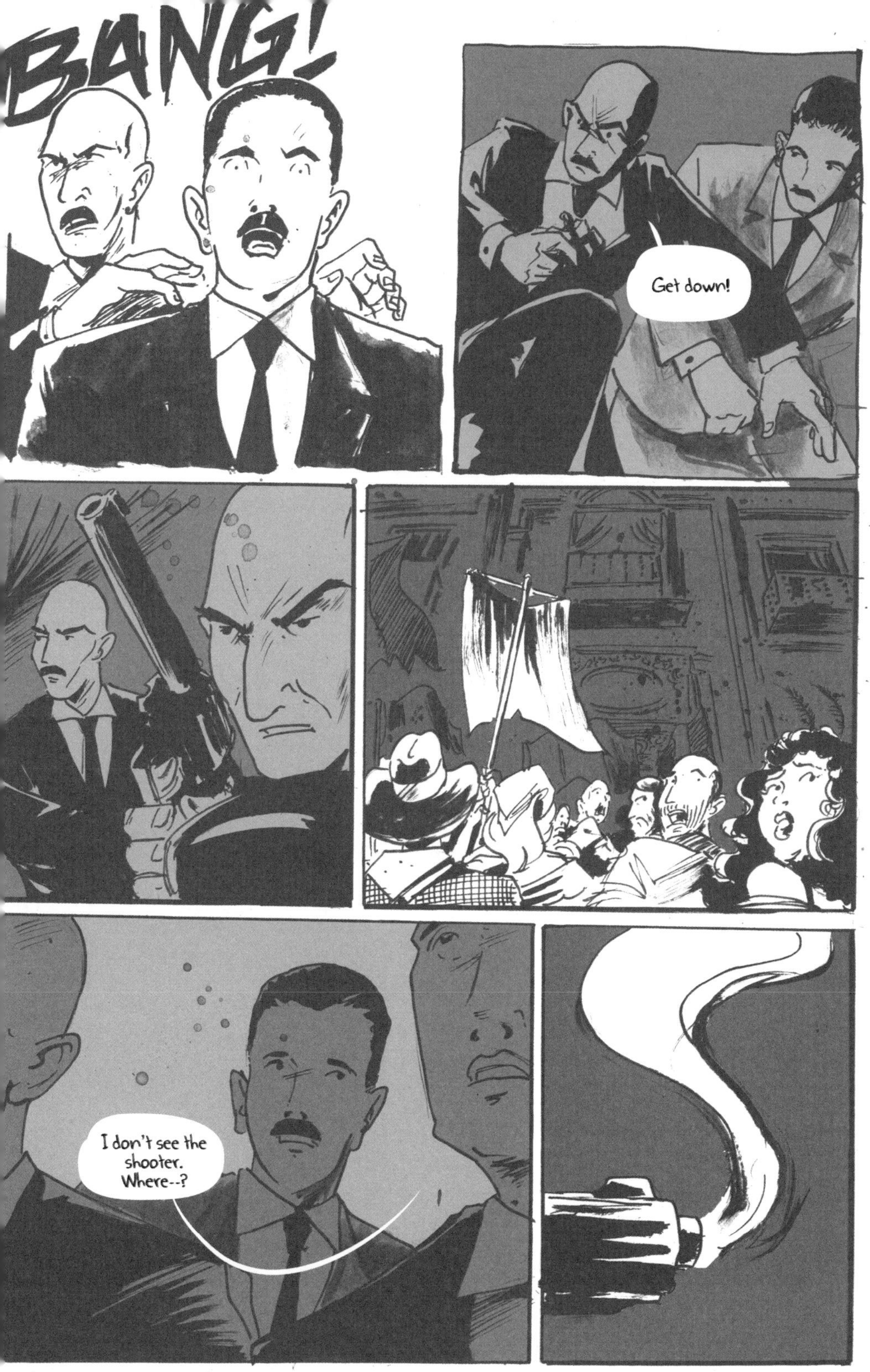

BANG!
Get down!
I don't see the shooter. Where--?

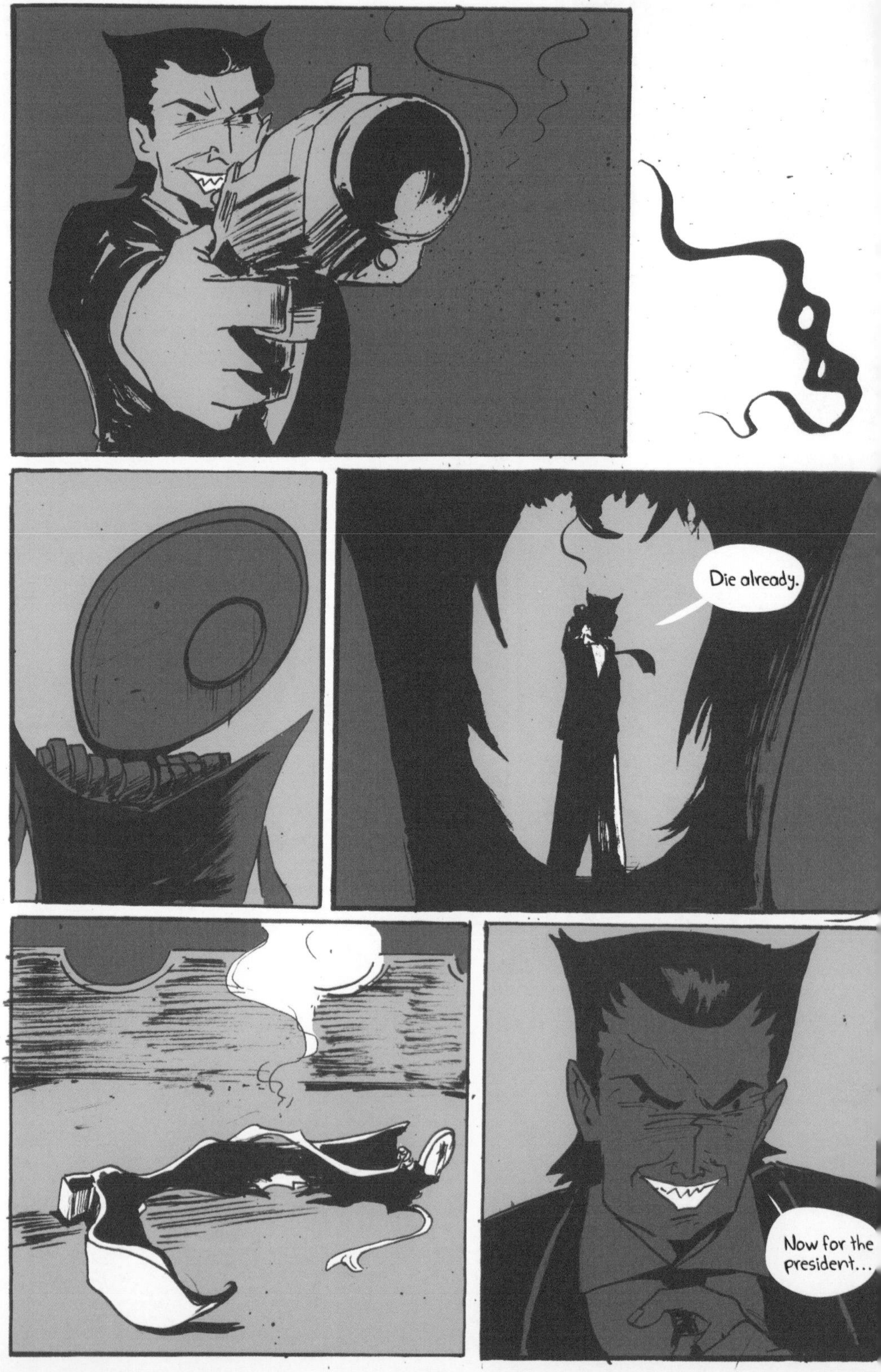
Die already.
Now for the president...

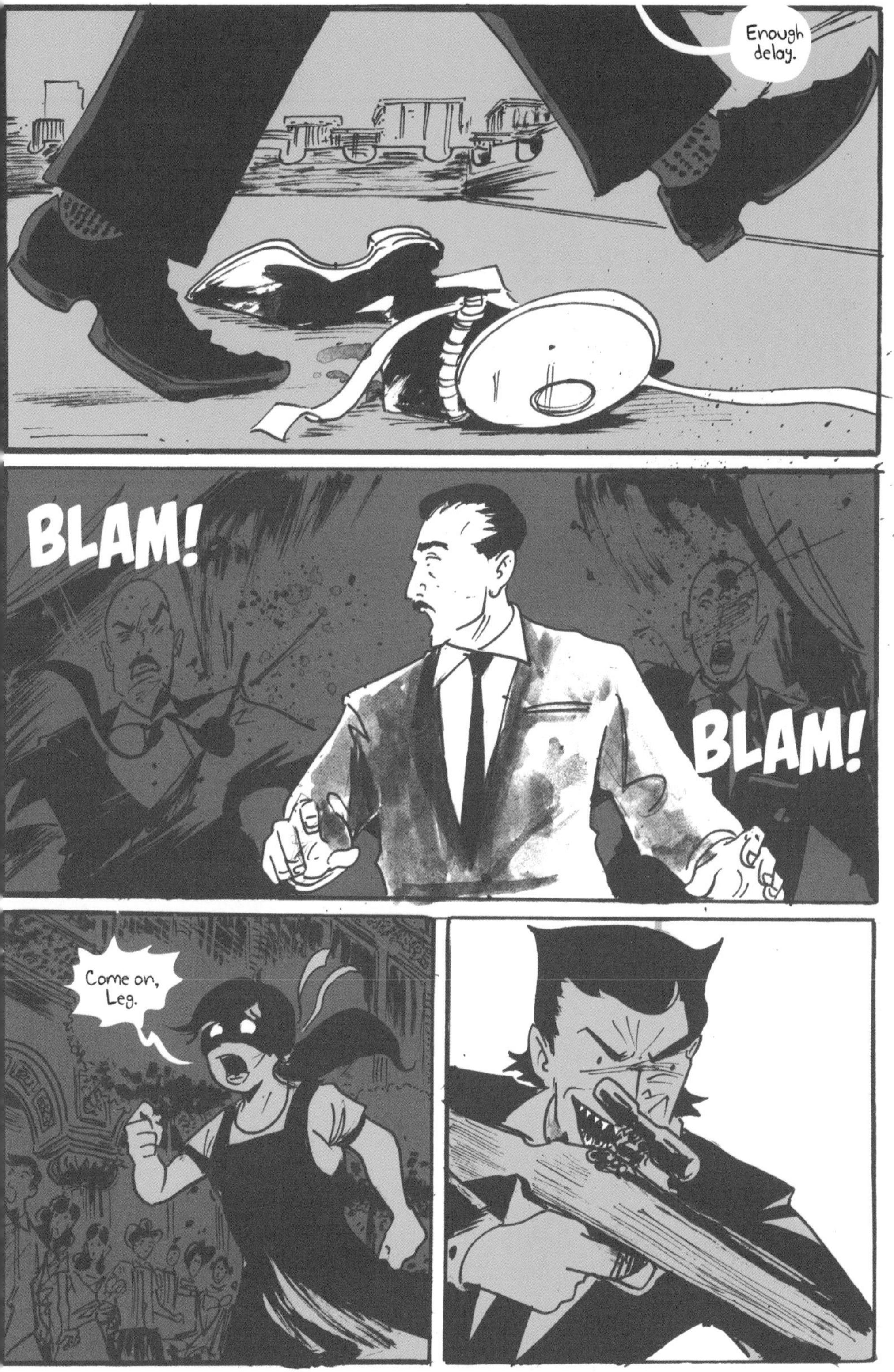
Enough delay.
BLAM!
BLAM!
Come on, Leg.

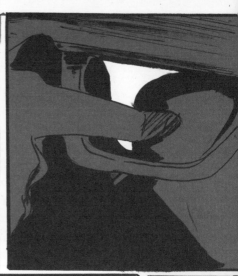

No!

Leg!

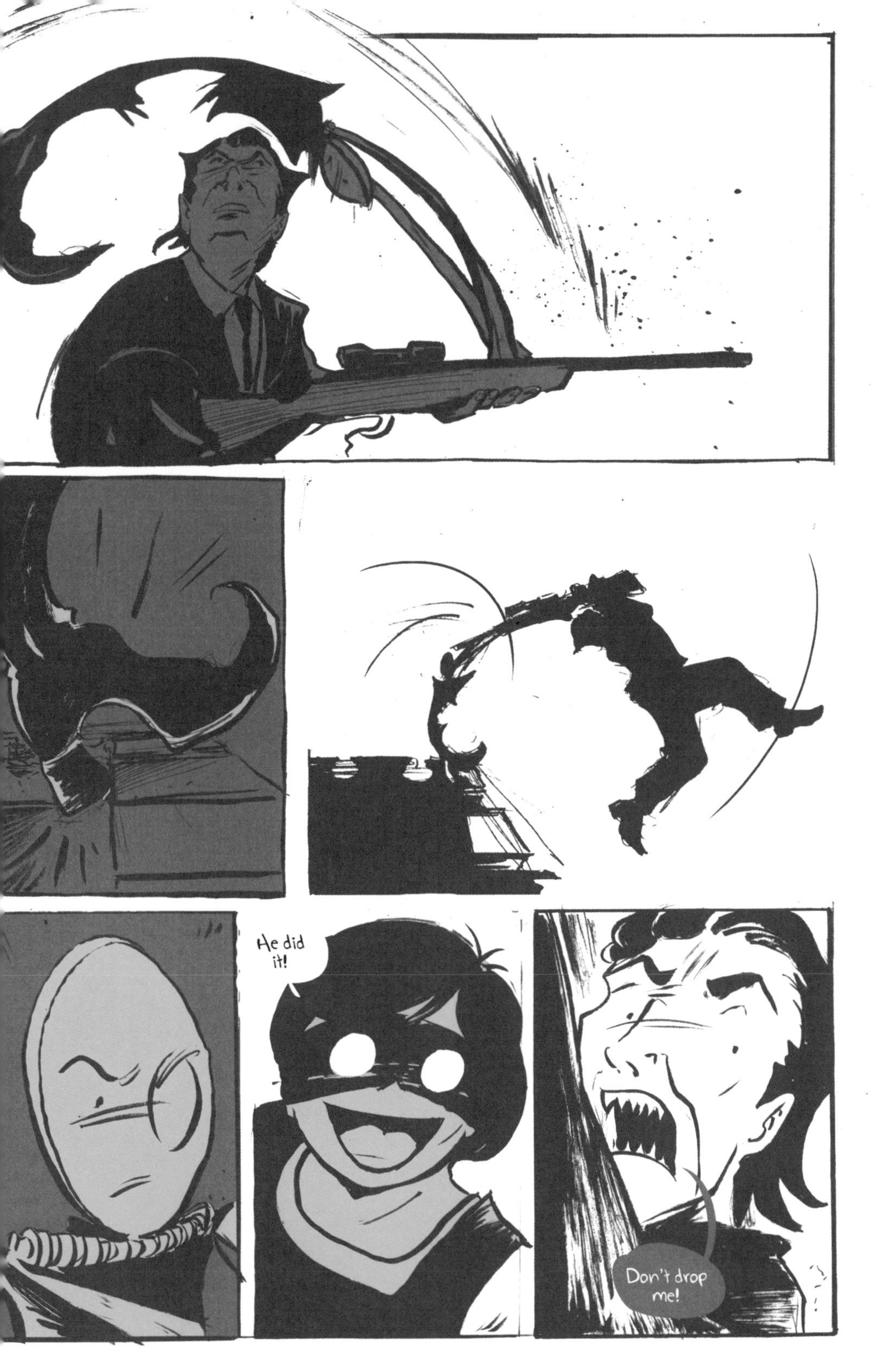
He did it!
Don't drop me!

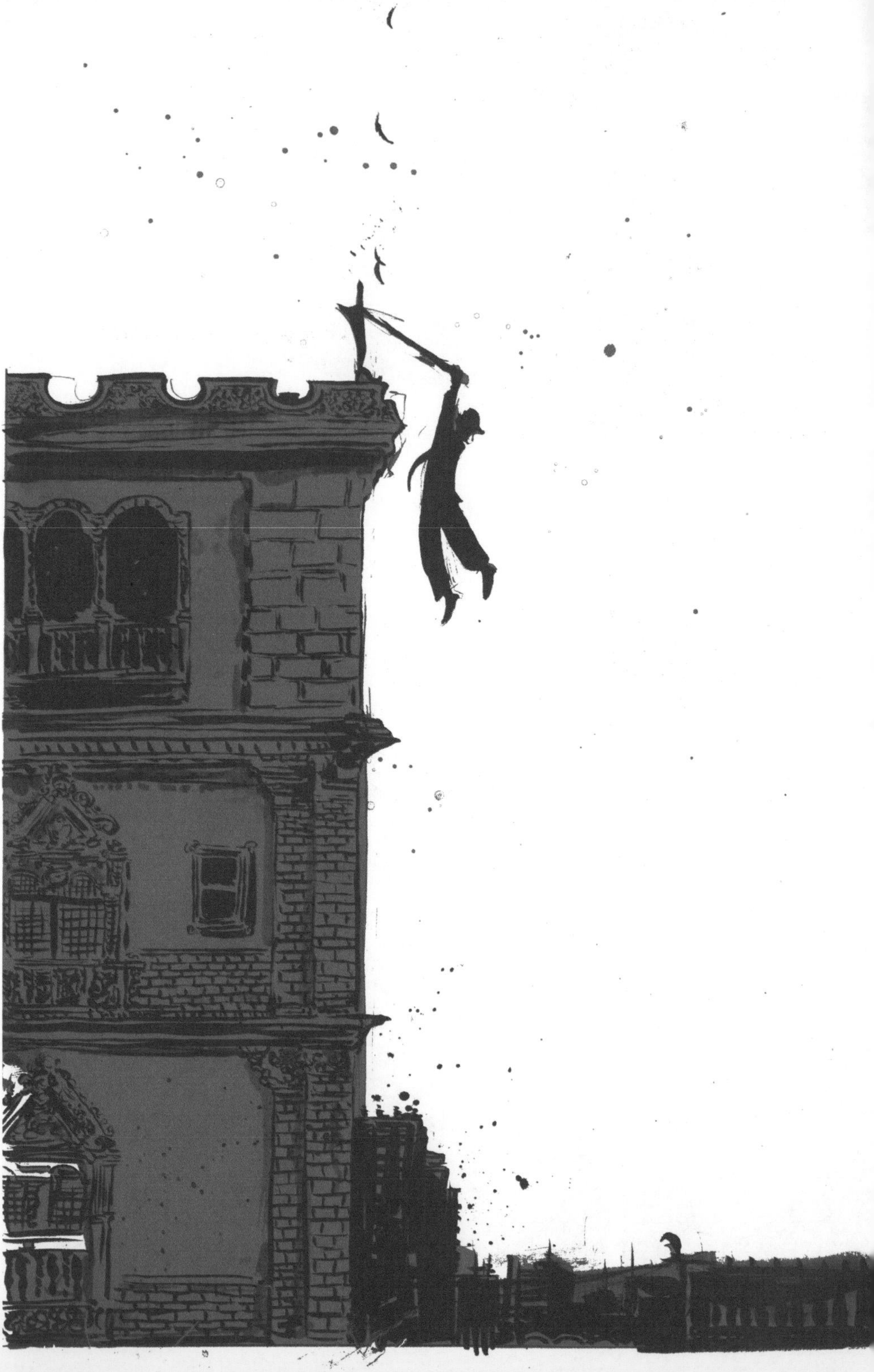

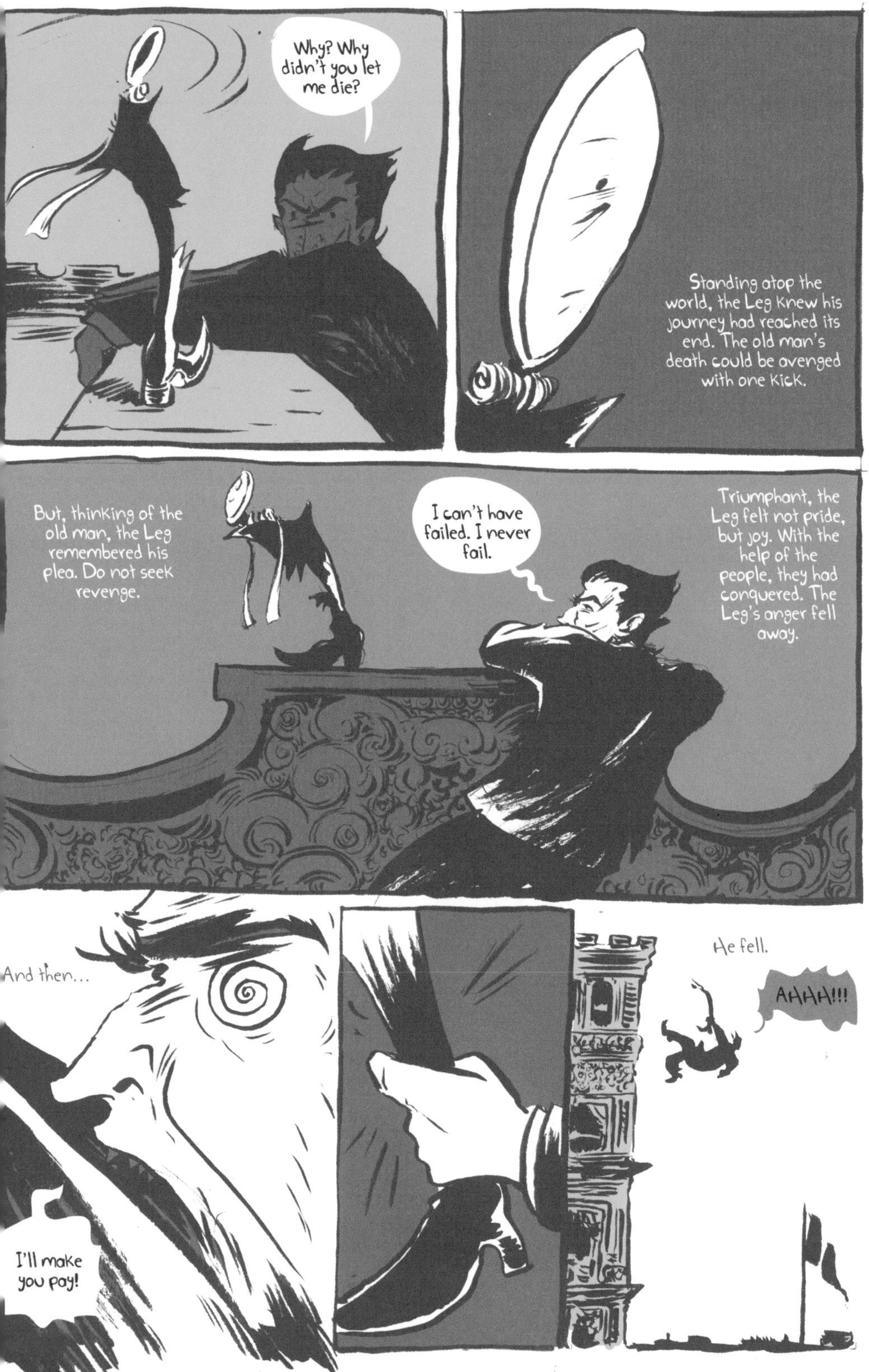
Why? Why didn't you let me die?
Standing atop the world, the Leg knew his journey had reached its end. The old man's death could be avenged with one kick.
But, thinking of the old man, the Leg remembered his plea. Do not seek revenge.
I can't have failed. I never fail.
Triumphant, the Leg felt not pride, but joy. With the help of the people, they had conquered. The Leg's anger fell away.
And then...
I'll make you pay!
He fell.
AHHH!!!

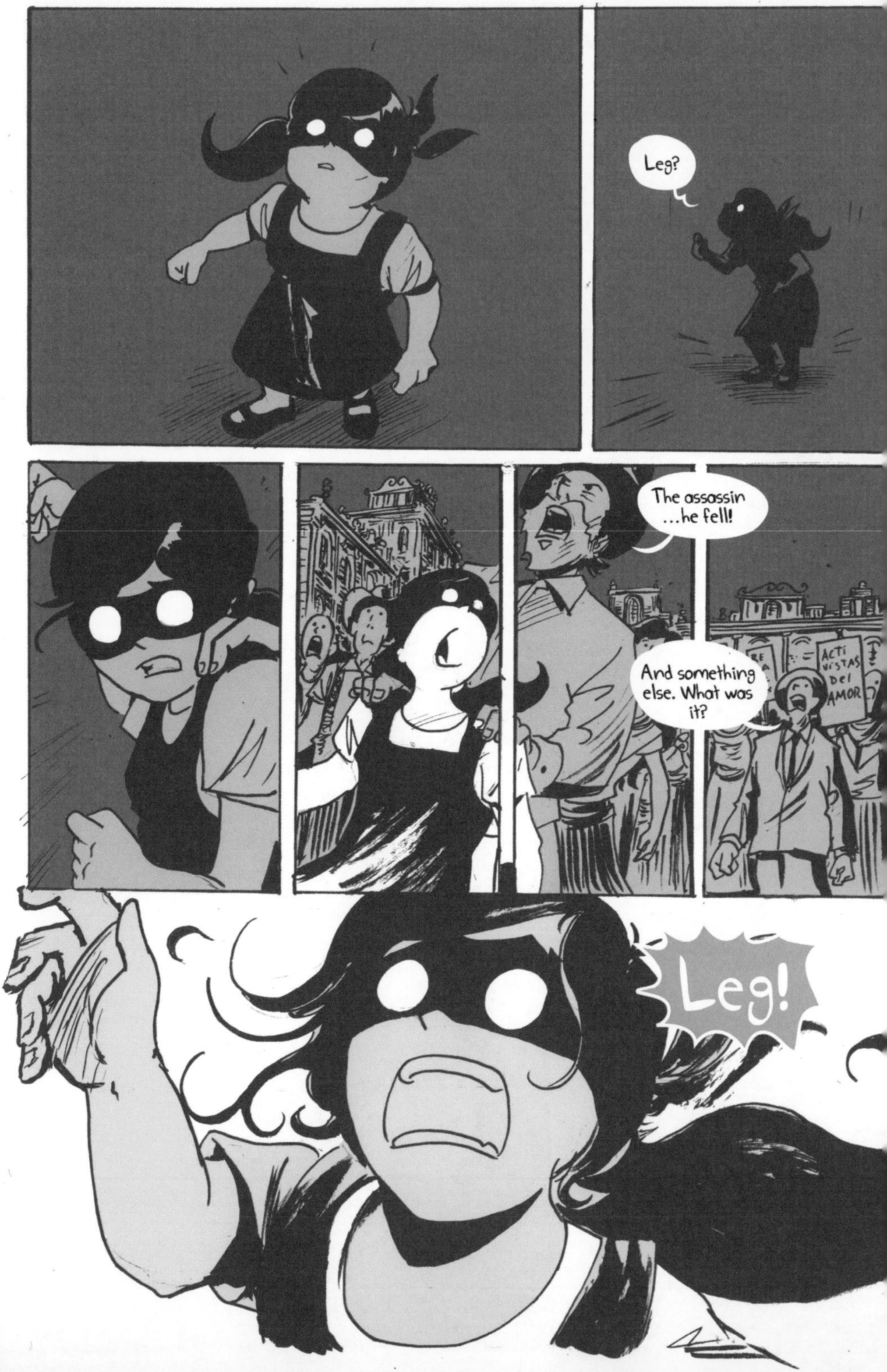
Leg?
The assassin ...he fell!
ACTI VISTAS Del AMOR
And something else. What was it?
Leg!

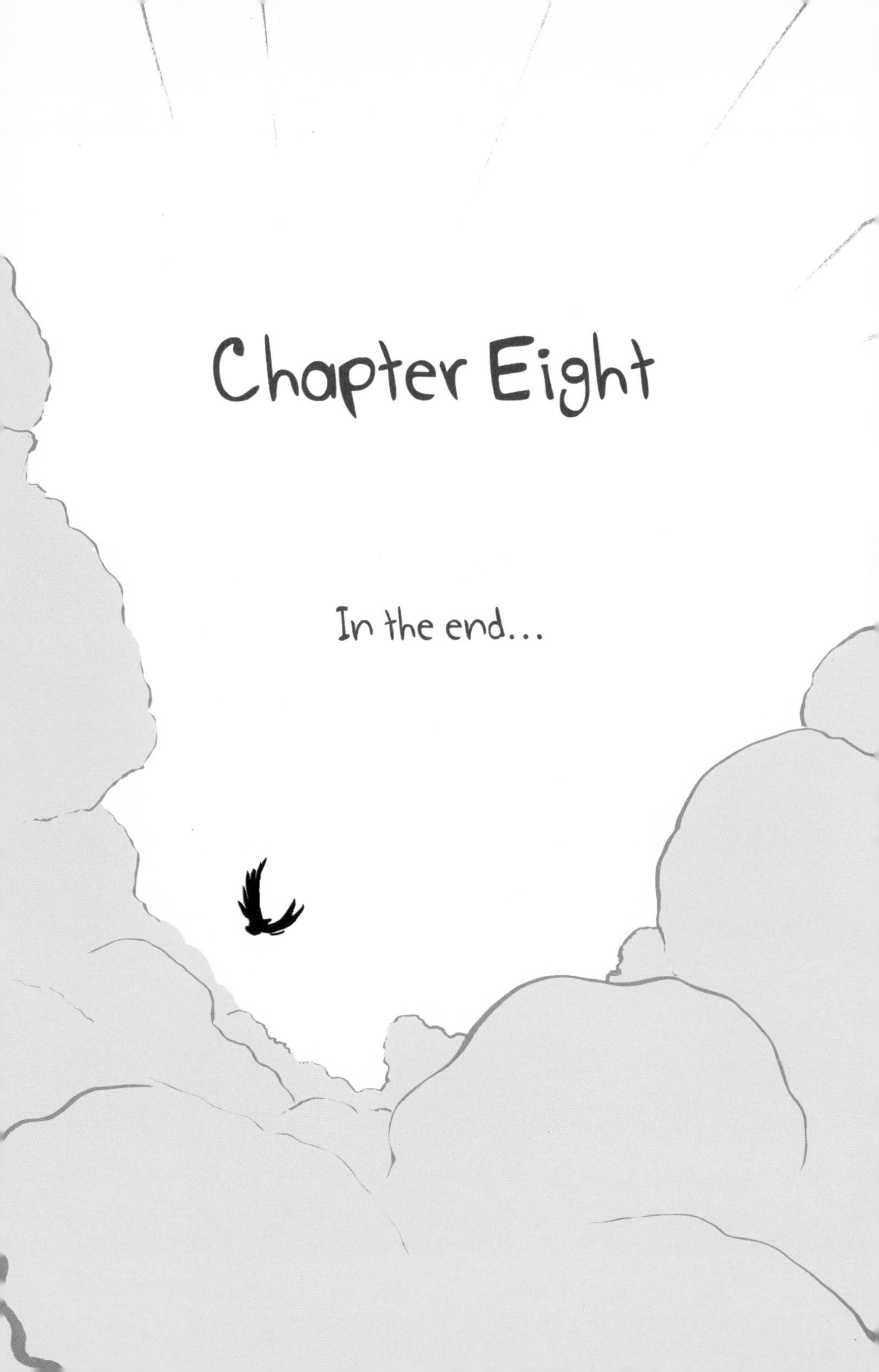
Chapter Eight
In the end...

Many miles, have I flown. …

Many sights, have I seen. …

And never did a child's dream come true …

So perfectly as that of Ana.

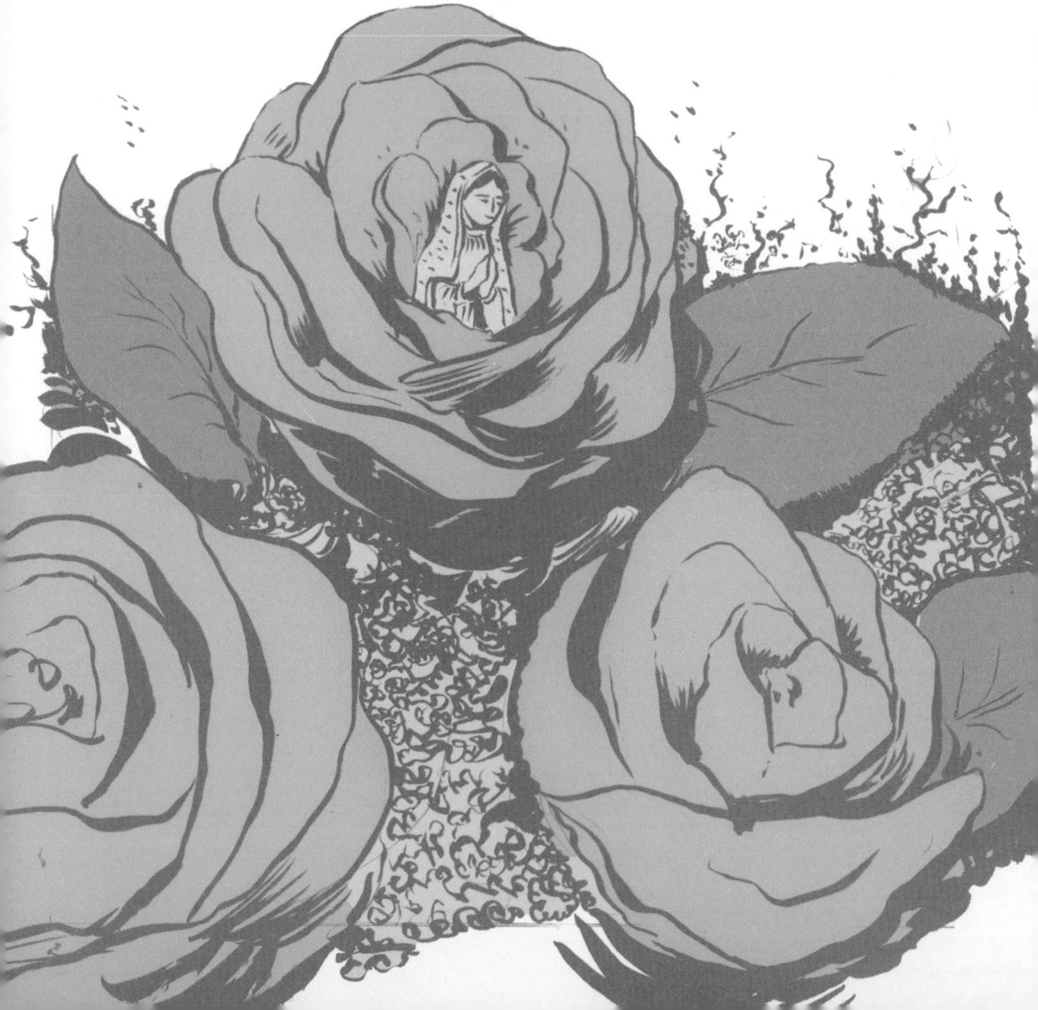

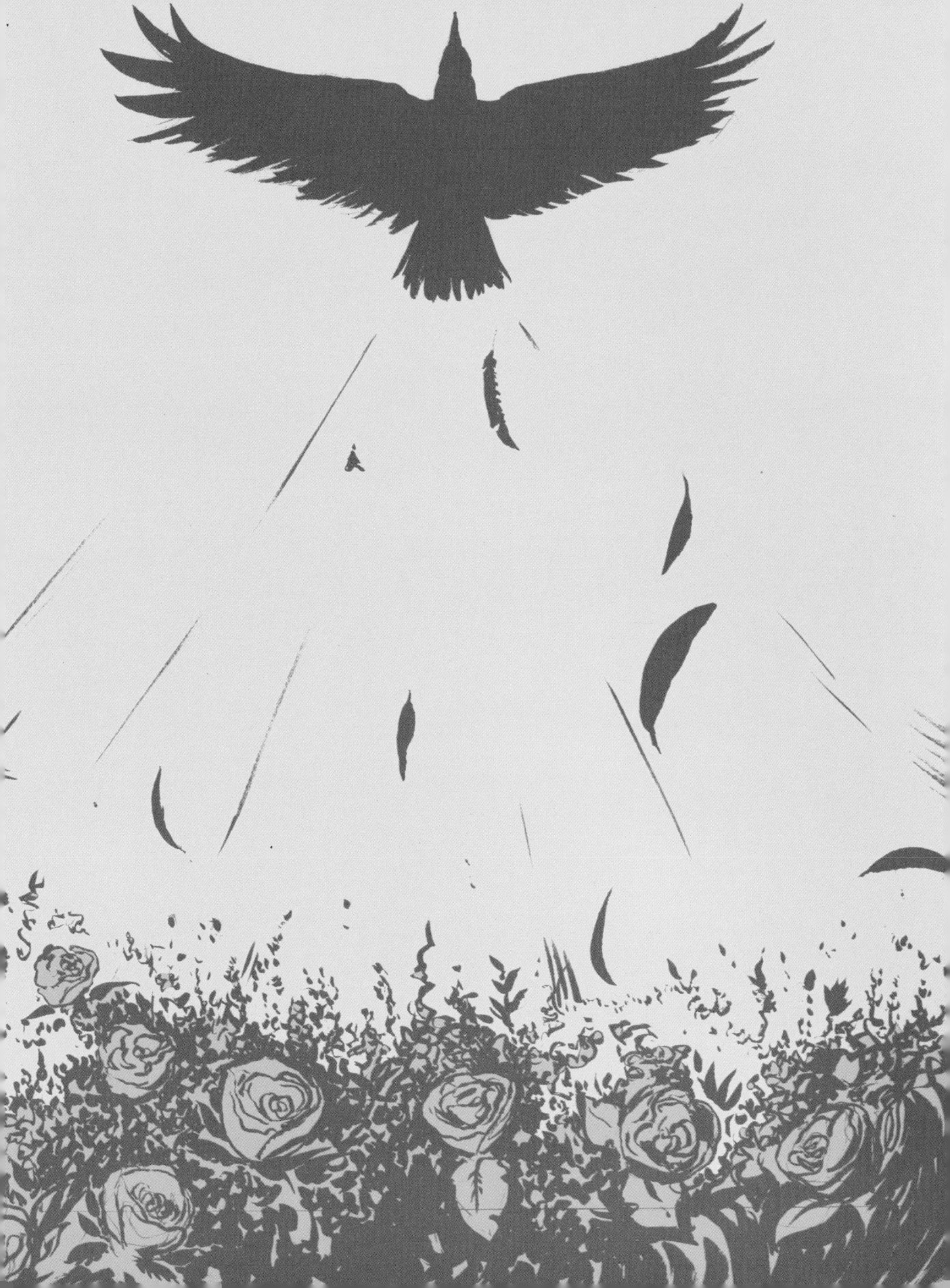

But even living as a princess, she was not content.

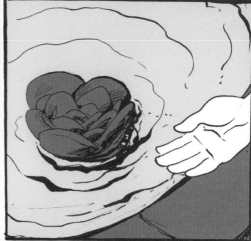

Oh, Leg...

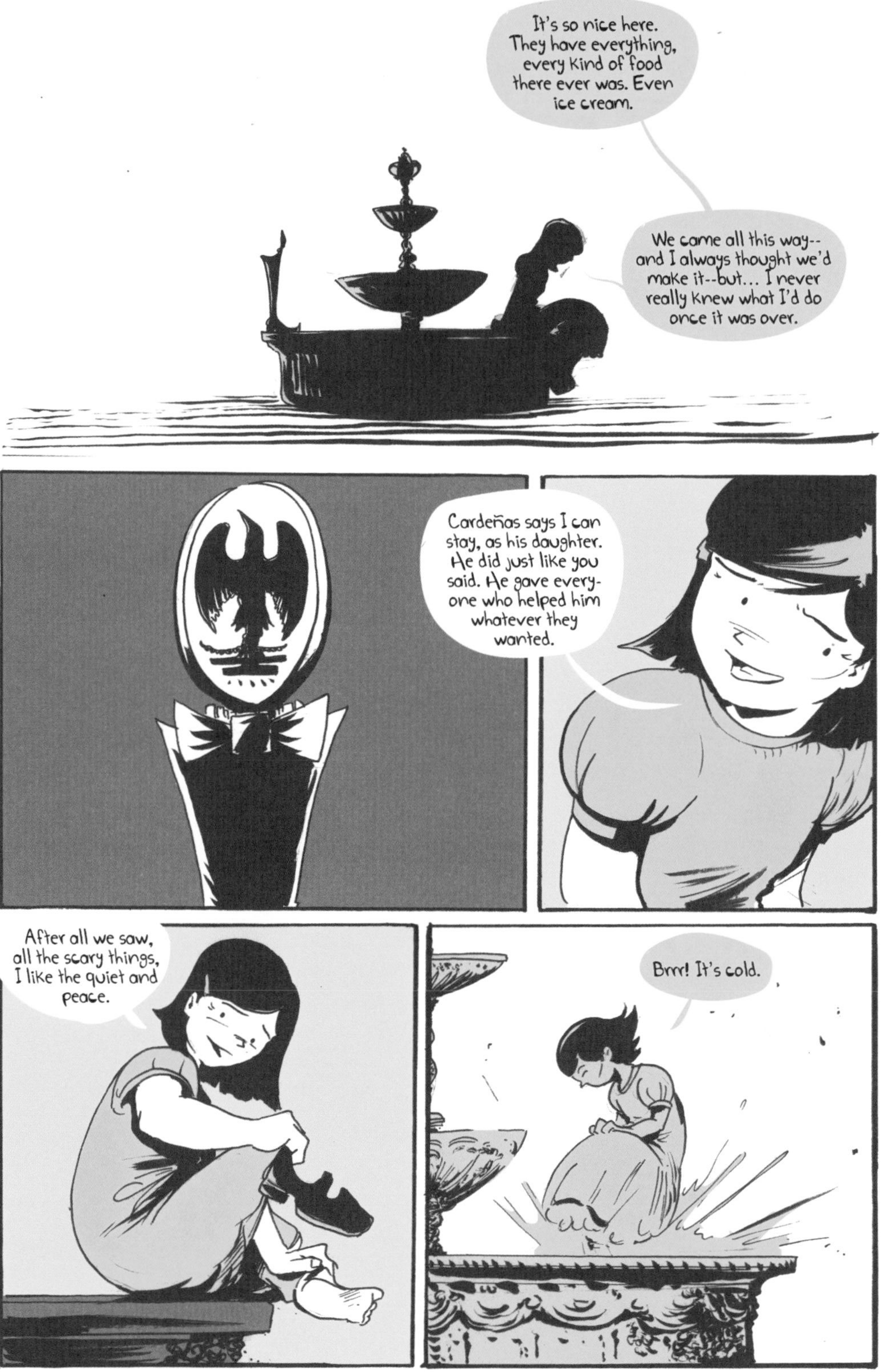
It's so nice here. They have everything, every kind of food there ever was. Even ice cream.
We came all this way-- and I always thought we'd make it--but... I never really knew what I'd do once it was over.
Cardeñas says I can stay, as his daughter. He did just like you said. He gave every-one who helped him whatever they wanted.
After all we saw, all the scary things, I like the quiet and peace.
Brrr! It's cold.

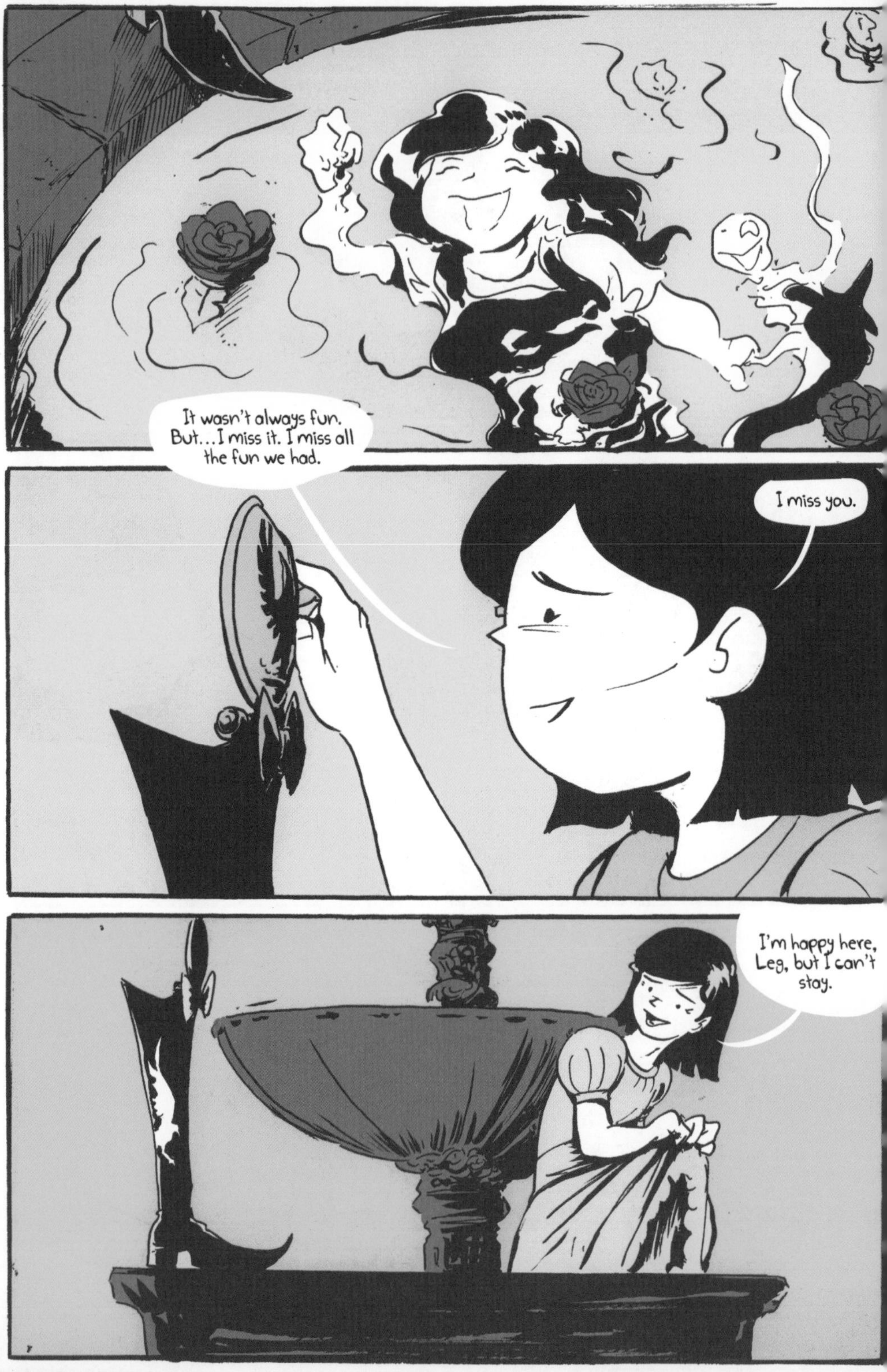
It wasn't always fun. But...I miss it. I miss all the fun we had.
I miss you.
I'm happy here, Leg, but I can't stay.

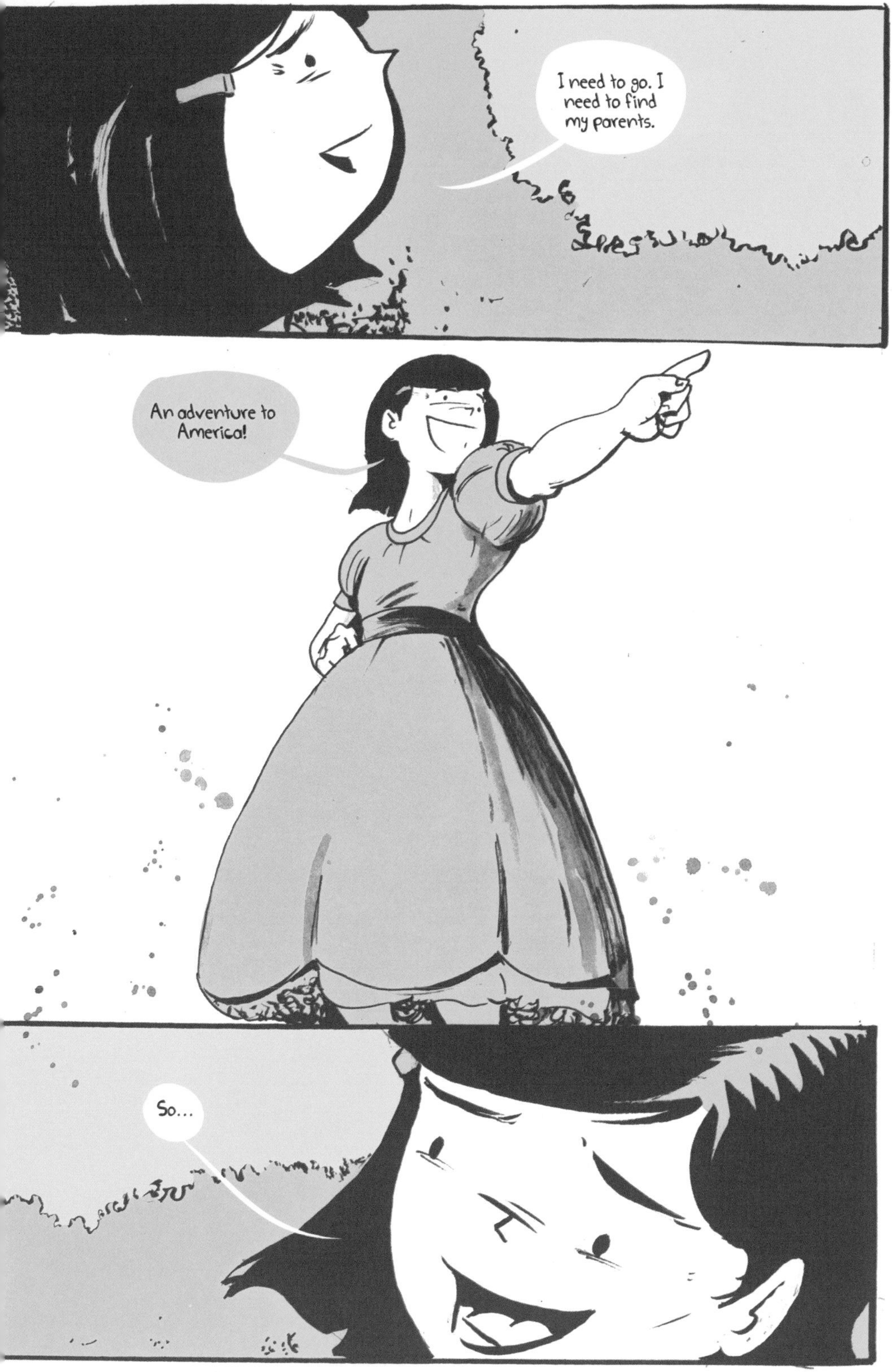
I need to go. I need to find my parents.
An adventure to America!
So...

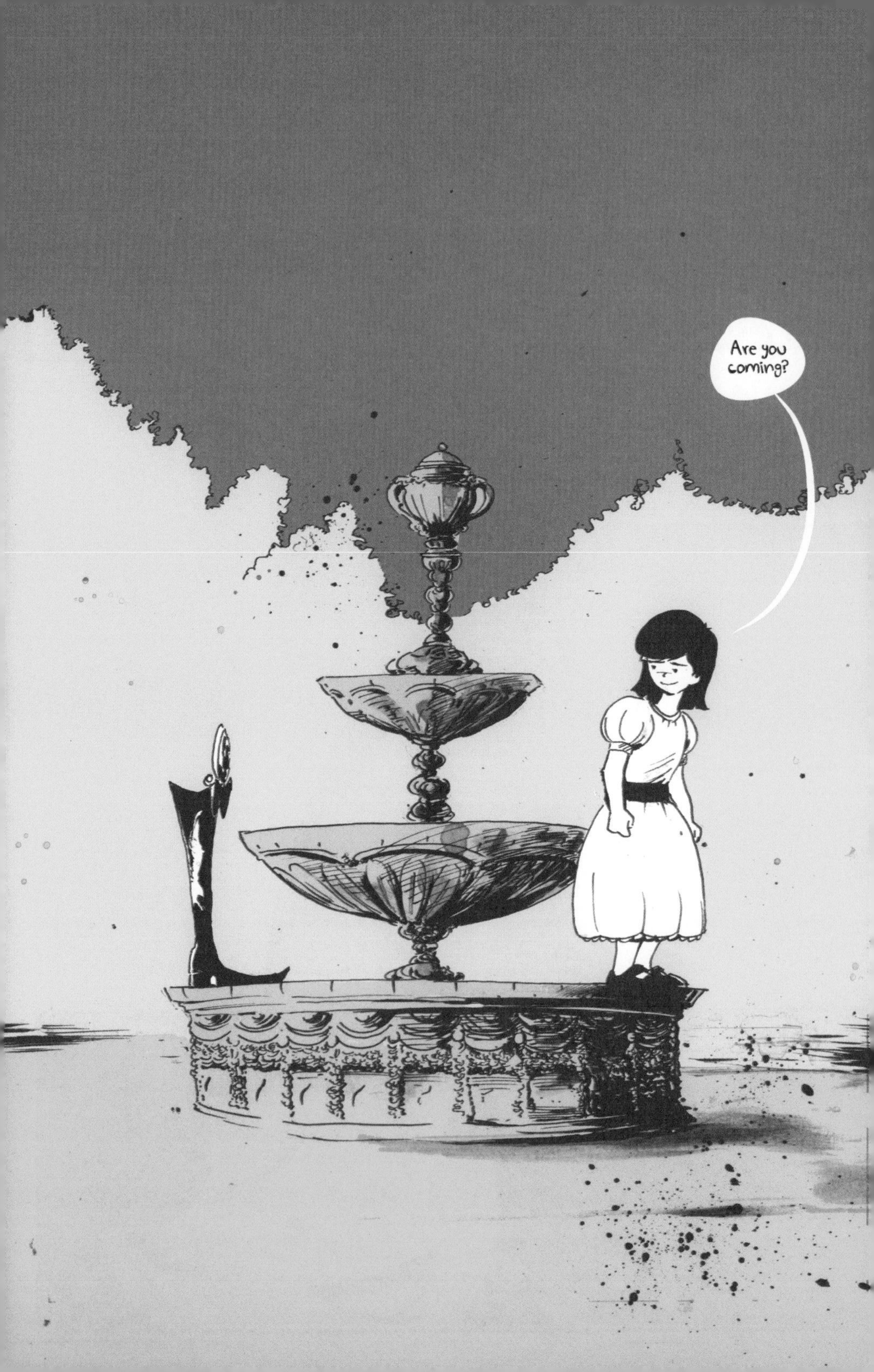
Are you coming?

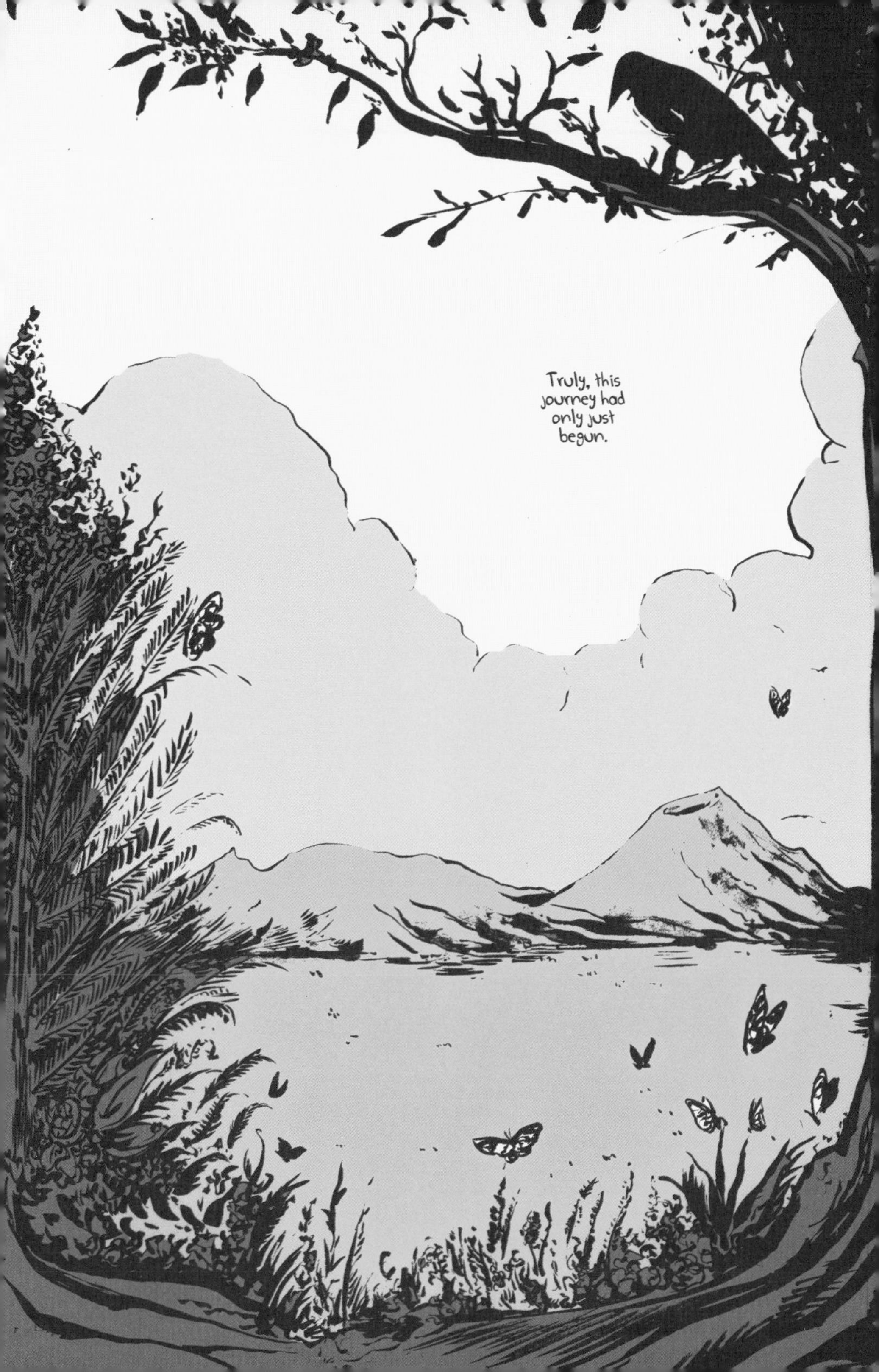
Truly, this journey had only just begun.

Van Jensen is a former crime reporter and magazine editor who now writes comic books such as *Pinocchio, Vampire Slayer* (Top Shelf Productions) and *The Flash* and *Green Lantern Corps* (DC Comics). A native of western Nebraska, he first heard about Santa Anna's leg in a history course at the University of Nebraska-Lincoln. He now lives in Atlanta.

Jose Pimienta grew up in Mexicali drawing and observing as many stories as he could get his hands on. His appreciation for movies ranged from animated family films to midnight horror shows. The other major influence in his upbringing was music, which remains a major part of his life. After high school, he moved to Georgia, where he attended the Savannah College of Art and Design. In 2009, he gathered his belongings and returned to the West Coast, where he enjoys as much coffee and drawing as he can.

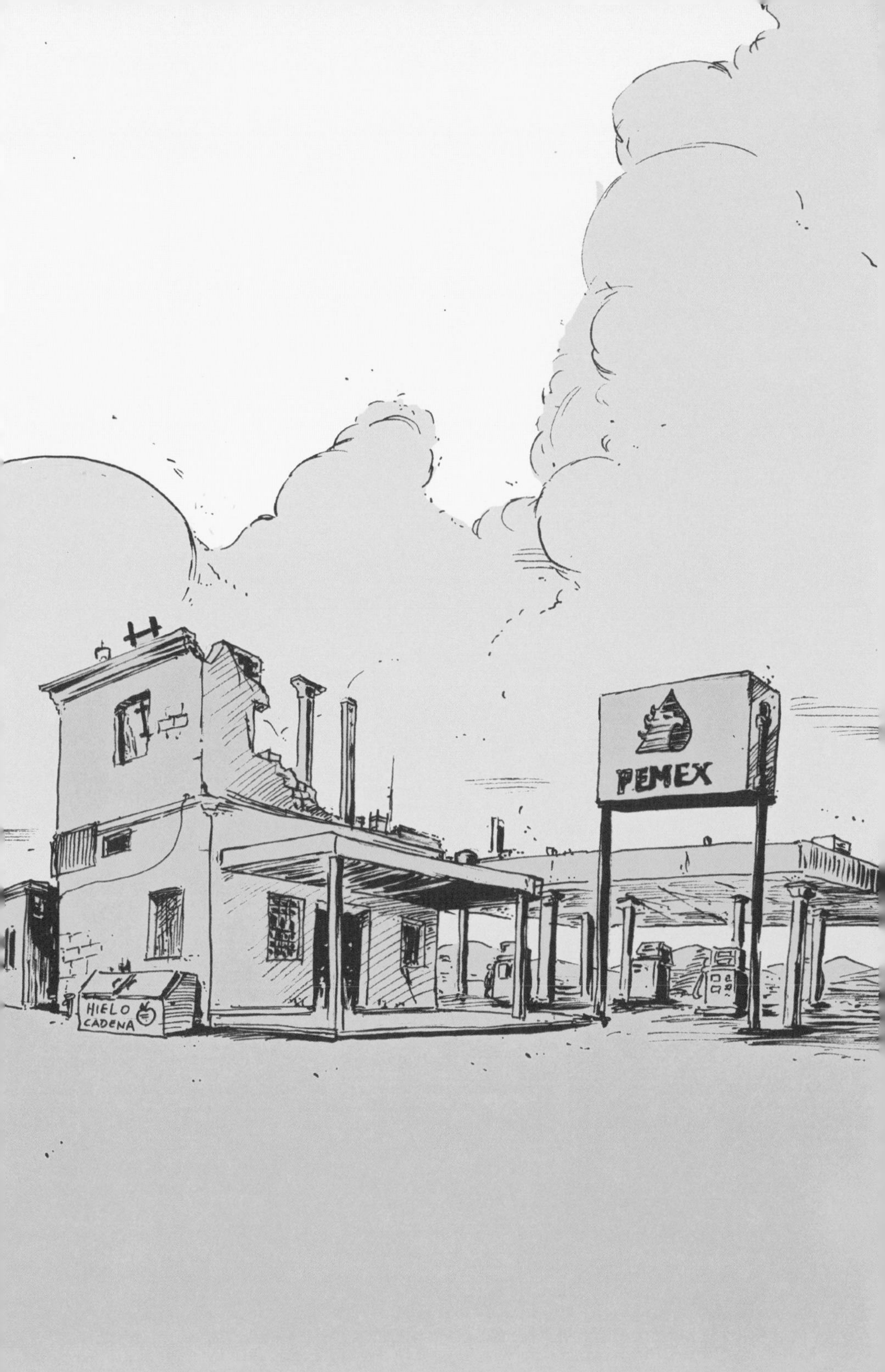
PEMEX
HIELO
CADENA

We spent years working on this book,
and without a special group of people
it would never have been possible to complete it.
A special thank you to those
who helped make this book a reality.

Jesse David Mulligan Parker
Mike Garvey
Jose Mario Pimienta
Tony and Lauren Inglis
Estrella Pereira
Brian Szente
Victoria D. Peraza
Evan Price
Dusty Higgins
Austin L. Ray
Asher Cook
Andrew Carl
Derek McConnell
Kyle Torok
Rafa Reyes
Bee Louise
Mario Candelaria
Tierra Incognita
Irma Judith Orrantia de Rodriguez
Peter and Carolyn Cobb
Lourdes Pimienta
Tim & Jean Jensen
Tim Vamplew
Andrew Aydin
Tessy Garcia
Alex Rennolds Smith
Jose & Maria Pimienta Rendon
Hortensia Franco
Familia Postlethwaite Retamoza
Maria Eugenia Garcia
Jim Hardison
Phil Smith
Ana Teresa Palma
Bradley Odom